ROSE OTIS, EDITOR

A Gift of Love

A daily devotional for women by women

REVIEW AND HERALD® PUBLISHING ASSOCIATION
HAGERSTOWN, MD 21740

Copyright © 1994
Review and Herald® Publishing Association

The contributors assume full responsibility for the accuracy of all facts and quotations as cited in this book.

This book was
Edited by James Cavil and Penny Estes Wheeler
Designed by Patricia S. Wegh
Type set: 10.5/11.5 Berkeley

PRINTED IN U.S.A.

98 97 96 95 94   10 9 8 7 6 5 4 3 2 1

Library of Congress Cataloging in Publication Data
A gift of Love : a daily devotional for women / by women ;
    Rose Otis, editor.
         p.   cm.
   1. Women—Prayer-books and devotions.   2. Seventh-day Adventists—Prayer-books and devotions—English.   3. Devotional calendars.   I. Otis, Rose Marie Niesen.
BV4844.G54   1994
242'.2—dc20   94-32834
                                                              CIP

ISBN 0-8280-0889-2

Scriptures credited to EB are quoted from *The Everyday Bible, New Century Version,* copyright © 1987, 1988 by Word Publishing, Dallas, Texas. Used by permission.

Scripture texts credited to NAB are from *The New American Bible,* copyright © 1970, by the Confraternity of Christian Doctrine, Washington, D.C., and are used by permission of copyright owner. All rights reserved.

Scripture quotations marked NASB are from the *New American Standard Bible,* © The Lockman Foundation 1960, 1962, 1963, 1968, 1971, 1972, 1973, 1975, 1977.

Texts credited to NEB are from *The New English Bible.* © The Delegates of the Oxford University Press and the Syndics of the Cambridge University Press 1961, 1970. Reprinted by permission.

Texts credited to NIV are from the *Holy Bible, New International Version.* Copyright © 1973, 1978, 1984, International Bible Society. Used by permission of Zondervan Bible Publishers.

Texts credited to NKJV are from The New King James Version. Copyright © 1979, 1980, 1982, Thomas Nelson, Inc., Publishers.

Bible texts credited to NRSV are from the New Revised Standard Version of the Bible, copyright © 1989 by the Division of Christian Education of the National Council of the Churches of Christ in the U.S.A. Used by permission.

Bible texts credited to Phillips are from J. B. Phillips: *The New Testament in Modern English,* Revised Edition. © J. B. Phillips 1958, 1960, 1972. Used by permission of Macmillan Publishing Co.

Texts credited to REB are from *The Revised English Bible.* Copyright © Oxford University Press and Cambridge University Press, 1989. Reprinted by permission.

Bible texts credited to RSV are from the Revised Standard Version of the Bible, copyright © 1946, 1952, 1971, by the Division of Christian Education of the National Council of the Churches of Christ in the U.S.A. Used by permission.

Bible texts credited to TEV are from the *Good News Bible*—Old Testament: Copyright © American Bible Society 1976; New Testament: Copyright © American Bible Society 1966, 1971, 1976.

Verses marked TLB are taken from *The Living Bible,* copyright © 1971 by Tyndale House Publishers, Wheaton, Ill. Used by permission.

Biographical Sketches

Betty Adams, a retired schoolteacher living in Placerville, California, is married and has three grown children. She enjoys her garden, reading, camping, and traveling. FEB. 9.

Deborah Aho lives at Riverside Farm Institute, a training school in Zambia. She and her husband coordinate the World Food Program to Prevent Malnutrition in their area. Deborah home-schools their three children, teaches sewing classes, and has organized a home industry for village women. FEB. 23, MAR. 3.

Ginny Allen lives in Vancouver, Washington, with her husband, an academy Bible teacher. They have two married sons. She is a nurse in a public high school, has spoken for retreats, seminars, and church weekends across the United States, Canada, Brazil, and Russia, and cohosts a TV series on Christian concerns for the Three Angels Broadcasting Network. JAN. 26, JULY 9.

Nettie M. Anderson is an administrative assistant and editor and lectures concerning effective family relations. She is a minister's wife, has three daughters, and enjoys jogging, sewing, crafts, and reading. FEB. 7.

Chelcie Sterling-Anim is a secretary at the Trans-European Division. She is the wife of a minister and has one daughter. She is a trained Bible instructor and lay preacher who enjoys working with young people and is actively involved in Pathfinder work. Her hobbies include badminton, music, reading, and needlework. MAR. 31.

Marilyn Applegate is a wife, mother of two sons, and writer living in Washington. For 30 years she and her husband have been involved in pastoral and hospital administration work. A current project of hers now that she is living in the Northwest is researching the missionary influence in the opening up of Old Oregon. JUNE 22.

Alma Atcheson, housewife, church communication secretary, assistant welfare leader, and mother of three, serves with the Pink Ladies in hospital visiting. She has written articles for local newspapers and church publications. Her hobbies are gardening, leathercraft, and ceramics. JUNE 23, OCT. 12.

Rosemary Baker, a freelance writer living in Le Claire, Iowa, enjoys working with children. Her children's book *What Am I?* was published by the Pacific Press Publishing Association. Her ideas have been published in the *Shining Star* magazine, *Kids' Stuff* magazine, and others. She also enjoys writing poetry and painting. OCT. 14, NOV. 21.

Audrey Balderstone is the mother of two sons, and she and her husband operate a garden landscaping company in England. She is studying for an honors degree at the University of London, conducts her bimonthly Home Fellowship group meeting, maintains her interest in community activities and flower arranging, and is active in her church and community. APR. 30, AUG. 30, SEPT. 10, DEC. 28.

Rosa Taylor Banks and her husband and two children live in Maryland. She is a writer, public speaker, and church administrator. Her hobbies include public speaking, playing piano, bowling, singing, and writing. JULY 17.

Mary Barrett is a pastor's wife, mother of two young daughters, and homemaker living in England. When possible, she works with her husband—preaching, giving Bible studies, and running programs. She also writes for Christian magazines. Her hobbies include being with friends, reading, and needlecraft. MAR. 9.

Jessie Beard and her husband live in Pennsylvania. The mother of three grown sons, she works as a customer service representative and serves as a superintendent in her local church. She enjoys writing, walking, bicycling, shopping, and public speaking. OCT. 15.

Dawna Beausoleil taught for 14 years on the elementary and college levels. She now lives in northern Ontario with her pastor husband. She assists him with visiting, seminars, and public speaking. Her hobbies include reading, writing, camping, and crafts. SEPT. 6, OCT. 20.

Joni Bell and her minister husband live in central New York. She is the mother of two and a psychiatric nurse. Joni enjoys singing, supporting her husband's ministry, traveling, archaeology, and snorkeling. **Mar. 21, Apr. 17.**

Miriam Berg has two daughters and six grandchildren. She's the daughter, wife, and mother-in-law of pastors in South America. She has been a missionary in Mozambique, Peru, and for the past 22 years, Brazil. She loves working with children. **June 24.**

Karen Birkett is an administrator in a financial planning firm in Toronto, Ontario. She has been involved in the children's and youth departments of her church. Her hobbies include reading, knitting, embroidery, and camping. **Oct. 22.**

Janet Staubach Bottroff lives with her husband, Stephen, in Grand Terrace, California. She holds a B.S. degree in accounting. Currently she is treasurer of her church and church school. Her favorite hobby is quilting, in which she holds many awards from local and county fairs. **Jan. 16, May 16.**

Carole Breckenridge is director of marketing for a chain of nursing centers in Maryland. She enjoys public speaking, writing, travel, reading, and nurturing friendships. **May 17.**

Ellen Bresee, the recently retired cofounder of Shepherdess International, has served with her husband in pastoral and evangelistic team ministry for many years and has taught elementary school. She is the mother of three sons and one daughter, and is a published writer, marriage counselor, and speaker. She and her husband have recently moved to Colorado. **Apr. 1, Dec. 31.**

Rosemary Brucken is a full-time honors student at Andrews University in Berrien Springs, Michigan, pursuing degrees in English and religion. A single mother of two college-age sons, her background is in journalism and advertising management. **Oct. 18.**

Jeanette Bryson lives at Atlantic Union College, where she is the dean of women. She is a widow, the mother of three children, has B.S. and M.A. degrees in education, and has served as a missionary. She is a board member of Adventist Singles Ministries, is actively involved in the college church and various women's activities, is the author of one book, and has written articles and short stories for several religious publications. **June 8.**

Darlene Burgeson, formerly a sales manager, enjoys reading, gardening, and working with creative family albums. She and her husband live in Minnesota and have both been involved with church leadership for years. **Mar. 14.**

Betty R. Burnett, from "Charlevoix the Beautiful," Michigan, works for the Department of Agriculture, has been married for 35 years, is a mother of five and grandmother of eight, and loves her church family and assists them by participating as an elder, adult Bible teacher, women's ministries coordinator, and friend. She enjoys reading, crocheting, children, and walking in the fields and woods. **Feb. 2, Sept. 5.**

Hazel Burns and her husband live in Kettering, Ohio, and have two grown children. She began a women's ministries program in her local church 10 years ago and is still actively involved in it. She is a homemaker, church and neighborhood Bible study leader, lecturer, and seminar instructor. Her interests include baking, quilting, painting, hiking, skiing, and family outings. **Oct. 1, Nov. 1.**

Andrea A. Bussue was born on the island of Nevis in the West Indies. She is a graduate student at the University of Maryland. She has been a superintendent at her local church in Hyattsville, Maryland. Presently she is the director of the children's choir. She loves children and enjoys reading, traveling, sewing, cooking, and meeting people. **May 31, July 20.**

Luan Cadogan is a secretary and lives with her husband and two children in Toronto, Ontario. She is the children's program coordinator of her church and has been actively involved with directing the children's choir and organizing children's programs for special occasions. She enjoys nature, music, writing, gardening, and making children's crafts. **Feb. 10, June 14.**

Monica Casarramona, an editor at a publishing house in Argentina, has taught elementary and secondary school and is a professor of education. Monica is a prolific writer and is actively involved in her church as a deaconess and children's ministries coordinator. **May 5.**

Mary Casler has recently retired from 12 years of being a chaplain in Ukiah, California. The previous 18 years were spent as a family counselor. Presently she is enjoying being a homemaker and working part-time as a chaplain. **DEC. 6.**

Virginia D. Cason, a homemaker and public speaker, lives with her doctor husband in California and has four grown children. She has written programs and lessons for Vacation Bible School and Bible classes, as well as songbooks for children. She teaches voice and is a DJ on the radio, a ham radio operator, and a private pilot. Virginia is the daughter of H.M.S. Richards, Sr. **FEB. 28.**

Joy Cavins is employed at Oakwood Academy in Huntsville, Alabama. If you want to find her, come to the Mount Calvary church, where she'll be somewhere with the kids. Joy teaches Vacation Bible School, primary, and children's chapel. **SEPT. 1.**

Mary Centerano is a biology teacher by profession, but temporarily is her husband's secretary. She is also a homemaker, mother, and active church worker in Buenos Aires, Argentina. **APR. 29.**

Janice Chamberlain, a former elementary teacher, minister's wife, missionary to the Pacific Islands, and editor of Ohio and Michigan's *Shepherdess Newsletter*, is now "retired." Janice lives in Avon Park, Florida, and cares for elderly people. She enjoys photography, writing, piano, family, church, work, and a good book. **AUG. 31.**

Shari Chamberlain began her career as a health educator. She has been an associate in pastoral care for 10 years and a chaplain for five years. She is currently a chaplain in California. She enjoys mountain climbing, a good book, chatting with friends, and adventuresome travel. **FEB. 20, JUNE 21, SEPT. 25, DEC. 8.**

Lyndelle Chiomenti is the editor of the Easy English edition of the adult *Sabbath School Lesson Quarterly*. She is married and enjoys writing, reading, crocheting, antiques, history, water gardening, and biblical studies. **NOV. 17.**

Birol C. Christo lives with her husband in India. She is a retired teacher, the mother of five grown children, and the Shepherdess International coordinator for the Southern Asia Division, and spends all her spare time sewing and making craft items to sell as fund-raisers to help orphans. **FEB. 25.**

Ginger Mostert Church, the mother of two grown sons, is a marketing representative for the Review and Herald Publishing Association. She teaches seminars on possibility thinking, and has had articles published in several magazines and local newspapers. She and her husband, Dennis, live in Maryland. She enjoys cross-stitch, reading, writing, sharing ideas in seminars, and flowers of all kinds. **JAN. 25, JULY 15, DEC. 4.**

Susan Clark lives in California with her husband and two active teenagers. She is a member of the local women's ministries council and enjoys leading a weekly women's Bible study. Her interests are quilting, gardening, reading, and supporting the music and sports activities of her children. **JAN. 30, JULY 3.**

Carel Sanders Clay lives in Napa, California, with her husband and daughter. She has two grown stepchildren. She teaches nursing and is currently completing her master's degree in that field. She has taught cradle roll, youth, and adult Bible classes. Carel enjoys quilting, sewing, writing, public speaking, cats, and being a mom. **FEB. 12, NOV. 15, DEC. 18.**

Dorothy Minchin-Comm is a professor of English at La Sierra University in California, and editor of a religious journal. A prolific writer, she and her late husband, Walter O. Comm, served as missionaries for 16 years in Central America and the Far East. Her "spare" time is given to her son and daughter, to travel, to helping conduct writing workshops, and to doing still more writing. **JULY 30, NOV. 11.**

Rae Lee Cooper has just completed 16 years of mission service in India with her minister husband and has recently moved to Maryland. In December 1994 she will be finishing a degree in nursing. Rae is a musician, and mother of a daughter and a son. Her hobbies include helping children and women, reading, and writing. **AUG. 9.**

Cynthia Coston is a homemaker, a veterinarian's wife, and mother of two young boys. She lives in Virginia and is a pianist, harpist, and vocalist. She is very involved in children's ministry at her church. **APR. 24.**

Alice Covey was a schoolteacher before her marriage, and is now a widow living in Canada. She is the mother of six and grandmother of 15. Alice enjoys writing, sewing, crocheting, playing the piano, and flower gardening. JUNE 25.

Judith Crabb was a single parent of two boys for 16 years. She makes her home in St. Helena, California, where she is the senior chaplain at the St. Helena Hospital. Her special joys include ministering to patients, families, and staff, trips with her husband, and Christmastime with both families together. FEB. 6.

Sharon Cress is the director of Shepherdess International. She and her church administrator husband live in Maryland. She enjoys water, the beach, and collecting antiques. APR. 25.

Faith Johnson Crumbly is on the editorial staff of *Celebration* magazine. Her articles have been published in various magazines and two preschool devotional books. She says the inspiration for and the heroes in much of her writing are her husband, Edward, their five children, and five grandchildren. FEB. 16.

Celia Cruz is the administrative secretary in the Office of Women's Ministries at the General Conference. A pastor's wife and mother of three adult children and two teenagers, she enjoys people, her family, teaching the preteen Bible class at her church, presenting seminars, and preaching. Some of her interests are needlework, reading, writing, and ceramics. MAR. 1, APR. 21, JUNE 30, DEC. 23.

Shonna Dalusong is a wife, mother, and registered nurse. She and her husband are currently assisting in the nursery at their church and helping with children's church and youth activities. One of her hobbies is writing; she writes a monthly column for her church newsletter. MAR. 20, JUNE 3, OCT. 7.

Sandy Lee Dancek, a literature evangelist, is a grandmother of four granddaughters and a published writer and speaker. Originally from Pennsylvania, she and her husband, Ed, now make their home in West Virginia. Her interests are piano, organ, flower arranging, kids, and grandchildren. AUG. 17.

Lynn Marie Davis, a sign language interpreter for the state of Georgia, coordinates the disability services for her church in Decatur, Georgia. She has served on the Commission for People With Disabilities for two years. Walking, cooking, writing, and facilitating workshops and seminars on finding one's niche are some of her favorite things to do. SEPT. 23.

Brenda Dickerson writes from Omaha, Nebraska, where she is a wife and the mother of a 2-year-old daughter. She enjoys teaching Sabbath school, sewing, gardening, and writing. FEB. 17, MAY 14, JUNE 17.

Nelma Drake writes from the beautiful state of Idaho. OCT. 29.

Crystal Earnhardt is an evangelist's wife, mother, and freelance writer. She has written two books published by the Review and Herald Publishing Association. Her articles and stories have appeared in various religious magazines. She lives in Misenheimer, North Carolina. MAR. 15, JULY 21.

Christina Ennis is a medical technologist at the Veterans Administration Medical Center in Denver, Colorado. She has written several skits for young people and enjoys gardening and reading. MAY 15, AUG. 16.

Sharon Estrada, a victim of childhood sexual abuse who has drawn close to Jesus for healing, is the founder and president of Victims of Hurting Childhood, Inc., in Dickson, Tennessee. Her story, *In Search of Pearls*, is to be released in 1995. She often travels to speak to groups, establish support groups, and counsel victims of abuse. Sharon's pastor husband, John, is her number one encourager! She is a mother and a grandmother. APR. 12.

Doris Jenner Everett is a mother and grandmother, assistant Sabbath school superintendent, women's ministries coordinator, assistant deaconess, and assistant church clerk, and has a nursing home ministry and tells children's stories. Her interests are reading, writing, and keyboard. OCT. 10, NOV. 3, DEC. 30.

Alice Fahrbach and her doctor husband make their home on the shores of Lake Superior in Michigan. Alice is a retired nurse and mother of four grown children. She enjoys the outdoors, camping, and music. MAY 20, AUG. 28.

Esther I. Fayard lives in Buenos Aires, Argentina. A mother of two and grandmother of five, she worked as a Bible instructor for 20 years, then as an editor until her retirement. APR. 8.

Cristina Fernandez, a secretary, teacher, and counselor, was born in Chile. She has dedicated her life to helping youth, adults, and families through her counseling. AUG. 24.

Linda Hyder Ferry is a physician at Loma Linda University Hospital and teaches in the preventive medicine and family practice residency programs. Her current interest is studying the relationship between depression and lifestyle diseases. She and her husband are amateur ornithologists and have conducted research on hummingbirds in southeastern Arizona. JULY 26.

Karen Flowers is working herself out of a job as the mother of two college-age sons, but codirecting family ministries at the General Conference with her husband, Ron, will likely keep her busy enough. She reads and knits and practices her long-neglected flute for fun. DEC. 13.

Carol Foote is a registered nurse working at a small northern New York hospital in an alcohol and drug rehabilitation unit. She is active in her church—especially in women's ministries—enjoys playing the piano and guitar. APR. 28.

Heide Ford is the assistant editor of *Women of Spirit*, the new magazine for Adventist women. She is a minister's wife living in Maryland and holds a master's degree in counseling. Her interests include reading, different cultures, rollerblading, and the outdoors. JAN. 31, APR. 1, MAY 1, NOV. 4.

Sharon Fujimoto is a student at Pacific Union College majoring in international communication with a French emphasis. Her home is in Yokohama, Japan, where her parents have been missionaries since she was 9 years old. JAN. 23.

Edna Maye Gallington lives in Riverside, California, and works in communications. She is a graduate of La Sierra University and has taken public relations work at the University of California at Riverside. She enjoys playing the piano, creative writing, hiking, and working in her church. MAY 2, JUNE 4, OCT. 9.

Sonia Gazeta writes from Brazil College, where she teaches Portuguese for the theology seminary. She is also a translator and secretary. APR. 13, MAY 11.

Lila Lane George is a medical secretary and Arizona pastor's wife who enjoys her six grandchildren, oil painting, hiking, and reading. The church activity she finds the most fulfillment in is leading a Twelve-Step support group. In 1988 she realized her dream of receiving her bachelor's degree (after 30 years' absence from college). DEC. 2.

Margaret Mondics Gibbs and her first husband, Ben Mondics, were missionaries to Lebanon and Turkey. She became a widow with two teenage sons, then married Donald Gibbs, M.D., and became a stepmother of 10 children from first grade to college. She is a volunteer teacher in a church school, plays in a bell choir, and is a member of a ladies' literary society that is more than 100 years old. AUG. 25, DEC. 20.

Evelin Harper Gilkeson lives in California with her husband and two daughters. She teaches, and is working on a master's degree. AUG. 12.

Bertha Appleton Glanzer taught church school and public school in southern California, both in regular classrooms and as a special education teacher. She also directed the United Cerebral Palsy Center at Loma Linda University. She is retired and lives with her husband, Ben Glanzer, in Yucaipa, California. JULY 7.

Evelyn Glass, a homemaker, mother, farmer, and local church clerk and elder, is also the women's ministries director for the Mid-America Union. Her articles have appeared in local and state newspapers and Christian publications. She enjoys folk painting, sewing, knitting, refinishing furniture, reading, speaking, and community programs and committees. JAN. 21, MAY 24, AUG. 7.

Carmen O. Gonzalez, from New York, is a teacher and a single mother. She has served as a church elder, superintendent, head deaconess, youth council member, and a translator for several Maranatha mission projects in the Dominican Republic. She enjoys praising God, praying, writing letters, walking, bicycling, reading, people watching, and playing with her nephew Danny. JAN. 8, MAR. 18.

Hazel Marie Gordon is the women's ministries advisor for the Southern Union Conference, where her husband serves as president and she works with him in a team ministry. Hazel is known for her musical abilities in both voice and piano, as well as public speaking. She has two daughters, three grandchildren, and many friends. DEC. 25.

Kathryn M. Gordon served as a student missionary to Japan and Korea while she was in college. She is employed at Andrews University and is currently working on her master's in social work. She enjoys gardening, canoeing, and studying automobile mechanics. AUG. 18.

Ramona Perez-Greek is the assistant director of women's ministries for the North American Division of Seventh-day Adventists, mother of one preschooler, and administrator's wife. She travels extensively as a public speaker and seminar presenter, and recently was given an honorary doctorate in humane letters from Andrews University for dedication and commitment to church life. NOV. 16.

Rebecca J. Grice is a secretary. She and her husband have two married sons and two grandchildren. She enjoys working with youth and Pathfinders. She conducts workshops on teaching this age group (10-16) using active learning. Her other interests are writing, painting, mountain biking, snorkeling, waterskiing, and camping. AUG. 23, NOV. 13.

Meibel Mello Guedes, a seminar presenter, writes from Brazil, where she is involved in women's ministries. MAY 4, SEPT. 24.

Jo Habada is deceased. At the time she wrote, she was teaching English and was the guidance counselor at Bass Memorial Academy in Lumberton, Mississippi. MAR. 2, OCT. 30.

Patricia A. Habada has a doctorate in education curriculum and supervision and is a curriculum specialist. She has authored and edited countless instructional manuals and has written numerous articles for denominational journals. Her hobbies include writing, boating, walking, music, and reading. JAN. 15, DEC. 5.

Cherry B. Habenicht is a teacher, guidance counselor, and vice principal at Wisconsin Academy. She and her husband have served in ministry for 27 years and have three children. She is a published writer who has been active in women's ministries. MAR. 13.

Barbara Hales is a wife and mother living in New Carlisle, Indiana. She serves as a financial aid advisor at Andrews University, is a member of the Indiana Conference women's ministries committee, and lectures on women's issues. She enjoys writing, sewing, and cooking. AUG. 11.

Barbara Jackson-Hall is the editor of *Vibrant Life*, a health magazine. Before moving to Maryland, she was a television news reporter in Columbus, Ohio. She is married and enjoys tennis, reading, and aerobics. DEC. 9.

Sali Jo Hand is a mother of three sons and has one daughter-in-law. She is a homemaker, artist, and senior pastor of two churches in southeastern Arizona. NOV. 27.

Lea Hardy, formerly an English teacher, now as a church elder promotes women's ministries, leads Bible study groups, and does some speaking. She is a published author and has written a Bible lesson series, "Women Discovering Jesus," primarily for overseas use. She writes for and acts in a local group called Maranatha Players. FEB. 5.

Beatrice Harris is a retired Bible instructor and church school teacher. She is a local church elder and an associate personal ministries leader, and has written articles for religious magazines. She has two grown children. JAN. 28.

Peggy Harris is an elder and church growth director in her local church. She is also a musician, and is actively involved in ministering to women. She has her own business as an insurance agent and also presents biblical hospitality seminars. She and her husband have two children and grandchildren. FEB. 27, MAY 7.

Jeanne Hartwell, an English teacher by profession, is a pastor's wife, assistant pastor, and mother of two children. She enjoys people, sewing, flower gardening, crafts, reading, and writing. JUNE 12.

Susan Harvey lives in Hagerstown, Maryland, with her husband, Rhea. She is the director of promotion and women's resources at the Review and Herald Publishing Association. She previously had a career as a professional interior designer and design teacher.

She has two grown sons and enjoys keeping up with their creative and interesting lives, as well as reading, walking, and traveling. **Jan. 4.**

Susanne Hatzinger, a mother and grandmother, lives with her husband in Vienna, Austria. She is a personal ministries leader in her local church, has supervised a vegetarian restaurant for many years, and has conducted about 150 nutrition seminars during the past few years. **Feb. 18.**

Sue Hayford teaches at Parkview Junior Academy in Syracuse, New York. She enjoys gardening, reading, and traveling. She and her husband are ham radio operators. **Feb. 14, Apr. 11.**

Lorabel Hersch is on the pastoral staff of the Collegedale church, where she serves as community chaplain. She is a former librarian and English teacher, writes articles for religious magazines, and has authored a number of Bible lesson quarterlies for young people. She is the mother of six adult children, and enjoys traveling with her husband, reading, writing, and meeting new people. **Apr. 10, Aug. 15.**

Wilma Hertlein is the mother of two sons and is a missionary in Brazil, where she translates to English. When retirement comes, she will be happy to spend it in usefulness anyplace she and her husband will be. **Oct. 28.**

Norma Hilliard, a former missionary to Japan, is retired and lives in Ukiah, California. Birdwatching, sewing, flower gardening, and music are among her many interests. **Dec. 14.**

Karen Holford is the mother of three young children. She is the wife of a pastor in Essex, England. Karen has written for a variety of Christian journals, including *Ministry*. She also designs church banners and Christian cross-stitch kits. **May 12, June 15, July 12.**

Tamyra Horst lives in Pennsylvania with her husband and two young sons. She is a homemaker and public speaker who loves people, reading, writing, and family. She is involved in women's ministries in her local church and teaches the young adult Bible class. **May 29, June 26, Aug. 29, Dec. 1.**

Fannie L. Houck is a freelance writer living in Washington. She and her husband have three grown children. She is a local church elder and women's ministries leader, and holds several other church offices. She is a published writer of five books and hundreds of articles, poems, and puzzles. **Oct. 3.**

Lorraine Hudgins is a retired administrative secretary. She has coauthored pageants and written songs, 30-minute dramas, and numerous articles and poems. **May 30, July 4, July 11, Sept. 15, Oct. 27, Dec. 17.**

Barbara Huff writes from Mound, Minnesota. She is the wife of a church administrator, the mother of two adult children, and a grandmother. She is a freelance writer and also the communication director and women's ministries director for the Minnesota Conference of Seventh-day Adventists. **Jan. 14, May 28, Sept. 9.**

Charlotte Ishkanian is the editor of a denominational magazine and lives in the metropolitan Washington, D.C., area. She is the mother of three teenagers, and is active in children's ministries in her home church. **Feb. 4.**

Ruthie Jacobsen has spent most of her professional life in nursing education and nursing service administration. She served her church as the director of women's ministries for the Oregon Conference for the past eight years, and has recently moved to Maryland. Ruthie is the mother of two grown sons and enjoys walking, flying, reading, and entertaining. **Mar. 16.**

Mary Johnson, *Bouquets* editor, is married and the mother of a teenage son and daughter. She is also a part-time secretary and lives in the northwest corner of North Dakota. Her devotional first appeared in *Bouquets*. **Sept. 2.**

Madeline S. Johnston writes from Berrien Springs, Michigan, where she and her husband make their home. She is a freelance writer and mother of four grown children. A former missionary, she has written several books and numerous articles. Writing, knitting, genealogy, Scrabble, photography, traveling, and bird-watching are among her special interests. **Jan. 5, June 2, July 13.**

Marianette Johnston is the treasurer for Planned Assistance for Troubled Children. She and her pastor husband spent 42 years in ministry, several of which were in mission service. Her special interests are family, her grandchildren, cross-stitch, and quilting. **Mar. 12.**

Fredi Rayline Jones is a native Californian, where she is the Community Services Federation president for the Napa Valley. She and her husband own a florist business. They have four married children and nine grandchildren. They are both active in their local church and in disaster response. **Dec. 19.**

Jeanne Jordan, a retired teacher, lives in Michigan with her husband. They have been married for 44 years, served as missionaries for 12 years, and have two grown children. She has authored three books and countless articles in church magazines, and enjoys reading, traveling, and words. **Jan. 9.**

Marilyn Bennett Justessen is a pastor's wife, nurse, nursing instructor, and assistant pastor. She enjoys entertaining, people, reading, walking, swimming, sewing, and teaching. **May 10.**

Sophie Kaiser, a retired widow, has been active in children's ministry, Pathfinders, women's support groups, and cooking schools. She enjoys gardening, cooking, baking, reading, singing, traveling, and young people. **June 6.**

Faith Keeney, a retired accountant, administrative secretary, and pilot, has flown many missions over the past 25 years into Mexico to bring physicians, dentists, and other health-care workers to isolated villages that have no other care. She loves reading, poetry, painting, and hiking. **May 13, Dec. 26.**

Vi Keith is the bookkeeper for a family ministry, Family Matters, based in Tennessee. She has served two years as superintendent in her local church, and is currently in her second year as the women's ministries leader. She enjoys poetry and songwriting, along with quilting. **Jan. 20.**

Marcia A. Keller is director of career services and international student affairs at Oakwood College in Alabama. She holds a master's degree in public administrative science and is also a registered nurse, wife, and mother of two daughters. **Nov. 12.**

Collene Kelly is an elementary teacher by profession but a homemaker by choice. She enjoys spending time with her minister husband and two preschool boys. Collene also likes gardening, walking, writing, trying new recipes, and attending family gatherings. **July 23, Sept. 11.**

Birthe Kendel is from Denmark and writes from St. Albans in England. She is a minister's wife and the happy mother of two teenage daughters. She is the director of children's ministries and women's ministries for the Trans-European Division of Seventh-day Adventists. **Mar. 24, May 22, Sept. 4.**

Marilyn King is a retired registered nurse. She and her husband live in Oregon, where she is active in the local church and school, working with youth and with the Red Cross as a volunteer nurse. She enjoys family, music, nature, and teaching a Bible class in her church. **Apr. 9, Aug. 22.**

Fylvia Fowler Kline completed her undergraduate and graduate degrees in Pune, India. She now lives in Maryland and works as an administrative secretary in media services; however, she considers motherhood her primary occupation. **Jan. 22.**

Karen Ann Knight is married, has three children, and lives in Delaware. She is a personal ministries assistant, communication secretary, children's Bible class teacher, and choir member in her church. Karen also works at Kent General Hospital as a television representative. **Nov. 19.**

Hepzibah G. Kore writes from southern India, where she is the women's ministries director. **June 29.**

RosaLynda Kosini, a business correspondence specialist, aspiring writer, church communication secretary, and health major, lives near the Texas hill country in San Antonio. In her quiet time she enjoys reading, Impressionist art, experimental cuisine, and getting her hands dirty in potting soil. **Mar. 11.**

Betty Kossick, a freelance writer, wife, mother, and grandmother, has been very active in her church as a church elder, Bible worker, teacher, church secretary, and receptionist.

Her personal philosophy is "others." Betty and her husband live in Ohio. **Feb. 1, Mar. 17.**

Kay Kuzma writes from Tennessee, where she and her husband make their home. Kay is founder and president of Family Matters, and hosts a daily radio feature and weekly television program for families. She is a public speaker and author of numerous books, and the mother of three grown children. **Jan. 1, June 10.**

Marion Lake is the mother of three married children and grandmother of four lovely granddaughters. She hosts a weekly women's prayer group and is a women's ministries coordinator and local church elder. She enjoys reading, music, quilting, knitting, walking, and reaching out to other people. She and her husband make their home in the state of New York. **Feb. 24.**

Eileen E. Lantry is from north Idaho. She is a librarian, teacher, homemaker, minister's wife, and Bible worker. She spent 14 years as a missionary in the Far East. Eileen has authored 13 books and loves nature, gardening, hiking, and cross-country skiing. **Jan. 2, Feb. 26, May 23.**

Lillian Lawrence is retired from teaching church school and managing a supervisory home for adults. For 60 years she was church pianist and organist, and held most church offices. Many of her poems and several articles were published in hometown newspapers years ago, as well as by church magazines. She raised seven children, including Lorna Lawrence. **Nov. 7.**

Lorna Lawrence is a school principal and teacher, composer, and concert soloist living in California. She is currently enrolled in a Ph.D. program in crisis counseling and is a published writer. Her special interests include counseling, traveling, marketing, composing, and arranging music for guitar, keyboard, and vocal arrangements. **Apr. 14, Oct. 13.**

Gina Lee is an accounting specialist in Burbank, California. She lives with her four cats in a trailer full of books and dolls. She has contributed articles to five books, including the two previous women's devotionals. **Jan. 11, July 28.**

Aileen Ludington is a board-certified physician with more than 25 years of practice experience. She spent seven years as medical advisor for the *Westbrook Hospital* television series and is presently the medical director of the Lifestyle Medicine Institute in Loma Linda. She is married and has six grown children. **Apr. 6, May 21, June 20, July 8.**

Ellen MacIvor and her husband are enjoying their retirement in British Columbia. She worked as a medical secretary for her husband while her two children were going to school. The grandmother of five children, she loves the outdoors, reading, writing, and walking. **Oct. 2.**

Lois Magee has been a Bible instructor since 1978. She has a B.A. in speech pathology with a minor in psychology. She is based in New Orleans and enjoys singing in the chancel choir and the ladies' ensemble. Her hobbies include in-depth Bible study and a variety of word games. **June 13.**

Anita Marshall lives with her husband in England, where she is a writer and computer typesetter for Stanborough Press. She is actively involved in Vacation Bible School, has written a manual on VBS, has had many articles published in magazines, and has written two books for teenagers. **Dec. 7.**

Jamisen Matthews is a transcriptionist for a nursing agency in New Haven, Connecticut. She is the mother of two teenage daughters, has a ministry for the deaf, and also assists in distributing food in the community. **Oct. 8.**

Wilma McClarty is an English and speech professor at Southern College in Tennessee. Wilma is a wife, a mother of two, a public speaker, and a writer. She has received many honors and awards, one of the most recent being the Sears-Roebuck Teaching Excellence and Campus Leadership Award for 1991. **Jan. 7, Feb. 22, Apr. 15, Apr. 16.**

Maria G. McClean lives with her husband, Wayne, and daughter Kamila in Canada. She is a registered nurse and an ordained local church elder, and serves on various committees in her church. She enjoys singing, playing the guitar, reading, exercising, and lecturing. **Apr. 20, May 26.**

Gloria C. McLaren, a hospice chaplain and nurse, was born in Jamaica. A wife and mother of five children, she enjoys writing, sewing, crocheting, and singing, and is a group facilitator on grieving. **Jan. 29.**

Marge Lyberg McNeilus is a homemaker, mother of four children, and grandmother of four. Her husband owns McNeilus Auto and Truck Parts, and she works as his bookkeeper. Her hobbies include traveling, grandmothering, photography, crafts, writing, and music. **Apr. 22, Oct. 4.**

Mary Kay Milam and her husband of 53 years own a farm in Missouri. She is involved in her local church as a teacher and leader in Community Services. She uses her hands to write songs, stories, and poems, create toys, and host multitudes of meals to delight family, friends, and strangers. **Sept. 30.**

Dorothy Montgomery (1926-1989) and her husband, Bob, had four children and 11 grandchildren. Dorothy was a nature lover and an avid swimmer who loved the Lord and giving Bible studies. She worked as an administrative secretary for her denomination's headquarters for almost 20 years and was bedridden with cancer and other complications the last four years of her life. **June 18.**

Lois Moore is a public health nurse in Caldwell, Idaho. She is head elder in her church, and teaches a weekly adult Bible study class. She served as a missionary in Indonesia and in South Korea before her marriage. She has two stepchildren. **Sept. 7.**

Mailene Ferreira Moroz was, at the time this devotional was written, a gifted speaker, organizer, administrator's wife, and actively involved in women's ministries in Brazil. She died in a car accident just a few weeks after writing it. **Nov. 18.**

Anita Requenez-Moses, a social worker, lives with her husband and two daughters in California. She and her husband have served as missionaries in Peru, Ethiopia, and Kenya. She is a speaker at women's retreats. **Apr. 19.**

Lillian Musgrave and her husband have made their home in northern California for more than 30 years. They own their own business, and have three children and three grandchildren. Lillian enjoys reading, writing, music, church work, cooking, needlework, and family activities. **Oct. 19.**

Joan Minchin Neal was born in Australia, lived in England, and now makes her home in Dayton, Tennessee, where she is a registered nurse. She and her husband have four grown children. She is the women's ministries leader at her local church. She enjoys nature, sewing, journalism, and her grandchildren. **June 1.**

Beatrice S. Neall is a professor of religion at Union College. She and her husband served as missionaries for 17 years in Southeast Asia. Her hobbies are gardening, growing African violets, and writing. **Feb. 3.**

Bienvisa Ladion-Nebres was born in the Philippines. She and her husband are missionaries in Zaire. They have three adult children. She enjoys music, stamp collecting, teaching, and helping in her church. **Oct. 26.**

Joyce Neergaard works with her husband in the Adventist Development and Relief Agency as an assistant for project development and as a shepherdess coordinator in Cyprus. She is a nurse and enjoys working with her local church in community health promotion programs and preteen and teenage Bible classes. Singing, reading, writing, snorkeling, and skiing are some of her leisure time pleasures. **Aug. 13, Nov. 25.**

Esther Nestares is a teacher and secretary. She has dedicated her life to child evangelism and working for the young people of South America and Asia. She is now retired but active in her local church in Argentina. **Apr. 2.**

Mabel Rollins Norman is a wife, mother, and grandmother. Her articles have appeared in many newspapers and magazines, and she has written a book on organizing for ministry. She organized a women's ministries group in her local church in 1988, and continues to serve as women's ministries coordinator, organist and pianist, and communication secretary. She is also a certified prison fellowship volunteer. **Aug. 27, Oct. 21.**

Sheree Parris Nudd, a vice president of a 243-bed hospital in Rockville, Maryland, is also an accomplished speaker and published author. She is the youngest alum to have established an endowed scholarship fund at her alma mater, a college in Keene, Texas. She and her husband have two daughters. Dec. 12.

Kathleen Tonn-Oliver, also known as Katie, lives in Angwin, California, where she works as a creative and commercial writer, and a fund developer and grant proposal writer for nonprofit organizations. Author of 11 books and numerous articles, Kathleen is a recovering victim of child abuse who currently has a handful of major writing projects on the subject, including a book, *Welcome Home, Exiles!* July 22, Aug. 5.

Rose Otis is the director of women's ministries for the General Conference of Seventh-day Adventists. Since the office was established in 1990, she has helped to develop programs that benefit women in countries around the world. Her work includes training leaders and speaking to women's groups. She enjoys her grandchildren, writing, and being home. Jan. 6, Apr. 23, Aug. 14, Nov. 30.

Norma Jean Parchment and her minister/administrator husband make their home in Ontario. She is a pioneer of women's ministries in Canada. Mar. 28, Aug. 19, Nov. 6.

Sonia Paul is the director of student housing at Oakwood College in Huntsville, Alabama. Married and the mother of two children, Sonia still manages to find time to write. Mar. 27.

Julia L. Pearce is a nursing instructor and a consultant in women's health services, and has written articles regarding women's health issues. She makes her home in California, and is the coordinator of women's ministries in her local church. She enjoys women's history, reading, sewing, and giving women's medical presentations. Aug. 4.

Lois Pecce lives in Ohio with her college professor husband. The mother of three young adults, she is a freelance writer, and cofounder and president of Dayton (Ohio) Christian Scribes, a writers' group. Lois is active in nursing home ministry, writing to prison inmates, and her local church. She enjoys gardening, sewing, reading, knitting, and snorkeling. Oct. 25.

Lori Peckham is the editor of *Insight*, a magazine for Christian youth. She and her husband live in Falling Waters, West Virginia. Lori is active in the youth department of her church and enjoys snorkeling, jet skiing, and traveling. Mar. 29.

Ivy M. Petersen was the women's ministries director in Cape, South Africa, until she took early retirement recently. She spent 34 years of teaching and lecturing in 23 church institutions and is still very involved in women's ministries programs, speaking, and writing. She and her husband, Louis, have five grown children and 10 grandchildren to fill all their spare moments. Nov. 2.

Eunice Peverini is a homemaker and mother of three adult children and grandmother of two. She and her husband, the speaker/director of the La Voz de la Esperanza radio ministry, live in California. She does volunteer work and enjoys interior decorating, flower arrangement and crafts, gardening, sewing, reading, and community work. Jan. 3, Aug. 8.

Mari Gibbs-Pickett is a professional artist and art educator. She has won many awards, and her work is in international private collections. She believes her greatest masterpieces are the children that her husband, Dale Pickett, and the Lord have given her. She hopes that she may help them become portraits in the likeness of the living Lord. Mar. 4, Apr. 5.

Birdie Poddar is from northeastern India. She and her minister husband live in Poona, India. Birdie has three adult children and two grandchildren, and worked as an elementary teacher, cashier, cashier accountant, and statistician before retiring in 1991. May 25, July 14, Oct. 5.

Ellen Rockel Dos Reis, from Brazil, is married and has two children. She has dedicated her life to ministry in various departments of her church, and has for the past few years concentrated her efforts in children's ministry. Aug. 26.

Sylvia Renz is a minister's wife, mother, and homemaker living in Darmstadt, Germany. She is a published writer of articles, radio programs for Adventist World Radio, and books. She loves reading and discussing issues with young people. June 16, Sept. 18.

Linda Reynolds and her husband live in northern California. They have three children. She has been active for many years in her local church. Since the birth of their daughter, she has worked to improve the rights of handicapped children and their parents. She also worked with a group that gave support to parents of newly diagnosed children. Sept. 12, Nov. 8.

Jill Hines Richards lives in Montana, where her husband is a teacher at Mount Ellis Academy. Jill is presently working on her doctorate in curriculum instruction and running for the office of county superintendent of schools. She enjoys cross-stitch, birdwatching, reading, crafts, skiing, and interior design. MAR. 25.

Kay D. Rizzo writes from Tulare, California. She and her husband have two married daughters. Kay is a monthly columnist for *Listen* and *Signs of the Times*, in addition to the 25 books she's published. She is an international guest speaker for women's ministry retreats, student Weeks of Prayer, churches, camp meetings, and civic groups. JAN. 12, SEPT. 13, SEPT. 14, SEPT. 29, NOV. 29.

Leona Glidden Running is a retired professor (emeritus) of biblical languages at Andrews University, where she still teaches several ancient languages. Three books she has written have been published, and she enjoys swimming, reading, knitting, and crocheting. OCT. 11.

Deborah Sanders is a housewife, mother, and writer. She and her husband make their home in Canada with their two children. She has written a collection of poetry and goes by the pen name "Sonny's Mommy," and enjoys doing community service work. NOV. 5.

Sheila Sanders has been a teacher and speech therapist, and currently works with retarded adults living independently in the community. She has been married and has two grown daughters and three stepchildren. She enjoys people, good music, and photography. JUNE 11, JULY 24, NOV. 24.

Hannah Priscilla Sandy is working toward a master's degree in public health. Her husband is the president of the Sierra Leone Mission in western Africa, where she has written a paper on female circumcision, which is practiced in Africa. MAY 18.

Susana Schulz, college professor and mother of three daughters, is the former women's ministries director for the South American Division. She has just moved back to River Plate College in Argentina, where her husband is the new president. During their previous years of work at the college she was the dean of women. She enjoys good music, good company, and laughter. MAR. 10.

Susan Scoggins is a secretary in West Des Moines, Iowa, where her husband is in administration. She is the mother of three young adults. NOV 14.

Karon Scott is an attorney's wife, mother of one married son, stepmother to two daughters, and stepgrandma to one little boy. She is secretary to the president and secretary of the Mid-America Union Conference in Lincoln, Nebraska. She loves animals, but her specialty is cats. DEC. 16.

Jean Sequeira, born in England, now lives and writes in the United States. She has worked as a Bible instructor, teacher, and office manager. She spent 18 years as a missionary in East Africa with her minister husband and two children. Her interests are calligraphy, flower gardening, photography, and writing. SEPT. 26.

Roberta Sharley and her husband, Lawrence, are retired—both from the health field. Roberta is a registered nurse. They have lived all their lives in the northwest United States. Roberta is active in her church. MAY 9, JUNE 27, DEC. 24.

Carrol Johnson Shewmake worked with her minister husband for 43 years, 15 of them as a school librarian. She is the mother of four adult children and seven grandchildren, has written numerous articles and authored several published books, and presents seminars on prayer. Her hobbies are nature, writing, reading, speaking, dolls, sewing, and people. JULY 31.

Judy Shewmake is editor of *The Adventist Home Educator*, a newsletter for parents who are home schoolers. The five Shewmakes are Californians. Judy collects blue plates, does cross-stitch, and likes working with children. FEB. 15.

Sheryl Walter-Shewmake is the wife of a professional auto technician, a home-schooling mother of two daughters, a part-time church secretary, and a children's Bible class teacher in her church. She lives on 30 acres of wooded land in northeast Washington, and enjoys painting, sewing, calligraphy, and the great outdoors. SEPT. 28, OCT. 17.

Iris Shull is an administrative assistant in marketing at the Review and Herald Publishing Association. Iris is married and has two sons, Matthew and Dennis. She is active in her local church and is a member of the Hagerstown chapter of Professional Secretaries International. Her pastimes include music (singing or playing her flute), reading, travel, and embroidery. **Apr. 3.**

Marion Simmons is a retired educator who spent 50 years in church work at the elementary and college level, and in departmental work. She is a published writer and enjoys traveling, public speaking, reading, and promotional work. **Aug. 3.**

Jackie Ordelheide Smith writes from Silver Spring, Maryland. She enjoys traveling, volleyball, camping, and spending time with her husband, Robert, and her dog, Jake. She is the coordinator for Global Mission Pioneers at the General Conference. **Dec. 11.**

Janice R. Smith, the mother of four young children, is an elementary teacher, homemaker, and recording artist, and plans to home-school her children. She is involved in ministry to families and is the kindergarten leader at her local church in Canada. She enjoys outdoor activities with her family, sewing, craft making, and music. **May 8.**

Marie Spangler, founder of Shepherdess International (a support system for ministers' wives), is a retired teacher, mother of two grown children, and a minister's wife. She is a published writer whose special interests include music, memory books, people, pastors' wives, and early childhood development. **Oct. 16, Sept. 22, Nov. 23, Dec. 20.**

Glenice Linthwaite Steck writes from northern California, where she lives with her husband and two children. She works as an administrative secretary at St. Helena Hospital, and is actively involved with the children's department at her church. Her hobbies include collecting Dickens Village lighted miniatures and walking. **Jan. 27.**

Ardis Dick Stenbakken was an active Army chaplain's wife for 23 years; however, her husband retired to serve at the administrative level in their church. She is most proud of their adult son and daughter. Ardis is concerned about women's issues and enjoys church work, crafts, reading, travel, and public speaking. **Jan. 19, May 3, July 19, Sept. 21.**

Elizabeth Sterndale, a psychiatric nurse, is a general field secretary and the director of women's ministries for the North American Division. She has written several articles on health topics and enjoys reading, gardening, traveling, listening, and walking. **Jan. 17.**

Beulah Fern Stevens is director of pastoral care at Portland Adventist Medical Center in Portland, Oregon. She is a chaplain, nurse, published author, and speaker. **Mar. 7, May 27, June 5, July 1, Aug. 20, Sept. 19, Dec. 27.**

Marilisa Foffa Stina is a women's ministries leader in São Paulo, Brazil. She is a pastor's wife and enjoys playing the piano, swimming, and nature. **June 28.**

Cindy Sumarauw came far from her home in Indonesia to study at Pacific Union College, and graduated in June of 1994 with degrees in psychology and predentistry. **Feb. 11.**

Laura Lee Swaney is presently studying to be a certified alcoholism counselor and plans to counsel adult survivors of incest. Her goal is for a ministry in helping battered women and people with drug addictions find freedom in Jesus. She and her family reside near the Ithaca, New York, area. **Feb. 13, Apr. 27, July 10.**

Loraine Sweetland, a librarian, writes book reviews for *Library Journal* and is a director and editor of the local Rotary Club newsletter. She taught school for 14 years, has served as personal ministries director for her church, and has held many other church offices. She enjoys reading, antiques, gardening, and computer work. **Mar. 26, July 25.**

Arlene Taylor is president and founder of a consulting and education service, and director of infection control at the St. Helena Hospital in California. She is a published writer, hosts a one-hour weekly radio program, *Causerie*, and is an internationally known lecturer. **Jan. 13, July 16, Aug. 6, Sept. 3, Oct. 11.**

Audre B. Taylor is an administrative assistant for ADRA, and serves as a local church elder. Her hobbies are writing and choral conducting. She is a published writer, and a practicing psychotherapist in the metropolitan Washington, D.C., area. **Sept. 8.**

Wendy Piner Taylor is married, has a 20-month-old son, and lives in California's beautiful Napa Valley. She is an English major in college and plans to pursue a career in writing. She enjoys snowboarding, sailing, and hiking. **July 18.**

Edna Thomas, a missionary, is a native of Memphis, Tennessee. She is currently living and teaching primary school in Freetown, Sierra Leone. MAR. 23.

Peggy Tompkins, a church administrator's wife and a homemaker, is the mother of two married children. She has been editor of *The Heart of the Home*, a publication for mothers at home, since 1986. She enjoys houseplants, reading, hiking, and other adventures with her four grandsons. JUNE 19, AUG. 21, SEPT. 20.

Rita Van Horn is an assistant professor at Pacific Union College, where she is teaching nursing. She recently returned from mission service in Lesotho. She is actively involved in women's ministries in her church and enjoys reading, cooking, and visiting with friends. JAN. 18, OCT. 31.

Nancy Van Pelt, a certified family life educator and home economist, is an author and internationally known speaker. She has written 17 books on family life, a prayer notebook, and has her nineteenth book under way. Nancy coordinates a women's ministries group that meets in her home in Fresno, California, where she lives with her husband, Harry. Her hobbies are getting organized, having fun, and quilting. JULY 5, JULY 6, NOV. 22.

Janis Vance is president and founder of Take Heart retreats, a ministry devoted to spiritual healing for women who have been sexually abused in childhood. She is a registered nurse and a licensed rehabilitation counselor with a master's degree in education. She teaches an adult Bible class at her local church. Janis and her husband live in California and are the parents of three grown children. JULY 27, DEC. 15.

Corrine Vanderwerff, a missionary and freelance writer, manages REACH child sponsorship projects in Zaire, where her husband is the ADRA director. She has two new book releases, one being the 1994 junior devotional. MAR. 8, MAY 6.

Evelyn VandeVere is the director of women's ministries for the Southern Union Conference. She has had articles published in *Our Little Friend*, *These Times*, *Adventist Review*, and *Among Friends*. Her hobbies and special interests are putting together family albums of pictures and mementoes, reading books, and writing articles. APR. 7.

Nancy Cachero Vasquez, an administrative secretary in the North American Division office, is the wife of a church administrator and mother of three young adult children. Her special interests are reading, writing, crafts, shopping, and baking. FEB. 21, OCT. 6, DEC. 10.

Maria Cristine Vicente lives and works in Brazil. She has one son and enjoys working with children and young people. NOV. 28.

Nancy Jean Vyhmeister is a professor of mission at the Seventh-day Adventist Theological Seminary at Andrews University in Michigan. She has written various articles for religious publications and textbooks. Nancy enjoys homemaking, writing, friendships, and her grandson. FEB. 8, OCT. 23.

Jackie Phalen Wait graduated in 1994 from Southern College with a B.S. in nursing and married in August. She and her minister husband are currently working in Louisiana. At the time this devotional was written she was a student, and engaged to be married. She enjoys singing, camping, hiking, and skiing. MAR. 19.

Ellen Swayze-Ward is the wife of a retired minister. Although she is in her 80s, she remains active in church work. Her hobbies include reading and flowers. DEC. 21.

Anna M. Radke Waters is enjoying her retirement in the state of Washington. She and her husband have five children and seven grandchildren. Anna does cross-stitch, plays Scrabble, writes, and works in her yard—for fun! JULY 2.

Sharlet Briggs Waters, director of medical records at St. Helena Hospital, is a wife and mother of two young children and is involved in children's Sabbath school. Sharlet's interests are gourmet cooking, travel, home remodeling and redecorating, and shopping. MAR. 6.

Elizabeth Watson, an associate professor of social work at Andrews University and the associate director of the Center for Cultural Diversity, is also the director of GENESIS, a program designed for single parents to earn a college degree. She is a local church elder and women's ministries coordinator, and presents workshops and seminars. The mother of three, she enjoys writing children's stories, cross-stitch, reading, and letter writing. JUNE 9.

Dorothy Eaton Watts, a freelance writer, editor, and speaker, is a church administrator's wife in Canada. She was a missionary in India for 16 years, founded an orphanage, taught elementary school, and has authored 10 books and numerous articles in religious publications. Her hobbies include bird-watching, gardening, and hiking. JAN. 10, FEB. 19, SEPT. 17.

Kit Watts is an assistant editor of the *Adventist Review*. She has been a pastor, teacher, and librarian. Kit lives in Silver Spring, Maryland, and her interests are traveling and photography. OCT. 24.

Davena Wellington, a single parent for four years, is now remarried. She and her husband have two children and live in St. Louis, Missouri. She is involved in her church in family life, women's ministries, and working with youth. She enjoys volleyball, reading, and nature activities. NOV. 20.

Veryl Dawn Were writes from South Australia, where she is a homemaker. She is a nurse by profession, served as a missionary for eight years, is the mother of one grown son, and has written articles for various religious publications. Currently she is involved in community service work with her husband and enjoys gardening, bird-watching, stamp collecting, and knitting. NOV. 10.

Penny Estes Wheeler is the editor of a new women's magazine, *Women of Spirit*, and the author of eight books and numerous articles for religious publications. She was also the editor of *Guide* for three years. Her other interests include flower gardening and walking. AUG. 1, AUG. 2, DEC. 3.

Robyn Wheeler, at the time she wrote this devotional, was in her second year of teaching history and English as a second language at a public college in the People's Republic of China. In her spare time she enjoys reading, swimming, photography, and traveling. DEC. 22.

Carlene Will teaches seminars on home organization and personal devotions. She is the women's ministries leader for her local church. She is the mother of four boys, and works in her opthalmologist husband's medical office in Issaquah, Washington. AUG. 10.

Rhoda Wills is an English teacher at Andrews Academy on the banks of Lake Michigan. She's the mother of three grown children and enjoys gardening, reading, and music in her spare time. JAN. 24.

Debby Gray Wilmot, a registered nurse, homemaker, piano teacher, pastor's wife, and mother of two, lives in California. She is the church choir director, an accomplished accompanist, and a coordinator for the Northern California Conference Shepherdess organization. Debby enjoys acrylic painting, flower gardening, and composing music for voice, keyboard, and guitar. JUNE 7, JULY 29, DEC. 29.

Marcedene V. Wood is a retired secretary, copy editor, and Bible instructor. She worked in Kansas, Hawaii, the western United States, and the Washington, D.C., area. At the present time she is the leader in the children's department for ages 7-10 in her church in Kansas. Her hobby is working with these young children. MAY 19.

Kathy Jo Duterrow Yergen spent 16 years in Washington and 17 years in Alaska. She currently resides in Beltsville, Maryland, where she and her husband work together in team ministry. Her interests include watercolor, drama, music, and poetry. SEPT. 27.

Opal Hoover Young died July 1993 at the age of 92. She was a college professor of literature, and an editor, writer, and poet. APR. 18.

Leni Zamorano is an elementary school teacher and a homemaker in Buenos Aires, Argentina. She has two children, and works in the music department of her church. Her favorite hobby is embroidery of tapestry. MAR. 22, APR. 4.

Sandy Zaugg currently teaches English as a second language to international students at Walla Walla College. She is a widow with one adult daughter. Her hobbies include reading, traveling, wood carving, and writing. MAR. 5, SEPT. 16, NOV. 9.

Gabriele Ziegler is editor at the *Voice of Hope* in Darmstadt, Germany. She writes radio programs that are broadcast from different local radio stations in Germany. She likes reading, gardening, and having long talks with her husband and friends. MAR. 30.

January 1

How He Leads

When my heart is overwhelmed: lead me to the rock that is higher than I. Ps. 61:2.

My mom was a pack rat in the most positive way. She saved everything that had to do with her family. Every newspaper article. Every report card. Every letter. And I'm glad she did, or I wouldn't have found an old letter I'd written to her that helped me recall how God opened the door for me to get my education.

I remembered I wanted to go to Michigan because I had fallen in love with a man who was getting his doctorate in biostatistics at the University of Michigan. Mom was less than enthusiastic. She couldn't imagine any daughter of hers traipsing off across the country "chasing" a man. But for some reason my selective memory had forgotten that I had gone to the University of Michigan for summer school (where Jan was a student), in spite of her opposition. She felt it was foolish when I had no money. I just knew that if God wanted me to get a graduate degree in child development from Michigan State University (70 miles away from Jan and the University of Michigan), He'd somehow provide a way. Here's what I wrote to Mom on July 25, 1962:

"Last night was the worst night of my life. I was torn as I thought about everything you had said and wanted me to do. How did I know this was where I should be? Was it really God's will, or was it my own willful way that got me to Michigan? I can't remember when I have been so confused.

"About 11:30 p.m. I couldn't stand it any longer. I had heard of the Bible comforting people—but I didn't know what to read. Finally I thought I'd just open the Bible and see what I'd find. My eyes fell on this verse: 'When my heart is overwhelmed: lead me to the rock that is higher than I' (Ps. 61:2). I couldn't believe it. I was sure no other text could be more appropriate. Then I turned a few pages, and these words caught my eye: 'In thee, O Lord, do I put my trust: let me never be put to confusion' (Ps. 71:1). I memorized these verses and determined to make them mine, and finally fell asleep.

"This morning as I was walking to class I repeated these verses and then forgot about my conflict until a few moments ago, when I returned to my room. A call was waiting for me from Dr. Borgman, my advisor from MSU. She was calling to say that one of the graduates who had a two-year teaching assistantship had just resigned, and was wondering if I would want it for next year. Can you believe it? The experience will be worth as much as the schooling, plus my tuition will be paid!"

The Lord is watching over each one of us. Sometimes things seem dark, but if we trust in Him, our faith will be rewarded. If I had gotten this scholarship before going to Michigan, it would not have meant nearly as much. I would have known for sure where to go, and it wouldn't have taken any faith. But having to wait—not knowing, searching my heart, praying for guidance, stepping out against others to do what I thought was right, but not having a sure sign—has strengthened my faith. It's stronger than ever before. God has taught me a lesson that I would have learned in no other way— that of utter dependence upon Him, "the rock that is higher than I."

May we each depend completely on Him every day this new year as we prepare to go home with Jesus when He comes again.

KAY KUZMA

January 2

DECEIVED

Do not deceive yourselves. 1 Cor. 3:18, NRSV.

Preposterous! How could I, who loved the truth, deceive myself? And then it happened!

For weeks I'd waited for this moment. Several years had passed since our son and his wife had visited us. Now they were bringing our grandson for his first trip to Grandpa and Grandma's home.

Traveling 120 miles to Spokane Airport, we had spare time before the 10:30 p.m. arrival. Approaching the Alaska Airlines counter, we saw the attendant leave. A sign read "This office will reopen at 5:00 a.m." The posted schedule gave no indication if the plane had arrived or was late.

"Let's go to gate 8," my husband suggested. "We've only 10 minutes to wait."

Skirting the baggage claim area, we climbed the stairs to the concourse.

"Strange," I commented. "No attendant, and the plane's due in minutes."

My husband looked out the window. "There's an Alaska Airlines plane parked at gate 8. It'll be a tight squeeze to get another plane into the empty space beside it."

Just at 10:30 a plane landed. "Right on time!" he announced.

My heart skipped a beat as I watched it taxi down the runway. Soon I'd be holding our dear little grandson in my arms. But the plane went elsewhere. Time passed. Another plane landed, but it wasn't Alaska Airlines.

"Wonder why nothing's posted on the signboard," my husband observed.

More planes landed. By 11:00 p.m. we were almost alone.

"I'm going to find someone who can give us information on Alaska Airlines," I said.

Again I passed the baggage claim area without a glance. I hurried toward the only open ticket counter. "Sorry, lady," the agent replied, "we have information only on our airline."

Returning to gate 8, I saw my husband still looking.

"Something's wrong!" I cried. "No one's waiting for this flight." In desperation I approached a pilot standing by gate 6. "Pardon me, but may I ask your advice? We arrived here 10 minutes before the Alaska Airlines plane from Los Angeles was due, have waited for more than an hour, and can't get information from anyone."

"Try calling Alaska Airlines to see if it arrived early or has been canceled."

"Thanks. I don't know why we didn't think of that."

My husband called. Concern covered his face.

"How dumb can we be!" he pointed out the window. "That plane arrived almost two hours ago."

Rushing to the baggage claim area, we saw our tired daughter-in-law holding the baby. Our son was desperately calling his brother, trying to decide what to do and to find out what had happened to us.

We'd ignored every clue: the closed ticket counter, no gate attendant, the parked airplane, the lack of people waiting. Blinded by what we believed was truth, we'd blocked out the facts.

This year may we each not be deceived, but choose to pay attention to the Holy Spirit as He draws us in love to Him.

EILEEN E. LANTRY

JANUARY 3

WITH THE FAITH OF A CHILD

He called a little child and had him stand among them. And he said: "I tell you the truth, unless you change and become like little children, you will never enter the kingdom of heaven." Matt. 18:2, 3, NIV.

We were on our way home from the optometrist. My 10-year-old daughter was thrilled, wearing her first pair of contact lenses. Now she could see 20/20 and could make out signs on stores, names of streets, and even distinct leaves on the trees.

The lenses had cost a lot of money, but it was a sacrifice we were willing to make so that she would be able to see better, and never again be called "four-eyes"! I took advantage of the short drive home to explain again that she needed to be very careful with her contact lenses, especially until she was more used to wearing them.

Two days later as I glanced out the window I smiled to see my daughter happily playing with a friend, turning somersaults on the green, somewhat overgrown lawn in the backyard. Suddenly I remembered, *Susana has her contact lenses on. Will she lose them playing like that?* I got up to remind her to be careful, but on my way out I ran into her coming to tell me, in a weak voice and near tears, "I think I lost one of my contact lenses."

"Where?" The question was almost ridiculous. Of course, somewhere in that long grass.

"Can you tell me what area you were playing in when you lost it?" Another senseless question.

"Around here, Mom," she said, pointing to an area about 10 feet square.

After looking for a while I said, "Who can find a tiny contact lens in this thick, tall grass? It's simply impossible! We've tried. We'll just have to buy another one."

Susana looked at me with her innocent face and said, "Jesus knows where it is. He knows where everything is. He can show it to us. Let's pray, Mom."

The sun was getting low in the sky. We knelt right where we were, our hands still on the lawn we'd been combing through, and closed our eyes. In my heart I asked the Lord to give me words to explain to her that He can't always take charge of all our little problems for us.

We both prayed. When I opened my eyes, my index finger was

pointing directly at the contact lens, which glinted in the last rays of the sun, seemingly saying, "Here I am!" I felt something very special at that moment. I was ready to cry tears of joy, to laugh, to shout at the top of my lungs, "Thank You, Lord! My daughter will always know that there is Someone who cares about the big things and the little things."

Many times through the years contact lenses have been lost in our house, but the Lord has helped to open our eyes, reminding us that if He counts the very hairs on our head and knows when the sparrows fall, He no doubt watches over us and will guide us as we, like little children, give our hearts into His hands. EUNICE PEVERINI

JANUARY 4

CONFESSIONS OF A LIST-MAKER

Create in me a clean heart, O God; and renew a right spirit within me. Ps. 51:10.

There's a pad of paper on my desk, a nice brand-new graph paper pad—the kind I like to use for making lists. It's untouched, except for three words at the top of the first page—"New Year's Resolutions," it says. I've been meaning to fill up the rest of the page, just as soon as I figure out how.

Making lists is one of my favorite pastimes. I love to "get organized." I've even been known to write something on my list of things to do after I've done it, just so I can have the pleasure of crossing it off. Anyway, my New Year's resolutions list still lies untouched. An unfamiliar uncertainty has kept the page blank for days now. I've been making nice neat New Year's resolutions lists every year since I was a child. Last year I even made them publicly, in front of several of my friends. Funny, I don't remember what all the items on the list were—obviously I achieved very few of them.

My resolutions in the past have read like a grocery list of past flaws and future hopes—a reminder to myself to replenish things I have run out of, such as patience and kindness, and to try to stock up on abilities I've never had.

When I make the list, I plan to be able to cross the items off one by one, as I push my grocery cart up the aisles that mark the months of the new year. Perhaps my problem is that I never actually get a new year. I carry my old years along with me and write my new list on the same old dusty slate. "Stop eating between meals." Could be that's one of yours, too. It certainly has been on my list year after year. When I write it down, I'm thinking about last year's bad habits. I also write, "Be a better parent, wife, daughter, friend, worker"—somehow again just steering my way back to the shelves that hold last year's faults.

But the tradition of New Year's resolutions is an acknowledgment that despite all we've done in the past, we can change. It's a way to tip your hat to the possibilities within yourself, to the idea that the future can be different.

As a Christian, I get really excited about this concept. And the more I pray about it, the more I know that not only can I do better, but I can really be different, through the grace of Jesus Christ.

Today's text is perfect for a list-maker! Item 1 on my list: clean heart. Item 2: renewed right spirit. In the spirit of joy that putting one's life in the hands of Jesus brings, I resolve to sort out some of my priorities this year. Rather than trying to improve myself, I can humbly seek God's help, and with His assistance be a better parent, wife, friend, daughter, and all those other things I want to be.

I invite you to join me and take this verse as your New Year's resolution. You'll be free to break old patterns, and even take a risk or two. — SUSAN HARVEY

JANUARY 5

IN HIS KEEPING

For he has charged his angels to guard you wherever you go.
Ps. 91:11, NEB.

Our family was driving through Manitoba wheat fields one Sunday, hurrying to a North Dakota workers' retreat. The undulating grain offered a certain beauty, but we'd seen no real towns—only an occasional block or two of houses huddled around a closed gas station/store.

"I'm getting sleepy," Bob said. "Would you drive?"

He pulled over and turned off the engine. We switched places. I turned my key in the ignition. Nothing happened. I waited, tried again—nothing. The nearest farmhouse was barely visible on the horizon.

Bob looked under the hood, but we knew any automotive illness had to be extremely obvious before we could diagnose it.

"Guess I'll have to hitchhike to Winnipeg," Bob announced.

"No way," I countered. I knew that even if he got a ride, Winnipeg was two hours away, which meant four hours' travel. And finding any mechanic on Sunday, much less one who would know what our problem was and have the parts to fix it, would be next to impossible. Furthermore, I'd be left sitting by the road with three children. More out of fear than piety I offered, "Why don't we pray about it first?"

We reminded God that Bob was the retreat speaker and that we mustn't be late. We had no solution, but knew He could help.

"Now what?" we asked. What's the proper response after requesting a miracle—look under the hood again? Fiddle with something? Try once more? Wait for an angel? If so, how long?

I finished a game our son and I were playing, then tried again. Nothing.

But before Bob could say "I'm hitchhiking to Winnipeg," a pickup slowed beside us. "Got some trouble?" asked the driver.

"Well, yes. But it's one of these foreign cars you probably don't see many of here."

He parked behind us and got out. "I may not be able to help, but I'll be glad to take a look."

Bob asked, "Do you live around here?"

"About a mile and a half down the road," he replied, nodding in the direction from which he'd come. "We farmers pretty much have to fix our own equipment. There's just no other way. Winnipeg's too far."

I fixed my eyes on him. If this was an angel, there'd be none of this sudden-disappearance stuff while I turned away for a moment. I turned the key and pressed the accelerator when told to, but kept observing him through the crack formed by the raised hood. Definitely a farmer—flannel shirt, sleeves rolled up, worn and stained jeans, sunbaked face, and stout, sturdy hands.

"With our vehicles we just have to keep trying until something works," he commented. About then something did. The engine roared to life.

As the farmer returned to his pickup we thanked him profusely, but he replied, "No trouble. I just noticed you seemed stuck." He started his engine, then waited to make sure we got onto the road without killing ours.

I drove away slowly, keeping an eye on the rearview mirror to preclude missing anything if this real farmer and pickup suddenly vanished. They didn't. But I watched clearly as he backed into a dirt path in the wheat field and headed back down the highway—*in the direction from which he had come.* MADELINE S. JOHNSTON

January 6

A Never-ending Task

But he knows the way that I take; when he has tested me, I will come forth as gold. Job 23:10, NIV.

While enjoying a rare, quiet day at home I turned on the television to a program that was offering helpful hints to homemakers. The advice that caught my attention concerned a homemade solution for cleaning brass. The host instructed the television audience to make this solution, in an amount proportionate to the size of the pieces needing to be cleaned, using a ratio of one cup of water to a teaspoon of both salt and vinegar. I watched her polish to a fine sheen the items she'd been soaking in this mixture. Her recipe seemed to work like magic!

Over the years I have accumulated several silver-plated serving pieces and miscellaneous brass items, including a brass headboard. I admire these things, but they continue to cost me precious time. In order to be beautiful, each piece must undergo repetitious polishing. Cleaning the bed is the most time-consuming, but because it looks so beautiful when I'm done I continue to repeat the process when it begins to look tarnished.

While preparing to entertain guests recently, I got out a couple silver-plated serving trays. Even though they'd had a recent cleaning, they wouldn't pass scrutiny on the buffet table.

I considered arranging some leafy lettuce around the edge of the salad tray, but decided against it. I was sure that as the guests helped themselves to the food the tarnish would become obvious. I was frustrated with the frequency that these trays needed polishing in order to be useful. I didn't have time to spend polishing tarnished metal. I put the trays away and used glass.

As I continued to prepare the meal I reflected on a spiritual parallel to my decision. I was reminded that just like my silver and brass, I too require an ongoing polishing if there is to be real beauty in my character. Without God's frequent polishing it would be impossible for me to "shine" for Him. However, there is a major difference between my attitude and God's concerning the polishing process. While the frequent need to polish my things frustrates me, the Master Designer finds joy in "polishing" the characters of His children. Praise God, He never grows weary of this process.

I can't begin to comprehend God's patience, because the only gauge I have with which to measure is the yardstick of my own human experience. But I remind myself that my heavenly Father has promised to be present in my life moment by moment. "I will never leave you nor forsake you" (Joshua 1:5, NIV). His omnipresence is one of the greatest sources of peace in the Christian life.

Today I want to be more conscious of my heavenly Father's tender concern for the polishing process necessary in my life. I want to invite Him to continue this process until I am ready to meet Him face-to-face. I want to be more like Him. ROSE OTIS

JANUARY 7

EVERYTHING STARTED WITH WORDS

In the beginning God created the heaven and the earth. . . . And God said . . ." Gen. 1:1-3.

God could have stamped His feet. He could have commanded Gabriel to do it. He could simply have *thought* the world into existence.

But He spoke.

In the beginning there were words. Before the world there were words. The God-chosen means of creation: words.

The internationally famous Helen Keller coped with a triple disability, the complications of a fever at 19 months having left her blind, deaf, and basically mute. For almost seven years she lived in a sightless, soundless, wordless world, a pathetic, frustrated child. One memorable day her teacher, Annie Sullivan, finally made her understand that there were such things as words. Helen testified she went to bed that night for the first time a happy child, her joy dependent on words.

In 1904 Helen finished college, graduating with honors from Radcliffe. Incredibly, she learned to read in *five* languages. For such accomplishments Mark Twain called her one of the two most remarkable people of the nineteenth century. Her achievements with words distinguished her from other deaf-mutes.

Although doctors never helped her regain any sight or hearing, Annie Sullivan did have limited success in teaching her to talk. But Helen's voice quality was such that she needed an interpreter. Interestingly enough, she stated her greatest personal disappointment was her inability to *speak* clearly, not her deafness or blindness. Helen defined her life, as it were, by words.

Words . . . the medium of the creation of all life and the medium in which life continues to be enlarged, explained, enriched, and controlled.

So now in the beginning of a new year there are still words: words of promise and words of despair; words of praise and words of condemnation; words of truth and words of lies—in short, words used or abused.

As we reflect this year on scriptural passages relating to words, let us resolve to make our own use of them more accountable. As we heighten awareness of language concerns, let us resolve to make our response to words more sensitive. Impressed with their potential for good or evil, let us resolve to take our communications gifts more responsibly.

Let us resolve because . . . in the beginning were *words*.

WILMA MCCLARTY

JANUARY 8

A JOYFUL HEART

Delight thyself also in the Lord; and he shall give thee the desires of thine heart. Ps. 37:4.

As a fairly new Christian, I had been anxious and eager to please the Lord in everything I did. I had read the above promise before and had wondered when and how He'd answer it. I was a single parent living in New York City, and I had many concerns for my little boy. I wanted to do all I could to give him a Christian home and education. I'd pray with him at night and send him off to church school each morning. I was thrilled to be able to send him to a Christian school, and thanked the Lord for the privilege. Yet from time to time I'd watch many mothers as they happily walked their children to and from the nearby school. I longed for the privilege of walking my son to school too. My heart ached as I wished to share that part of the day with him. But it was useless since I worked full-time and could not even be home when he returned from school in the afternoons. He'd stay with a neighbor until I arrived. I imagined his longings to have me there when I arrived (I had longed for my working single mother as a youth).

Several months passed, and one evening I received a call from the driver of the van who drove my son to school along with other children. He explained that he could no longer drive the children to school. At the time I thought it would be a big problem, but after praying about it, I realized that the only solution was to get up hours earlier and take him to school myself before going to work. I didn't have a car, so the only choice was public transportation. It was rather stressful at first, but after a while we enjoyed the time together. The Lord guided and protected us through the many hours of travel in the crowded and at times dangerous railways.

Although I didn't see it at first, the Lord had answered a desire of my heart. With great joy I still thank Him today.

Each one of us must acknowledge daily His marvelous answers to our deepest desires. Isn't He wonderful!   CARMEN O. GONZALEZ

JANUARY 9

A GOOD MEASURE FOR ME

Give, and it will be given to you. A good measure, pressed down, shaken together and running over, will be poured into your lap. Luke 6:38, NIV.

I was working my way through college during World War II. I was a new Christian, barred from my home because of my new beliefs. All the money I earned in my job went toward my tuition and dormitory fees, except $3 a month to cover my personal needs. I was very careful with that money.

One of the requirements at the college was that female students wear stockings everywhere on campus. Bare-legged indignity, even in the steamiest of Michigan summers, was not to be tolerated, on pain of a $1 fine. Rayon hose, costing an unbelievable $1 a pair, had replaced the newly minted nylon hosiery when they went out of production because of the war and into filmy parachutes "for the boys."

With a little mending gadget available at the time, most of us had painstakingly closed up the "ladders" in our last pair of nylons. Finally, when they became too fragile to be mended further, we had been forced to wear our rayon stockings.

I was faithfully wearing and washing nightly my one and only pair of these less dainty hose, careful not to risk my last dollar, when the Week of Sacrifice at church rolled around. Serious about entering into all church programs, I was sad to discover I had nothing to sacrifice for the offering promoted in the nightly worship.

It struck me that sacrifice did not mean giving up something one didn't want or could do without; it meant giving up something one needed. I would sacrifice $1, Lord sparing my hose.

It had been a stressful week of late-night study and lack of sleep. I had given up my bed to my roommate's mother, who was visiting for a week. As I walked to church I realized that my venerable, much-washed rayon stockings had developed a run. Now what was I to do? The run in my stocking was devastating, and I cried as I entered the church. But when the offering plate came by I gave the $1 that I had pledged.

That evening I sewed up the run in the obligatory stockings into a clumsy seam, not to be confused with the normal seam in the back, featured on all stockings in those days. The next day I hurried from work to the dorm to bid goodbye to Ruth's mother. I was too late; she had already left. A thin box was on my bed with a note from Ruth's mother on top—a thank-you for the sacrifice of my bed. Inside the box? A pair of nylon stockings. JEANNE JORDAN

January 10

GOLDEN MESSENGER

I will never leave thee, nor forsake thee. Heb. 13:5.

It happened four days after my surgery for breast cancer. Although the surgeon had made only a three-inch incision to remove a small lump, my right breast was sore and ugly-looking. Several blood vessels leaked, causing heavy bruising. The swollen breast turned from red to purple to black, then yellow and green.

I was feeling sorry for myself, but at my husband Ron's urging I rode along to the river to watch the sunset while he walked Matt, our golden retriever, along the dike.

It was a glorious sunset! The whole river appeared as liquid gold, with here and there shadows of waves making patches of turquoise blue. I started to cry. The beauty and peace of the scene contrasted starkly with my tumultuous feelings of fear for the future. What every woman dreads had come to me.

My tears flowed unchecked, and my throat ached from the tension of wondering what the end would be. For those few moments it was hard to remember that God was still in control.

As I watched the gold change to softer shades of peach, apricot, and soft mauve I thought of Ron and Matt walking off into the sunset of life without me. How would they manage? He'd surely marry again. The thought brought a fresh river of tears. (I was really getting into this!)

Just then I heard the rapid beat of feet on the hard path. I looked up, and through my tears I saw Matt racing, tongue hanging out, straight toward the car. He came around to my side; I opened the door. He laid his head on my knee and looked up at me with those wonderful adoring eyes as if to say, "Whatever is wrong with you?"

I forgot myself as I tried to get him to go back to Ron. He refused to go without me. Ordinarily he follows the one who moves the fastest. This was unlike him. No amount of coaxing would make him leave. He stayed by my side, refusing to enjoy the walk without me. Amazing! I know that somehow that dog sensed something was wrong and wanted to help.

Feeling warmly cherished, I wrote in my journal a prayer of sudden realization and gratitude: "Thank You, Lord, for sending Matt to comfort me, to make me smile, to restore my sense of balance and my trust in You! As Matt nuzzled against me, refusing to leave my side, I heard You whisper to my fearful heart, 'Dorothy, I will never leave you nor forsake you.'"
DOROTHY EATON WATTS

JANUARY 11

WHAT DO ANGELS LOOK LIKE?

What are the angels, then? They are spirits who serve God and are sent by him to help those who are to receive salvation. Heb. 1:14, TEV.

The car was packed, and I was just starting to pull out of the parking lot when one of my tires went flat. I had a friend in the men's dorm and I called him to come to my rescue, but unfortunately he was no mechanic. We struggled fruitlessly just trying to get the jack together.

"Don't tell me you've never changed a flat before," I said in exasperation.

"All right, I won't tell you," Tom said agreeably.

"What am I going to do?" I wailed. "My parents are expecting me. I'll never make it home on time."

"Need any help?"

Startled, both Tom and I turned around. Neither of us had heard anyone approach, but there he was in all his glory—a genuine mechanic, dressed in a blue gas station uniform complete with grease stains.

"I'll say we need help," Tom said gratefully. "Can you change a tire?"

"Sure. No problem." He knelt down to examine the flat. "Where's your jack?"

The smiling man changed the tire while the two of us more or less looked on. I tried to make light conversation, but apparently he wasn't much on talking.

"I really appreciate you helping me out like this. I was on my way home for the weekend when I discovered that I had this flat, so I called Tom."

"But I don't know anything about cars, so I wasn't much help," Tom finished. "Thanks for bailing me out."

The mechanic just smiled as he tightened the lug nuts and then pushed the hubcap back into place.

"There you go," he said. "All fixed."

Tom picked up the jack, and I went to open the trunk lid. By the time I got it closed, the mechanic had vanished.

"Where did he go?" I asked Tom. "I didn't get a chance to thank him or ask him his name."

"I don't know. He just vanished." Tom looked thoughtful. "Say, you don't think he was . . . an angel, do you?"

"No. He probably just had someplace else to be in a hurry."

"Yeah, probably."

What do angels look like? Do they wear long white robes and have wings? Or were they, like people, created in God's image?

Perhaps they're like Christians, serving as the arms and legs of God. Just as in the story of the good Samaritan, our neighbor—our "angel"—could be anyone with the courage and love to do God's work here on earth. Christ said that when we help others, we are really helping Him. Maybe instead of wondering whether angels look like people, we should be wondering if people could look a little more like angels.

GINA LEE

JANUARY 12

HARD-BOILED TRUTH

Fools think their own way is right, but the wise listen to advice. Prov. 12:15, NRSV.

It was quite simple, really. I'd read the instruction book and all the warnings, but in my mind I questioned the manufacturer's advice. *It's a matter of timing,* I told myself. *If I watch it carefully, I can make it work.*

I dropped a raw egg into a teacup of hot water, placed it in the microwave, closed the door, and set the timer. I waited a few seconds, then peered through the microwave window and smiled. The water was beginning to bubble. I straightened and walked across the kitchen to the sink.

Ka-boom! I whirled about to see the microwave door burst open. Scalding water and bits of egg flew like shrapnel in all directions. I would never have imagined that one medium-sized egg and a half cup of water could make such a mess. I wiped pieces of egg and puddles of water from inside the microwave, the floor, the kitchen counters, the ceiling, and the refrigerator door on the far side of the room.

When Richard ran to the kitchen to find out what had caused the terrible explosion, I told him about my experiment. My husband shook his head in disbelief.

"Kay, I can't believe you did that!" Carefully he explained why the egg had to explode in the confines of the microwave.

All the while, I held up bits and pieces of egg—hard-boiled. "But honey, see? I was right. It did hard-boil the egg. I just had the timing wrong, that's all. Next time I have to . . ."

He groaned, shook his head, and disappeared down the hall to our bedroom and his "reading" corner. And I returned to my cleanup, certain I had been right.

Unfortunately, the next time we used the microwave I discovered that the manufacturer had also been right. The timer and the door on the appliance never worked properly again. Last year we bought a new microwave. The fool in me still believes I can microwave/hard-boil eggs—all I need is to know the exact moment the egg hardens and to be able to remove it from the appliance quickly enough. However, the wise woman in me restrains the inner fool from further scientific experimentation.

Learning by experience is painful. (In the case of my exploding microwave, it was also expensive.) Learning by precept (the manufacturer's instruction booklet) and by example is a safer, saner way to become wise. When I read the manufacturer's warnings but did not heed them, I ruined an expensive appliance. When I choose to ignore my heavenly Father's warnings, the price tag for my foolishness is much, much higher. It involves my eternal salvation.

"Lord, make me wise when it comes to You and Your Word. Teach me not to play the part of the fool when it comes to my eternal salvation." — KAY D. RIZZO

JANUARY 13

AHEAD OF TIME

The Lord has done this, and it is marvelous in our eyes. Ps. 118:23, NIV.

Early morning, and I was leaving for a speaking appointment. The actions came so automatically: press the garage door opener, turn the ignition key, lock the car doors, back out onto the driveway. It was such a familiar routine.

At the end of the driveway I became aware of an overwhelming urge to go back into the house for a pair of panty hose. My first response was simply to ignore the thought. After all, I had never before carried extra support hose with me. Why start now?

The impression would not go away. It was as if the words were imprinted across the video screen of my mind: "Go back into the house and get another pair of hose." I stepped on the brake. One of my New Year's resolutions had been to pay attention to intuition—even when I could not immediately offer any rational explanation. No time like the present to start paying attention, I mused, reversing all my actions of a moment ago. Within 60 seconds I was back in the car, a new pair of support panty hose in my briefcase.

As always when starting out on a trip, I spent the first few minutes talking with my best Friend—outlining my plans for the day and asking for guidance that I might be an exemplary role model. Traffic was congested, and I was glad that I had left home early. The directions sent me to the center of the city, and I parked underneath a skyscraper. Briefcase in hand, I checked the information board for my destination—conference room on the mezzanine.

When I was halfway up the escalator, the moving stairs caught and jerked. I was momentarily thrown down on the metal plates—and then they stopped moving altogether. Walking up the rest of the now-stationary escalator, I assessed the damage. While I was essentially uninjured, the fall had started runs in both legs of my panty hose—wide runs that were rapidly expanding in two directions. Help! My presentation was due to begin in less than 10 minutes.

My thoughts suddenly focused on the extra pair of hose in my briefcase and on the ladies' dressing room—the door of which was directly in front of me. I started to smile. Before I knew of my need, God had answered—*ahead of time* (Isa. 65:24, NIV). I knew beyond a shadow of a doubt that while I could have completed the presentation with runs in my hose so obvious to all, the potential outcome had just been enhanced. I could better concentrate on my talk because my appearance would be intact!

Dr. Luke wrote that God remembers even the sparrows, little birds that are sold five for two cents—and that we are of much more value than many sparrows (Luke 12:6, 7). Once again I had tangible proof that my heavenly Parent was concerned about me as an individual human being—interested in helping me to be all that I could be. God had answered my need before I even knew there would be one. How fortunate to be a daughter of the King.

ARLENE TAYLOR

January 14

No More Tears

He will wipe every tear from their eyes. There will be no more death or mourning or crying or pain, for the old order of things has passed away. Rev. 21:4, NIV.

Have you ever stopped to think that *all* of God's creatures cry? Animals cry when they are in pain or when they are lonesome for their mate or their master. Birds cry too.

I heard a cardinal cry one day. Everyone knows that birds sing, or chirp, or even squawk. But this cardinal was hurting, and he didn't know that birds don't cry, so he cried.

From our bedroom window one afternoon I heard this distressed sound about the same time our son Tom heard it and called to me. There was a male cardinal lying in the grass in our backyard. He couldn't fly, and he was crying.

I picked him up and inspected him the best I could. When he grabbed the web between my thumb and finger, I fully understood how it was that he could crack open sunflower seeds! As soon as he released his grip, he began crying again. I put him down and sat there, feeling stunned and helpless.

Finally Tom brought me gently to my senses and said that we should either help him or put him out of his misery. I decided to call a veterinarian. She said she'd be glad to take a look at him, and as we drove to her office the little bird continued to cry. And so did I.

Once the bird was on the examining table, the vet stretched out his wings and felt him all over. She really couldn't see anything wrong. Then the cardinal became quiet and limp. The doctor grabbed her stethoscope, determined that he still had a pulse, and said she needed to put him in an oxygen tent and incubator immediately.

Tom and I went home, and in a couple hours the doctor called and said that even though she had given the red bird a shot of epinephrine, she couldn't revive him. He had no doubt received a severe concussion.

I love to hear birds singing, and I recognize many of their calls. I am amused when birds scold, but I hope I never again hear a bird cry. Birds aren't supposed to cry—but they do.

Strong, assertive career women aren't supposed to cry—but they do. Articulate elders and hospitable deaconesses aren't supposed to cry—but they do. Some cry loudly, some cry almost inaudibly. Let's be tuned in to our sisters and lend a listening ear or a helping hand when we can. Someday there will be no more tears.   BARBARA HUFF

JANUARY 15

CHOSEN

In him we were also chosen. Eph. 1:11, NIV.

I wish you would reconsider," I said to my daughter, Shirley. "Think about your age. Think about your children. Tammy's in college now, and Kevin will soon be in academy."

"Mom, we've thought about it. We've talked about it. I just can't leave her there," Shirley responded.

"There" meant Honduras, where Shirley and Tammy had gone to participate in an academy mission trip during Tammy's senior year. They had volunteered to do some needed work at an orphanage. In just 10 days those students had accomplished a great deal—and my daughter, a nurse, had helped out in the orphanage, taking care of some of the sick children.

"Just imagine it, Mom," Shirley continued. "All those little ones in metal cribs, whitewashed walls, no stimulation. They are rarely held—just fed and diapered, because the people just don't have time to do much else. You have to see her, Mom. She's so tiny for her age. She needs someone to love her."

"Honey," I said, "by the time she's ready for college, you and Don will be ready to retire!"

"I know," she replied. "We've thought of that too. But Mom, if she never goes to college, she will have had a better life with us than if she stays there. We just can't leave her there."

And she didn't. Shirley and Don and the whole academy and church got involved. After several months the final adoption arrangements were made, and we became grandparents again.

Three-year-old Ana could not even walk. She looked more like an 18-month-old baby. She had an ear infection. Her body was full of parasites, and her head was full of lice. Her foot had been broken, probably from a fall. But she had the biggest, brightest eyes and the most wonderful smile you could imagine! In just one hour she worked her way into our hearts, and we too could never let her go!

Ana is 6 now, still catching up physically and developmentally. She speaks clearly—you can't stop her! And she has a constant glowing twinkle in her eyes. Leave her? Never! She's our precious granddaughter!

And that's the way God is. With all our defects, problems, and cares, He loves us. No, He will never leave us nor forsake us. "He chose us . . . before the foundation of the world. . . . He destined us for adoption as his children through Jesus Christ" (Eph. 1:4, 5, NRSV). "In him we were also chosen."   PATRICIA A. HABADA

JANUARY 16

ICE CREAM

"For I know the plans I have for you," declares the Lord, "plans to prosper you and not to harm you, plans to give you hope and a future." Jer. 29:11, NIV.

With the start of a new calendar year, I am reminded of an experience I had when I was the "ripe old age of 14." I thought I knew everything! (After all, I was in my teens and no longer a child!) While on a vacation trip I ordered an ice-cream cone.

Now, this may not seem to be such a big event—I mean, I used to get ice-cream cones even when I wasn't on vacation! And I would always order the same thing—chocolate! Was there anything else? Chocolate was my favorite—my whole family knew that. But since this was a vacation (a time of change), I decided to order something new, even though I was afraid I might not like it.

To this day I'm not sure why I ordered the flavor I did—mint chip! I think I liked the pretty shade of green—or perhaps someone recommended it. Wow! Was it good! *Whoever invented this was a genius,* I thought. This was even better than chocolate! I was no longer a die-hard chocolate ice-cream fan. I had changed.

I am a few years older (and wiser) now and realize that change is part of the cycle here on this earth. We see it in nature with the changing of the seasons. From the dead of winter springs forth a spark of life in new little buds. As summer unfolds we see the flowers in full bloom. Fall turns the world to more golden tones before we once again see the chill of winter drop the leaves from the trees.

I don't know who started the idea of making New Year's resolutions, but it is a custom that the world has accepted as a way for people to make drastic changes, hoping to carry these changes through the rest of the year.

As Christians we have the opportunity to start each day new, and begin each day with the Creator of the universe. Can you think of anything better than to make changes daily—not just once a year? Just as nature moves slowly from season to season, we too can make these gradual transitions in our own lives.

So before the holiday season is far behind, I usually take this time to reinforce those qualities that I hold dear from Christmas:
- Cheerfulness to one and all
- A spirit of love
- Fellowship of family and friends
- A sense of concern for the well-being of others
- The acknowledgment of God's precious Gift—His Son—for me

If I remember these things each day, I believe I'll see those changes in my life that are for the better. I look forward to a closer walk with my Lord throughout this year. I don't know what changes the Lord will take me through, but I'm sure it will be even better than mint chip ice cream!

JANET STAUBACH BOTTROFF

January 17

Earthquake!

Therefore I tell you, do not worry about your life, what you will eat or what you will drink, or about your body, what you will wear. Is not life more than food, and the body more than clothing? Matt. 6:25, NRSV.

I was in Los Angeles, California, in January 1994 on business and was delighted to have dinner with Anna and Ben, longtime friends. I had grown up with Anna and roomed with her in college, and was happy that we could enjoy an evening together before going back to my hotel room.

At 4:30 a.m. (Pacific time) on January 17 I had awakened and was sitting on the side of my bed getting ready to begin to work on some notes of the previous day's activities. At 4:31 my bedroom began to quake, as did a good many other bedrooms in the Los Angeles area. It was then that I learned that I could pull on a pair of slacks and a sweatshirt, grab my shoes in one hand and my flashlight in the other, and be in a doorway in 32 seconds. Thirty-two seconds was the length of time of the quake. I turned on the TV and learned that it had been a severe earthquake centered in the Northridge area, where Anna and Ben lived. I saw pictures of destruction very near their home. I tried calling them, but was unable to get through. Their telephone was dead.

In the middle of the afternoon Anna was able to contact me. She was OK, as was Ben. But she said, "Liz, everything in my house that can break is broken." Later in the conversation she said, "The most frightening part was having to pry open the doors to get out of the house."

They left their house for one week, going back only to do what cleanup they could do. Cleanup included opening the back door and taking a shovel to empty out their kitchen of pots, pans, broken dishes, broken china, silverware, salt, applesauce, cereal, and beans all mixed together on the floor and counters. Their fireplace and chimney were severely damaged. They had no electricity or water, and gas lines would have to be repaired.

Three weeks later work took me again to the Los Angeles area, and I thought about my friends. In vain I looked around my house for some little thing hanging on my wall that would remind her of our growing-up years together, something to take to her as a replacement for some of her loss. So I called her on the phone and said, "Anna, when I come next week, is there some little thing I can bring you for your house?"

"Oh, no," she responded. "I have learned not to get too attached to my things."

What a lesson for me! "I have learned not to get too attached to my things."

Dear Lord, thank You for the safety You provided Anna and Ben and me and the thousands of others in the Los Angeles area during that horrible quake. Help me, Elizabeth Sterndale, not to get too attached to things. In Jesus' name, amen. ELIZABETH STERNDALE

JANUARY 18

HE HEARD MY CRY

Answer me when I call to you. . . . Give me relief from my distress; be merciful to me and hear my prayer. Ps. 4:1, NIV.

I love reading the Psalms because David as well as other writers have felt the way I have when the worries of this world weigh down my soul and God seems very far away.

The budget of the school was not balancing, a letter from home came saying that my sister was sick, and a conflict with a staff member had brought sorrow into my heart because I could not find a solution to the problem that was there and it had caused a breach in the relationship. Even when I tried to explain how I felt, the words were not comprehended by those around me.

It was not surprising to me that when I listened to a prayer being offered at a meeting I was attending, praising God for His wonderful works and for answering prayer, the words were too much for me to bear. I slipped out of the room quietly before the prayer was finished.

I struggled within myself, trying to find the peace and assurance that God was listening. I felt embarrassed about my action; perhaps I had let people down by showing disrespect to God. Although some people came to remind me of my poor example to the students, it was not until a friend came and listened to my moanings about God and then offered to pray with me that my self-pity began to disappear. Her prayer was beautiful, bringing both of us to the throne of God.

That evening as I was reading Psalms again, I realized that when David cried out for mercy or in distress, God answered his prayer.

David wrote, "You have filled my heart with greater joy.... I will lie down and sleep in peace" (Ps. 4:7, 8, NIV). "The Lord has heard my cry for mercy; the Lord accepts my prayer" (Ps. 6:9, NIV).

Rita Van Horn

January 19

Football Versus Fellowship

One thing I ask of the Lord, this is what I seek: that I may dwell in the house of the Lord all the days of my life, to gaze upon the beauty of the Lord and to seek him in his temple. Ps. 27:4, NIV.

It is near the end of another football season, and I've had many opportunities to go to a game, but have not done so. I used to live near the Aloha Stadium in Honolulu, but I never went to a game there either, even though I was invited to go to one of the Pro Bowl games. You may wonder why.

Every time I go to anything like a football game, all they want is my money. They even charge for the programs! Some of those who receive the money don't use it very wisely, either. And the people are so noisy that sometimes I can't hear the announcer. I did go to a game several years ago, and believe me, I don't want to go through that again! The seats were hard, the parking situation was bad, and I didn't have anything appropriate to wear.

Furthermore, it looked like it might rain. And I was afraid the game might run into overtime and make dinner late. Besides, I didn't know most of the people we were going with, and I didn't like some of those I did know. I found out some were hypocrites: they just went for the tailgate parties, not to see the game at all. I was tired, and to top it all, I had company.

As you can probably tell, I don't go to football games because I really don't like football. But did you notice how many of the complaints and excuses I gave sound like those that people give for not going to church? As far as I know, no one in the entire world cares whether I go to a football game or not. But Someone cares very much whether or not I go to church. Christ cares. He died that I might fellowship with Him. The church is a body of believers, and when a part of that body is missing, it matters.

Ardis Dick Stenbakken

January 20

"Why Are You So Afraid?"

He said to his disciples, "Why are you so afraid? Do you still have no faith?" Mark 4:40, NIV.

Waves of confusion, indecision, and fear swept over me; I felt as though I would drown in an ocean of circumstances beyond my control. For months I had been in severe pain, and there were only two ways to relieve it, neither of which was acceptable in my mind.

In June I had fallen and severely damaged my right knee; I had already had four surgeries on that knee. The last surgery was to last from 10 to 15 years, and only three had passed. As the pain grew less and less tolerable, the doctor said he could put me in a wheelchair or I could have a total knee replacement. I was proud and independent, so the wheelchair was out, and I was reluctant to face more surgery. I had a valid fear of surgery, as I would need blood transfusions. Whose blood would I get? Would my heart stop on the operating table, as it had once before? Who would take care of my family?

I trusted God and had faith in Him; I agreed to the surgery, but was searching for some answers from Him. He had always been there before when things were beyond control. The waves of fear and pride were really capsizing my ship.

I was asked to help with a women's spiritual retreat as a prayer group leader. God knew just where He wanted me. The first day our group study was on Mark 4, which I had studied in small groups at our church. As I was reading the passage in my devotions that morning and got to verse 40, my eyes became glued to that verse. I read and reread it. Tears came to my eyes. "Why are you so afraid? Do you still have no faith? I was with you when James was healed from his heart attack; I answered the very hour you prayed for guidance for a job." As I sat there and thought of every time God had visibly answered my prayers, I could feel His presence there in the chair by my side, reassuring me. A calmness came over me, and I knew I was doing the thing He wanted so I could be of help to Him in the future.

The surgery took three and a half hours, and I did not need any blood other than my own. I woke up from the anesthesia feeling better than I did at any other time after surgery that I can remember.

Seven weeks later the doctor said I had healed amazingly well, and after two more months I would be walking better than I did before I went in for surgery, with no assistance and no pain.

I know God is the Great Healer and will pick me up when I stumble.

When things get rough I try to keep these favorite texts in my mind:

Matthew 21:22: "If you believe, you will receive whatever you ask for in prayer" (NIV).

Second Timothy 1:7: "For God hath not given us the spirit of fear; but of power, and of love, and of a sound mind." VI KEITH

JANUARY 21

HOARFROST

He giveth snow like wool: he scattereth the hoarfrost like ashes. Ps. 147:16.

We awoke this morning to a world of beauty. Every tree, branch, weed, and piece of grass is covered with hoarfrost. The sun sparkling on the frost particles gives us a twinkling, glittering panorama of the countryside. Chickadees flit in and out among the tree branches, at peace with this transformation of their habitat. Sparrows and blue jays add their movement and color to the view. The scene is so beautiful it almost defies description—a truly delightful Christmas card scene.

Hoarfrost forms when air is cooled to freezing temperatures and the moisture in it condenses on objects. It differs from ordinary frost in that the ice crystals are long and needle-shaped. The shape of the crystals is what makes it so visible as it coats everything with an exquisite covering of frost particles.

This cold, brisk January morning in northern Minnesota again reflects the beauty that God has chosen to bestow upon us. His creative decoration of the vegetable matter above the snow-covered ground is another reason for me to ponder His goodness to me. I am reassured that He delights to fulfill my need to observe beauty in my surroundings. Stepping out the door, I breathe deeply of the fresh air. My nostrils feel pinched and my lungs are stimulated as they feel the cold air rush in; my whole body feels invigorated. It is an environment that commands me to move so that I will stay warm.

As I walk across the yard I look more closely at the frost formations. I marvel at how the frost is able to cling to every surface. When I touch the crystals with my warm hands, they quickly melt, leaving a cool dampness on my skin. Their connection with their mainstay is so tenuous, and I know that the wind will soon blow the frost from the trees. Quickly we will lose our picturesque scene and go back to the ordinary landscape.

Just now, Lord, I want to praise You for the beauty You bring into my life. Thank You for giving me the ability to appreciate Your wonders. I thank You for making our world so awesome. You have shared with me the intricacies and beauties of nature and brought cheer and joy into my life. Because You care about the visual beauty before me I know that You care for the beauty of my soul. Because of Your caring You died for me that I might live to continue to enjoy Your gifts throughout eternity. Thank You, dear Jesus. I love You for giving the beauty of hoarfrost.   EVELYN GLASS

JANUARY 22

YOUR HEART'S DESIRE

Delight yourself in the Lord and he will give you the desires of your heart. Ps. 37:4, NIV.

Chippy was the community mongrel—everyone fed him, but he had no home. Then came a missionary couple who adopted India, its ways, its food, its people—adopted Chippy, too.

Over the next six months we became friends, and Chippy and my young son, Jez, became inseparable. They took walks together and played together. Then the time came for us to leave India. It was time to say goodbye to grandparents, friends, neighbors' pigeons, stray cats—and Chippy. I knew Chippy would be the hardest!

One afternoon, reminding Jez that this would be the last time he would see Chippy, we went up the hill to have our farewell dinner with Chippy's family. As soon as we stepped into their home Jez began his usual hunt. "Thippy, Thippy," he called, looking in all their favorite hiding places: under the table, behind the door, in the kitchen pantry, in the closet, behind the couch. However, Chippy was not to be found. In the past Chippy had often disappeared, only to return several days later, looking happy and well cared for. And of course, being a dog, he had no idea his little friend was leaving on the next plane to America.

Our plans to have a pleasant dinner were ruined with Jez's wails of "I want Thippy *now*!" Nothing would stop him. Not hugs, not explanations, not reason, not even bribes. My sympathy slowly turned to frustration and was on the path to anger. The situation seemed totally out of control—and all over a dog!

Just as I was ready to apologize to Chippy's family and take mine home, Jez stopped crying and said, with a huge smile, "Mama, Jezan will pray. Jesus will bring Thippy."

Oh, no, I thought to myself. *Now he's really going to bawl.* Knowing Chippy's escapades, I realized that his return that afternoon, let alone that week, was far from possible. Besides, Jez was too young to understand the philosophy that every prayer is answered, but sometimes you don't get what you ask for, because God knows what is best for you. And so I tried getting him to compromise: "Jesus knows where Chippy is, sweetheart, but maybe Chippy doesn't want to come right now. Why don't you thank Jesus for making Chippy your friend? We'll ask Jesus to take good care of Chippy while you're away."

"No," he replied firmly. "Jesus will bring Chippy *now!*"

We watched the innocent child live out his faith. Jez folded his hands, closed his eyes real tight, lifted his head up high, and called out: "Bear Jesus, can you hear Jez? Please, please, bring Thippy."

With a confident smile he pushed himself off the floor, and even before he could get back on his chubby legs Chippy came bounding into the room!

As grown-ups, we had our doubts about Chippy's return that afternoon, but Jez did not. Jesus' prompt reply was exactly what he expected. In response, he hugged Chippy and yelled out, "Thank You, Jesus!"
FYLVIA FOWLER KLINE

JANUARY 23

A VERY PRESENT HELP IN TROUBLE

God is our refuge and strength, a very present help in trouble. Ps. 46:1, NKJV.

Even though the world was dark with the news of wars and conflicts among nations, my life began in the calm and serene security of my family with my loving parents, three older sisters, and a brother. I remember the lovely Japanese garden with ponds, a bridge, and a little hill with countless varieties of trees and shrubs, pomegranates, figs, loquats, etc., where as a child I played hide-and-seek within the garden enclosed by walls and two gates.

But this security was shattered after the war, when things were scarce all over Japan, and when my father, after being confined to bed for three years, took his last breath, leaving his beloved wife and children.

It soon got much harder for my mother to care for and educate all her children, and when an opportunity to study abroad opened for me, I decided to go to America, an unknown place with unknown people. At the age of 14 I left the port of Yokohama, alone on a huge vessel, leaving my mother, brother, and sisters behind, not knowing then that I was not to return to my home country for the next 12 years, and not knowing that many raging storms were waiting for me in the unknown world.

But by God's providence I met a dedicated Christian couple, missionaries to Hawaii, who extended help when I felt I was in the midst of those raging storms with such insurmountable problems and who introduced my precious Redeemer and Creator to me. Now when I look back, I can see God's hand in my life helping me to meet the many fierce storms I experienced.

We all have trials and heartaches, and we do not know what tomorrow holds. But we don't need to know, for God knows all our trials.

The Storms of Life

As weather does not always clothe the earth with tender
  warmth and radiant light, life is not continually serene.
At times angry winds tear at the fragile leaflets of security
  that enclose the trunk of life.
In the midst of these storms, broken relationships, fatal accidents, sickness, depression, and dependency threaten
  to topple one's life by uprooting faith.
But the storms of life are lessons through which one may
  learn the true meaning of life.
Be courageous when the storms of life thrash against your
  tree. Dig your roots firmly into the soil of faith.

The Master who silenced the storm on the Sea of Galilee will stand by your side. Grasp His hands, and when the storm has passed, you will discover that the pinnacle of your tree is reaching higher and straighter to the heavens. SHARON FUJIMOTO

JANUARY 24

GOD'S CHILD

Not one [sparrow] is forgotten before God. . . . Even the very hairs of your head are all numbered. Luke 12:6, 7.

Rejoice, because your names are written in heaven. Luke 10:20.

In the 1950s on one of her weekly television shows Loretta Young posed the question "Who are you?" She suggested that most people would first of all say their own name.

"But," she persisted, "besides your name, who are you?" In the program that followed, she dramatized important concepts of relationships and values that affect self-esteem, thereby shaping our lives.

What we are called and what we value have an influence on what we become. Our names then become synonymous with our very personalities, characters, and reputations. Unlike the rose, which "by any other name would smell as sweet," a human being by another name would somehow be different.

In the film *A Patch of Blue* Sidney Poitier plays a young Black man who befriends a blind White girl named Selina. Her father carelessly blinds her, then leaves. Her mother and grandfather seem cynical and uncaring, addressing her roughly as "Sleena," or by other coarse epithets. The young man sees her sitting under a tree in the park and courteously engages her in conversation. When he calls her Selina, she says softly, "Nobody never said my name that purty way before." From him she learns about loving relationships.

Isaiah and other Bible writers remind us that our heavenly Father tenderly calls us by a new name (Isa. 62:2). Over and over in Scripture God assures us of our worth to Him: "He that toucheth you toucheth the apple of [My] eye" (Zech. 2:8). "Behold, I have graven thee upon the palms of my hands" (Isa. 49:16).

Old and New Testament characters alike witness to us by their own experiences that we are children of a loving, caring God. Moses records Jacob's experience as if he were a lost son and God goes looking for him. He finds him "in a desert land . . . [a] waste howling wilderness; he led him about, he instructed him, he kept him as the apple of his eye." God fluttered over him as a mother eagle "spreadeth abroad her wings," and bore him up (Deut. 32:10, 11). The vividly tender language leaves no doubt about the strong parent-child relationship developing between God and Jacob.

Because of God's great intervention in his life, the apostle Paul declares that whereas once he was a child of darkness, he, and all of us, are become the children of Light (Eph. 2; Rom. 8:16, 17). Through his imagery we see that we are raised from our low estate to the level of royalty.

When people speak our name roughly, or mispronounce it, we are affected, sometimes cut to the heart. So God is also sensitive to how we speak His name, our tone of voice, the names by which we address Him. It's about joining a relationship. When God wrote, "Thou shalt not take the name of the Lord thy God in vain," He was not being petulant; He wanted to preserve a special relationship between Himself and His children. Jesus took time to teach His disciples to call on God by the name He loves best of all, "Our Father." As a loving Father, He knows all about us, even how many hairs are on our head. He recorded our names in His family register.

Loretta Young closed her show that day by saying, "If you identify yourself as a child of God, you have discovered a priceless identity."

RHODA WILLS

JANUARY 25

THE LORD AND HIS PEOPLE

The Lord will give strength to His people; the Lord will bless His people with peace. Ps. 29:11, NASB.

What a promise! Each time I repeat it I receive joy and hope. As my Bible lay open to this verse, my eyes wandered back to the beginning of Psalm 29. Under the chapter markings, written in italics, I found the words *The Powerful Voice of God*. A footnote a few verses later sent me hunting for 2 Chronicles 20:21, 22.

Here I began reading about Jehoshaphat readying his people for battle. My eyes moved upward again, and I found Jahaziel (someone I'd never really been introduced to) speaking.

"And he said, 'Listen, all Judah and the inhabitants of Jerusalem and King Jehoshaphat: thus says the Lord to you: "Do not fear or be dismayed because of this great multitude, for the battle is not yours, but God's"'"(2 Chron. 20:15, NASB).

But Jahaziel hadn't finished. He went on: "'"Tomorrow go down against them. . . . You need not fight in this battle; station yourselves, stand and see the salvation of the Lord on your behalf." . . . Do not fear or be dismayed; tomorrow go out to face them, for the Lord is with you.' . . . The inhabitants of Jerusalem fell down before the Lord, worshiping the Lord" (verses 16-19, NASB).

It goes on to say how some of the people stood up to praise the Lord God with voices loud and high. How I would love to have been there.

And when Jehoshaphat had "consulted with the people, he appointed those who sang to the Lord and those who praised Him in holy attire, as they went out before the army and said, 'Give thanks to the Lord, for His lovingkindness is everlasting.' And when they began singing and praising, the Lord set ambushes" (verses 21, 22, NASB), and the enemy was defeated.

What is your battle? Could it be discouragement, fear, looking at others instead of God? Perhaps you lament your seeming lack of talent or the fact that you seem to be doing more than your share of the work.

As you fight this battle, you must know who your enemy is. The Israelites knew theirs. Is your enemy God's people, your family, a non-Christian? Perhaps you see clearly that your enemy is yourself, or Satan and his angels.

Now that you have seen and know your enemy, you're ready to fight! What will happen if you position yourself, then stand still and go into your battle with singing and praising? Can you imagine things getting better or worse? Maybe your greatest problem is that you've seen this battle as yours instead of the Lord's.

The Lord's people will not, cannot, fail. Each of us must give Him our battles. We can't fight them alone. But our God is able. Face each new day with Him. GINGER MOSTERT CHURCH

JANUARY 26

THOUGHTS FROM MY QUIET TIME

And night shall be no more; they need no light of lamp or sun, for the Lord God will be their light, and they shall reign for ever and ever. Rev. 22:5, RSV.

Lord, are You looking forward as I am
to our first walk together in heaven—
just the two of us?

I think about it all the time.
What will we talk about?

Where will we go?
What are the first words You will say to me?
Sometimes I imagine You will say, "Ginny
[and I know my name will sound beautiful when You say it!],
I love you,
and I'm so glad you're here!"

And I'll say,
"Thank You!
Oh, thank You, Lord, for inviting me!"
Maybe then You'll ask me what I like best about heaven.
I already know what I will say.
"You, Lord! Knowing that You are here!"
Will we go exploring together?
Will You show me some of Your secret delights,
maybe some little unexpected thing that You made
just because You knew I would enjoy it?

Lord, I can think of heaven only in earthly terms,
the things I know—
mountains for climbing,
lakes for swimming,
and streams for wading.
Creeks that bubble and bounce just to delight my senses.
Apple trees for climbing
and weeping willows for sitting under.
And most of all—dogs and cats and coons,
bunnies and bears and maybe a yellow-eyed wolf
for holding and hugging.

(Lord, You already know I'm not much for fins and feathers;
and flowers interest me
only if I don't have to take care of them!)

Have You already planned our first walk
knowing what I like to do?
Do You have a spot picked out under a weeping willow tree
(we'll have to change the name in heaven, won't we!),
a spot where the critters will climb all over us
as we sit and talk?

Lord, there's so much I want to tell You
and so much I want You to tell me.
I hope I won't be so overwhelmed by it all

that I won't be able to talk!
Wouldn't that be funny?
Me—speechless in heaven!

Do You know what I want, Lord, most of all
on our first walk together?
I want to see You smile because of Your joy in me!
I want to hear You laugh with delight
at the things I say.
God's laugh!
There's not much to laugh at right now, but someday,
Lord, I want to hear You laugh.

And when our first time together is over
(I know Your appointment book will be full),
I'd love to hear You say,
"Ginny, this was so much fun!
I love being with you.
Let's do it again real soon!"

GINNY ALLEN

JANUARY 27

SPOT-MICKEY

For the kingdom of God belongs to such as these. Mark 10:14, NIV.

I have always disliked mice; they give me the creeps. Consequently, my heart was not overflowing with joy when my little boy received a real live mouse as a gift. Christopher, on the other hand, was wildly excited. He undertook to make friends with it immediately, named it Spot-Mickey, and took great pains to care for it in the finest style possible.

One day Chris had just finished cleaning out the mouse cage when I told him it was time for us to go shopping. During our trip he talked excitedly about his pet. In fact, he could hardly wait to get home again. But alas, when we arrived back at the house, he discovered an empty cage. Somehow the mouse had gotten out, and my son was inconsolable.

I had to explain to Chris that because of our two house cats, it was highly unlikely that Spot-Mickey was still alive. Chris insisted that we pray about it, which we did. I didn't hold out much hope, however. "It would take a bit of a miracle for that mouse to avoid the cats, Chris," I said.

Finally it was time for bed, and Christopher was still crying. "Please, Mommy," he begged, "I want to pray one more time. I want to ask Jesus to please send back my mouse." We prayed one more time, Chris tearfully telling Jesus how much Spot-Mickey meant to him. Finally he headed back to his own room and to bed.

Suddenly I heard a scream. Rushing into his room (expecting the worst), I saw the little mouse perched on top of one of my son's tennis shoes, smiling up at him! Christopher tenderly placed the mouse back in its cage and then jumped up and down enthusiastically. "Jesus did it, Mommy! Jesus sent my mouse back."

Sometimes I have questioned whether or not our heavenly Parent really does pay attention to our individual prayers—especially those about a lost mouse. As I stood watching Christopher and his precious little pet, I experienced a renewed sense of belief in the personal watchcare of a God who sees the sparrow fall (Matt. 10:29).

With Christopher, I want to have the humble faith of a little child (Matt. 18:4), the faith that may be as small as a tiny mustard seed (Matt. 17:20) but strong enough to move a mountain. "Thank You, God," I breathed. "Thank You for rewarding my son's faith—and help me to exhibit that kind of faith every day in my own life."

GLENICE LINTHWAITE STECK

JANUARY 28

TERROR IN THE NIGHT

The angel of the Lord encamps around those who fear him, and he delivers them. Ps. 34:7, NIV.

Nancy opened her eyes as the dark room in which she was sleeping seemed to come alive with light. At the same time, smoke filled her eyes and throat. As she jumped out of bed, she looked back at her 4-year-old daughter, who was asleep in the same bed. Flames were surrounding the young child as Nancy snatched her up in her arms, unhurt, then ran to the kitchen and out the door.

Looking back from the outside of their mobile home, Nancy saw flames already leaping high in the air, and heard windows exploding in the bedroom in which she and Lisa had so recently been sleeping.

The fire spread quickly through the whole mobile home. They watched as their possessions were ruined or destroyed.

Nancy, recently baptized, said that she had been praying for a miracle in her life, but not that kind of miracle. She felt that she had been saved from a "burning, fiery furnace," as had the three Hebrews in the book of Daniel.

It is said of the three Hebrews that "the fire had not harmed their bodies, nor was a hair of their heads singed; their robes were not scorched, and there was no smell of fire on them" (Dan. 3:27, NIV).

Although Nancy and Lisa were protected, it was not to the extent of the three Hebrews. The ordeal left them exhausted. Their voices were husky from smoke inhalation, and the threat of pneumonia hovered. Lisa was afraid to be in a room by herself—of the dark.

Nancy was a single parent with no supportive relatives. She stayed with various friends until an insurance settlement provided the means for her to obtain another home.

Nancy and Lisa stayed in our home for several days. One evening Nancy went to the bedroom early, leaving Lisa under our care. Finally we said, "Lisa, it's time for you to go in with your mama. It's bedtime."

"No," Lisa, thinking of her own fear of the dark, replied. "My mama's all right. She's not afraid."

Psalm 91 describes the confidence the person who "dwells in the shelter of the Most High" can have. God promises, "You will not fear the terror of the night. . . . He will command his angels concerning you to guard you in all your ways" (verses 1, 5-11, NIV).

BEATRICE HARRIS

JANUARY 29

NEW LIFE, NEW FRIEND

I am the resurrection and the life. John 11:25.

It was a busy day for me. I had made up my mind to see a patient who was very much alone and depressed, but it turned out that another patient was in the dying process, and I was asked to be present for the patient and family.

When I got to the facility the patient had died, but the family was still present. Spiritual support was given, and the presence of the Holy Spirit was felt. The family was reassured of God's continued love and presence. After the family left the facility to make other plans, the nurse and I were left in the room with the dead. She affirmed me in my work, and I gave God the glory.

God had made it possible for me to work as a hospice chaplain, and I regard it as a great privilege. The nurse and I really got involved in conversation. We were open and willing to share our feelings. She has a wonderful relationship with Jesus, and we were connecting as never before.

During our interaction we came to the conclusion that people who are hurting with grief or loss are usually healed as the pains of others are shared. The death of the patient had led to a reviving of our spiritual lives; we had gotten to know each other, and a bond of friendship had developed between us. I was reminded of the words of Jesus when He said to Martha, "I am the resurrection and the life."

We know that the patient who had died was awaiting the resurrection, but right there in the room both of us were experiencing a new life, the inner being renewed as we focused on the love of Jesus. The place and time were very sacred to us. We left that room with a new experience, a new commitment to share what we possess with others.

This experience will be unforgettable. I gained a friend, a deeper love for Jesus, a deeper meaning of the concept of sharing. Sharing even when there may be pain, because the joy of sharing will bring new life to us. We can never forget that when Jesus shared Himself to the whole world through pain of the cross, He gave life to all. Life to be enjoyed in the new earth, where we will know each other better.

GLORIA C. MCLAREN

January 30

LET ME WALK WITH YOU

How beautiful upon the mountains are the feet of the messenger who announces peace, who brings good news, who announces salvation, who says to Zion, "Your God reigns." Isa. 52:7, NRSV.

In my closet I have a variety of shoes. There are some shoes that are well worn—they have trod many miles in their short life. How many thousands of other shoes have they met toe-to-toe or crossed paths with, or trod side by side with.

One pair of my shoes are my "muckers." These shoes in particular have traversed some diversified terrain, while hunting or tracking behind a search-and-rescue dog. There is a certain thrill to following 30 feet behind a well-muscled dog who is concentrating intently on an invisible path and pulling you along. The reward at the end of the track, when the dog finds the lost person, is tremendous.

I have a number of other types of shoes that can also go to great lengths to find someone lost. A person may be lost in nature's wilderness, or the wilderness of everyday life. The man lost in the mountains missed the trail because of a rockslide; the person you meet daily has perhaps lost the Lord's marked-out path because of the slide of life's burdens.

We don't have a well-trained dog guiding us when we wear our shoes, but we have the One who gave the dog her good nose—the Creator Himself. Have your shoes experienced the thrill of being pulled to someone who can be led to the Saviour?

Shoes have a particular problem. They are not self-propelled. Shoes need feet in them to make them move. Shoes can't find someone lost in life's forest of problems without a spiritually whole person filling them. Where are they going to find a spiritually whole person?

Two thousand years ago Jesus wore a pair of sandals. Our shoes need to tread the same path with Him. Sometimes our shoes will get muddy if we step off the well-formed path. Our Father can dry the muddy shoes off and set them back on the dry road once again.

Make a point of allowing your shoes to carry you to someone who needs to find the Way today. SUSAN CLARK

JANUARY 31

BEEP BEEP

He who refreshes others will himself be refreshed. Prov. 11:25, NIV.

Reflecting on friendships, I realize how thankful I am to be a woman. Women seem to enjoy deeper levels of friendship than most men. There is comfort and peace in sharing inner feelings and struggles with another woman. Though Jewish men of old prayed daily, "Lord, I thank You I wasn't born a woman," I thank the Lord I was.

What a precious gift friendship is. God has made us to yearn for His friendship, as well as to desire human companionship, kindred spirits. Recently a friend of mine said, "Heide, you minister to me by visiting me." She is an elementary school teacher, and I enjoy dropping into her classroom occasionally after school just to chat. We are both pastoral wives, so we are used to giving more than receiving. I understood her explicitly when she said, "I often visit other people, but you come and visit me." The blessing I give comes immediately back to me, because the moment she sees me her face lights up and her eyes sparkle. I have no doubt this friend loves me dearly.

Friendship—it gives meaning to life. With our society and homes becoming ever more fragmented, it is time to cherish and nurture friendships. The world out there is often cold and competitive. We need the warm fires of friendship to banish the chill air, to bring comfort and affirmation.

During graduate school I developed a friendship with one of my classmates who lived a few blocks away. Every day on her way to work, Pat would beep her horn as she drove by. Even with the windows shut on a cold and snowy Michigan day, I could hear that *beep beep*, and it would warm my heart. A simple thing, but it represented caring and affirmation. Since Pat's house was not on my travel route, I pondered how to show I cared in a distinctive way too. My husband came up with a brilliantly crazy idea. He made a wooden sign and painted on it the words "Beep Beep." We snuck over to her house one evening and planted the sign in her front yard. Now we could both be encouraged by these tangible affirmations.

Silly things, simple things, but it's what we remember and giggle about in later years. We don't need money to show that we care. Money can't buy a listening ear, an understanding heart, or simple, crazy ways to show we care. Go ahead, plan today to share a *beep beep* with someone you love.   HEIDE FORD

FEBRUARY 1

THE POEM

There are different kinds of gifts, but the same Spirit. 1 Cor. 12:4, NIV.

Plastic ID cards and photos swell my wallet. There are a few dollars, too. And there is the frayed-edged poem. I've been carrying this poem, "My Prayer," by Anna Modine Moran, for many, many years. It was clipped from the pages of the predecessor of the

Adventist Review.

Why would I carry a poem around for more than a generation, nearly two? Simply because my world was made more wonderful because of the poet's challenge. A challenge she gifted me with by using her gift of wisdom through her poetry.

As a young Christian, I often prayed the words of the poem because it was indeed a prayer. Soon the prayer poem became a way of life. It remains a joy to repeat the words:

My Prayer

Lord, give me discernment,
The insight to see
That many lost souls
Are depending on me.
To tell them of Jesus,
To show them the way
That leads up to heaven's
Eternal day.
Lord, give me remembrance
To quote from Thy Word
The truths that so many souls
Never have heard;
To teach Thy commandments,
Salvation explain,
And to pray for them, with them,
Again and again.
Lord, give me the courage
Thy love to proclaim
So all who may hear me
Will reverence Thy name.

If not for the steady urging found in God's Word and this poem, I might not have said "Yes" to do His bidding. "No" might have been my response to varied responsibilities along the way. The souls who were influenced for God's kingdom might not have been, and I'd have missed a lifetime of blessings. Thus, I return again and again to the poem—and I'm lifted up, and continue to be spurred on.

Just as a child needs a hero, as a young Christian I needed something I could relate to, that which would encourage and enable me. Poetry, clear and simple, was one of the tools I needed, to read, to guide (and as I later found, to write myself). God used poetry to move me along His path.

Poetry provides much of the salve for life's bruises. Poetic phrases bring encouragement to the soul and set the stage for music of the heart. Undoubtedly the uniqueness of poetry is one of the reasons the Psalms continue, even in this state-of-the-art era, to be a constant source of help to the wounded soul, as well as a platform for rejoicing.

May poetry add to your joy in Jesus' love—and let's together thank God for poets and the blessings they provide. BETTY KOSSICK

FEBRUARY 2

THE LUMP

Another parable spake he unto them; The kingdom of heaven is like unto leaven, which a woman took, and hid in three measures of meal, till the whole was leavened. Matt. 13:33.

Sunday was the busiest day of the week. All the beds to change, biggest wash of the week, bread and cookies to bake for the week's lunches. If the milk hauler came, the milk tank had to be washed and sanitized. A growing energetic family on a dairy farm surely didn't get very bored with life. But this particular Sunday the bread didn't get set in the morning, and the day slipped by so quickly. I knew it would have to be "store bread" for lunches that week.

Then Friday came, and with the weekend, expected family from out of state. I could not serve my loved ones that store bread. I simply must set a batch of bread. But the morning again quickly passed, and it was after lunch before the ingredients were hastily thrown together in a flurry to make the regular 12-loaf batch. Then bustling the youngest children into the car and giving last-minute instructions to the older boys to be sure to bring the cows up early for evening chores, I flew into town to buy extra food supplies. You know you can count on Murphy's law when you are in a hurry—if anything can go wrong, it will.

It was three hours before I got back home, and I was frantic worrying about the boys and that batch of bread. I could just envision bread dough overflowing my kitchen table.

When I drove into the yard, my sister's car was there, and I had not even been there to greet her at the end of her long journey. After hugs all around, I dashed into the kitchen to finish the bread, only to find a lump sitting in that bread pan! The bread dough had not even risen! A quick memory check told me I had forgotten the leaven, and without the yeast all I'd get was a lump sitting in a bread pan.

Nearly every time I set a batch of bread I remember this experience, even after 30-plus years of baking. To learn that lesson, I needed to forget only once.

Among the Jews of Jesus' day leaven was sometimes used as an emblem of sin. But leaven can also represent truth. The leaven of truth in our lives changes us as thoroughly as leaven within the bread dough changed it from being just a lump. The leaven of truth, when received into the heart, will regulate our desires, purify our thoughts, and sweeten our disposition.

O that today we all might choose to have within our hearts the divine grace our Lord spoke of, that leaven that will make us beautiful vessels to be used by God, enlarging our capacity for loving and feeling.

BETTY R. BURNETT

FEBRUARY 3

THE FASTIDIOUS GUEST

If I do not wash you, you have no part in me. John 13:8, RSV.

I was expecting a special Guest in a few hours, and still had to clean the house. Everywhere I looked were jobs crying out to be done. Dishes in the sink. Dirty laundry. Closets, cupboards, basement, garage . . . I was appalled at all the work. I would have to do a superficial job—as I had been doing for some time.

I worked fast, shoving things into closets, straightening here and there, cleaning up obvious dust and dirt, until the front rooms looked fairly respectable.

Soon I heard His knock—at the back door! I wondered which would be worse—keeping Him waiting while I tore into the kitchen, or letting Him come in and see everything as it was. Reluctantly I opened the door and motioned Him toward the living room.

He didn't follow me. Instead He took off His coat and put on an apron. Then He filled a bucket, took a towel, got down on His hands and knees, and began scrubbing the floor.

I was mortified. "You don't like my housekeeping," I said.

"If I don't do the cleaning, I can't be your Guest," He replied.

I relented. "Don't just scrub the floor—do the walls, the cupboards, everything!"

He was glad I stopped resisting. As He went from room to room, the cleaning agents He used put a gleam on every surface. He even had a special red solution for stubborn stains.

I hoped He wouldn't want to see the attic. There was stuff in there too private for anyone to see. But the look in His eyes told me a cover-up was worse than the mess. Right away He spotted my tiny treasure chest, inlaid with mother-of-pearl. Inside were secret notes and a dried rose—scented keepsakes of a forbidden relationship, each one evoking powerful memories. "This little box that you cherish so dearly," He warned, "will ignite a fire that will burn down your whole house."

"I can't give it up, but You may take it," I faltered. He did. He also cleared out the accumulation of unresolved guilt, fear, and resentments that had collected there.

He even went through my wardrobe. My taste had run heavily to positive image builders for my job, and baggy grubbies for home wear. He wanted clothing more genuine and consistent. The clothes He provided are truly lovely—enhancing, but not overpowering the special qualities He has given me. He thinks white is becoming on me.

After a while He looked at me and smiled. "There is one job we must do yet—the windows. We must remove the soot and dirt so that the light in your house will shine through clearly to the neighborhood."

I cannot express the joy I have experienced since my special Guest has come to stay. Though the cleaning work is never done, it's great to be rid of the accumulated baggage that once narrowed my life. The King of glory, who "dwells in the high and holy place," also lives in me.

BEATRICE S. NEALL

FEBRUARY 4

HIDDEN BEAUTY

The Lord does not see as mortals see; they look on the outward appearance, but the Lord looks on the heart. 1 Sam. 16:7, NRSV.

Geologists call them geodes, but I like the Indian name better: thunder eggs. The Warm Springs Indians of central Oregon first discovered these peculiar, rough, round rocks lying in the loose volcanic gravel around the base of Mount Jefferson and Mount Hood in the snow-capped Cascade Mountains of the Pacific Northwest.

The Indians believed these rocks were missiles thrown by the fighting thunder spirits who lived in these two volcanic peaks.

They thought that when thunderstorms occurred these rival gods hurled the round stones at each other in anger. This is how they explained finding the thunder eggs scattered over the plateaus surrounding the mountains.

They aren't much to look at. Usually about the size of an orange, the stones are dull gray, rough, and quite round. One could walk over an entire field of thunder eggs and never give them more than a passing glance—or toss.

The stones apparently began as mud balls or air pockets trapped in the lava flows that poured out during volcanic eruptions of these mountains ages ago. Geologists believe that the air pockets acted as molds into which mineral-laden water seeped. The minerals settled out of the water and lined the pocket, then eventually filled them, hardening over time into agates or crystals. The varying composition of the minerals account for the beautiful contrast in colors found in some of these rocks.

The minerals that formed the geodes was leeched from the surrounding layers of lava in which the agates were formed. The mineral-poor lava decomposed more quickly than the harder agate-filled geodes, leaving them lying on the surface and hastening their discovery.

No one knows who first broke one of the thunder eggs open to discover the beauty inside, but today geodes are hammered or cut in two, and the most beautiful are filed and polished to a brilliant and beautiful finish.

The thunder egg reminds me of people I've known—dull, uninteresting, easily overlooked on the outside, but filled with promise and beauty inside.

The beauty in a thunder egg didn't just happen. It was formed in the crucible of fire and water. But the beauty is brought out only after hammering, filing, and polishing. The same process makes people beautiful. But it also is painful.

Some thunder eggs, like some individuals, display no apparent inner beauty. But the eye of God sees beauty where we might pass it by. We must see with caring, loving eyes, as God sees. Or we may destroy something God intended to be a thing of beauty.

We look at these gems and see beauty. We too can be beautiful to God and to others. But we must be willing to open ourselves to God's fire and to His sometimes painful polishing, or we may never fully reflect His character as He designed.   CHARLOTTE ISHKANIAN

FEBRUARY 5

"PLEASE, GOD, DON'T LET HER DIE!"

Bless the Lord, O my soul, and forget not all his benefits: who forgiveth all thine iniquities; who healeth all thy diseases; who redeemeth thy life from destruction; who crowneth thee with lovingkindness and tender mercies. Ps. 103:2-4.

"Mommy!"

The plaintive cry roused me for the second time that cold November night, and I hurried to my daughter's room. Again finding her asleep, I decided to rest beside her where I could reach her more quickly if she called.

I must have dozed, for suddenly I opened my eyes to find my tiny 4-year-old standing there, eyes glazed and dull, trying with all her might to shake the sturdy old four-poster. As I led her back to bed, I discovered that her skin was dry and burning hot. I had to get that fever down!

Frantically, futilely, I searched for something—anything—to reduce the fever. I panicked. My little daughter was extremely ill, I had no telephone, and the only help in the house was a sleeping 5-year-old.

Briefly I considered waking my son and sending him to the neighbor's home. But how could a child of that age be sent out into a snowy midnight to trek a half mile on the hopes that he *might* be able to rouse someone?

I dashed back into my little girl's room. She was so thin that her body barely made a mound in the covers. My mind froze. I could see no movement, no breathing, only that still, white face.

"Please, God, don't let her die!" The words were torn from my throat, and I threw myself down by her bed. God? How long had it been since I had spoken that name?

Raised in a Christian home, I had been taught love and reverence. But I had drifted far from any relationship with my Lord. Now I was overwhelmed with the enormity of my sin. I cried out my grief, my confession, my need.

I don't know how long I stayed there, weeping and pleading with God. At last, however, I opened my eyes and looked at my daughter. There was a faint flush on her cheeks, a bead of moisture on her forehead. As I lifted her tiny hand to tuck it under the covers, I found it moist and warm. Again I closed my eyes in prayer, this time in gratitude to a merciful God. Again the tears flowed, but now in joy. I bent to kiss the child's brow. Two deep chocolate-brown eyes opened briefly, a smile flitted across the tired face, and two precious arms encircled my neck. Oh, thank You, my Father!

Many years have passed since that frightening night. I watch my children as they nurture *their* children, and my heart rejoices in a loving and merciful God who answered a mother's prayer for healing: healing for a dying child, and healing for a sin-sick soul.

LEA HARDY

FEBRUARY 6

RISK WITH GOD

By faith Abraham . . . obeyed and went, even though he did not know where he was going. Heb. 11:8, NIV.

When I look ahead in life, I have not always seen a clear path stretching out in front of me; when I look back, however, it is very plain to see the many ways in which the Lord has led me. Sometimes I have felt like Abraham: I believed that God was calling me to step out in faith, to take a risk with Him, and yet I did not always know exactly where that would lead.

For example, in 1982 I prayerfully risked leaving the Midwest with my two sons to return to California after being away for 14 years. At the time it was not clear where we would live or even where I would work. We arrived in California on a Sunday. On Tuesday I was interviewed and hired for a job, and on Thursday I started working. Two months later the three of us moved into a home that the Lord had found for us to rent.

Still later God had plans for me to continue my education and to marry. Today I am serving the Lord as senior chaplain at St. Helena Hospital in California. Back in 1982 I had no idea where God's plans would lead, but in my wallet I carry these words printed on a tiny piece of paper:

"Although I may not be able to control the winds that blow, I can always set the sails."

Sailors tell me that setting the sails involves taking a risk. Just so, following God's plan for our lives involves taking a risk—but not a chance! With God the trials of life can blow into wonderful changes.

Looking back, I praise God for the trials in my life because I can see how He used them to bring about positive change in my life. I know that when I am unable to set the sails, God will help me to do that also, if I let Him.

Taking a risk with God is always worth temporary inconvenience, even pain, because our Creator desires us to have life "more abundantly" (John 10:10).

Our challenge is to stay close enough to God so that we can hear His voice behind us saying, "This is the way, walk ye in it" (Isa. 30:21). So set your sails; take a risk with God. It is more than worth it!

JUDITH CRABB

FEBRUARY 7

JUST DON'T LOSE YOUR FAITH

For we walk by faith, not by sight. 2 Cor. 5:7.

In recent years our family has gone through some of the most stressful situations that any family could experience. My own mother passed away; my husband's mother, who was in her early 50s, died suddenly of a heart attack; and my brother choked to death while eating breakfast. I said to the Lord, "Nothing else that comes our way could be worse than this!" Was I ever wrong!

Our eldest daughter, a college junior, started complaining of fatigue during her first year at college, but she assured me she was getting enough rest living in the dorm.

During the Christmas break our family doctor examined her but couldn't find anything wrong. I was sure the stress of living away from home was just too much for her. I made sure she got extra rest while she was home. Her symptoms persisted, and I grew more concerned.

Our physician wanted her to see a neurologist. During the examination the neurologist could find nothing wrong with Daphne that would contribute to her fatigue, but he suggested that she have an MRI to eliminate the possibility of overlooking something. It was on the MRI screen that we got the first glimpse of our nightmare. Daphne had a brain stem malformation. The neurologist advised immediate surgery. Our family was in total shock! I prayed as I had never prayed before. All kinds of thoughts went racing through my mind. Who would perform this delicate surgery? Certainly not the neurologist we had just met.

Shortly after we got the news, the Lord brought to mind a visit

I'd had with an assistant to a Johns Hopkins neurosurgeon. This person had told me about Dr. Benjamin Carson, a young surgeon who put God first in all his decisions and credited God for his successes. I called Dr. Carson's office, and he said, "Send the MRI scan by overnight express, and I'll call you tomorrow morning."

When the time for the life-threatening surgery arrived, I knew that God was in control. I could hardly believe the peace I was feeling in the face of danger. In fact, I never cried that day, because I felt I had to be strong for my daughter, who never lost faith or showed any signs of fear to her family. But there were plenty of tears afterward. Tears of joy! Even though it's been almost a year since the surgery, I cry every time I think of how close I came to losing my daughter.

I praise God for seeing us through all our trials. He will see you through your trials also. —NETTIE M. ANDERSON

FEBRUARY 8

GOOD GIFTS

Is there anyone among you who, if your child asks for bread, will give a stone? Or if the child asks for a fish, will give a snake? If you then, who are evil, know how to give good gifts to your children, how much more will your Father in heaven give good gifts to those who ask him!" Matt. 7:9-11, NRSV.

The emphasis is on *good*. I can usually tell the difference between a good gift and a bad gift. It's not always the cost that makes the difference. A costly yet useless gift brings no real joy! A beautiful gift from a person I hardly know may mean little. A good gift is one that fits the giver and the receiver—one that will be remembered with pleasure for years to come.

I think of the record of Vivaldi's *Four Seasons* on my first birthday after we were married. Not a terribly expensive item—we could not have afforded anything that cost more than $5! But my husband of two months had come home on the overnight bus just to be there for my birthday. I played that record again and again, year after year.

Jesus was talking of good gifts for children. I recall my daughter's wanting—needing, she said—shoes that just did not make sense. They were not sturdy enough for our gravel streets. At that time she would have thought them a good gift. I got her something else. Our little boy was fascinated by anything shiny. Knives were especially attractive. He would have thought a knife to be a good gift. We deemed otherwise, and kept knives and razor blades where inquisitive hands could not reach. Children, apparently, do not always know what a good gift is. Sometimes I too have difficulty knowing which of God's gifts is good for me. In my mind, good gifts are the ones I want, either for myself or for those I love. But I don't always get what I consider a good gift.

And while I am trusting, not really understanding the whys and wherefores, a quotation from *The Desire of Ages* reassures me: "God never leads His children otherwise than they would choose to be led, if they could see the end from the beginning, and discern the glory of the purpose which they are fulfilling as coworkers with Him" (pp. 224, 225).

Perhaps I should read that differently: "God never gives to His children anything but good gifts for which they will be thankful when, at the end of the road, they look back and see how and why God chose to give them."

Just for today, dear Father, let me enjoy Your good gifts of sunshine, home, work, family, and above all, peace in knowing that Your definition of *good* is really best.   NANCY JEAN VYHMEISTER

FEBRUARY 9

STOPS AND STEPS

The human mind plans the way, but the Lord directs the steps. Prov. 16:9, NRSV.

About four years ago we were helping our son and his wife move to their new job in southern Mexico. Since he would be teaching industrial arts at a school in a remote mountain area, he was taking quite a bit of heavy equipment and supplies. Much of this was stowed away in our 20-foot travel trailer. Before long the heat and the weight of our load began to take its toll on the tires, but changing a tire did give us a little break in the monotony of the long trip. Then as we started to pull ahead after stopping for a red light in a large Mexican city, there was a bang, and we realized that we had broken an axle. Finally our son was able to get his vehicle ahead and tow us to a side street. Just a block away was a repair shop, and although it took several hours to find an axle and install it, we were able to continue our trip.

Our son decided to transfer some of the load to his vehicle, and then he began to have problems. First one and then another wheel broke, which quickly caused the tires to deflate. But each time, even when it seemed that we were out in the middle of nowhere, within a few miles we would come to a roadside repair shop. We reached Mexico City in the middle of a very heavy rainstorm. As we were struggling to negotiate the flooded streets, a passing motorist signaled that we had another flat tire on our trailer. We were able to pull over to a place that wasn't flooded, and changed the tire. Just a few blocks away we were able to get the tire repaired, so we didn't have to travel without a spare.

All these problems had slowed us down considerably, and we were a day behind schedule as we came to the last 60-mile stretch of road before we reached the school. As we stopped to buy gasoline the attendant told us that the road had been closed for the past several days because of mudslides and rockslides. This was the first day it was open to traffic! Even though we didn't realize it at the time, our stops had been ordered by the Lord.

Only in heaven will we know the reason for many of our unscheduled stops, but we can be sure that they were ordered by the Lord. Our prayer should always be "Heavenly Father, although I cannot always understand Your ways, I know that I do not need to. I submit myself gladly to Your direction and to Your loving care."

BETTY ADAMS

FEBRUARY 10

GOD IS REAL

Fear thou not; for I am with thee: be not dismayed; for I am thy God: I will strengthen thee; yea, I will help thee; yea, I will uphold thee with the right hand of my righteousness. Isa. 41:10.

God, I just had to get out into the open this morning, to see the bright sunshine, breathe the fresh air, and feel the wind on my face. The tension was building inside, and I had to talk to You to tell You how I was feeling; I had to come to You, the source of strength.

And so I walked over to my open cathedral behind the church next door, by the fence, nature, the trees, the birds singing, alone. The tears just started rolling, and I sobbed, soothing myself and pouring out my heart to You. It's been tough; I've been trying to be strong, to be positive, but today I am breaking.

Over there, through my tears, I see a groundhog standing tall, checking out its surroundings. I see a rabbit scampering through the grass, its ears nervously sticking up in the air. I'm reminded of Your constant love and Your promise to be with me.

As I lean on the wire fence, in my hand I'm holding a paper that I pulled from my bag. I had hurriedly grabbed it from my books this morning. Incredibly, the story is about how the storm arose as You slept in the boat on Galilee; when the storm was raging, Your friends were frightened. You stood up and calmed the sea, and then there was peace. I claim the promise of Your power to calm the fears, anxieties, and worries of my life. You are with me, Lord.

It's 8:25—time to head back to work. But I'm still weeping; I need the assurance of Your presence with me. I don't usually ask for signs, but today I feel I need a sign to reassure me of Your love and care. Lord, can You send me a bird? Just let it fly in front of me.

A dove flies a little way from me; I hear birds singing, but none in front of me.

It's 8:28—time to go. I think to myself, *Maybe I'm being silly asking for a sign*—and then, a red-breasted robin flies down and lands right on the fence to the left of me! And it stays there! I am stunned. Lord, You are real, You care, You are with me and will make me strong. "Fear thou not; for I am with thee: be not dismayed; for I am thy God: I will strengthen thee; yea, I will help thee; yea, I will uphold thee with the right hand of my righteousness." As I turn to leave, the robin flies to the ground right in front of where I was standing. I leave at peace.

I stop to pick some wildflowers so their beauty will inspire me with God's love and care. I feel so much better, Lord; I'm praising and thanking You for peace and joy, and for drying my tears.

Thank You, Lord; I love You! Groundhog, rabbit, reading, dove, robin on the fence, flowers—You are with me, Lord, and You are real.

Luan Cadogan

February 11

Love Is Being Together

Let not your heart be troubled; ye believe in God, believe also in me. In my Father's house are many mansions: if it were not so, I would have told you. I go to prepare a place for you. And if I go and prepare a place for you, I will come again, and receive you unto myself; that where I am, there ye may be also. John 14:1-3.

At the last half of the year that I was a student missionary my ex-boyfriend and I started thinking about renewing our relationship. The many months we had away from each other had apparently brought us to the conclusion that perhaps our relationship was one of the better ones to pursue. Letters began to come and go. Sometimes the letters were frequent enough to keep the communication going, but there were times when the next letter felt as though it came just a day too late. With my being a student missionary and his adjusting to his new job, both of us were kept very busy. It was hard to write as often as we wanted to. We tried communicating our experiences and thoughts, as well as our feelings and emotions. Reading his thoughts in writing, I could almost feel our togetherness, as if he were right there with me. Oftentimes it really comforted the longing. But I realized that there was so much more in store for us when we would actually be together again.

When Jesus had to leave His friends, He sent the Holy Spirit here so that His friends would always feel His presence here on earth. And His presence is real. But there are still so many things that get between God and His beloved people. We often get distracted with the struggles of this world, and look to heaven just for relief from our suffering. While God will bring an end to this suffering, He has the greater purpose of getting us to His home. He longs for His people to be in heaven so that this separation is no more, so that nothing can come between God and us. In the last phrase of the text above, I found such profound love. God's purpose of preparing a place for us is so that, as Jesus said, ". . . where I am, there ye may be also."

God longs to have His loved ones back. His is a love too great for this finite life to manifest. It is a love only eternity can comprehend.

This kind of love is my strength. This love is my life.

CINDY SUMARAUW

FEBRUARY 12

THE LIONS' MOUTHS

Then Daniel spoke to the king, "O king, live forever! My God sent His angel and shut the lions' mouths, and they have not harmed me." Dan. 6:21, 22, NASB.

Before I stood up I breathed a quick prayer. "Oh, Lord, please send the words." I walked to the front of the large classroom. It was my turn to present my master's research proposal to the class and the two professors. I could almost see the critical one sharpening her knife and fork as if to eat me alive when I began my presentation. Public speaking has never been difficult for me; however, the atmosphere here was not one of collaboration but of dissection.

Throughout the preparation of the proposal I repeatedly gave this overwhelming task to the Lord. Each step of the process had been fraught with difficulty, and I agonized daily over the content. I did not find the professors particularly helpful, even during out-of-class appointments.

As my presentation got under way, I began to relax. I felt an incredible calm as I sought to introduce my topic and the need for research in this area. Spontaneous applause broke out as I finished speaking. During the time for questions I received only compliments from my classmates and a commendation from one of the professors.

I returned to my seat feeling the absolute deliverance of Jesus. Into my mind slipped the text in Daniel. For me this had been a modern-day lions' den. I had been accepting of the possibility of public humiliation, but instead God had blessed me with public appreciation. I had been delivered.

When I arrived home, my husband anxiously asked how the presentation had gone. I smiled and said, "'My God sent His angel and shut the lions' mouths.'"

Do you face adversity in your life today? Just as God took care of the prophets, He promises to take care of us. Let Him be your deliverer. "Trust in the Lord with all your heart, and do not lean on your own understanding. In all your ways acknowledge Him, and He will make your paths straight" (Prov. 3:5, 6, NASB).

CAREL SANDERS CLAY

FEBRUARY 13

A Prayer for Help

Our help is in the name of the Lord, who made heaven and earth. Ps. 124:8.

Lord, please help me to do the right thing
    when all is not right.
Lord, please help me to say the right thing
    when I have no words to say.
Lord, please help me to love
    when I feel empty of any love.
Lord, please help me to give
    when I have nothing left to give.
Lord, please help me to reflect Your light
    when I feel so dark.
Lord, please help me to think Your thoughts and feelings
    when the world has its own.
Lord, please help me to be all You want me to be
    when I'm told I can't be anything.
Lord, please help me see You
    when all I see is me, and the world.
Lord, please help me to feel Your power working
    when I feel so powerless.
Lord, please help me to be full of the Spirit
    when I feel so full of me.

LAURA LEE SWANEY

FEBRUARY 14

I HAVE PLANS FOR YOU

For I know the plans I have for you, says the Lord, plans for welfare and not for evil, to give you a future and a hope. Jer. 29:11, RSV.

It was one of the worst times of my life. My grandfather had died, and my husband and I made a rushed trip back to Michigan over a holiday weekend to attend the funeral. When we returned to our home in Connecticut, we learned that while we were gone the organization my husband worked for had eliminated his department as part of their budget-cutting process. In two weeks he would be unemployed. It didn't take much figuring to show us that we couldn't afford to continue living in that high-rent area on my teacher's salary alone.

    We checked the usual options—he searched the job ads, and I searched for a cheaper but acceptable apartment. No doors seemed to be opening for us. We tried to refigure our budget again and again, but came up with the same result every time—a quickly dwindling savings account.

My quiet time began to take on the appearance of an interrogation session. "Why, God? We want to serve You. You promised to supply our needs. Why aren't You? Are You just going to let us go broke? become homeless?" Every time I thought about our financial situation I panicked.

Then I got a letter from a former student. We had been out of touch for several years. She knew nothing of my circumstances. In her letter she mentioned that she had accepted Christ as her Saviour and had a wonderful, growing relationship with Him. She also mentioned a text that was very special to her—Jeremiah 29:11. When I looked up the text and read it, it was as though God was speaking directly to me, answering all those questions I had been throwing at Him over the past few weeks. "I know the plans I have for you . . . plans for welfare and not for evil, to give you a future and a hope."

God's plans for us did unfold, although not overnight. They involved some things we never expected—including a move to another state. But they also brought blessings we hadn't dared hope for—including our own home in the country. We have had to face other tough times since then, but I don't panic anymore. I know that God does have a plan, and He will let me see the next step in His own time.

SUE HAYFORD

FEBRUARY 15

I AM LOVED!

Before they call I will answer, while they are yet speaking I will hear. Isa. 65:24, RSV.

It had been a particularly trying day, and I was exhausted. Not only was I trying to do the shopping with my three children and the distractions they bring, but my mind was burdened that day with a myriad of details complicating my life at the time.

The grocery store was my next-to-the-last stop. I hurriedly put the groceries in the back of the car, helped the children into their seats, and drove across town to my last errand.

As we got out of the car, I looked around for my purse. It wasn't in front where I usually put it. I looked in the back by the groceries, hoping I had put it there. After searching futilely, I realized that I had left it back at the grocery store.

We got back into the car. I said a silent prayer and started driving. Every light was red, and it took at least 15 minutes to get back to the grocery store. The entire time, I was alternately praying and worrying. I was thinking of how complicated it would be to cancel the credit card and ATM card, and to get a new driver's license. I wasn't carrying much money, but we could not afford to lose any. I hoped that some honest person would turn in my purse, and then I worried about how I would find it or whether it was gone for good.

I drove up to the grocery store. There, in the front of the grocery cart, was my purse, right where I had left it in the return cart rack!

A wave of peace washed over me. Amazement filled me. God cared about me! I felt completely loved by my heavenly Father. I believe that an angel covered my purse to show me that my Father cares for His children, including me! JUDY SHEWMAKE

FEBRUARY 16

THE HOME REMEDY

We are filled with joy. Ps. 126:3, NIV.

She looks like a cartoon, I thought, studying the crooked smile on Xandi's tiny face. Her lip line momentarily staggered upward, plummeted downward, then began a feeble ascent. The twisted arrow of lips directed my gaze to her big brown eyes, where all thought of humor ended in a pool of tears. My little granddaughter was engaged in sibling rivalry, and she was the only one who wasn't laughing.

I wrapped Xandi in my arms, and we rested in the caring of hugs. An instant replay of tearful scenes featuring my own "funny" faces and those of my two siblings filled my memory's screen. Newly found humor collided with twinges of old pain. Involuntarily my finger traced my smile, an irregular outline running up, down, up.

Even as I murmured, "I know, I know," into Xandi's ear, I knew that we'd both need caring therapy again sometime. That's life—"even the Christian life," my own mother had gently informed me. So I continued administering Mama's remedy for healing hurt feelings. Her prescription of hugs, anecdotes, kisses, prayer, and happy songs had always revived both the wounded and the comforter. More important, they provided padding for life's wound in waiting.

As Xandi focused on the sunshine in her life, she regained her cheek-lifting smile, and in the days that followed, God gave us a new song to sing. —FAITH JOHNSON CRUMBLY

Joy
(Xandi's Song)

Words and Music by Faith Johnson Crumbly

God has begun to do a good work inside of me.
When I opened my heart, He planted a seed.
A little joy started growing there, And now it's in full bloom, deep down inside.

CHORUS
Joy! It's an inside job. It's an inside job. Joy starts on the inside. Ooh. Joy's an inside job.

2. I can sing in the rain and smile on a cloudy day.
I know the sun will shine again for me.
And like the rainbow that spans the sky,
My joy spreads far and wide for all to see.

© 1990 Faith Johnson Crumbly
All Rights Reserved

FEBRUARY 17

ALREADY READY

You also must be ready, because the Son of Man will come at an hour when you do not expect him. Luke 12:40, NIV.

During our family vacation last summer we stopped at the Precious Moments Chapel near Carthage, Missouri. As the guide led us inside the chapel and enthusiastically began telling the stories behind each cherubic painting, I found myself compellingly drawn not only to the expressive faces of the little characters but also to the themes they portrayed.

Many different scenes from the Bible were illustrated, beginning with the Creation story and proceeding through the Old Testament stories and into the New Testament parables of Jesus and the Lord's Prayer.

As we walked from one display to another I couldn't help noticing a man and his little daughter walking directly in front of me. With her hand tucked snugly into her father's, the girl was practicing her newly developed reading skills on the captions for each scene while the father patiently coached her along. I could clearly hear their conversation as we stood in front of one particular display.

The tiny figurines seemed to be involved in various activities of everyday life while in the clouds above them Jesus was returning to this earth. The caption read: "Will you be ready?"

When the little girl had finished reading those four important words, her father looked down at her and asked, "Will you?" She turned her innocent little face up to her father and without hesitation replied, "Yes. I'm already ready."

Her simple, confident reply stopped my heart. What precious childlike faith! She hadn't said "I think so" or "I hope so." She was sure of her standing with Christ!

While tourists continued to press around me, Jesus had indeed brought a little child and set her in the midst of us and said through her innocent faith, "I tell you the truth, anyone who will not receive the kingdom of God like a little child will never enter it" (Mark 10:15, NIV).

Are you ready today?

BRENDA DICKERSON

FEBRUARY 18

THE DREAM OF A SMALL HOUSE

And it shall come to pass afterward, that . . . your sons and your daughters shall prophesy, your old men shall dream dreams. Joel 2:28.

There are different sorts of dreams: hopeful dreams, chaotic dreams, and in exceptional cases, dreams used by our heavenly Father to enlighten, answer, or encourage us.

God, by way of such a rare dream, blessed me; to this very day the dream has been a constant encouragement.

Our congregation in Vienna, Austria, made plans to do missionary work in an area near Vienna called Klosterneuburg, on the Danube.

Led by our pastor, we distributed religious leaflets and health material, took opinion polls, and gave lectures on biblical themes; we did our best to awaken the public's interest. All to no avail.

Then, to my surprise, I was called upon to conduct a series of lectures on nutrition. I was delighted at the prospect. But a sister who had pledged to help me had a change of heart. After much prayer, however, she agreed to help if there were a sufficient number of enrollments in the course. Failing this, we would give up. I concurred. But, lo and behold, more than 50 people signed up.

Confidence and courage returned to all of us. Although I interspersed a good measure of our Christian beliefs in my lectures, I had no opportunity to talk of the fast-approaching end of time and the soon coming of our Lord Jesus. We continued to present programs in public halls, but I was beginning to be concerned about the possibilities of maintaining and intensifying the contacts with the people attracted by the lectures. We were fearful about prejudice if we gave Bible studies in a public hall.

I humbly beseeched God for direction. That very night I had a dream in which I saw a small house and all of us were busily coming and going. Interestingly, such a small house did exist in a neighboring village. Part of the house was occupied, but part was vacant. Our pastor and volunteers set to work renovating this section of the house. When the job was completed, a sign that read: "Health Center of the Division for Life and Health" was put up.

During the past year our pastor has been able to launch a Bible study series and a lot of activity has gone on in the house, just the way I dreamed it would.

When I am feeling low and discouraged from poor health or criticism and would consider relinquishing the work I've set to do, my dream of the small house serves as an encouragement. Indeed, it is on the Lord's behalf and not on my own that sharing the good news continues in Klosterneuburg. — SUSANNE HATZINGER

February 19

Help, Lord! I'm Drowning!
And . . . they escaped all safe to land. Acts 27:44.

I struggled awake fighting awareness and a million things to do. I wanted to hang on to oblivion, the absence of pain, pressure, and everyday living. After several attempts to get my feet on the floor I finally gave in to the demands of another day.

I picked up my long to-do list and groaned. *I'll never get it all done! I've no time for devotions this morning, Lord. I'm sure You understand.* I sent up a silent prayer as I tried to decide which job to tackle first.

I fixed breakfast, dropped my husband at the office, and drove to the church school to teach a class. Then I rushed to the doctor's office, only to wait for nearly an hour. From there I hurried to the supermarket for groceries and picked what I thought was the shortest line. Mistake. Everyone in front of me had unpriced items, and the clerk called for price checks.

I rushed home to get lunch ready, then back to the office to pick up my husband, eat, and do dishes. As Ron left he said, "I need an article written by tomorrow morning. Think you could do it?"

I felt like screaming! How could I add one more thing to my list that was not half done when it was already 3:00? I was getting further and further behind. Then I went to my desk, picked up my journal, and wrote out my frustration:

"How, Lord, how? I just want to hole up in front of the fireplace and do nothing, but I must press on. I have a manuscript to finish, a Sabbath school program to get ready, a Thanksgiving meal to prepare. This week is getting away from me."

To make sure the Lord got my point, I drew Him a picture. I sketched an ocean scene with big waves and a stick figure with head and outstretched arms sinking beneath the surface. I wrote the caption, each word one line lower on the page, until the last was at the very bottom, "Help! Lord! Help! I'm drowning, and I've no strength to swim!"

Then I opened my Bible to Acts 27, the story of Paul's shipwreck, where I had last stopped reading. The words of verse 44 seemed to leap out at me, and I chuckled at their appropriateness: "And . . . they escaped all safe to land."

I could hear God speaking to my frustrated heart, "Dorothy, just as I was able to see Paul safely to land, I can see you safely to the end of this day, this week. You will not drown!" DOROTHY EATON WATTS

FEBRUARY 20

A SAFE PLACE—PLUS

In keeping with his promise we are looking forward to a new heaven and a new earth, the home of righteousness. 2 Peter 3:13, NIV.

"Kevin, get off the railroad track!" I yelled. My 6-year-old brother seemed paralyzed as he gazed at the oncoming train. Seconds seemed like hours to me as I ran across our backyard toward the track. His foot was stuck under a tie! The train was slowing as fast as it could, tooting incessantly. With only seconds to spare, Kevin freed himself and escaped.

This near-death experience precipitated family prayers for a safe new home. Within a week we had found a country home with lower monthly payments than the urban home. It was within walking distance of our church and school.

This house was a home of atmosphere and great character. At one time it had been the central home on a large farm. Every time I see a Christmas card of children peeping through the white spindles of an oak banister it reminds me of this home.

It was a heavenly place for children. We picked raspberries, climbed to the top of a shed to mount a tire swing for Tarzan-like rides, played hide-and-seek in the huge yard, went for long rambles in our woods. We harvested roses of 50 different varieties, hyacinths, daffodils, an enormous vegetable garden, honey from our beehives, and eggs from our chickens. Grandpa installed a sturdy merry-go-round that we rode until we were dizzy. In winter we sledded for hours on a slope the size of a skier's training hill. In summer motorists stopped and helped themselves when they saw 100 feet of lilac hedges that filled our abode with sweet perfume for months. In spring we had long Easter egg hunts and for weeks afterward would uncover Easter eggs. In fall there were always crisp apples in the root cellar, and the aroma of something appetizing baking in the kitchen.

I lived there only four years, but have been back many times to visit my childhood home. Today it is in a busy metropolis. Farmlands surrounding it have been turned into subdivisions.

Although the huge yard still remains, the house does not look quite as large as I remember it. But a plethora of pleasant memories sweep over me each time I return.

Part of the magic of returning is the reminder of how God held my family gently in protecting hands and provided for us. This memory reassures me that today as I set my heart on a safer, more peaceful place to live than this earth, God will delight in fulfilling this dream. I chuckle as I think of the pleasure My provider must have by planning extra bonuses too good even to imagine.

SHARI CHAMBERLAIN

FEBRUARY 21

WHOLE-WHEAT RELIGION

Jesus said to them, "I am the bread of life; he who comes to me shall not hunger, and he who believes in me shall never thirst." John 6:35, RSV.

We moved across the country a couple years ago. Coming from the West Coast to the East Coast in wintertime was a "cold" culture shock, but we weren't discouraged. We decided we'd make friends with our neighbors and enjoy our new surroundings.

What we didn't figure on was that once the cold weather set in and the sun set before we even got home from work, there was never anyone around the neighborhood to even say hi to without aggressively going up and knocking on their doors. Southern California weather had been conducive to having people outside all year round, at all times of the day and night. But this was different. A challenge.

Around Christmastime I decided to make a couple batches of my favorite cranberry bread. Then my husband, daughter, and I, wrapped up in our winter clothes and arms loaded with cranberry bread, braved the winter storm to go knocking on our neighbors' doors. When some weren't home, we went to others. But the north wind and blowing snow proved too much for us thin-blooded Californians, and we were forced to retreat to our own warm castle with the remaining loaves. However, at least some ice had been broken.

It was a few days later, when I was out shoveling snow off the driveway (while my husband was traveling on business in Florida), that the neighbor across the street made her way over to tell me how much she had enjoyed the cranberry bread. We talked for a while and became friends.

A couple months later I had an opportunity to buy a mill to grind wheat for breadmaking. "Lord, if You help me get it, I'll dedicate it to You," I said. "I'll use it for missionary work. We can go into a partnership." The Lord must have thought that was a good idea, because He worked it out so that I could buy it.

After doing a trial batch of homemade whole-wheat bread for my family, I offered a prayer and began making a batch for our neighbors. "I just baked a batch of bread and thought you might like a loaf," I said as I handed my neighbor a fresh loaf of 100 percent whole-wheat bread.

We've developed friendships with three couples on our block, partly because of the whole-wheat bread. One neighbor, Mary, won't let me give her anything without reciprocating. She's given us flowers to plant in the garden, vegetables from her garden, and some of her crafts. The others have shared from their gardens also.

According to Ellen White, "there is more religion in a loaf of good bread than many think" (*The Ministry of Healing*, p. 302). I'm hoping that we can soon get well enough acquainted with our neighbors that I can introduce them to my Partner in the bakery business. He's the expert on bread. After all, that's His middle name ("I Am" the "Bread" of "Life").

NANCY CACHERO VASQUEZ

FEBRUARY 22

OFF-KEY

Be sure your sin will find you out. Num. 32:23.

According to the band program, I played the piccolo, and according to that same program, my last name was identical to the band director's. A definite connection existed between those two facts. I played the piccolo in my husband's college band because I wanted to be involved with his trips and concerts, not because I was the most gifted musician in the school. But I got along, letting the fast, difficult passages be played by the first flutist.

I got along, that is, until Raphael Mendez—*the* Raphael Mendez—came on campus as guest artist for the fall concert. This world-famous trumpeter commanded respect, making us band members apprehensive, so nervous were we about making an error.

The Thursday evening rehearsal was a long one, musically

challenging, emotionally intense. A master performer, Mendez played brilliantly, flawlessly, his one-finger rendition of "Variations on the Carnival of Venice," leaving us awestruck. A demanding teacher, he'd persist until we too played to his satisfaction, stopping the band often to emphasize a rhythm, correct a note, or suggest a different interpretation.

Sitting comfortably at the end of the flutes, I reminded myself how lucky I was not to be first trumpet or first clarinet. My relief was short-lived.

"Piccolo player"—Mendez looked straight at me—"will you please play that run again? I thought I heard an F-sharp; it's supposed to be an F."

Nothing did I want to do less at that moment than to solo that fast, long chromatic run while the whole band listened.

"The note is an F, sir," I offered, hoping words would suffice for music.

"Please—*play* the run, the presto section." He was getting impatient.

Only one thing was more embarrassing than not playing the run, and that was playing the run and messing up, a "guaranteed" for me. The band members were enjoying themselves immensely, since they knew something Mendez hadn't found out yet: I was the director's wife.

"Perhaps the first flute could play that section; she'd be more accurate," I volunteered, my face the color of my red blouse.

Found out. Betrayed by my own lack of practice.

"You can fool some of the people all of the time and all of the people some of the time, but you can't fool Mendez even once," I mused.

Nor God.

To live one's life as if there were never to be an accountability is the most unrealistic of attitudes.

The Bible's words of warning are still true, often in this life and always in eternity: "Be sure your sin will find you out."

Wilma McClarty

February 23

Guns and Mad Dogs

When you pass through the waters, I will be with you; and when you pass through the rivers, they will not sweep over you. Isa. 43:2, NIV.

When we first started planning our move to Africa, it was with the intention of working at one of Riverside Farm Institute's isolated agriculture projects. The thought of managing three children on a small island homestead surrounded by desolate African bush concerned me. Feeling that currents of danger were threatening to flood their banks, I looked for a remedy to my anxieties. It seemed to me that under the circumstances a gun made sense, and understanding the psychological importance of my solution, my husband agreed to our owning a small pistol.

As events turned out, we never did move out to the agriculture project in the bush. We ended up living at Riverside Farm, and the gun stayed packed on a high shelf in the bedroom closet.

Then early one morning, while my husband was away, I awoke to discover a rabid dog outside my window, snarling in a mad frenzy. Getting the gun down from the closet, I slipped the clip of bullets into the shaft and rushed to the door. Shaking from an overdose of adrenaline, I aimed at the raging dog 20 feet away and pulled the trigger. Nothing happened. The dog snarled and eyed me viciously. Hurriedly I tried firing again, but there was no doubt about it—the gun had jammed. To my relief, the campus guard came driving up at that moment with rifle in hand, and I slipped back into the house, leaving him the task of keeping the world safe.

After I calmed down a bit, it occurred to me that my solutions in life have often turned out to be jammed guns. On the shelf they have had a way of making me feel a little more brave and in control, but in my hands they have left me feeling foolish and vulnerable. As a child I was taught that angels are by my side, but that didn't stop me from taking flying leaps into bed to escape from being ambushed by Indians underneath. Those fears and solutions seem silly to me now, but despite repeated evidences of God's watchcare, I still find myself looking for a big stick to carry when danger threatens to flood its banks. Oftentimes I think my solutions are all that stand between myself and disaster, but in moments when my plans fail I suddenly see how really powerless I am, and how my only real security in life is trusting in my heavenly Father. Thank God my guns jam every now and then.

Deborah Aho

FEBRUARY 24

PRAYER AND PRAISE

Are any among you suffering? They should pray. Are any cheerful? They should sing songs of praise. . . . Therefore confess your sins to one another, and pray for one another, so that you may be healed. The prayer of the righteous is powerful and effective. James 5:13-16, NRSV.

When the words "Your tumor is malignant" penetrate your mind, many thoughts start buzzing around your head. A prayer goes up, and you immediately start drawing on God's strength. A woman of prayer gathers strength from her moments with God for the times when the chipping and polishing of God's precious jewels takes place.

Yes, I had been on my knees asking Him to change me, for I knew there were some rough edges that needed to be smoothed. I am so grateful for my prayer experiences. They gave strength through a difficult two years of playing the most difficult waiting game.

Many people have prayed for me: pastors, elders, friends, my children and grandchildren, and my husband, who was my strongest supporter. My larger family who met together the evening of my anointing also prayed for me.

Through it all there have been many precious times spent with Jesus as He gave me a deep settled peace in my soul. Oh, there have been tears along the way, but those tears seemed only to remind me of my frail humanity. My heavenly Father understands and considers my human frame. He knows I am made of dust. Oh, what a wonder that He is ever mindful of our individual needs.

Claim His promises as your own. Keep a prayer in your mind always.

People "ought always to pray and not lose heart" (Luke 18:1, RSV). Prayer and praise move mountains! MARION LAKE

FEBRUARY 25

THE BROKEN CUP

Let us therefore come boldly unto the throne of grace, that we

*may obtain mercy, and find grace to help in time of need.
Heb. 4:16.*

We children gathered around the table while our parents carefully opened a carton that contained a new tea set. One by one Mother unwrapped the cups, the saucers, the side plates, the milk jug, the sugar bowl, and last of all the teapot. I remember how excited we were! With oohs and aahs we gently touched the fragile dishes. To us this was the most exquisite and beautiful china anywhere.

At first the treasured tea set was used only for guests. Once after the guests had gone, Mother asked me to pick up the dishes and wash them. I carefully carried them to the kitchen, and while I was cleaning up, a cup suddenly slipped from my hands and crashed on the hard concrete floor. With horror I looked at the broken pieces. No one was around. With the trembling hands of a 10-year-old I tried to put them together. It was like putting Humpty-Dumpty together again. Fear overwhelmed me as I struggled with the temptation to bury the broken pieces. No one would be any wiser—at least that's what the tempter told me. But I had been taught to tell the truth no matter what the consequences. With the broken cup in my hand and with faltering steps I timidly approached Mother. One glance at my face, and she knew the heartbreak and fear that I was silently going through. "Never mind," she said. "What would the manufacturers do if somebody didn't break the dishes? They would starve."

Within a twinkling of an eye my fears vanished. My heart rejoiced, and love for Mother filled my whole being. The treasured sugar bowl is still in my possession, and when I look at it I remember Mother's words and the broken cup. We cannot always predict how our earthly parents will respond when we are remiss or do wrong. I expected to be punished or at least scolded for my apparent carelessness. But with God we have the assurance that our confession will always be forgiven. There may be consequences for our negligence, but He never fails to pardon.   BIROL C. CHRISTO

FEBRUARY 26

CHASED BY BABOONS

The Lord will rescue me from every evil attack and will bring me safely to his heavenly kingdom. 2 Tim. 4:18, NIV.

On a recent trip to South Africa we saw the signs all along the road: "Don't feed baboons. They are dangerous." We'd read of a baboon who snatched a child, then nearly killed the father, who had tried to retrieve his boy by hitting the baboon with a stick.

These large, adaptable monkeys usually travel in troops of 10 to 70. We watched them forage for food, eating wild fruit, leaves, seeds, and insects. A big male baboon stands almost five feet and may weigh more than 90 pounds. They have arms almost as long as their legs, a muzzle that looks like a dog's, and sharp teeth that make them look fierce when they open their huge mouths.

Looking for a place to eat, we spotted a troop of about 14 baboons in a picnic area.

"Not here," I said. "Let's stay far away from them."

Down the road we found another table on the edge of a cliff overlooking the ocean. Because of the strong wind, we kept most of our food in the basket. I put the loaf of bread in my lap and began making avocado sandwiches. Suddenly a hand snatched the whole loaf. I looked up to see a baboon disappearing over the cliff.

My husband turned around and yelled, "The whole troop's coming! Run for the car!"

He took the basket and I grabbed the rest, heading for the car door. I'd opened it a few inches when another baboon reached for the food in my hand, and squeezed ahead trying to get in first. Slamming the door, I raced around the back. I felt his sharp claws scratch my upper arm, and turned to look. His open mouth and two-inch-long canines were almost touching my face.

"Hurry!" my husband shouted. "Others are just behind you!"

Somehow I slid under the steering wheel, with my husband following. Just as he shut the door, baboons jumped on the car, growling, barking, and screaming. Some men working on the road saw them, grabbed some shovels, and drove them away.

I know my caring heavenly Father kept that large baboon from biting me. And He'll keep me from every evil attack from Satan and bring me safely to His kingdom. Have you claimed this promise and thanked Him for His care for you, too? —Eileen E. Lantry

---

February 27

Friends

Go therefore to all nations and make them my disciples; . . . and

teach them to observe all that I have commanded you. I will be with you always, to the end of time. Matt. 28:19, 20, REB.

This poem is a paraphrase of the thoughts contained in Matthew 28:19, 20.

>Friends come in all sizes and shapes:
>to comfort,
>to listen,
>to help,
>to teach,
>to share,
>when times are good
>and not so good.
>
>Friends encourage me,
>laugh with me,
>and care about me.
>
>True friends lift my spirit,
>speak my language,
>understand my aches,
>share my sorrows,
>take time from their busy lives
>to brighten
>my corner of life.
>
>I am thankful to my friends for
>the inspiration they give to me,
>for pointing me heavenward,
>for helping me to better understand my complex self,
>for the giving of their self.
>
>God wants me for a friend,
>to comfort,
>to listen,
>to help,
>to teach,
>to share
>His love with others
>when times are good
>
>and not so good.

PEGGY HARRIS

FEBRUARY 28

FOUND!

Or what woman, if she has ten silver coins and loses one coin, does not light a lamp and sweep the house and search carefully until she finds it? And when she has found it, she calls together her friends and neighbors, saying, "Rejoice with me, for I have found the coin which I had lost!" Luke 15:8, 9, NASB.

I have some friends who live at the edge of their own beautiful lake. Schubert and Tiger Lily are the white swans who live there too. There are also four Canadian geese, a pair of mallards, and some domestic geese. Six tan-colored adults, and best of all—13 fluffy babies!

At breakfast time all of them come for a handout. The grain is tossed onto the ground for the ducks and into the water for the swans. Swans need water in order to swallow the grain. It's always a contest to see who gets the most in the shortest time. But one day while I watched—well, let me tell you about it.

The host let me help her toss grain onto the ground near the edge of the lake. And almost before the grain hit the ground, those handsome Canadian geese were out of the water. Then the mallards. The swans began swallowing as soon as the grain hit the water. But where were the domestic geese? They must be hungry too.

"Oh, here they are," I called. "No, there's just one little fluffy baby." It came foraging up on the bank. "Where are the others?" We strained our eyes.

"Look, there they are," my friend replied, pointing far out on the lake. I could barely see them. What I saw were three adult geese keeping the 12 fluffies corralled between them. The other adults were running frantically back and forth on shore, searching behind and beneath every shrub and tree.

We watched as the searching geese moved slowly closer to where we stood. The babies and their "sitters" swam closer too, and the breakfast on the shoreline was disappearing like magic. Finally the search party was close enough for us to hear their frantic calls. Immediately the little "lost" fluffy who had been foraging near us quit pecking breakfast, stretched its tiny neck, and looked out over the water.

"Peep, peep . . . peep, peep," it called. The searchers stopped dead still and listened.

"Peep, peep . . . peep, peeeeeeep!" You could almost see what they were thinking!

With one mighty splash they were out of the water. There was much fluttering, flapping of wings, and geese talk as they greeted the "one who was lost, but is found."

Our loving Father is not willing that any of His children should perish. Where are you this morning, my friend? Have you wandered from His care?

Listen. Do you hear the Searcher's call? Do you want to be found? Let Him hear your voice just now—"Here I am, Father. Here." And there will be great rejoicing in heaven! VIRGINIA CASON

March 1

BURGLARS AND ANGELS

The angel of the Lord encamps around those who fear him, and delivers them. Ps. 34:7, RSV.

It was a very foggy March night in 1976 in a sleepy little Southern town. My husband was gone on a business trip. My four children were sound asleep in their large bedroom. I could hear the rhythm of their breathing as I checked the door that opened from their room onto the long wooden front porch. I had already checked the foyer door and the French doors in the living room, which also opened onto the front porch, and the back door. I walked into my bedroom, turned out the light, got down on my knees to pray, climbed in bed, and was soon fast asleep.

I awoke with a start and lay awake in my bed listening. Had I heard a noise, or was I dreaming? There it was again! It sounded like metal scraping on the front screen door. Again I heard the scraping sound! Burglars must have been watching the house and noticed that the car and dogs were gone. They must have thought we had all gone on a trip. They had no way of knowing that we had just sold our dogs the day before my husband left on his trip, and that the children and I were home.

I got out of bed, put on my robe, and walked barefoot in the darkness to the children's room. In my mind I visualized the layout of the furnishings as I cautiously walked through the house. I cracked the side of the curtain on the front window and peeked out, but even the light from the corner streetlight was hidden by the dense fog. I crossed the house again, stopping at the three beds and the crib to check the boys. As I quietly walked down the hallway to my bedroom I again heard the scraping sound, this time on the back screen door!

I thought of calling the police but was afraid of making a noise or of being seen through the window if the burglars had flashlights. Would we be killed? Instead of taking chances, I fell on my knees by my bed and prayed, claiming God's promise to send His angels to encamp around us! I climbed back into bed and waited.

Suddenly I heard a loud crashing noise like rolling thunder coming from the front porch just outside the French doors in the living room and footsteps running away from the house! I quickly made my way to the living room in the darkness, and peeked through the French door. A three-legged iron table had been knocked over on the wooden porch.

Needless to say, I thanked God for sending angels to scare the burglars away, went back to my room, and fell soundly asleep with the assurance that God was watching over us. CELIA CRUZ

MARCH 2

LET THERE BE BEAUTY

He has made everything beautiful in its time. Eccl. 3:11, NIV.

There are certain words in every culture that evoke an instantaneous, measurable, emotional response: Mother. Baby. Blood. Fire. Laundry.

Laundry?

Well, OK, maybe not in every culture. However, in America the word "laundry" conjures up definite emotional responses.

On television, for example, laundry seems to bring out a frenzy of emotions. In one scene a whole family watches dear old dad labor and sweat in the backyard all day and then won't let him come near them until his clothes have been laundered.

Television commercials are also loaded with people who go crazy over spots. Earnestly they explain how they did comparison washing to see which soap got their laundry whitest.

I picked up a most charming magazine recently. It was devoted to promoting the nostalgia of bygone eras by offering advice on furnishings and describing old-fashioned ways of entertaining, such as tea parties and croquet tournaments. There were delightful articles about gentle, restful rooms filled with charming, elegant things. In the middle of this elegant magazine was an article about, of all things, a laundry room.

Of all the places to make elegant, the laundry room would not be the first to pop into my mind. The laundry room is probably the last-named, last-decorated, last-cleaned, last-listed-in-the-real-estate-ad room in the house. Many houses don't even have a laundry room; they have a utility room, or a laundry closet, or a it's-really-for-something-else-but-the-laundry-is-stuck-there-too room.

The writer of the article collected antique linens, which she then used to ornament her home. And guess what? She had a beautiful laundry room with a stone floor and walls, a lovely antique oak cupboard painted in soft green and white, potted plants, and a splendid bay window overlooking a wooded hillside. It was a place of beauty—for laundry!

Suddenly the laundry room had new possibilities for me, a place not just for doing a chore, but to enjoy beauty while doing it. I saw that there is value in adding beauty to even the most humble places. Now I have new images and associations for some old familiar hymns and Bible texts: "Create in me a clean heart." "Wash me, and I shall be whiter than snow." (God's laundry room must be awesome!)

Most of us have "laundry rooms" in our lives, in our relationships, even in our spiritual lives. We all have areas we take for granted, places that need to have the cobwebs and lint cleared away. Even our most commonplace words and actions could be better used to contribute to loveliness.

Excuse me for a moment now, won't you? I've got some potted plants I want to put out in my laundry room. JO HABADA

MARCH 3

MOTIVES

I tell you the truth, you are looking for me, not because you saw miraculous signs but because you ate the loaves and had your fill. John 6:26, NIV.

The drought-stricken land had taken its toll on its people, and the little villages began to send out convoys of men and women to Riverside Farm Institute, where they hoped to secure maize and relieve their hunger. As a leader in Zambia's famine relief program,

I knew the word had traveled deep into the hills that the agriculture training school was distributing food. Eagerly the villagers arrived, weary but hopeful that the days of hunger were over. Gratitude filled their eyes, and precious words of blessing were bestowed on our team of volunteer workers.

Wherever our trucks appeared, letters came in the mail thanking us for our willingness to organize and carry out the maize distribution.

Then came the days that the maize stopped. Transportation problems at government levels were so bad that nothing moved out of the cities. Fortunately the surrounding villages had surplus maize stocked up to see them through such a crisis, but as they saw their surplus dwindling they began to panic.

Irate village leaders began showing up at our office accusing us of starving the people. False rumors circulated that we were hoarding the maize for ourselves, preventing it from reaching them. They believed it was our fault they were suffering, and they wanted justice. How quickly opinions had changed. Obviously the good favor we'd enjoyed with the people had been in direct proportion to their receiving the loaves, if not the fishes.

The transportation matter was eventually settled, and the trucks began rolling the maize in again. Once again the villagers were receiving large stocks of food, and once again they were eager to befriend us. Like little children they rallied around, eager to let us know that they had never doubted we would come through.

The turn of events came as no surprise to us. Call it human nature. But seeing it acted out so vividly got me thinking about my own relationship with God. It's not such a quantum leap of the imagination to see that same streak of human nature in my heart. Unless I allow the Holy Spirit to crucify self, I welcome God's love and blessings, only to turn away when I realize that following Christ means denying self and taking up my cross. Today the haunting question put to His disciples comes down through the ages to all of us: "Will you also leave Me?" And unless our hearts are seeking for more than a few bags of maize, our answer won't be any different than that of the multitude that ate the loaves and fishes.

Deborah Aho

March 4

Simple Truth, Sensationally Saving

If you confess with your mouth Jesus as Lord and believe in your heart that God raised Him from the dead, you shall be saved. Rom. 10:9, NASB.

How long has it been since you realized the basic "born again" principle is simple? Within your plans do you forget that Jesus said, "I am the way" (John 14:6)? Are you tempted to believe that you can't receive Him because you lost your temper, or became too busy with your life of being Mom, student, and/or career-possessed?

Do you make the time during the day to praise Him for His glorious sunshine after days of threatening rain or snow? Maybe you didn't notice the sun because you were too busy checking your list to see if all the items you had on it were indeed finished. You may have even lost that moment of belief and assurance out of aggravation with yourself because you forgot your list or never made one.

Perhaps the idea of believing in Jesus in simple childlike faith was at the top of your list today, but got crowded out as you fretted in your mind points of doctrine that your brother, daughter, or friend criticizes or refuses to interpret exactly as you do. Maybe you felt eager to share with a stranger the Sabbath truth as you understand the New and Old Covenant.

Rippling through you may be the desire to give healthy habit hints to everyone you see. Perhaps surging up in your suggestions may be the latest seminar with details on the state of the dead. To be certain, these and other beliefs are cornerstones and sharp tools of truth. But does that stranger know of the love lavished by our Lord who died? Will that friend, daughter, or brother know today that if they believe on the Lord Jesus Christ they shall be saved, they and their household (Acts 16:31)?   MARI GIBBS-PICKETT

MARCH 5

MY NEW CEILING FAN

Because the Lord God helps me, I will not be dismayed; therefore, I have set my face like flint to do his will, and I know that I will triumph. Isa. 50:7, TLB.

"Lord, I need help!"

The parts of my new ceiling fan and light fixture were spread out on the table before me. I'd assembled as much as the directions advised, turned off the circuit breaker, and taken down the old light fixture.

Now I was in trouble. From the hole in the ceiling a black wire and a white wire hung down. From the fan on the table a black, a white, a blue, and a green wire stuck up. (The real estate man had assured me that this would be a simple job!)

I slumped into a nearby chair and prayed out loud, "Lord, I need help!" Almost at once a name popped into my head—the father of a friend of mine. "But Lord, he's probably busy, and maybe he doesn't know about wiring—and I really don't know him well enough . . ." I sat and thought of lots of reasons not to phone the man. "Lord, it would be so simple for You to make an angel appear at my front door. He could fix this mess easily." The name stayed in my head.

So I finally called and explained my problem. I was right. He was busy. He was in the middle of a big garage sale, but he said he'd see what he could do.

About 15 minutes later his 88-year-old brother-in-law arrived at my door. He said he wasn't a professional, but he liked to help people. He said he thought he might be able to help me. He said he'd rather help someone than sit at a garage sale anyway.

For the next hour he stood on the stepstool and I stood on a chair handing him tools. Now I have a new fan and a new light fixture and a new friend.

Does God care about our little day-to-day worries? You bet He does. And sometimes He sends willing Christian people to do the work of angels.

Thank You, Lord, for sending me a human angel. Now use me to be a blessing to someone else today. Amen. —SANDY ZAUGG

MARCH 6

AS TREES . . .

Then the trees of the forest will sing, they will sing for joy before the Lord. 1 Chron. 16:33, NIV.

The highway followed the irregular coastline—up, down, and around. It was early morning, and I was beginning a four-hour drive to be with my mother while my stepfather underwent surgery. The sun had not yet risen, and ground fog clung to the land in gauzy patches. Windswept headlands, dotted with sweeping Monterey pines, signaled that civilization would soon be far behind. Before long the car radio began to crackle with the waning signal. I was tired and unsure of what I would find at my destination. Surgery always carries an inherent risk.

Another hour, and the highway entered a forest. Rounding a bend in the road, I suddenly caught my breath at the glorious beauty spread out before me. Beams from the rising sun were streaming down through the giant redwoods. The rays had caught in the branches, pierced the mist, and turned everything into an ethereal and sparking fairyland. Pulling into a small turnout, I stopped the car and rolled down the window. How I wished for brush, paints, palette—and an ability to capture the scene on canvas.

The engine quieted, and I became aware of sounds all around me. There was the rippling of a creek, the morning song of a bird, the murmur of wind through the leaves, and yes, it was as if the trees themselves were softly singing in joy and praise to God.

My mind turned to thoughts of the many scriptures that refer to trees. The Bible tells us that human beings who delight in the Lord are like trees planted by streams of water (Ps. 1:3); that they will be called oaks of righteousness, "a planting of the Lord for the display of his splendor" (Isa. 61:3, NIV); that the trees of the Lord are well watered (Ps. 104:16).

My reason for making the trip expanded beyond the need to be with my mother. Like Isaiah, I was on a mission to bind up the brokenhearted, to bestow the oil of gladness instead of mourning and a garment of praise instead of a spirit of despair. I could hardly wait to tell my family about the trees—they would understand and enjoy my description of the painting that had been captured in my memory.

The engine began to hum once more, and I was on my way again—rested, rejuvenated, and rejoicing. Metaphorically, I, a tree of the Lord, had been well watered. SHARLET BRIGGS WATERS

MARCH 7

WINDS OF LIFE

Then he rose and rebuked the winds and the sea; and there was a great calm. And the men marveled, saying, "What sort of man is this, that even winds and sea obey him?" Matt. 8:26, 27, RSV.

March is known for wind. Winter cold changes to springtime warmth, with resulting turbulence in air currents. According to the Severe Storms Forecast Center there are official terms describing wind speeds. From 3 to 31 miles per hour is a breeze; 32 to 63 mph is a gale; 64 to 75 mph is a storm; and wind at 76 mph or more is a hurricane.

Have you ever noticed how we use weather terms to describe life experiences? "Oh, it's a breeze," we say of something we sailed through easily. "They've had a stormy relationship," we might reply when describing interactions that are more turbulent than tranquil. And there are times when we feel like life is pressing against us with full hurricane force.

How is it with you today? Are you skipping through the day enjoying the sunshine of life? If so, enjoy. Or is life whirling around you with frightening speed? If that describes your day, remember you have a Friend who says to storms, "Peace; be still."

BEULAH FERN STEVENS

March 8

THE VISA

Now Samuel did not yet know the Lord: The word of the Lord had not yet been revealed to him. 1 Sam. 3:7, NIV.

An incident a few weeks before my trip with the governor made me think of young Samuel's experience. When God called, Samuel didn't know Him well enough to recognize His voice, but not until recently did I really consider the implied parallels in that story for today's Christians.

My husband and I have experienced instances of God's unmistakable intervention and guidance in our lives. Recently a friend suggested that a close relationship with God includes listening for Him. I'd not thought about that before.

We are missionaries in Zaire. Our mission's main postal address, though, is in Zambia, where we go for the bulk of our mail and to have telephone or fax contact with the outside world. It's only 150 miles (240 kilometers) from the mission, but the trip contains many variables—road conditions, border formalities, and police checks, which may be as few as five or as many as 15. Therefore, to allow time for business and to avoid the dangers of night driving, we usually take two full days to make the trip.

Not long ago our mail needed to be collected and several business matters required attention. Since I had a Wednesday afternoon school board committee to chair, we decided to drive down on Monday afternoon and return Wednesday morning. My Zambian visa had expired, so my passport was taken to the Zambian consulate for a new visa, but the one responsible neglected to get it back as agreed on Friday morning. On Friday afternoon on the way home from shopping I thought of going for the passport. "No," I told myself, "it's almost closing time, and it's a few blocks out of the way. I'll have it picked up Monday morning."

But the Zambian consulate will be closed Monday; it's a holiday for them, my thoughts immediately warned me.

I don't know that; nobody's said anything about that, I argued with myself. And we went home without the passport.

"The Zambian consulate is closed," the messenger told me Monday morning when he returned empty-handed. "It's a public holiday for them, and there's no one there."

We had no choice but to postpone our trip until Tuesday and leave business unfinished in our rush to be back for the Wednesday meeting. God does want to be involved and to help us in our everyday lives, but it is up to us to learn to know Him and to listen for Him.

CORRINE VANDERWERFF

MARCH 9

ACCEPT ONE ANOTHER

Accept one another, then, just as Christ accepted you, in order to bring praise to God. Rom. 15:7, NIV.

I was convinced that I had made a mistake! As I sat at the edge of the swimming pool watching the members of the group near the water, I *knew* that I was in the wrong place!

Most of the members were stroke victims; slowly they made their way to join me, their damaged limbs making the process difficult.

There was the woman who sat in a wheelchair, unable to move, and had to wait for help to be hoisted into the pool. There was another in obvious pain from arthritis of the spine; another struggled with the consequences of polio. Behind them came a man who hobbled toward the swimming pool, one of his legs shorter than the other. And finally there was the young girl with only one leg.

This was no ordinary swimming group, but a disabled one. So what was I doing there?

A few months earlier I had been diagnosed as suffering from ankylosing spondylitis. This disease is an inflammation of the spine, resulting in lack of mobility in various joints in the body. There is no cure, but exercise slows down the rate of immobilization. So there I sat at the pool's edge awaiting my first lesson.

I had been convinced that God had led me to this group through a succession of answered prayers. But now I doubted His leading. I felt a fraud being there when there were so many people with obvious disabilities and much greater needs.

How wrong I was! Once in the water I was oblivious to their disabilities and focused only on mine. While my companions swam like ducks in the water I struggled with my inability to move as I wanted. I had made the mistake of comparing myself to others and their handicaps, and had forgotten about mine!

That experience made me aware of the judgmental attitude we sometimes have toward others. So many times we focus on their faults and conveniently forget about ours. We pride ourselves on not being as insensitive as Mrs. Blunt or as critical as Mr. Grumble or as hurtful as Mr. and Mrs. Perfect. How many times we pat ourselves on the back and tell ourselves we're OK.

But what happens when we stop comparing ourselves to human beings and begin comparing ourselves to Jesus Christ? What happens when we step into the water and are forced to look at ourselves?

Then all our pride is stripped away and our sins, our "disabilities," which we cleverly conceal from others, glare angrily at us. We become totally aware of the ugliness and wretchedness of sin that permeates our inner selves. We are awed that Jesus can love and accept us the way that we are.

The Bible says that just as Jesus accepted us, we need to accept others. We need to be tolerant and understanding of their "disabilities," or weaknesses.

If our relationship with Christ is as it should be, we will have no desire to focus on the disabilities of one another, but rather be more concerned with Jesus making our disabilities whole.   MARY BARRETT

March 10

Is There Victory?

Do not grieve, for the joy of the Lord is your strength. Neh. 8:10, NIV.

A picture has been hanging on the wall on my side of the bed in my bedroom for many years. It does not contain a beautiful landscape or flowers or even children; actually, it has nothing more than letters . . . united as words . . . making a sentence—a sentence that states a philosophy of living.

I inherited this picture when its owner died; I knew her very well. Her joy of living was a song in her life; it shot forth as a smile. She had been successful in multiplying her talents, transforming them in service, and it seemed that life was easy and pleasant to her.

But no, life had not been very charitable to her. In her 20s an illness had appeared that would stretch for long years. Sedatives had been insufficient, and the suffering had been intense. The doctors had struggled to win the battle, but in vain.

No, life had not been very generous. The only solution had been drastic, and the technical skills had only disguised her difficulties. Have you ever thought how difficult it would be to live with only one leg? Have you imagined how troublesome, how traumatic, how cumbersome the results would be?

But there at her own bedside my mother had had the picture hanging. At the beginning of the day, at the end of the day, she could read its text:

"If you wished to be grateful to God for everything He gives you, there would be no time left for complaining."

How many "reasons" would we have today for complaining? How many "justified reasons" will we find (or invent) today for complaining? Will we be deprived of a leg, an arm, or another element that we imagine vital for our happiness? Are we going to continue our habit of transforming every small or medium frustration into a terrible amputation? Or are we going to hide under unreal armor, pretending that the problems do not exist?

When today the battles of life come close, remember the words of the picture and be thankful, "for the joy of the Lord is your strength."

Susana Schulz

March 11

Tired of Running?

Come to Me, all you who labor and are heavy laden, and I will give you rest. Take My yoke upon you and learn from Me, for I am gentle and lowly in heart, and you will find rest for your souls. For My yoke is easy and My burden is light. Matt. 11:28-30, NKJV.

Once I ran in the race of daily living—going nowhere. Feeling the yoke of life, I examined my priorities; changes had to be made. From those changes I wrote:

> Watch my feet . . .
> running to work,
> running to school,
> running to church,
> running from God.
>
> Watch my self-deceit!
> My work can train another,
> my school can teach another,
> my church can reach another.
> For none has sacrificed for me.
> None saw death's cruel face and
> resurrection's glorious light!
>
> Watch His arms unfold.
> Watch my feet . . .
> running to the cross.

When it's all said and done, Jesus is still there waiting for us to come unto Him—to give us rest and peace, and to exchange life's yoke with His. No one else promises and delivers like that. Yet we give all our waking hours to things, causes, or people, most of whom won't remember us in the end. I learned to take Jesus at His word; He's good for it. Spend time with Him before running any further. He will make the race shorter and the road sure.

RosaLynda Kosini

MARCH 12

GOD'S TIMING

But let all who take refuge in you rejoice; let them ever sing for joy. Spread your protection over them, so that those who love your name may exult in you. For you bless the righteous, O Lord; you cover them with favor as with a shield. Ps. 5:11, 12, NRSV.

Early on an April morning I read this psalm, then copied verses 11 and 12 into my prayer journal, claiming this promise for each one on my prayer list. (Of course, my children are at the top of the list.) I wrote my prayer, specifically asking, "Look down on each one, because You know their needs far better than I do. Help them to be aware of Your favor wherever they are. Remind each one of Your love and mercy and that they can look to You with complete confidence that their Father doesn't see their sins, only the sinless life of Jesus."

A couple mornings later my daughter and her husband were abruptly awakened by a shot fired just outside the window of their home, which was on a vast ranch in New Mexico. Two men with guns began to harass them with such taunts as "I am the devil, and I've come to take your soul." My daughter crawled to the living room, hid behind a bookcase, and telephoned the police, who were 60 miles away.

They hid their two little boys in a closet and prayed. The threats went on for more than an hour. Several windows were broken as the men tried to get in. Just as one man raised himself to a back window, lights appeared from the highway five miles away, giving evidence that the police would arrive shortly. Immediately the would-be intruders took off across the valley, but were soon apprehended.

It was a shattering experience for this little family, yet through it all they felt the protection of God, which kept the assailants outside their home until help arrived.

What assurance it brought to their hearts as they learned later the text I had claimed for them. Many other providences of God through the whole experience showed them His tender care.

MARIANETTE JOHNSTON

March 13

Beauty

Make a lampstand of pure gold and hammer it out, base and shaft; its flowerlike cups, buds and blossoms shall be of one piece with it. . . . Three cups shaped like almond flowers with buds and blossoms are to be on one branch, three on the next branch, and the same for all six branches extending from the lampstand. Ex. 25:31-33, NIV.

I enjoy reading these detailed instructions for the wilderness sanctuary, because I like to think of God as a lover of beauty and elegance.

In a throwaway society in which tables are cleared by rolling up the paper cloth with all the plastic plates, cups, and cutlery inside, I appreciate all attempts to keep aesthetics alive.

Twenty-six years ago Dick and I selected delicate stemware as we filled out a bridal register. We received one goblet as a gift and bought another ourselves. That "set" of two seems symbolic now. As I lay a lovely table, I'm reminded that relationships need careful protection if they are to survive.

Though I've never given an afternoon tea, I own a hand-painted set once promised me by my grandmother. I was no more than 10 years old when I first looked with awe at the bright poppies and gold trim on each piece of china and traced the artist's name, "Emily Chase," with my finger. To know that such exquisite beauty would one day be mine made me feel rich and honored. I think now of how I might bless my own children with such vision.

So heavy it seems to defy destruction, a vase of thick crystal that now occupies a prominent place in my home was shipped across the Atlantic by my aunts in Sweden. Its simple lines and fine etching represent the art of my people. Meant to display a dozen roses, it is still the perfect container for any large bouquet. It speaks to me of loving artistry and also of faith.

These are some of my treasures on earth. They are easily damaged and irreplaceable—certanly not for everyday use! Or are they? Exodus reinforces for me that color and richness, visual and sensual delight, are part of knowing God. Ugliness is not holiness; unattractiveness is not spirituality.

Cherry B. Habenicht

MARCH 14

A Voice in the Night

And the Lord came, and stood, and called as at other times, Samuel, Samuel. Then Samuel answered, Speak; for thy servant heareth. 1 Sam. 3:10.

One warm fall day our 6-year-old daughter went to play in a friend's yard after school. She had taken her new school shoes off while playing, and when she was ready to start home, they were nowhere in sight. The girls helped her look, but with no success. No matter how hard she tried, she could not remember where she had put them, and worried that a passerby had taken them.

Heidi was crying as she came in the back door. She knew there was not enough money in the budget to replace them.

"Perhaps we'd better pray about this," I said. "The Lord knows where the shoes are even if we don't." We knelt down right then and asked Him to help us. At bedtime we asked Jesus again to let us know about the shoes. Heidi went to bed, fully believing they would be found.

Everyone slept soundly that night, but at 2:00 a.m. we were awakened by a shout and the sounds of footsteps running down the hallway in the dark. "I know where my shoes are!" Heidi cried. "God called my name in the night, just as He did Samuel's. He told me to look way back under the big bush at Lynn's house. That's where they are! I saw a picture of them right there!" She was so excited. We could hardly wait until morning to see if they really were there.

At dawn we went over and looked. Sure enough, there they were, pushed way back under the bush where no one would ever have found them. We knelt down right then and thanked the Lord for showing us where her shoes were—and just in time, too, for a cold rain fell continuously the next day.

I was so thankful that our little girl remembered the story of Samuel and how God had called him with a message in the night. What a blessing we would have missed if we had not taken time together to read those precious Bible stories.

That was more than 30 years ago, but our daughter still talks about the incident to this day. She never will forget how God called her name in the night.   DARLENE BURGESON

MARCH 15

THE BUTTERFLY'S PROMISE

He makes me to lie down in green pastures; He leads me beside the still waters. He restores my soul. Ps. 23:2, 3, NKJV.

It had been a long cold winter, the kind in which the sun refused to shine and the sky dressed in an ugly coat of gray. The ground alternated from being a solid frozen hazard to a slushy, muddy mess. I'd spent most of my time wiping runny noses, calming irritable cabin-fevered kids, and job hunting.

It probably wouldn't have been so bad if I'd had a friend to chat with, but a recent move had separated me from the best female friend I'd ever known. Oh, how I missed her! I'd probably never find another who would actually exchange housework with me because she knew I hated mopping the kitchen floor, or call me once a day to see what I was cooking for supper. Somehow an occasional card or phone call didn't fill the void.

The butterfly appeared during the height of my depression, when I thought spring would never arrive. It had been a particularly dreary day, so I decided to keep busy and clean the house thoroughly.

I washed windows, vacuumed curtains, and dragged freshly washed quilts out to the backyard to air-dry.

The soggy ground penetrated my shoes and my thoughts. Would the sun ever shine in my heart again? Why did I miss my old home so badly? Would I ever feel contented and happy in this friendless town?

I reached up to pin the quilt on the clothesline securely. A burst of bright orange and black flitted past me. I stopped and stared, my thoughts unconsciously lifting higher. That butterfly was so small—seemingly insignificant—but it carried on its tiny wings a message of hope and assurance. "Hold fast," it seemed to say. "Brighter days are coming."

Since then I've learned that depression is caused by various sources, and you and I must each deal with it in our own way. Statistics show that it reaches epidemic proportions in the winter months, when people tend to stay indoors. For me sunlight, fresh air, and exercise are a must in keeping a healthy outlook on life. Yes, even in the winter we must appreciate the beauty of a naked brown tree and compare it to the nakedness of our own soul. Nature is healing, and when combined with the Word of God, it is preventive medicine for the soul.

CRYSTAL EARNHARDT

March 16

What a Mighty God We Serve

I say to you, Don't be afraid; I am here to help you. Isa. 41:13, TLB.

It was 2:00 in the morning, but suddenly Judy was wide awake. It seemed strange that she would be so alert at this hour. Glancing out the window at the falling snow, she saw sparks in the air—not unusual with a big fire, but now there should be only embers in the wood-burning stove downstairs. Then she heard the roar of a chimney fire and quickly woke her husband, Dave.

The fire department's efficient crew lost no time in getting to the house, and before long, they were satisfied that the fire was out.

The firefighters commented on how "lucky" they were to awaken and discover the fire. Judy and Dave knew it was not just luck. As they sat in the living room with their Bibles, they thanked God for His deliverance; then they both gave in to exhaustion and slept.

Judy had dozed on the sofa just a short time when once again she was alert—but why? She sat very still and listened, and heard the now-familiar roar. She again woke Dave. When Dave found their phone was dead, he quickly dashed to the nearest neighbors to call the fire department while Judy ran upstairs for the children. She took both sleepy children out the front door and through the snow to the car parked outside, and quickly headed back upstairs to collect necessary items. But when she opened the door to the stairs, she was stopped by smoke and fire.

There are still many questions to be answered about this experience. Though the answers will have to wait, Dave and Judy realize that the old farmhouse could have burned quickly and without warning, and are amazed at the timing of events that early morning. Judy knew that God had awakened her, not once, but twice. His timing was so precise.

Someone has said that "a coincidence is when God works a miracle and chooses to remain anonymous." Sometimes in dramatic ways, as with Judy, sometimes in smaller ways, God may choose to intervene providentially for His children.

Many times in Scripture God says, "Don't be afraid." In Isaiah 41:13 He says, "I am holding you by your right hand—I, the Lord your God—and I say to you, Don't be afraid; I am here to help you."

There's a little chorus that could be a response to this promise:

What a mighty God we serve,
What a mighty God we serve;
Angels bow before Him,
Heaven and earth adore Him.
What a mighty God we serve.   RUTHIE JACOBSEN

MARCH 17

POTPOURRI WORDS

Let no corrupt communication proceed out of your mouth, but that which is good to the use of edifying, that it may minister grace unto the hearers. Eph. 4:29.

Tainted communication? But you're a Christian; certainly you don't speak corruptly, do you?

What might this unsavory speech be? Swearing comes to mind, of course, but that's too obvious. What about complaining, gossiping, or nagging? God wants you to refrain from using unwholesome words. He wants you to develop the habit of building up others, to meet their needs. (Perhaps a hurting heart needs a gentle word from you at this very moment.) Your speech is to be a blessing to others.

I have a friend in California who made me aware of the importance of my voice and words. Jackie Naipo, who for many years was the administrative assistant to the late *Roots* author, Alex Haley, told me, "I call you to be comforted by the tone of your voice and the words you speak." (We became friends as a result of my interviewing Haley.) Our Christian oneness is shared each time we converse. In essence, we edify each other.

To "minister grace unto the hearers" actually means giving a favor. Those who come into your sphere of fellowship are favored by your speech. Your words become like a fragrant potpourri to them. By doing this, you carry out your responsibility to edify.

Have you ever surprised someone (even a stranger) with the joy of your words? Make someone's day! Speak in love, uplift them, so that they might praise God.

Many religious writers give counsel on the matter of voice and speech. To magnify Scripture, we must speak in such a way as to nurture the hearer.

Like Moses, some of us are slow of speech, actually afraid to speak much. We may even feel that what we have to say is unimportant. We must ask Jesus to give us a sanctified mouth, to be the incorrupt voice communicator God wants us to be. Perhaps this prayer will help: "Lord, direct Your Spirit to put the right words in my mouth, at the right time, for the right people, to bless them and You. Amen."

BETTY KOSSICK

MARCH 18

AT THE BLINK OF AN EYE

There hath no temptation taken you but such as is common to man: but God is faithful, who will not suffer you to be tempted above that ye are able; but will with the temptation also make a way to escape, that ye may be able to bear it. 1 Cor. 10:13.

Have you thought recently about how often God has provided a way to escape your temptations? I don't think we give that much thought. I believe we have taken the fulfillment of the above promise for granted. But I know that He has done it for me every single day. Although there are things from my previous life without Him that have ceased to be temptations, there are those that nag me daily and may stay with me until the Lord's coming. You and I have hopefully learned to allow the Lord to help us cope with the daily temptations and not allow ourselves to be enslaved by them.

One morning I awoke with a strong temptation to indulge in a sinful behavior. I wondered what could have caused such strong feelings. I prayed and asked God to remove the temptation. I had prayer and Scripture readings and tried thinking of other things, but this temptation still kept nagging at me. I had not yielded to it, but it was on my mind.

I walked into another room to dress for the day. Within a few seconds my thoughts were suddenly turned to a sick coworker I had been witnessing to in previous weeks. At the blink of an eye the temptation was no longer nagging at me. I almost could not believe it. I immediately recognized that God had made a way of escape! Praise God! What a wonderful Saviour. His promise was fulfilled once again.

I am reminded of how God provided for a friend at a time of extreme emotional agony, discouragement, and despair. My friend thought that the best solution was to end it all. He couldn't see any other way out of his dilemma and pain. So one night he decided to get in a canoe and go out to the deepest part of a lake. There he planned to take his life once and for all.

Suddenly the call of a loon distracted him. He knew that loons were not inhabitants of that area. Intrigued by its call, he went out to find that loon. God had provided a way of escape for him. Praise God! Today this friend of mine shares his testimony for the glory of God and serves the Lord fervently and faithfully.

The next time you are tempted, seek for His way of escape. You'll find Him true to His word. CARMEN O. GONZALEZ

MARCH 19

THE BLOND-HAIRED LADY AT THE DOOR

Dear friends, since God so loved us, we also ought to love one another. 1 John 4:11, NIV.

It was a crisp morning. My heels clicked sharply as I walked in the early-morning sun through the quiet residential neighborhood. Today was a very special day. I was going to church for the first time in years. I wondered to myself: *What will the people there be like? Will they send strange, questioning looks my way?* Although this happened several years ago, the memory is etched in my memory forever. I reassured myself with *It's OK if I'm alone, with no friends. People go to church alone all the time. It's no big deal.* Other than these few insecure feelings, my heart was really rejoicing.

The little stone church was so beautiful with its lovely stained-glass windows. As I reached to open the door, I could feel my heart pounding with nervous excitement. The next moment I was standing in the little foyer with a blond-haired lady holding a stack of bulletins and wearing a very big—and genuine—smile and saying something along the lines of "Welcome" and "Glad to see you." I don't remember her exact words, but they were warm and welcoming. Her next move took me by surprise. She gave me a great big, warm hug—not a stiff, uncomfortable one. She didn't seem to notice the smell of tobacco or what I was wearing, and she didn't give me any strange, questioning looks, either.

As I took my seat in the back row on the end, several people came to shake my hand and wish me a happy Sabbath. These were people I had never seen before, but it occurred to me that they all seemed so happy. I don't remember the sermon that day or even the special music, but I do remember feeling welcome and even loved by that little church.

What if I hadn't been so warmly received? What if I had gotten strange, intimidating looks or stiff, phony smiles? I may not have stepped foot in another church for a long time.

Our Saviour and very best Friend is just waiting to fill us with His love so much that it can't help overflowing to all those we come in contact with. The blond-haired lady at the door may never know how very much God used her that day, and what a difference she made in my life.

Friends, let us always love and accept all those whose paths we cross, though ever so briefly. A precious soul for Christ may be at stake. Praise God for the opportunity to serve Him in loving others.

JACKIE PHALEN WAIT

MARCH 20

SHOPPING SURPRISE

Your Father knows the things you have need of before you ask Him. . . . Seek first the kingdom of God and His righteousness, and all these things shall be added to you. . . . Ask, and it will be given to you. Matt. 6:8-7:7, NKJV.

My husband and I were expecting our first child. What a time of anticipation and joy it was to prepare our home for this new little addition. It was a big transition for us, as I would be staying home and we would go from two incomes feeding two people to one income feeding three people. Finances were already tight because I had fought three months of incessant nausea, missing most of my work schedule for this time period. Then I became borderline toxemic and had to have scheduled periods of rest each day. Our life was slower and our budget stretched much tighter than expected much earlier than we had anticipated.

When I was about seven months along we began crib shopping. The prices were overwhelming! For even a simple quality crib we were looking at $400, not including the mattress and linens. A good mattress would cost us at least another $100. We began to pray that God would direct us to make wise choices with our money.

About this time a friend suggested checking in the classifieds for used baby furniture. We initially balked at putting our new little one into something used, but decided it wouldn't hurt to look around. After two entire discouraging days making phone calls and traveling around to look at different used cribs, I was ready to give up. I made one last appointment for my husband and me to see a crib. Imagine our delight when we discovered the very crib we had been looking at in the store, mattress included, for $110! We went home the excited owners of a gorgeous cherry wood crib.

The next day we found a letter in our mailbox from a very dear friend and mentor. She had enclosed a check for $100, for us "to buy something for the baby." Truly God had answered our prayers beyond all our expectations! What a God of love and miracles we serve!

Shonna Dalusong

March 21

Welcome, Spring!

See! The winter is past; the rains are over and gone. Flowers appear on the earth; the season of singing has come. S. of Sol. 2:11, 12, NIV.

Spring has arrived! The promise of long, light-filled days, multicolored flower gardens, and humming insects occupies my thoughts.

However, the scene out my window is anything but springlike. Snow covers the ground in ragged patches. Trees are black and naked against the dirty white backdrop, and a few withered stems jut out of the cold, wet ground where last summer's flower gardens flourished. No evidence here of velvet-petaled roses or blossom-laden branches with their little twig homes encircling speckled blue eggs.

Ah, but what promise this little patch of frozen ground holds. All the beauty of spring is only inches below the surface. It could happen any time now. The bright-green shoot of a daffodil. The flute-like whistle of returning orioles or a warm gentle rain. How eagerly I anticipate each new day, awaiting the miracle of new life nature is about to unfold.

How much like the dreary winter landscape our lives can be. Bleak and utterly barren. Hostile to God. Oriented toward gratifying, pleasing, exalting, and esteeming self. Incapable of living a spiritually fruitful and meaningful life. How eagerly the Father must watch us, waiting and hoping for some sign of our hearts opening to the warm

rays of His Son. A repentance of sin, receiving the Lord Jesus Christ into our lives, and as a new creation living in faithful and loving obedience to His Word.
JONI BELL

MARCH 22

SPRING GARDEN

I have come that they may have life, and that they may have it more abundantly. John 10:10, NKJV.

Have you ever felt like not going on with the household chores after having enjoyed your garden on a spring afternoon?

My garden is small, but I manage to have different kinds of plants and flowers all year long. For example, the hydrangeas will not bloom until midsummer, but now in spring the leaves sprout again with new freshness and vigor. The other flowers, in the meantime, are resting.

There are dark, reddish lilies, and pretty soon the yellow ones will bloom. Since spring is here and the sun is warmer, the hibiscus flowers have grown larger.

"They seem to be smiling," my mother says happily as she watches the colorful daisies in the flower beds. She has spent hours pulling out weeds and watering the plants in the evenings.

I take good care of the plants that are in the flowerpots. I cannot forget the pergola with the jasmine that extends their branches toward my window, perfuming my bedroom in the evenings. After a hard winter, everything sprouts full of refreshed life, abundant life, which I also want to grasp to renew myself.

My heart has been sleeping for a long time in the winter of indifference. The sun of the love of God is illuminating me. It is calling me back to life. To an abundant life. It is spring in God's garden. You and I are plants that receive His tender care. This is the moment to listen to God's voice to renew ourselves. I have decided to open my arms, take His hand, and come into blossom this spring.

Do you blossom and have joy, connecting yourself with "the Life"? Jesus has come today for us to have a plentiful life. Let's take advantage of that vitality!
LENI ZAMORANO

MARCH 23

WHILE YOU ARE YET PRAYING

And it shall come to pass, that before they call, I will answer; and while they are yet speaking, I will hear. Isa. 65:24.

After I had been married five years and had two sons, married life seemed to be threatening to enter the doldrums. All the mystery was gone, and the reality was not as exciting. The temptation was just to make the best of a so-so situation. But then I remembered Isaiah 65:24 and my glorious visions of what a Christian marriage should be like, and although my husband and I were from different cultures, our original intent was to let the Lord bless us spiritually through our marriage. Self, of course, had been getting in the way a lot, and I'd found that to be determined to allow the Holy Spirit to mold you was a lot easier said than done!

Therefore, at the commencement of my husband's three-week absence I determined to agonize with the Lord to give me *all* in my marriage that the Lord had intended. I would not settle for less!

When my husband returned, there was no dramatic sign of change—nothing for *four years!* Then suddenly, while I was sitting in church one day while on vacation, out of the blue the Lord spoke: "When you return home you will find that your prayer will have been answered!" That's all. No details. Not even a mention of which prayer. But in my heart I knew which prayer it was.

I had not prayed about it again consciously and was not even thinking about it when the Holy Spirit "interrupted" my thoughts during the worship service. The assurance was so complete that I felt no need to discuss it with anyone nor felt any anxiousness about getting back home to my husband. "For I am God, and there is none else; I am God, and there is none like me . . . ; I have purposed it, I will also do it" (Isa. 46:9-11).

As I passed through immigration checks with my two boys, I looked into my husband's face. Something was present there that let me know that my prayer had indeed been answered. Praise the Lord!

I am certain that my husband will confirm that we are truly experiencing the Lord's blessing in our home even amid disagreements, arguments, pressures, and pleasures. These blessings are from heaven, not the world. "O give thanks unto the Lord, for he is good: for his mercy endureth for ever" (Ps. 107:1).   EDNA THOMAS

MARCH 24

HOLD FAST

In my distress I cried unto the Lord, and he heard me. Ps. 120:1.

While Job and his wife were leading a comfortable life, a debate was going on in heaven. Satan felt provoked by God praising Job to his face, and his cynical question "Would Job worship you for nothing?" made at least two things very clear. First, that Satan believed people to be incurably selfish, even in their relationship with God, and second, that he was convinced not only of Job's selfishness, but also that God protected Job and favored him regardless of what really went on in his heart. When Satan left the heavenly courts, he had God's permission to prove his points.

Suddenly calamity after calamity fell on Job. When the messengers had told their terrible news, Job tore his clothes, shaved his head, and worshiped God. He had been brought up to believe that all he possessed was not his own, but had come to him from God, and he could possess it only as God permitted. Job put that lesson into practice.

But what about Mrs. Job? Did she not go through the same experience as her husband? Did she not lose all her children, her servants, her position in society, her friends—everything except her husband, who was covered with boils and who smelled so bad that it was difficult for her to be around him? She certainly did, but at the time of her loss her reaction was different from her husband's.

As long as everything went well, Mrs. Job enjoyed a good relationship with God. She had raised 10 children and taught them well, but when things started to go bad, it looks like her faith disappeared as quickly as her possessions. At that moment, stripped of almost everything she treasured in life, she could see no reason to continue her relationship with God. Nothing could be gained from it. She walked down to the rubbish heap where her husband sat scraping his sores with a piece of pottery. "You are still as faithful as ever, aren't you? Why don't you curse God and die?"

Job's and Mrs. Job's test was the same, but their reaction to the testing was different. Why? Job stood the test because of his close relationship with God. The relationship, however, did not begin when all the troubles began; on the contrary, that was the time for the relationship to stand its test. Their friendship had grown during all the good years. Mrs. Job, however, had failed to build up this kind of relationship, and in the time of trouble her incomplete faith did not sustain her trust in God.

The story of Job and his wife gives us an opportunity to consider our own relationship with God. Do we worship God because we love Him, or for what He can do for us? Could Satan rightly accuse us of worshiping God to gain the blessings we receive? Yesterday is in the past, tomorrow is still in the future, but today is ours. Ours to seek a relationship with God that is strong enough to say: "Though he slay me, yet will I trust in him" (Job 13:15).   BIRTHE KENDEL

MARCH 25

A LETTER

As cold waters to a thirsty soul, so is good news from a far country. Prov. 25:25.

When leaving home to attend a Christian college out of state, I left many things behind, including a male acquaintance. To reassure me his feelings had not changed, he sent me a letter daily, and this became the highlight of my day.

After spending more time together during a vacation, we mutually came to the decision that our life goals were not the same. So we discontinued our relationship. Though I was not emotionally broken about the decision, I still missed the daily letters of encouragement and cheer.

It didn't seem that many things cheered me up on those long dreary days of that quarter. Not until I discovered another letter.

> Lord, today I need something to cheer me,
>   to lighten my step.
> Today I need a letter.
>
> Quickly He assures me,
>   "You do have a letter today!"
>
> "Good news?" I ask excitedly.
>   "A promotion? Money?
> Or perhaps the sweet thoughts of a loved one?"
>
> Emphatically, encouraging, He whispers His reply.

"Good news," answers He.
"The greatest promotion,
   Riches beyond compare,
With sweet words from the One who loves you the most."

JILL HINES RICHARDS

MARCH 26

GOD-SIGHTINGS

And God made the beast of the earth according to its kind, cattle according to its kind, and everything that creeps on the earth according to its kind. And God saw that it was good. Gen. 1:25, NKJV.

I had never heard of "God-sightings" until a church member spoke of such things. "A beautiful sunset, a fragrant rose, or a loved one's phone call," she explained, "are all God-sightings." She encouraged other members to watch for those enjoyable moments in our lives that point us to God's love.

I had occasion to remember her words one morning as I drove to work over a back road near a reservoir. Often I would come upon mallard ducks and Canadian geese waddling slowly along. Coming from a rural background and loving all the beautiful flora and fauna that God has provided for us, I'd always drive carefully down this stretch of my route.

On this February morning, barely daylight, I almost passed them before I realized what they were. I slowed as they tipped up their white tails and fled into the woods. I quickly counted them. A herd of eight white-tailed deer! Now, as a native Vermonter, I've seen deer herds by the hundreds, but this wasn't Vermont. This was Maryland, and only 20 miles from Baltimore in one direction and Washington, D.C., in the other. In Maryland I have seen one or two deer at one time, but never a herd of this size.

I slowed my car from my usual mad dash to work and silently thanked God for this God-sighting. It made me feel that God was in charge and had arranged this special treat for me. Perhaps as you go about your work today you'll want to look for some of these God-sightings in your life and thank our Creator for providing each one of them.

LORAINE SWEETLAND

MARCH 27

LET GOD

But it is good for me to draw near to God: I have put my trust in the Lord God, that I may declare all thy works. Ps. 73:28.

A young friend of mine experienced a traumatic event in her life. She decided in her heart that she had been forsaken by God. She determined to write God off. Her sorrow overwhelmed her until it was all that she could do to pour out her hurt to God on paper. Through written prayers she began to find that her source of strength could come only from God. It was only then that she realized that the peace that she sought would come ultimately from Him. And so she wrote and shared this heartfelt prayer with me:

"O God! I'm so unhappy. Why did this have to happen to me? I've always prayed that it wouldn't happen. You know it has always been my biggest fear. I can't handle it. I just want it to go away. I want the hurt to stop; I want my tears to dry up. When will the fears ever leave? I want my security back—now! Help me, God. You have promised that old things shall pass away and all things will become new. I claim this promise. I want newness of life, a new, pure, unbreakable heart. One with resilience. What am I to gain from this experience? Please bring joy and peace back into my life. You promised to comfort those that mourn. My heart is broken, torn out of my bosom. Oh, Lord, I don't want a band-aid; I need healing from inside out. The band-aid continues to slip off—exposing the soreness. I'm pleading for healing. Take Your healing hand and return my heart to its rightful place. Reconnect each heartstring with Your compassion. Delicately knit each fiber in place with understanding. And then, Lord, cup Your hand as a shield over this pounding muscle to protect it from the snares of sin and heartache. Dress me with the whole armor of God to protect my soul from the wiles of the devil, so that I may encourage others and be a testimony of Your compassionate love. Amen."

Like my young friend, we have to discover that God alone is our source of power. And this power can be received only by believing, entrusting our lives to Him, and totally committing to His will.

SONIA PAUL

MARCH 28

ENCOUNTER

Taste and see that the Lord is good. Ps. 34:8, NIV.

The flight attendant, making a last check before takeoff, discovered an attaché case that was ill-placed. She heaved it into the compartment above and slammed the lid. Crash! The lighting panel came tumbling down, missing my head by a few inches. Immediately the maintenance crew was notified. We were deplaned and informed that repairs would take about a half hour.

Hours later it was announced that the plane was incapacitated because of navigational problems and we would not be able to get a flight out until the next morning.

I lugged my baggage to the motel and to what I anticipated would be a long and boring evening. Wending my way to my room, I made a left turn and discovered I was in a group waiting to enter a meeting room. A friendly woman stepped forward and asked, "May I help you?"

I responded, "I thought this was the hallway to Room 110."

With a smile she replied, "The bedrooms are down one more hall; this is a meeting room." I thanked her and, on turning, recognized the logo on her name tag, which represented a program designed for strengthening marriages.

"Oh," I exclaimed, "you're Marriage Encounter!"

"Yes. Do you know about us?" she asked.

"Do I!" I replied. "My husband and I have been encountered."

With that she threw her arms around me, welcoming me to the group. On entering the room, I was immediately encircled by friends. Friends whom I had never met or heard of before. Friends who were from different faiths, different experiences, different geographical locations. Friends because we shared a common bond, a source of reference; we had all experienced the Marriage Encounter program.

Later I went to my room with a warm feeling of being loved and welcomed, one of purpose and seeing God's hands lead once more in my life. The anticipated lonely evening had turned into a rich experience.

Did God use the loose screw from the panel to delay the flight so that a more serious (possibly life-threatening) problem could be detected?

Was the plane delayed for the purpose of allowing me to meet this lovely group of people? Did God also use the experience to reinforce His constant presence and individual care regardless of my circumstances?

I'll probably never know the answers. Yet the joy and excitement in meeting these strangers, yet friends, gave me a taste of what I believe it will be when, in heaven, I will walk into room after room where the saved from all ages, faiths, and nationalities will warmly respond to me as friends because we will have all shared in an encounter with Jesus.　　　　　　　　　　　Norma Jean Parchment

---

March 29

Blood on the Ceiling

[God] has said, "I will never leave you or forsake you." So we can say with confidence, "'The Lord is my helper; I will not be afraid. What can anyone do to me?'" Heb. 13:5, 6, NRSV.

I lay on a stretcher in the emergency room staring at the only thing I could see: blood splatters on the ceiling.

Someone came to take my blood pressure. I couldn't look at the person, since my head and back had been taped to a board.

"Could I please make another phone call?" I whispered.

"Sorry, miss," a man responded. "There have been two big accidents brought in. We don't have time to make calls." He hurried off.

I inhaled and bit my lip. Then I wriggled my toes. Yes, I could still move them.

A nurse brushed by. "Excuse me," I called. No response.

The ambulance paramedics had told me I'd be taken to the hospital with "spinal cord precaution." That meant taped down to a hard board so I couldn't move anything.

I'd read about Joni Eareckson and others who were paralyzed permanently. I knew what the paramedics feared—a spinal cord fracture.

Just a few hours earlier I'd been stopped at an intersection waiting for the light to turn green when I'd heard a bang and felt my car lurch into the car in front of me. The paramedics had pulled me out of my car and immediately taped me to the board.

"But I can walk," I'd protested. "I can move my toes and fingers."

"Stay still," they had insisted.

"But if I'm paralyzed, why can I move?"

"Listen," one of the paramedics had replied, "about half the people we take in with spinal cord fractures are paralyzed immediately. The other half have it happen afterward. They move, and then their cord gets severed."

That sobered me quickly. I swallowed and allowed no other part of me to move. I hardly wanted to breathe.

Now I'd been lying in this position for more than an hour, just waiting for my turn for X-rays. I guess they had to help the bleeding people first. I wasn't dying.

I was alone, looking up at the blood on the ceiling, unable to move. But suddenly I looked beyond and began to pray, "God, I've never felt so alone. I don't know anyone here, and I'm facing the hardest thing I've ever faced. This is tough, God. Please comfort me. I know You're here with me."

Suddenly I knew that was true. I wasn't alone. God's presence surrounded me and filled me with peace. I remember thinking, *Yes, even if I'm paralyzed I can still talk to You, God. I can still enjoy music and chocolate and talking to friends and reading good books. I can still feel the warmth of the sun on my face and the wind in my hair and hear ocean waves.*

I wanted to hug God and jump up and down when it was determined that I had only a ruptured disk in my neck.

I'm thrilled to be able to walk and move freely today. But I also remember how God's presence was clearest to me when I needed it most—when I felt most alone and scared and vulnerable.

LORI PECKHAM

MARCH 30

GOD, PLEASE HELP ME!

The Lord is with me; he is my helper. Ps. 118:7, NIV.

It's Monday morning. The alarm goes off at 6:00. After a few minutes my brain starts working. Already I'm thinking of the day's deadlines: I have to be at the office by 7:30. I wonder how much mail there will be after the weekend. There will be a meeting with the other staff members at 9:00; after lunch there is an interview with the Adventist Development and Relief Agency; following that there will still be letters to write and radio programs to produce.

My thoughts go faster. When will I manage to do all that ironing? It continues to pile up in the corner. I also need to go birthday shopping for my husband. The plants wait for a drop of water, and a friend is waiting for a phone call. How am I possibly going to manage this day? In desperation I cry, "God, please help me!"

I am sure you know the situation. You don't know where to start, what to do first. Through experience I have found that the more I have to do, the more time I need to take in the morning because first of all I need to talk to God. "God, You are the only one who can help me get today's work well organized. I don't want to run round all day, not noticing that someone needs a smile or a listening ear. God, give me the wisdom to decide what is most important to be done today so I know where to start."

That helps me to calm down. Now I can think clearly. I take time to eat a good breakfast and perhaps even listen to the news. I find it very helpful to make a priority list. I write down all the things I need to do today, so I don't have to be afraid of forgetting anything. Then I think about the importance of each item. I realize that some things can wait until the next day.

Finally, when I look at the list at the end of the day, it is very satisfying to see all the things I actually managed to do in what looked like an impossible day. "Thank You, God!"

GABRIELE ZIEGLER

MARCH 31

THE JOY OF SERVICE

And we know that all things work together for good to them that love God. Rom. 8:28.

For as long as I can remember it has been my dream to be a missionary, so in 1982, when I was asked whether I would like to work in Côte d'Ivoire, West Africa, I jumped at the chance. It was certainly a dream come true! And yet after only two weeks there I was back in England, in traction in a hospital bed, with at least nine months of recovery ahead of me. I had hardly gotten to know the other missionaries. It was my third Sabbath and we were on our way to church when the car I was traveling in was hit by another car. Two days later I was flown home. The days in the hospital were long, and the nights even longer. The tears flowed freely when no one could see them. I could not understand why God had allowed this to happen to me when all I ever wanted to do was serve Him. A member from the local church gave me a book to read about praising God in all situations. This was difficult!

I had been in the hospital for about a week when a mother and daughter joined me in the ward. Their family had been in a tragic accident that had killed the father and left another daughter in a coma (she had been taken to another hospital). I began to realize that I did have a lot for which to thank God. We soon became friends, and the mother asked me how I could be so cheerful under these circumstances. I told her of my faith in Jesus and began sharing Bible promises with her and her daughter. Often she would ask me to read my Bible aloud for her or share my sacred music with her. I knew I had to be strong for them. In an effort to cheer them, I forgot my depression. I knew there were difficult days ahead, but I was thankful for the opportunity to share my faith, even while in traction in a hospital bed. For three and a half months we shared our joys and our sorrows.

She was not from this area, and she did not want to have any contact with anyone after leaving the hospital, but she now knew she had a friend in Jesus. I returned to West Africa nine months later to continue my work. Day by day I have learned more and more of the great joy of serving the Lord and serving others.

CHELCIE STERLING-ANIM

April 1

SPRINGTIME

The old order has passed away; now all is new. 2 Cor. 5:17, NAB.

Spring is just around the corner. I can see the tips of my spring bulbs cautiously peeking out above the sod. A few unusually warm days may have caused them to be overly optimistic, but growth is in process. As I watch the green coming through the brown earth I feel happy knowing that sometime in the not-too-distant future, blossoms will appear and reward every passerby with their beauty.

Watching this process of growth brings me to examine my own spiritual growth. I want to grow quickly and bloom profusely. Sometimes progress seems so slow. Just when I think I'm making good growth a cold spell hits, and like the tips of the emerging bulbs, I halt and end up with some dark, frozen parts.

It's so easy to become discouraged with one's Christian growth.

We expect it to be like the Jack and the Beanstalk fairy tale—just throw a few magic beans out the window and climb to heaven the next day.

Flower growth requires many days of basking in the sun's warmth. Spiritual growth requires steady, everyday warming from time spent with God's Son. Be patient but persistent in His presence. Gradually you will grow and one day bloom in the fullness of His beauty.

Ellen Bresee

April 2

"The Lord Is My Shepherd"

The Lord is my shepherd; I shall not want. Ps. 23:1.

The birth seemed impossible. It seemed that it meant death for the baby and mother. After a difficult delivery, a girl was born—the only child that this couple would be able to have.

In such a significant and important moment of the couple's lives, they asked the doctor, who also was a pastor, to dedicate their baby to God so that she might serve Him wherever she was called. Dr. Robert Habenicht suggested the name for this little one. The parents agreed to the name because it matched their feelings so well.

When the baby was 4 months old a terrifying electrical storm arose while she was sleeping peacefully in her cradle. Her mother picked her up and took her to another room. As soon as they were out of the bedroom, lightning rushed through the baby's bedroom, destroying part of the wall where the cradle was.

Through childhood and into her teen years this young woman studied, and life seemed to go happily on, but she never forgot that she had been dedicated to God by her parents. While in college she met a young man who wanted to be a missionary. They began to like each other and soon made plans to marry and serve the Lord wherever He needed them.

After a while a test came. The young woman was struck with a terrible illness and had to interrupt her studies just months before her graduation. After trying everything, the doctors came to the conclusion that she had no chance for recovery.

One night, while she was at the hospital, God answered the faithful prayer of her boyfriend, who asked God to give him a sign if it was His will to see these two servants joined in matrimony. That night he received the positive response to his prayer, more clearly than he expected. Only he knows how God had answered his prayer.

God's hand was evident as the recovery progressed day by day, until it was complete. Soon all was forgotten, except the sincere thanks from both to the Almighty.

Three years later we, Daniel and Esther, joined our lives in marriage and began a long journey with the Lord's work, wherever He needed us: in Uruguay, Argentina, Brazil, the Philippines, and Nepal, with the permanent blessings of God during 50 years of service. We thank Him for His guidance during those years and through the many storms and dark times. As long as we live, let's all live with God as our guide. Blessed be His name!   ESTHER NESTARES

APRIL 3

ARE YOU COMING BACK, FATHER?

Let not your heart be troubled; you believe in God, believe also in Me. In My Father's house are many mansions; if it were not so, I would have told you. I go to prepare a place for you. And if I go and prepare a place for you, I will come again and receive you to Myself; that where I am, there you may be also. John 14:1-3, NKJV.

I want my grandpa!" Matthew wails because of his fever and aches. In the beginning stages of chickenpox, Matthew is hard to console. There isn't much comfort in telling him that Grandpa is far, far away in Russia. So I hug Matthew and hold him close to me. I whisper to the still-snuggled form in my lap, "I miss Grandpa too." It's silly, but I wish I could somehow take my son to Russia immediately to see his grandpa! Why does Matthew mostly miss his grandpa when he is sick or has just bumped his head? Because he knows that Grandpa loves him and will sympathize. This love and attention distracts him from the hurts.

When it was my turn to leave home for a year of mission service halfway around the world, I did miss my parents. I soon made lots of new friends and became busy with life in Hong Kong. Now, having my parents leave me and my brother and sisters is different. We can cope by filling our days with plenty of activity. We also know that Mommy and Daddy are doing well in their new duties.

When I don't feel up to par, do I look to my heavenly Father as Matthew looks to his grandpa? Being a parent has given me the most vivid picture of what He must be like. He is everything I am not—patient and understanding, slow to anger, constantly loving and giving. What do I put my heavenly Father through when I scream and pout at life's obstacles? I find that I need to study Him more to continue growing like Him. Only then can I show Him to my son, Matthew.

I'm grateful that Matthew will get to see his grandpa in a few months. He's not the only one counting the days. My excitement about my parents' next visit with us reminds me that I am also waiting for my heavenly Father's return. Often I find myself asking, "How much longer will I have to wait to see You?" IRIS SHULL

April 4

Painful Boots

Come to me, all you who are weary and burdened, and I will give you rest. Matt. 11:28, NIV.

When my children were young they always enjoyed being Boy Scouts. We used to live in the city because of my husband's job, so they had great pleasure camping away from home. The night before leaving, they made happy comments and were very excited.

On one occasion, even though the weather was bad, the excursion wasn't put off, and both boys decided to go in their rubber boots. When the tents were ready, everybody went to sleep except Ron. He was the smallest one, restless but very shy. As his boots had water inside, it was impossible for him to take them off. He waited until everybody had gone to bed, to make sure that he was not going to be noticed, and then he went to bed with his boots on!

When my son returned home three days later, he looked tired and had an elevated temperature, so I could tell that something was wrong. When I opened his bag and saw his clothes as tidy and clean as I had sent them, my suspicions became real: he had not taken off his boots during the three days! He had not dared to approach somebody who could help him with his problem. He did not want anybody to notice his suffering.

I helped him take off his clothes to take a good bath, but when I started with the boots he shouted in pain. Very gently I took them off, and there were his little feet, dirty, wrinkled, wet, and blistered.

"How nice, Mom," he exclaimed. "What a relief!"

"If you had asked for help, you would have enjoyed yourself

much more, son," I explained later.

Do you approach your Saviour with your burdens and rest in Him, or do you support them anxiously and painfully by yourself? Trust Him. Leave your sorrows and anxiety in our lovely Jesus' hands, and you will find rest. LENI ZAMORANO

April 5

GOD STILL WORKS MIRACLES

Arise, shine; for your light has come, and the glory of the Lord has risen upon you. Isa. 60:1, RSV.

Eating too much is a difficult habit to break. It certainly isn't the only bad habit I have. Even now I felt like the commercial for some stain remover that runs something like "you've tried washing it out, you've tried brushing it out, you've tried scrubbing it out . . ."

Well, I tried brushing my teeth so I wouldn't eat more, I tried working more hours, fasting, praying. But I did not want to go to a clinic. You see, I had a major eating disorder. I tried reading books and talking to their authors. But over time the Lord was patient with me. By now I had all the head knowledge, but I was weak at the practical action that showed I knew how to overcome.

Finally with the help of parents and husband I opened a small business that gave me the opportunity not only to help with financial pressures but also to witness to all kinds of people.

You may wonder what a closet overeater could witness to. But God had been working in my life. Every step of the business opening had been miraculous, and as we would pray that the Lord would bring people to us that needed our type of work, we added that He would bring those who we could especially present to Him. We saw this happen daily. Not only that, but overeating became less and less a part of my life and trusting and glorifying God became a precious ray of joy to me, so that soon I had no thought of anything but the persons we were serving. What a mighty God we serve.

After years of struggling with self-disgust, distrust, and guilt, our gentle Shepherd led me as quickly as I would allow. Now He shows me new secrets to success. I wish I could tell you that I always remember how He has made my weakness a strength, and that this exceptional quiet miracle continually comforts me. But honestly, in my daily struggles with self-employment issues and family relationships,

I sometimes forget the tremendous victory He has given me over a potentially disabling disorder that crippled my productivity for years.

Today, please remember what victories He has given you in your life, and let those memories explode in a brilliant smile and song to all you come in contact with. MARI GIBBS-PICKETT

APRIL 6

A COLOR-LOVING CREATOR

See how the lilies of the field grow. They do not labor or spin. Yet I tell you that not even Solomon in all his splendor was dressed like one of these. Matt. 6:28, 29, NIV.

Last spring was a good year for California poppies, and my husband and I drove to Antelope Valley to view the golden panorama. There were *millions* of flowers, carpets of dense orange gold, as far as the eye could see. We walked among the blooms, taking pictures and rejoicing in their beauty. What a love gift from our color-loving Creator-God! What a foretaste of heavenly glories to come!

We hiked up to the ranger station to look at photographs and paintings of other desert flowers. A narrated slide show immersed us in further beauty. Happy and satiated, we were heading for the door when we noticed a descriptive placard. It went something like this:

"Although today we revel in the breathtaking beauty of the desert flowers, did you know that nature did not evolve them for human enjoyment? Their colors, textures, and designs came about through the evolutionary ages in order to attract insects and birds, which carry the pollen that enables the flowers to survive."

As we drove home I reflected on the lengths people must go to bypass the concepts of a loving Creator-God. To my (logical) mind, couldn't "nature" just as easily have evolved insects and birds that would be attracted to gray "generic" flowers?

It reminded me of a trip we'd made one summer into the high mountains of Colorado. As our group four-wheeled around the highest peaks, we encountered one meadow after another blanketed with virtual rainbows of wildflowers. We counted 86 varieties that afternoon.

Around the campfire that night our conversation went like this: We've discovered the best argument yet against evolution. The world doesn't *need* these flowers. Hardly anyone even sees them. They don't perform a vital service. We could exist without them. But they are here to remind us of the kind of God we have—a generous God who lavishes His world with beauty, even in unseen and inaccessible places.

Yes, the "evolutionary ages" people do have a problem. How would *you* explain the infinite varieties, shapes, and colors of flowers apart from a caring Creator-God? — AILEEN LUDINGTON

April 7

THE WORD IS "FLEXIBLE"

Be kindly affectioned one to another . . . ; in honour preferring one another. Rom. 12:10.

We were on "holiday" in England, touring the beautiful countryside complete with stone fences, hedgerows, and sheep on the rolling hills surrounding quaint little villages.

One day we came to a very narrow bridge with a very large sign that said "Yield." As we were approaching the bridge, a driver on the other side pulled over. *That's curious,* I thought. *We are the ones that have the "Yield" sign.*

As my husband drove over the bridge, nodding to the other driver when we got to the other side, I looked back. To my surprise, the sign by this side of the bridge also said "Yield." Drivers from both directions were requested to give the other the right of way.

How very sensible and practical, I said to myself, and what a good way to prevent head-on collisions!

Again I was reminded of the word I have written in my Bible by Paul's words in Ephesians 5:21: "Submitting yourselves one to another in the fear of God." The word is "flexible."

Loving Father, today may I be flexible in my association with Your children, in honor preferring them over myself. Amen.

— EVELYN VANDEVERE

April 8

A RECIPE TO STOP DEATH

I am telling you the truth: a grain of wheat remains no more

than a single grain unless it is dropped into the ground and dies. If it does die, then it produces many grains. John 12:24, TEV.

Sarah Winchester didn't want to die. We are told that, obsessed as she was by the lethal power of the rifle her husband had invented, she consulted a witch, who told her that she would not die while a group of men were working on building her house.

For 38 years (from 1884 to 1922) carpenters, bricklayers, and artisans worked 24 hours a day, every day. Sarah invested $22 million in her obsession, the "heritage" she received from that famous gun.

As work could not stop in that splendorous mansion, now an attraction for tourists, it is possible to find many quirks: for instance, ladders that go to the roof, doors that open to a wall, a chimney that goes through three floors and stops some inches before reaching the upper roof, etc.

What a huge amount of money and effort was dedicated to her project to stop death! Nevertheless, Sarah died in 1922, when she was 82 years old.

If Sarah Winchester had invested her enormous fortune in an institution dedicated to help homeless children, or to help outstanding students with no economic resources, or to build good houses for senior citizens without a family, she would have gone on living in the memory and thankfulness of those receiving the benefits of her money, dedicated in this cause to the service of life.

Like the grain, we must die first in order to live. We must die to pride, to vanity, to envy, to foolishness, and to self. Then the grain will sprout, grow, and give flowers and a fruit that never dies, namely, liberality. If only Sarah had understood this!

ESTHER I. FAYARD

April 9

The Clean Linen That Wasn't

They have washed their robes and made them white in the blood of the Lamb. Rev. 7:14, NASB.

Midway in my nursing career I was fortunate to obtain the services of Margaret. An impeccable housekeeper, she came every Friday to do the weekly cleaning.

Margaret's thorough cleaning included changing the linens on our bed, something no other housekeeper had ever done for me. Each Friday when I arrived home I found the bed neatly made and the set of sheets folded to perfection on top of the washer in the laundry room; I would then put them into the linen closet. Margaret had the ability, which I had never mastered, to fold the sheets exactly as if they had just come from the store.

Several months passed, until one Friday I stayed home from work with a touch of the flu. Lounging about while Margaret made the bed, I observed her removing the used sheets and cases and immediately folding them to perfection.

Following her into the laundry, I saw her placing them on top of the washer. With a sense of shock, I realized that this was Margaret's perfectionist method of preparing the linens for laundering, rather than throwing them into the hamper, as I would have done! Thus, for some time the unwashed linens had been making the journey from bed to linen closet without benefit of washing!

So much, if not all, of our daily happenings have a spiritual counterpart, do they not? There I was complacent in my certainty that the bed linens were clean, when in reality they were not. How, I reflected later, was my "spiritual linen"? Has my life been bathed in the Lord's fountain, set up "for sin and for impurity" (Zech. 13:1, NASB)?

Will I be among those clothed in white robes, who have "washed their robes and made them white in the blood of the Lamb"? Have I received from Jesus His cleansing for my life, or have I complacently assumed that I am spiritually OK?

After this experience the linens returned to their weekly washing routine, and to this day I go to the Lord daily, to receive from Him the cleansing and renewal He provides. Praise His name!

MARILYN KING

April 10

REFLECTIONS ON A TEMPLE COURTYARD

What will it profit them to gain the whole world and forfeit their life? Indeed, what can they give in return for their life? Mark 8:36, 37, NRSV.

Shangzhen is China's newest city. Based on free enterprise, this 11-year-old city makes a bold statement for what can happen when a society wants to develop on its own. One still needs a passport to enter this experimental community. All outside newspapers are picked up at Immigration. Few Western movies are allowed. All immigrants must be under 45 years of age or very well educated.

On a cluster of centuries-old rice paddies this bustling little community has built a well-planned commercial center, many high-rise apartment buildings, and schools to accommodate their children. Education is free, but after finishing form 8 (equivalent to high school in the U.S.), a student is assigned to a lifetime job by the government. Higher education is optional. Morality runs high; prostitution is forbidden; and couples are asked to show their marriage license upon checking in at a hotel.

Most commercial buildings and many apartment complexes reach from 10 to 30 stories high. Bamboo scaffolding still proves to be their safest construction device.

Air-conditioning in homes is forbidden in old China, but permitted in this experimental city. Roads are built and maintained mostly by hand. Zoning is not known. Bicycles provide the main mode of transportation, and the one who owns a motorized cycle is to be envied. Buses and taxis accommodate the visitors; very few private cars are seen anywhere.

The community has developed a unique park called "Splendid China," in which all the major attractions in the country have been replicated in miniature. Most of these include temples, pagodas, monasteries, even segments of the Great Wall. The landscaping has been duplicated in exact detail, most of which is kept in bonsai form to ensure precise proportions. The people figurines are individually crafted in porcelain; of the thousands in use, no two are alike. In this exquisitely planned 600-acre park I entered the courtyard of a Buddhist temple. The guide and I stood alone while the others explored this particular exhibit. The following conversation ensued.

"Are you a practicing Buddhist?" I asked.

"No, almost no young people are Buddhists anymore."

"Is there a reason?"

"It's dead. The lectures are boring and not relevant to our future. Only the old people still believe."

"Have you considered Christianity?"

"Really, I have thought about it. But so far I can't see that it offers anything either. It doesn't suit my future."

"What do you want from the future?"

"I want to be educated—well educated. Then I want to be rich and successful, and I want to help the people in my country get a better life."

"Would becoming a Christian keep you from all of this?"

"It really doesn't offer anything I can't do on my own."

The others returned, terminating our conversation. My young university friend gave me more to think about than an interesting glimpse into today's China. How significant is Christianity in your lifestyle? Is it relevant? — LORABEL HERSCH

APRIL 11

REST FOR THE SOUL

Find rest, O my soul, in God alone; my hope comes from him. Ps. 62:5, NIV.

I've always been quite self-reliant. My mother tells me one of the first phrases I learned to say was "I can do it myself!" That attitude carried over into just about everything I did—from craft projects to schoolwork to shoveling the driveway. I've always been reluctant to let anyone help, and I've usually been successful in my endeavors.

Unfortunately, that "I can do it myself" attitude has also entered into my relationship with God for much of my life. Even after I accepted Him as my Saviour and committed the rest of my life to Him, I was very hesitant to ask Him for help. When I got into a tough spot at school, in my work, or in my relationships with others, I didn't rely on God to guide me. I figured I could fix things myself. I had confidence in my abilities—after all, God gave them to me.

Finally God let me see how helpless I really was all by myself. My husband and I had recently moved and were living in a small one-room apartment until we could find a house we wanted to buy. I was teaching in a one-teacher school, a new experience for me. Then everything seemed to go wrong at once. We were not able to find a house we liked in our price range, and we ended up living in that small room—with most of our belongings in storage—for more than a year. I found that being the only adult in a classroom full of children ages 7-14 was very different from any teaching experience I had had before. For once, I really wanted to ask for help. But there was no one else around.

I became more and more depressed as the year progressed. I began to have trouble sleeping and felt so tired that I could hardly drag myself out of bed in the morning, much less teach with any enthusiasm.

Then I remembered a memory verse my students had learned earlier in the year: "Casting all your care upon him; for he careth for you"

(1 Peter 5:7). I decided to try it. I had a long talk with God out in the woods near where we lived. I told Him how useless, discouraged, and tired I felt. Then I recommitted my life to Him. When I got home I read some of my favorite texts, including Psalm 62:5. It instantly became "my text." That night I slept soundly for the first time in weeks.

I still battled depression often during that year, but now I knew what it meant to find rest in God alone. I couldn't rely on my home, my job, or my abilities to provide hope and a sense of self-worth. My soul found rest in God alone.

Sue Hayford

April 12

Why?

I, the Lord, have called you in righteousness; I will take hold of your hand. I will keep you and will make you to be a covenant for the people and a light for the Gentiles; to open eyes that are blind, to free captives from prison and to release from the dungeon those who sit in darkness. . . . I will lead the blind by ways they have not known, along unfamiliar paths I will guide them; I will turn the darkness into light before them and make the rough places smooth. These are the things I will do; I will not forsake them. Isa. 42:6-16, NIV.

You tried to tell us,
    but we wouldn't listen.
You tried to show us,
    but we wouldn't see.
You tried to guide us,
    and we wouldn't follow.
You tried to love us,
    but we wouldn't believe!
We broke Your heart,
    yet You cared for us.
We turned our back,
    but Your death spared us.
You were here once,
    and we treated You badly.
Is it true
    You're coming again?

Sharon Estrada

April 13

Broken Chains

For God so loved the world that he gave his one and only Son, that whoever believes in him shall not perish but have eternal life. John 3:16, NIV.

"Where are you going, Mom?" I asked as I saw her holding her Bible, ready to leave. At that time we lived in a district north of São Paulo.

"I'm going to Romao Gomes State Prison," she answered. "We've finally got permission to study the Bible with a group of prisoners."

"That's wonderful!" I said. "But isn't it dangerous? You are the only woman in the group, and once in a while rebellion breaks out among the prisoners."

"Don't worry, dear," she replied. "God will send His angel to go with me! Many people need to be set free by the Word of God." She went with two faithful brothers, week after week, month after month, for three years before moving to another city.

Years later my mother was at a special meeting of prayer, worship, and personal testimonies at Brazil College. A Christian brother in his late 40s came to the platform to share his personal experience. He spoke with enthusiasm for the God of heaven, who had broken his chains. He had been sentenced to 50 years in prison and certainly believed he would die in a dark prison cell. Then one day he met a lady who came into the prison and told him the following words: "Because God loved the world so much . . ."

At first he could not believe in what he was hearing. *This woman doesn't know what she is talking about,* he thought. *How could God love a man like me—a criminal, a transgressor?* But those words followed him continually, like a broken record in his mind: "Because God loved the world so much . . ." Overcome by the power of God's Word, he accepted and believed, and the Lord changed his life, setting him free from his past and from 50 years in prison.

"I owe so much to that dear sister," he continued. "I'd like to hug her tightly to show how grateful I am to the Lord and to Sister Adelaide."

Then a wonderful thing happened! Mother stood up and went to the platform. They hugged each other, and tears rolled down faces in the audience, tears of joy and happiness, because a captive soul was now set free, because "God loved the world so much . . ." Sonia Gazeta

April 14

THE UNSEEN HAND

The angel of the Lord encampeth round about them that fear him, and delivereth them. Ps. 34:7.

Recently I experienced a graphic deliverance while driving the evening commute from my up-valley job. Rounding a sharp curve, I came upon a line of stopped vehicles—a huge tree had fallen across the road. With horror I realized that it would be impossible to avoid hitting the last vehicle in line.

I prayed as I slammed both feet on the brake, heading for the right side of the road. I hoped I could maneuver between the vehicles and the embankment. Instantaneously I was impressed to change my course of direction to the left lane, which was empty. This caused my car to slide sideways. As I prepared for the expected impact, my car pulled out of its skid and came to a gentle stop behind the last car in line.

Realizing that my life had been spared by an unseen hand, I sat in stunned amazement and then watched in my rearview mirror as another vehicle rounded the curve behind me. It too went into a similar skid across the highway and stopped gently, just inches behind me.

"Lord, once again You have extended my life." With awe I realized that I am valuable to God.

We can pray, as recorded in Psalm 63:7, "Because thou hast been my help, therefore in the shadow of thy wings will I rejoice." Using the gifts God has given to us, we can be partners in these exciting days of earth's history.

LORNA LAWRENCE

April 15

THE WORDS OF BETRAYAL

And after a while those who stood by came to him and said to Peter, "Surely you also are one of them, because your speech betrays you." Matt. 26:73, NKJV.

The situation was most awkward, even terrifying. His Best Friend was on trial. Peter knew that to be identified with Him would probably mean death, but not to be, he vaguely sensed, would mean something even worse. Torn between words of commitment and words of betrayal, Peter chose betrayal.

"I do not know what you are saying," he declared (Matt. 26:70, NKJV); then he left to go out to the porch. But a maid saw Peter and told all who would listen that indeed he had been with Jesus of Nazareth.

With an oath he again declared, "I do not know the Man!" But the crowd persisted: "'Surely you also are one of them, because your speech betrays you.' Then he began to curse and swear, saying, 'I do not know the Man!' And immediately a rooster crowed" (verses 72-74, NKJV).

Slinking in corners, cowering behind protective pillars, moving uneasily from room to room—where was Peter the Courageous then? Peter the Ear-slicer, Peter the Impetuous, now Peter the Coward, the man who denied his Best Friend, his Saviour, everyone's Saviour. He who was betrayed by his own words then in turn used words to betray Jesus.

"Your speech betrays you," said those around Peter. And because Peter knew they were right, he decided to eliminate any doubt by speaking in a manner no one would associate with Christ: he cursed.

But as with all words of betrayal, they gave short-term peace. The rooster crowed, and Peter remembered: "Then he went out and wept bitterly" (verse 75, NKJV).

Peter was not, however, the last disciple to deny Christ with words. Nor do His followers have to swear to betray Him. Jesus is betrayed anew with each prejudiced comment, with each sarcastic remark, and with each half-truth made by any of His disciples today. Christians deny Christ whenever they use language to harass, discourage, or make fun of any for whom He died: calling a slow learner stupid; labeling an awkward teenager clumsy; hollering at an aging motorist. Even silence can betray Jesus, if that silence substitutes for defending someone.

Just as Peter knew that swearing would disassociate him from Christ, so we too can be assured our abusing language betrays Jesus anew.

The deciding factor for language should be that it be pure and kind and true—reflecting Christ's grace. Whenever our language is not such, we should listen closely . . . for the cock will have just crowed.

WILMA MCCLARTY

April 16

WORDS THAT QUESTION BUT WANT NO ANSWER

Pilate saith unto them, What shall I do then with Jesus which is called Christ? Matt. 27:22.

If only Pilate had really wanted an answer. If only Pilate had sought truth in his inquiry. But desperation, not a desire for knowledge, prompted his question. He was, however, not the last person to ask a question to which no truthful answer is sought. Some today have mastered the process.

"Is there anything I can do?" you politely ask the family whose house has just been gutted by fire. But too busy planning your own relaxing weekend, you suggest they go to a community service agency, pointing out the convenience of its hours.

"Let me know if I can help," you halfheartedly volunteer to a single parent who has to move to another house in two days. But too much in a hurry to be sensitive, you fail to interpret a "Well, I think I'll be OK" for what it really is—a plea for help.

"If you need anything, be sure to call," you offer the parents of three preschoolers, the youngest of whom is in the hospital. But too involved with a second job, you dash off to make a business call.

Questions—easy to formulate, easy to ask.

Questions—hard to respond to correctly, hard to answer as you know you should.

What would you have done had you been Pilate? There you stand in your royal robes, officially in charge of chaos. The crowd, clamoring for crucifixion, you can't shut up; Christ, calm, in control, you can't get to say a word, even when you ask Him a point-blank question (Jesus "answered him . . . never a word" [Matt. 27:14]).

Yes, what would you have done? It's an intriguing question, as many rhetorical ones are. You're probably not powerful enough to be placed in anywhere near a situation comparable to Pilate's, so it's safe to answer what you wish. But if you *really* want to know how you would have answered, here's a hint: How would you have responded to the all-too-real human dilemmas of the burned-out family, the single parent, or the mom and dad with the hospitalized child?

"Have thou nothing to do with that just man," Pilate's wife counseled, "for I have suffered many things this day in a dream because of him" (verse 19). A rather straightforward supernatural directive for the governor. No need at all for him, really, to inquire, "What shall I do then with Jesus which is called Christ?"

Yes, that same question is still asked today: "What are *you* doing with Jesus?" And just as Pilate knew exactly what he should have done, you too have just as clear instructions: "Inasmuch as ye have done it unto one of the least of these my brethren, ye have done it unto me" (Matt. 25:40).
WILMA MCCLARTY

APRIL 17

ENGRAVINGS

See, I have engraved you on the palms of my hands. Isa. 49:16, NIV.

He was a senior, and I was a lowly freshman. He was good-looking, wrote for our school paper, and dated one of the prettiest girls in the senior class. I think he probably knew my name, because the school I attended was fairly small, but that was about the extent of our relationship. I, along with the other freshman "hopefuls," watched from afar, sighing at the "togetherness" those upper-class students' lives seemed to exhibit. After graduation Tom married his high school sweetheart, and a few months later we heard they were expecting a baby. This was the stuff freshman dreams were made of. Then the bubble burst. Tom was drafted and sent to Vietnam. A few months later he was sent home in a flag-draped coffin, never having seen his little girl.

I was sightseeing in Washington, D.C., enjoying the Smithsonian, the monuments, and the beautiful fall day. Quite by accident I found myself at "The Wall," that black stone monument erected as a memorial to the men and women killed in Vietnam. I paused; did I know anyone who had died in Vietnam? Yes! I knew Tom. I would find his name. I was unprepared for the flood of emotions I felt as I traced his name with my finger. Unwiped tears rolled down my cheeks as I felt the terrible loss of Tom and all the other young men and women whose names were etched into that monument. How young he was. What had become of his wife and child? What was it all for?

There is Someone Else who has watched and loved through the freshman year, through the war, and through all the ages before and since. He too feels the terrible loss, and He too has a personal stake in each of our lives.

He looks down at the palms of His hands and weeps. How He longs for us to be home with Him. He can't get us out of His mind. We are engraved on His hands.

JONI BELL

APRIL 18

HIS OMNIPRESENCE

If I take the wings of the morning, and dwell in the uttermost parts of the sea; even there shall thy hand lead me, and thy right hand shall hold me. Ps. 139:9, 10.

Following are meditations on Psalm 139 and the 1981 summer northern European tour, sponsored by the Andrews University Alumni Association.

If I take the wings of the KLM
And fly to the uttermost parts of the world,
Behold, You are there!

If I ascend to the top of the highest ski lift in the world,
Or stumble over centuries-old cobblestones to the dungeons of old fortresses and castles,
Behold, You are there.

Though our bus take us over broad highways or winding, tortuous mountain roads,
We shall not fear,
For You are there.

Whether our ferry take us on the broad, lighted canals of Amsterdam
Or through the mysterious waterways of the Norwegian fjords
That lose themselves between majestic snowcapped and glacial mountains—
Lo, You are there.

Your hills enfold us like encircling arms
And point us to the heavens whence cometh our help.
Whither shall we go from Your Spirit

Or whither shall we flee from Your presence?

Lo, You were with us in the tiny landscape of Holland
With the windows full of lace and flowers,
Where the cats answer to "pushey, pushey, pushey" instead of "kitty, kitty, kitty."

You walked with us in the city streets
Of Amsterdam, Copenhagen, Stockholm, Oslo, Bergen, and Stavanger.

You spoke to us through the sculptures and music
And tapestries made by the masters inspired to imitate Your creation
And through great old churches with the green patina of ancient bronze spires stabbing the sky.

We were taught by You through the ships the Vikings sailed
And by the *Fram* and the *Ra* and the *Kon-Tiki*.
Such knowledge is too wonderful for us.
It is high; we cannot attain unto it.

If we said, Surely darkness shall cover us,
Even the night in those lands near the midnight sun
Was made light.
Yea, the darkness hideth not from You.

And there was beauty in the clouds
And in the mewing of the sea gulls.
And Your voice was audible in the sound of many waters of glacier streams and waterfalls.

You know all about our downsittings—our window seats and aisle seats in the bus;
And our uprisings—our alarms reminding us of time to be on our way.
You have counted the repetitious omelets served to the vegetarians, and the inevitable cheeses.

You understand the plumbing mysteries
Of the bathroom-drenching showers.

You have understood our thoughts
And are acquainted with our dispositions—

For there is not a word in our tongues but, O Lord,
Thou knowest it altogether.

We cannot or would not flee from Your presence.
It is Your right hand that holds us and will lead us
    through all of life's vicissitudes.
In the way everlasting.

You have taught us that whatever life brings of good or ill,
Whatever fears we may have of sickness, aging, bereavement;
Whatever circumstances bring us to strange places
Or introduce us to strange faces—

Even there will Your hand lead us
And Your right hand will hold us.

For if we ascend to the heavens or make our bed in death,
You will be there.

And when we awake, we are still with You.

OPAL HOOVER YOUNG

APRIL 19

LORD, TEACH US TO PRAY

And it came to pass, that, as he was praying in a certain place, when he ceased, one of his disciples said unto him, Lord, teach us to pray. Luke 11:1.

Late one night I walked out into our garden. I could hear the African night sounds. The campus electric generator was turned off for the night. I felt tired, drained, and helpless. We were in Ethiopia; my daughter Debbie was ill with a low-grade temperature, and my trip to and from Addis Ababa seeking medical help for her seemed in vain. My husband, Keith, and two daughters, Maria and Debbie, had prayed daily for strength, but it seemed that God was at a distance.

That night I felt as though I needed to talk and feel the closeness of a "best friend" relationship. I cried out to God, "O Lord, I need You. I want to hear Your comforting words and feel Your strength.

Lord, teach me to pray. Lord, teach me to communicate with You. Teach me to listen to You and send me peace."

The very moment that I cried to Him He answered with the most wonderful peace and a feeling of being in the sustaining and caring arms of our Lord Jesus. I had claimed His promise that He hears our prayers even before we ask (Isa. 65:24). My daughter was healed, and the fever left her.

Prayer is the process of developing and building a special relationship with the very Best Friend, our God, through Jesus our Redeemer. We need to learn to communicate and experience that personal relationship with God that makes us feel secure, safe, protected, and loved. We need to cry out, "Lord, teach us to pray."

The Lord's Prayer was given twice by Jesus Christ, the first to the multitude in the Sermon on the Mount (Matt. 6:9), and the second some months later to the disciples (Luke 11:1). The Lord's Prayer is the model prayer given by Christ. The prayer is brief and covers the basic needs and aspirations of the devout believer (Matt. 6:9-13), and has seven steps:

1. Praise: "Our Father which art in heaven . . ."
2. Recognition of God: "Hallowed be thy name."
3. God's will: "Thy will be done." (In God's will and in God's time.)
4. Petition: "Give us this day our daily bread."
5. Confession and forgiveness: "Forgive us our debts, as we forgive our debtors."
6. Protection and deliverance: "Deliver us from evil."
7. Thanksgiving and praise: ". . . the kingdom, and the power, and the glory . . ."

The personal, genuine relationship with our precious Lord must be established and nurtured through daily prayer and the study of God's Word. ANITA REQUENEZ-MOSES

APRIL 20

"YOU ALSO MUST BE READY"

You also must be ready, because the Son of Man will come at an hour when you do not expect him. Luke 12:40, NIV.

My brother was invited to a graduation exercise. We helped to make him look his best. He was going with a friend who was scheduled to arrive at 7:00. At 7:00 his friend was not there. At 7:30 he loosened his tie. At 8:00 he took off his jacket. He was tired of waiting, and so were we. Then at 8:15 the friend arrived. Everyone jumped into action to help my brother get ready again. We learned later that the friend had been delayed because of heavy traffic.

Jesus promised to come again. We have been ready and waiting for this event for a long time. It is easy to become tired of waiting, especially since Jesus did not give the exact time of His arrival. It can find us becoming less vigilant. We can loosen our hold on Christ and become complacent. We can lose our zeal for witnessing to others. We can take off our "armor of God" piece by piece until we stand defenseless "against the devil's schemes" (Eph. 6:11, NIV).

When Jesus comes, it will be too late to throw on our garments and rush outside to welcome Him. We must get dressed—in Christ's robe of righteousness—and stay dressed. Jesus Himself will keep us in a constant state of readiness if we let Him. "Abide in me, and I in you" (John 15:4).

The daily stresses of life can cause us to lose our focus. We can become so involved with items on our packed agendas that Christ is forgotten, and is remembered and petitioned just before we crawl into bed at night.

We can stay prepared by learning from God's Word daily, talking with Him constantly, sharing His love enthusiastically. "Let us rejoice and be glad and give him glory! For the wedding of the Lamb has come, and his bride has made herself ready" (Rev. 19:7, NIV).

Maria G. McClean

April 21

The Shortcut

Call upon me in the day of trouble; I will deliver you, and you shall glorify me. Ps. 50:15, RSV.

The year was 1975. My husband was pastoring a district of three churches, in two states. Making the circuit was a challenge every week, with four boys of our own, ranging from 7 years old down to a newborn baby, and a 1-year-old foster boy.

One day we decided that between churches the next week we would make a visit to an elderly couple in their 80s who lived way out in the country and had no transportation to church, which was 40 miles away.

Their home was a log cabin that they had built when they'd first gotten married, more than 50 years earlier. They had electricity, but still used a hand pump in the kitchen for running water, and a handmade broom. Their walls were covered with calendars dating back to the early twenties.

When we got ready to end our visit and go on to the third church for the afternoon church service, our host told us about a shortcut that would save us at least 30 minutes' driving time. We wrote down the directions, said our goodbyes, loaded up the car, and started down the unpaved country road.

Several miles down the road we made a left turn according to our directions and soon found ourselves driving through the most beautiful woods. Since there were no speed limits, no houses, and no road signs, and we were running late, we were traveling quite fast. Suddenly we crossed over a new concrete bridge, and my husband yelled, "Hold on!" The car hit the dirt road, bounced, and came to a sudden stop.

By the time we'd realized there was a two-foot dropoff at the other end of the bridge, it was too late to stop. None of us were hurt, and the car looked fine—but it wouldn't start. We lifted the hood, looking for the damage. The fan belt casing looked like a twisted pretzel! There we were in the middle of the woods with no help in sight and no tools in the trunk!

After we'd spent several minutes assessing our situation and trying to untangle the fan belt casing, our oldest son, Greg, suggested that we pray and ask God to send us help. We prayed, and then waited.

In just a few minutes we saw a pickup coming toward us. The friendly driver stopped when he reached us, and got out of his truck. He was wearing blue jeans, a red plaid shirt, and cowboy boots. In just a few effortless moments he had the twisted casing off the car, got the car started, said goodbye, and drove away.

We drove many many miles down that dirt road looking for turnoffs, houses, any place where the man in the pickup could have come from, and finally decided that he must have been an angel sent in answer to our prayer.

CELIA CRUZ

April 22

God's Watchful Care

In your day of trouble, may the Lord be with you! May the God of Jacob keep you from all harm. Ps. 20:1, TLB.

Have you ever locked your keys in your car? No doubt you know the sinking feeling of helplessness.

Picture this—two women traveling to South Padre Island, Texas, 1,500 miles from home. It is a very remote rest area without a telephone, and nightfall is rapidly approaching.

I had given my friend Lois a set of duplicate keys so we would not get locked out, but now both our purses—everything—was locked in the car. "What do we do now?" a distraught Lois asked me. I didn't have an answer, but I did know that the foreign-made car had a theft-deterrent option that makes breaking in difficult. Some of the people at the rest stop looked undesirable; we felt uneasy. We pleaded with our heavenly Father to help us out of our predicament.

An 18-wheeler was nearby, so I asked the driver if he had any suggestions. He volunteered to call for help. Meanwhile Lois knocked on the caretaker's door.

Wishing she were bilingual, she did get the message across: we needed help. The caretaker had a two-way radio, but apparently he was new on the job and not familiar with operating it. The instructions were written in English, so Lois read and did as directed. She told the border control, "We have an emergency; two women are locked out of their car!" The location was relayed, and a reply came back, "Help is on the way."

Another trucker stopped. Although his attempt to open the car with a coat hanger failed, he did say he wouldn't leave us alone in this remote and dangerous place. "Thanks, Lord," I breathed.

Others tried their keys, hoping for a match, and a family with a car phone also called for help.

Darkness settled over us as we impatiently waited for help. "Lord, please forgive our foolishness, and help us in our time of need and keep us safe," I prayed. I wondered what to do if we could not get the car open. Where would one stay with no money or credit cards?

Finally a sheriff drove up. "Are you the women with the locked car?" We assured him we were. He had a door-opening tool, but warned us that sometimes the automatic power locks and windows will not work after it is used. We didn't care about that at the moment. It wasn't long before he had the car open.

Before pulling onto the road again, we both bowed our heads and thanked the Lord for His protection.

That night the automatic lock did not work, but the manual lock did. I prayed that both would work again. So why was I surprised the next morning when the automatic lock did work correctly? Matthew 14:31 came to mind: "'You of little faith,' he said, 'why did you doubt?'" (NIV).

I know I am always in the Lord's control, but it seems that sometimes I need a refresher course. Thank You again, Lord.

MARGE LYBERG MCNEILUS

APRIL 23

HEAVENLY NEIGHBORS

A friend loveth at all times. Prov. 17:17.

My friends are cherished jewels that I carry in a corner of my heart wherever I go. From time to time I take them out and examine their immeasurable worth. I have spent time with these women during certain periods of my life, and then we've moved on to other places. But no matter where I go, these friends have remained a precious part of the fabric of my life. Some of them I don't see often, but when we do get together our friendship picks up right where it left off when we last said goodbye. Our hearts are in tune. We've developed a bond of friendship that distance does not sever.

I often think of my friends who stood by me when I was facing challenges. For instance, the friend who showed up in the middle of the night at a hospital where our son lay critically injured. Or the one who came to help pack boxes, clean sinks and toilets, and cook for us, to help our family meet an unrealistic moving deadline. I'll always remember the friend God sent to my door just before I received some unexpected troubling news from my doctor. Still others have understood when my workload didn't allow for time together to nurture valued friendships. They too empathized without me having to say a word. These friends have stayed by me, never demanding time or expressing disappointment in me. The assurance of knowing that I have a network of faithful friends will always be one of the real treasures in this life and the life to come!

I think June Strong said it best—she often does! She and I had shared the program at a women's retreat in San Antonio. Although we both speak at women's retreats, our paths rarely cross. At the close of the San Antonio retreat we were saying goodbye when June said something I've never forgotten: "Rose, I don't expect that you and I will ever have much time to spend together on this earth, but I want you to know that you're one of the persons I want as a neighbor in heaven."

Why don't you make a list of the persons you want to have as neighbors in heaven, and then begin to cultivate these friendships? Pray for these friends with the desire that they will be your "forever friends"!

ROSE OTIS

APRIL 24

WHOSE VENGEANCE IS IT, ANYWAY?

Vengeance is Mine, and retribution, in due time their foot will slip; for the day of their calamity is near, and the impending things are hastening upon them. Deut. 32:35, NASB.

We had tried to work things out with our landlord. The reminders that we sent him were answered with letters of threatened eviction. His phone calls turned into screaming tirades of verbal abuse against me. Every confrontation left me frustrated and weak. Even on days when there was no incident, I could think of little else, so consumed was I with anger over the situation.

Our landlord's continued unwillingness to follow through on agreed-upon work finally led us to seek legal recourse. As I headed for the courthouse my hands shook so violently from pent-up anger that I was afraid I would have to stop the car. In frustration I cried out, "God! Help me humiliate this scoundrel in court—teach him a lesson he'll never forget."

No sooner were the words out of my mouth than I realized that my request was hardly something the Lord could grant. So, against my will, I prayed a more appropriate prayer. "Dear Father, I hate my landlord. I have every right to feel the way I do. I have been wronged, and he deserves to pay. But I am responsible for the way this is consuming me. Please change my attitude."

I had no illusions that God could actually change the way I felt. Let's face it, I didn't even want to change. But over the next few weeks an unbelievable change did occur! Though the threats continued, I no longer felt the overwhelming anger. I started thinking about the metamorphosis of Saul to Paul. *Worse people than my landlord have turned their lives around,* I thought. *Is there one thing that I could say to make the difference in this man's life?* My anger had turned to compassion.

Months later we were still seeking relief through the legal system, but I was no longer consumed by negative emotions. God took the vengeance and anger from me. I recognized that it wasn't my responsibility to teach this person a lesson.

Has someone done you wrong? Of course the answer is yes. Very possibly the offense was much worse than what happened to us. But if your anger is consuming you, you remain the victim. We say "Vengeance is the Lord's" through clenched teeth in self-righteous anticipation of the day God strikes down our enemies. But the reason God offers to take the vengeance is not to satisfy our primal need for retribution; God takes the work of vengeance from us to preserve us from the cancer of hate. God can remove that consuming anger, even when we are not sure we want to give it up.

Are you tired of anger's bitter taste lingering in your mouth? Does the nauseating knot of reprisal in the pit of your stomach make you physically ill? You have every right to feel that way. But as a beautiful child of God, you have every right to feel good, too. As you relinquish the responsibility of punishing your enemies, give up your hatred for them too. Don't make yourself the victim twice.

CYNTHIA COSTON

APRIL 25

CAR WASH CONFRONTATION

While we were still sinners, Christ died for us. Rom. 5:8, NIV.

We live in a terrible world in which human life has little value. Innocent people are killed for no reason. So it should not surprise us that sometimes people will strike out at us even when we are innocent of wrongdoing. It is easy to become upset with such people and think they don't deserve love or respect either.

The other day when we finally had a nice sunny afternoon, I decided to go to the car wash and hose all the nasty salt off my car. Coming from the South, I do not like winter dirt and grime on my car. I like a clean car. For mental health I need a clean car!

I drove up to the car wash; there was a tremendous line in the automatic lane. Since I intended to wash the car myself, I bypassed this lane and pulled around to the shorter "do-it-yourself" lane.

At that moment I heard someone using all kinds of vile language, shouting at me! I gingerly rolled down the window, and the man yelled that no one was going to cut in front of him and that I could be assured that he would see to it that I didn't get ahead of him even if he had to get out and show me! When he finally stopped for breath I tried to explain that I was pulling up beside him to get into the do-it-yourself line. Undaunted, he started in again. If I even looked as though I was going to try to cut in front of him he would take care of me. I had visions just then of the next day's newspaper reading "Woman Shot in Line at Car Wash"—and it would be in a dirty car at that!

Timidly I eased on up into the do-it-yourself lane with this man continually eyeing me and revving his motor. I felt as though I had received a few blows. More than a few blows.

It has happened to each one of us. We have been the target of another person's abuse. It makes us feel wounded and worthless. And usually we think even less of the other person. The hard part is remembering that Jesus loves the one that delivered the blows as much as He does the receiver. Jesus would have gone through all of His 33 years on this earth for that person alone. He would have died if it had been just that one man at the car wash. Or if it had been just me. What a marvelous Saviour! SHARON CRESS

APRIL 26

WHO ELSE MATTERS?

Whom have I in heaven but you? And earth has nothing I desire besides you. Ps. 73:25, NIV.

Asking people what they want to do when they get to heaven is always fascinating. Typical responses from children include sliding down a giraffe's neck, riding on a lion, or having a pet monkey. Teenagers are a little more creative. Heavenly fun for them might entail surfing on the sea of glass or hang gliding from Mount Zion. Adults dream of exploring the universe and talking with great saints of old. Only on occasion does someone mention that the first thing they want to do when they get to heaven is to hug God.

The psalmist asks, "Whom have I in heaven but you?" Who else in heaven matters besides You? "My soul thirsts for God, for the living God. When can I go and meet with God?" (Ps. 42:2, NIV).

When I was a teenager my grandmother in Germany paid for our whole family to visit for five weeks during summer vacation. It was great seeing "Oma" and "Opa." The strawberry torte and Black Forest cherry cake were scrumptious. What fun to sleep in a feather bed, explore my mom's hometown, and be doted over! But with no car, things became a little monotonous after a few weeks. One Sunday our family borrowed a vehicle and visited a wellness resort that was just getting established. Seeing a real need, I decided to stay for a few days to help out. I learned later that Oma was quite disappointed. After all, I had come to Germany to visit her. She had even paid for the trip, because she wanted to spend time with me.

Our heavenly Father is not unlike our earthly parents or grandparents. He loves us intensely. He has expended all of Himself to give us an opportunity to take a celestial trip. He doesn't want just a "Hi, how are you?" relationship. Closeness, bonding, intimacy—these are what He desires. We have an awesome God who orchestrates the galaxies, yet treasures time spent with us personally.

"Whom have I in heaven but you?" Who else in heaven matters besides You, dear Father? "My soul thirsts for God, for the living God. When can I go and meet with God?" — HEIDE FORD

April 27

AWAKENING

The Lord will guide you continually, and satisfy your soul in drought, and strengthen your bones; you shall be like a watered garden, and like a spring of water, whose waters do not fail. Isa. 58:11, NKJV.

Sometimes God can use the "have to" chores to reveal inspirational insight. It's sometimes hard for us, with our finite minds, to understand how He works. How does He mend and heal broken hearts, addictions, and dysfunctional families? I had often wondered how He had begun to change me from an alcoholic/cocaine addict to a loving, whole Christian. He showed me in the early springtime when the earth was first reawakening from its winter slumber. It was a beautiful day; the temperature was 64 degrees, and the bees were busily buzzing. It was the kind of day that gives one a hint of the beauty to come. Purple and yellow crocuses were barely bursting from the ground, showing their secondary colors with which the

Artist had brushed them.

God spoke to my heart that magnificent spring day. Tired of reading, writing, studying, and cleaning, I decided I needed some invigorating exercise outside. Grabbing a rake out of the barn, I headed for the flower garden. I had been longing for weeks to remove the dead leaves and see a hint of greenery. The sun on my face felt fabulous! As I lifted my face toward the sun, my heart lifted in praise to the Sun of righteousness. I praised Him for the ability to be a steward of His earth by this task of digging in the dirt.

As I worked, my mind began to ponder my course of study at college—chemical dependency and dysfunctional families. I had absorbed enough by this time to realize that I had had such an upbringing and needed further healing. I started to ponder the recovery process; I knew that I still had many issues that needed to be dealt with.

Rake in hand, I began the gentle process of uncovering the marvelous beauty held captive under ugly, dead foliage. I prayed as I worked. My mind began to contemplate the steps of healing that dysfunctional families and addicts take in the recovery process. To this point my own recovery had been lonely, draining, and often painful. How long, I pondered, before one feels normal again? How long before one feels loved and accepted; how long before one finally becomes what God has planned?

As I worked the earth, gently peeling back the soggy deadness from the newly blooming buds, I thought, *It is a delicate operation. It is the same with us.* God has to peel back all the old ugly growth that is choking the new. We need to surrender "our gardens," full of dead, rotting emotions of anger, resentment, bitterness, and binding shame, to Him so He can remove the debris of pain. All such destructive emotions hinder His nurturing, budding possibilities in our sin-choked lives. This process takes time and great care; damage results from careless, hasty tearing away of the old "mulch."

As each flower is a delicate individual, so are we. As flowers blossom with the sunshine each spring, so do we with the "Sonshine." Let God tend to your "garden"! Become the beautiful blossom He intended you to be!

LAURA LEE SWANEY

April 28

Rainbows

I do set my bow in the cloud, and it shall be for a token of a covenant between me and the earth. And it shall come to pass, when I bring a cloud over the earth, that the bow shall be seen in the cloud. Gen. 9:13, 14.

It was raining. The rain clouds were overhead, and the sun was low and shining brightly in the west; to the east, spanned like a giant archway across the gently rolling farmland, was a double rainbow.

As we came out of the house, the rainbow caught our attention, and my daughter, with all the wonder and excitement that lives in the heart of the young, looked at me and said, "Mommy, I want to run to the end of the rainbow; can I go?"

I knew that she could not run through the waist-high grass the half mile or more to the place where the glorious colors rested lightly on the grass and bushes before they faded; yet my heart said *Why not?* so I told her, "Run and touch the rainbow."

It was a beautiful sight, and as her lithe body moved out away from me and toward the beautiful light, my mind pondered many things. How quickly this child, the creation of the love my husband and I share, has grown! How lovely the tints of her emerging personality sparkle and intensify as the light and knowledge of understanding illuminate her mind. I thought of the "bow of promise" given so long ago to the seasick, weary inhabitants of the ark, who saw the first rainbow and received God's promise. I thought of God, who for His delight and ours created all the glorious beauty that we enjoy.

After about five minutes the rainbow started to fade; slowly Becca turned and started to retrace her steps. My heart had in a few beautiful moments seen a view of both God and my child that I will cherish all my life.

Just as we cannot hold the colors of the rainbow in our hands, so we cannot hold the changing, growing hearts of our children in our hands. But we may cherish memories, symbols of promises and loving relationships that will warm our hearts through the years.

Carol Foote

April 29

My Garden

He who goes to and fro weeping, carrying his bag of seed, shall indeed come again with a shout of joy, bringing his sheaves with him. Ps. 126:6, NASB.

When we were small my parents encouraged us to help them in the garden. They even assigned us our own areas, which were very carefully taken care of. I wanted my piece to be the best, the most fruitful. That is why I would water it daily and would pull out the weeds.

One afternoon I ate one fruit, and when I was going to throw away the seed, my dad said that if I planted it and took care of it, I would have a new plant in a given time. I was fascinated by the idea, and assured him that I would plant it in such a way and would take so much care that the very next day the plant would start growing.

He tried to explain that it was not possible, that I had to be patient, that the process would take time. I insisted that we would see it the next day. (I was sure I knew more than he.)

Very early the next morning, as soon as I got up, I ran to the garden to see what had happened, and just as I had stated, there was the plant! It was more than two feet tall! I ran to find my father.

"Did you see I was right?" I said with satisfaction. I was so excited that I did not notice his smile of understanding. I felt triumphant.

That afternoon I watered my plant. The next day I was very sad to observe the first signs of decay. The second day it was already a disaster. I called my father to help me understand what was going on. I was tied up in knots. He bent down and pulled up the plant, my plant, that had grown so easily. It had no roots.

He spoke to me tenderly: "This was just a branch I cut from a tree and placed where you had planted your seed. I wanted you to learn this lesson. Not everything is made in one day. You must be hardworking and persevere; only then will you be happy when you see the fruit of your labor."

What a simple, wise, and lasting impression was made on my childish mind! Dad related the great truths of the Word of God with everyday life. I not only learned this lesson (and many others), but also use the same efficient method with my own children.

Mary Centenaro

APRIL 30

LOVELINESS UNLIMITED

Consider the lilies of the field, how they grow; they toil not, neither do they spin; and yet I say unto you, That even Solomon in all his glory was not arrayed like one of these. Matt. 6:28, 29.

Apart from my family, flowers are my greatest joy in life. Their colors, shapes, perfumes, never fail to attract me, and wherever I am, if I have flowers, I am happy.

When I first went to the big flower market at 3:00 a.m. on a cold morning to buy flowers, I was overwhelmed by the sight and the fragrance. I wondered if I would ever lose the marvelous sense of excitement I felt that first morning. After many such trips I can tell you I haven't.

Jesus knew what He was talking about when He told us to "consider"—think about—the flowers and how they grow. Flowers come in all shapes and sizes and colors, but they grow together harmoniously. Each has its own beauty, and they do not vie with each other. Take a flower in your hand and look at it very closely. Its intricate beauty will take your breath away, and yet flowers do not trumpet their superiority. They live but a short time, but while they live they give, unselfishly. Their loveliness is there for all to see and to enjoy, and when they have given all they can, they quietly fade away.

When I work with flowers, they always bring peace to my soul. Theirs is a calming, gentle influence that never fails to turn my thoughts to the Creator. How I wish we could be more like the flowers, living in harmony together and giving out only beauty and fragrance. If we could live like this, what a wonderful world it would be. Today let us try to show the fragrance of the love of Jesus in our lives.

AUDREY BALDERSTONE

MAY 1

THE WINDOWSILL OF HEAVEN

For thus says the high and lofty One who inhabits eternity, whose name is Holy: "I dwell in the high and holy place, and also with him who is of a contrite and humble spirit, to revive the spirit of the humble, and to revive the heart of the contrite." Isa. 57:15, RSV.

Every morning lean your arms awhile upon the windowsill of heaven and gaze upon your Lord; then, with the vision in your heart, turn strong to meet the day" (*anonymous*).

The windowsill of heaven. Leaning recently on my windowsill at night, I gazed up into the glimmering sky. A million, billion light-years away, I wondered what my Father was doing at that moment. I picture Him on His stunning sapphire throne with glorious rainbow colors encircling Him. Bursts of lightning introduce the deep bass notes of thunder. His magnificent throne room is abuzz with activity. In continual praise and thanksgiving are the mysterious four living creatures. The 24 elders join in adoration while sharing administration. The angelic choir fashion and perform new masterpieces of exhilarating expression. Then there are the angelic executives with their reports from all sectors of the universe. The Hydrogalactic Division, the Astrological Division, and the Division of Cosmo-research and Infi-development. The Division of Video-chronology, the Communigraphic Division—and the list goes on. God in His omnipotence can do megatasks in microseconds. For amid all His multitude of responsibilities among His myriad of galaxies, I am assured that He sees me leaning on my windowsill and smiles upon me.

Fear not, He says; I call the stars by name and I also call you by name. I know what street you live on and even the color of your house. You are ever in My gaze. And how I love it when you "every morning lean your arms awhile upon the windowsill of heaven and gaze upon your Lord; then with the vision in your heart, turn strong to meet the day." — HEIDE FORD

MAY 2

PERFECT PEACE

Thou wilt keep him in perfect peace, whose mind is stayed on thee. Isa. 26:3.

I did not hear the swish of the rock, nor feel the pain as it plowed through the car windshield and struck the right side of my face. Blackness! Numbness! Slowly I placed my hand over my eye. "I can't see," I mumbled.

"We are driving to the nearest hospital," I heard someone say. Some friends and I were returning from an afternoon hike when a large truck passing us kicked up a rock the size of my fist and slung it through the car's front windshield.

At the hospital the emergency room doctor phoned Loma Linda University Medical Center to send an eye specialist to Riverside and began pouring a solution into my eye to wash out the glass. For what seemed hours I lay under bright lights trying not to move. My forehead above my eye was deeply cut, and the cut continued across my eyebrow, skipped my eye, and continued a little below it. They didn't know how badly the eye might have been damaged.

I thought of my mother at home (Dad had died a year before). I thought of my job. Could I continue writing and editing and doing all my work with only one eye? Then my thoughts turned to God and prayer. Somehow through all this I felt peaceful and unafraid.

Years before, I had taken time to type on 3 x 5 cards my favorite verses from each book of the Bible. At night before I went to sleep I'd read one or two of these verses and review and think about them, applying them to my life as I drifted off to sleep. When I awoke in the morning I read another verse to think about during the day. I didn't really try to memorize them, but the thought lingered the same.

Now lying in the emergency room, I let these encouraging, loving Bible statements wash through my mind, and I could feel the strength and peace they brought.

Twelve hours and 27 stitches later I was safely in my own bed at home, where I stayed for a week, not knowing whether I would see once the bandages were removed.

I did see; my eye was not damaged. Now about 15 years later only a tiny scar remains—as well as a memory of a God who sheltered me in His arms of love. That memory has lingered through later times of turmoil when I didn't feel God's peace and when for a time I felt alone and forsaken.

To each one of you I recommend filling your heart with God's Word—sometime you may need its love and courage.

EDNA MAYE GALLINGTON

May 3

Sarah's Baby

For it is written that Abraham had two sons, one by the slave woman and the other by the free woman. His son by the slave woman was born in the ordinary way; but his son by the free woman was born as the result of a promise. Gal. 4:22, 23, NIV.

Sarah was beautiful. But she wanted a baby. Like almost every other woman in her culture, she had status and a place in history only if she had children. God had promised a child—in fact, many children, children as the stars in the sky and sand on the seashore. But so far she didn't have even one.

It is interesting to look through the chapters of Genesis before Sarai, later to be called Sarah, is mentioned. Sarah is the first woman to be given much coverage, but like her, almost every woman is mentioned either in connection with her beauty or her children, or that she had no children. Those were the things that society considered important for women. Not too different from today.

The promise of a child had been made to both Abram and Sarah, so they decided to help God a little, and Abraham, as he was now called, slept with Sarah's maid, Hagar, and she had a baby. That should have solved the problem as far as they were concerned, but they forgot that God wasn't honoring just Abraham—He wanted to honor Sarah, too. She had received the promise as well, and for God, nothing would do but that she have the child of promise herself.

Then comes a part of the story that is not so pleasant to read, and one begins to wonder what kind of woman Sarah was. In this part of the story she seems to us to be mean and vindictive. It had been primarily her idea that Abraham have a child by Hagar, but when Hagar became pregnant and a bit too proud of it for Sarah's liking, Sarah became so mean to Hagar that she ran away.

God met Hagar in the desert and told her to return, but not before promising her blessings too. When Isaac was born, Sarah was ecstatic; so when Ishmael began teasing little Isaac, Sarah became furious. She demanded that Abraham send both Hagar and Ishmael away. This, of course, distressed Abraham, because Ishmael had been his only son for a number of years; in fact, Abraham had once thought that Ishmael was to be the son of promise. But now Sarah demanded that he be sent away.

It is then that God steps into the picture once more. He tells

Abraham, "Listen to whatever Sarah tells you, because it is through Isaac that your offspring will be reckoned" (Gen. 21:12, NIV).

Isn't that fascinating? God telling a husband to do whatever his wife said. But God was protecting the son of promise, too. He knew what would be best for Isaac. And He was keeping His promise to a woman. Not a perfect woman, but one through whom and with whom He was willing to work. That gives me courage. God honors His promises to women, and the son of promise had to come through Sarah as much as through Abraham. I can joyfully worship a God like that. ARDIS DICK STENBAKKEN

MAY 4

CHRIST LOVES YOU!

Whoso findeth a wife findeth a good thing, and obtaineth favour of the Lord. Prov. 18:22.

To you who have been exemplary mothers and faithful wives . . .

To you who have loved, encouraged, stimulated, and understood your husbands, and been happy to see them win the battles of life . . .

To you who have transmitted the Word of God by your personal testimony at home, at work, with your friends . . .

To you who have motivated and shown your love to abandoned children . . .

To you who have wisely been always ready to hold out a hand to those who have fallen, stimulating them to get up and try again . . .

To you who have found the time to speak words of sympathy, showing that Christ is real in your life . . .

To you who have clothed the needy and always had a word of comfort for those who struggle . . .

To you who have helped and cooperated, carrying forward the plans of the ministry of women . . .

To you who have living faith—an ongoing personal communion with God . . .

Thanks be to God! Thanks be for you women of noble ideals, who are active and dynamic, servants using your talents in favor of the building up of God, transmitting peace to your equals.

You have inestimable value; Christ loves you!

MEIBEL MELLO GUEDES

MAY 5

CROWN OF GLORY

The hoary head is a crown of glory, if it be found in the way of righteousness. Prov. 16:31.

In the spring of 1884 Oscar Wilde, after observing one of his friends draw the portrait of a young man, devised the plot of his famous work *The Portrait of Dorian Gray*. Wilde imagined that while Dorian lived his life of arrogance and eternal beauty, his portrait lay in the dark cellar, reflecting his complicated life and illustrating his moral and physical deterioration.

Doesn't the same thing happen to us? Our generation worships the beauty of the face and body. Wrinkles are fought with surgery. We spend thousands of hours in the gym (not for the sake of health, but because of beauty). We adopt fashions that make us look younger (although they cause us discomfort). We use color to hide our gray hair. We have reached the point of considering age a shameful thing. Face-lifts and tummytucks, gyms and diets, dyes and cosmetics, give us the collective hysteria constantly deifying these paradigms of eternal youth.

Today's teenagers consider getting old a liability. Old age and maturity are seen as the end of the "good life." It's possible that in spite of these aesthetic mothballs we run the risk of harboring moths and mildew inside. Like Dorian Gray, we don't realize that in the cellar of our life, time, pain, emptiness, distrust, insecurity, vanity, and the lack of spirituality may be destroying us. What if our faces revealed the very truth we are trying to hide?

Why fear old age and death? Old age is the price that we pay for a good life full of projects, goals, and service. Death is the final rest after hard work and a life full of cares. For this reason, wouldn't it be more beneficial to direct our energies toward these objectives instead of trying to hide the traces of our passage through time, hiding our mistakes by postponing maturity? Solomon wrote today's text as a wise reflection at the end of his life: perhaps this is the best way of staying young. MONICA CASARRAMONA

May 6

THE BLUE BOOK

Speak, for your servant is listening. 1 Sam. 3:10, NIV.

Darkness had fallen, and a sullen heat hung over us. Knots of people sat around the periphery of the large room, chatting, when I came back in and took my place by my new friend. At the moment I didn't link the blue book in the box beside me with her or with "listening." It was just there, because . . .

The governor and his wife sat across from us. Behind them a ragged swatch of bare brick showed where plaster had fallen from the wall, and a long, narrow crack snaked upward from one of the windows—work of the earthquake that brought us there. The first shock, the worst quake ever recorded in Zaire, had hit more than a week before. Houses crumbled, their falling walls injuring many, killing some. And now the provincial governor had come with a large entourage bringing relief donations. ADRA/REACH had contributed generously, and at the governor's personal invitation I'd joined that official group for the four-day trip—the only foreigner, the only missionary, the only woman.

We saw the damage, visited the hospitalized, and sympathized with the frightened population now living and sleeping in the open air. As a gesture to the area churches, I'd also brought Bibles for their pastors and six French Bible readings books. After I'd given the Bibles to the pastors, I started to hand the six study books to one of the pastors. *No,* my thoughts told me. *Keep one.* And having no idea why I should, I obediently slipped one back into the box and handed him the other five.

"My aunt advised me to become a Christian." The first words my new friend spoke when I rejoined her caught me by surprise. "But I had no one to guide me."

The wife of the top government official for that area and a trained nurse, she then explained how as a young woman she'd left a church sensing she'd been deceived, and that an aunt had written encouraging her to find another Christian church. But alone, she hesitated.

"I have just the guide for you," I replied, reaching into the box and taking out the book. "Do you have a Bible?"

She nodded.

"Then this book will guide you and help you to understand the Scriptures." To myself I thought, *The Holy Spirit's prompting*, understanding then exactly why I had the thought to put the book aside. "An excellent book," I added, pointing to the first part of the title: "God's Answers."

CORRINE VANDERWERFF

MAY 7

UNTO YOU, GOD

The people who walked in darkness have seen a great light. They lived in a land of shadows, but now light is shining on them. You have given them great joy, Lord: you have made them happy. Isa. 9:2, 3, TEV.

Unto You, God,
    I give my childish dreams, my all—
because my heart is tender,
yielded in love to You.

Unto You, God,
    I bring my gifts and talents,
because of an inborn desire
to give back what has so freely
been given to me in my youth.

Unto You, God,
    I give, and give, and give
because it is demanded.
Because of those who take away self-esteem,
    value, and then, drained
because of the losses experienced,
the hurt inflicted by those who say
    "It is required of you,"
I stand empty, a nothing.

I give You what is due You
because it is my duty,
giving without understanding,
giving through tears of pain,
because it is only in this way
that I can cling to any shred
of a sense of belonging to You.

Unto You, God,
    I open my cold, hardened heart
softened by You, loving Spirit,
when I could do nothing,
left, deserted, lonely, wandering aimlessly.

Because You came,
                found me where I was,
                              and loved me!

Dedicated to those thousands whose heart cry seemingly goes unheard by human ears. These cries have been heard and carried on the wings of angels to the Most High.   PEGGY HARRIS

MAY 8

SPRINGTIME LONGINGS FOR NEWNESS

"They shall be his people, and God himself shall be with them, and will wipe away every tear from their eyes. Death shall be no more, and never again shall there be sorrow or crying or pain. For all those former things are past and gone." Then he who is seated upon the throne said, "See, I am making all things new!" And he added, "Write this down for my words are true and to be trusted." Rev. 21:4, 5, Phillips.

It was Mother's Day, and we all got together at my husband's parents' place to celebrate. Fourteen adults and 11 children made a lively crowd that ranged in age from 5 weeks to 85 years. As are all of our family get-togethers, this one bubbled from prattle to serious Bible discussion, from the kids giving comments to the spicy opinions getting tossed back and forth among the adults. But in and through all the excitement was a calm sense of family love and loyalty. Mom and Dad were visibly pleased to have their children and grandchildren surrounding their table, and Grandmother and Grandfather glowed as they watched the goings-on.

When everyone left on a walk, I sat nursing Aimee in the sudden stillness, enjoying her smallness and perfection. My reverie was broken by Grandmother. I'd forgotten that she too had stayed behind. She apologized for falling asleep while we were visiting, and I assured her that I didn't mind. She wanted to know whose baby I had with me, and I reminded her that it was Byron's and my baby, her own great-granddaughter. "Oh, of course," she said. "How silly to have let that slip my mind."

We talked of crocheting and walking in the rain, and then she held Aimee. She looked so serene holding Aimee. She rambled about her babies and how it seemed like yesterday. As I watched and listened, Aimee suddenly seemed very, very young and fragile, and it struck me that these two daughters of God had been born at opposite ends of a century. Then Grandmother broke my reflections by saying, "What a sweet baby this is." I knew she'd forgotten, again, that Aimee was her great-granddaughter.

Suddenly the kids were at the door exuberantly insisting that Aimee and I join them on the walk. With reluctance I took Aimee and bundled her for our walk in the light rain. As we stepped out, the kids scampered around me telling me what they'd been seeing on their walk. I took Byron's hand, feeling very in love with him and our four children, yet my happiness was mingled with sadness. It just didn't seem fair to have to grow old and forget even your own great-grandchildren.

We strolled along seeing and smelling spring blossoming and budding all around us, and I was filled with a fresh perspective on a longstanding desire for heaven, when the old will become new.

JANICE R. SMITH

MAY 9

ONLY ONE THING

Remember how short my time is. Ps. 89:47.

"Forgive me, Father. Today I accomplished so little! How can I ever get caught up?"

I realized I had as much time as anyone else each day. My Father created time in the first place. Could He somehow extend it for me in my need?

I didn't consider myself a negative person. In fact, I thought I was generally quite upbeat, positive, and cheery. I recognized that the weight of so many unfinished tasks and projects that I needed or desired to accomplish constituted a large portion of the stressors that jeopardized my health more and more as I aged. There seemed no way that I could improve my situation. My moanings continued. I suspected that not even God could help this problem.

In mid-December 1991 I entered more negatives regarding my lack of time into my prayer journal during my morning devotions.

Suddenly I "heard" definite though soundless words distinctly in my mind: *Try to accomplish one thing each day—and be thankful!* That was all.

Stunned, amazed, I recognized God's voice, for never would I have thought of such a concept—trying to do only one thing! I marveled at its simplicity, its lack of wordiness, clear, concise, direct.

I knew immediately that this was the answer to my prayer of many days. Yet I pondered that message several days before I realized its full impact. Those simple words, followed and obeyed, would bring about a whole new concept in my life. I would thank my Father for strength and time for accomplishing a task. Gone would be my anxiety over unfinished projects, and my unhealthful stress would lessen. Perhaps I could even hope for an improvement in my health problems. The change could conceivably add some years to my aging anatomy.

My Lord is able! "Impossible" finds no place in His greatness! My trust in Him keeps growing toward totality, by His amazing grace!

Now I understand better my Lord's 10-word intervention. My body was even then—unbeknown to me—developing a life-threatening disease. My heart was wearing out.

"Try to accomplish one thing each day—and be thankful!" has become my daily meditation and reminder. With my old worry habit I might not have lived through those months of illness in 1992. Thank You, my Perfect Parent!   ROBERTA SHARLEY

MAY 10

I AM GOD'S WORK OF ART

For we are God's workmanship, created in Christ Jesus to do good works. Eph. 2:10, NIV.

My Bible's study helps indicate that the Greek reference to this verse portrays the phrase *God's workmanship* as meaning a "work of art." So I have paraphrased this verse to read as follows:

"For I am God's work of art, created in Jesus Christ, beautiful, perfect, and lovely. I am a work of art that God enjoys looking at; but I've also been created by God to be a blessing to others, and therefore my actions will be beautiful, making me a special object inside and out: God's precious work of art."

I have always had a struggle feeling good about myself. As a teenager I felt ugly, and I buried my personality in these feelings. Through the years my self-esteem has improved as I have matured. But the battle to feel adequate still rages very strongly at times.

These feelings have led me to try to fill the "hole in my soul" with too much work, which has at times left me exhausted and unable to enjoy life. Or I overeat and jeopardize my health and body, deteriorating my self-worth. I have also looked to shopping and new clothes and "things" to fill the void. The results of this have been financial imbalance and lack of control, plunging my self-worth even further.

Then there are the spurts of overachievement coupled with people-pleasing and trying to make everyone happy. So on and on I go, trying frantically in many ways to compensate so that I can feel good about myself.

Then in desperation I turn to Jesus again, and these are some of the thoughts He floods me with. I recently discovered this verse from Ephesians 2:10, and it quietly struck me that God created me as His work of art. Not only that, but He created me in His image. He created me for His good pleasure. I am so precious to Him He wrote my name on His hands. He has said that Jesus would have left heaven to die for just me if I had been the only sinner.

He has also promised to guide me continually; to keep His eye on me as He guides me; never to leave me nor forsake me; to turn my ashes of burned dreams and aspirations into something beautiful; to come to take me home with Him soon so He can enjoy His work of art in person, continually and forever.

Oh, praise His name! God will make us into His treasured works of art if we just cooperate with Him and let Him work.

MARILYN BENNETT JUSTESSEN

May 11

Coincidence or Providence?

Are not five sparrows sold for two pennies? Yet not one of them is forgotten by God. Indeed, the very hairs of your head are numbered. Don't be afraid; you are worth more than many sparrows. Luke 12:6, 7, NIV.

As a Christian I do believe God is guiding my way on earth. One may wonder how He can provide for His whole creation, maintaining all the natural laws, sustaining the worlds in their pathways through the universe, naming the stars, ruling over the deepest secrets of wisdom, and even caring for small things of the daily routine of His children. Isn't it amazing? This greatness might have inspired the words of the well-known song "How Great Thou Art."

This conception of grandeur became more real to me one day sometime ago. It was Friday, and I was about to finish a sermon that I would preach in my Brooklyn church. As the subject was Christian education and how the educational work had increased during recent years, I realized I needed some current data—number of schools, teachers, students, etc. Normally I could get the information from the church headquarters, but it was Friday and office hours were over. Nobody I knew had the information I needed. But God was looking at me, and He knew my needs even before I did.

Some minutes later Pastor Joao Rabello came to my office. Pastor Rabello, a good friend of mine, is now retired and researches denominational history in Brazil. After we visited together, he handed me an envelope and said, "I received this from the church headquarters recently. It is for your historic files. After he left, I opened the envelope and could hardly believe what I saw—all the information I needed for my sermon! Was it a coincidence? Certainly not.

Our wonderful Father provides for our great and small wants. It makes me more thrilled about the God I know. It gives me assurance that He cares for me day by day.

I invite you to take your wants, joys, sorrows, cares, and fears to God. You cannot burden Him; you cannot weary Him.

Sonia Gazeta

May 12

Heavenly Motherhood

He will wipe every tear from their eyes. There will be no more death or mourning or crying or pain, for the old order of things has passed away. Rev. 21:4, NIV.

As soon as I found out that we were expecting our third child, I decided to let 5-year-old Bethany in on the secret. I was always very sick when I was pregnant, and we thought the children would be less worried about me if they knew that I was sick for a special reason. But I didn't want to excite them too much. I'd had two miscarriages before Bethany and Nathan were born, and knew that pregnancy held many hazards.

"Bethany," I said, "we have something special to tell you. Mommy is pregnant, and there is a little baby growing inside her, which is why she is so sick."

"Oh, Mommy, I'm so pleased! I was praying you'd have another baby!"

"But Bethany, I want you to know that not all babies work out. Some of them die before they are born. It's very sad. We hope and pray this baby will be all right, but we'll have to wait and see."

"Never mind, Mommy," she said. "If your baby dies, then you'll be able to have a little baby in heaven when you get there. Won't that be nice?" We'd never talked about such things, but somehow children have a way of understanding God that we seem to have lost touch with.

I'd always found comfort in the thought of angels bringing babies to their mothers at the resurrection, but my thoughts had never gone much past that point. Now I found myself imagining being a mother in heaven. What bliss! But I could hardly envisage rows of pearly-white diapers hanging on a celestial washing line outside a golden mansion! The heavenly babies in my imagination didn't need diaper changes!

It would be wonderful to be a mother with boundless energy and minimal housework. There would be no teething pain, no croup and fevers to struggle with at midnight, no days feeling heavy-headed from lack of sleep, no temper tantrums, no teenage terrors, no fear of dangers—just the joy of being together in a perfect world, sharing the delights of Paradise, watching the child grow to its fullest potential, naturally and perfectly. Motherhood as it was meant to be.

We don't know all that heaven has to offer. My wildest imaginings probably seem completely inadequate compared to the reality that God has prepared for us. But I do know that God is making it a place where all our sadnesses will end and pure, eternal happiness will begin. God's love is preparing an eternity of unimaginable joys for each one of us, whatever our earthly sorrows have been.

KAREN HOLFORD

MAY 13

LITTLE GIRL

Jesus saw her weeping. . . . Jesus wept. John 11:33-35, NKJV.

Lauren, 7 years old, slammed into the house, threw himself across the bed, and cried out, "Oh, that I had my life to live over again!"

Somehow I knew how he felt when I opened a birthday package from my sister. As I lifted the lovely frame from its encasement of tissue paper and ribbons, a small girl of 2 years peered solemnly into my face. I recognized it as one that had been lifted by a clever photographer from a family group picture of years ago.

The impact was so great that I could hardly keep my composure. This little girl looked so innocent and trusting. I wanted to cry without knowing exactly why. Maybe it was because I knew the mistakes she would make. I would like to have told her what to do if she "could live her life over again." I wanted to reach out and protect her from mistakes.

She was a sunny-dispositioned little girl with a keen mind and a merry laugh. She loved to read and usually received a book for birthdays and Christmases.

She helped to heal the wounds in her parents' hearts for the little girl they had lost before she was born. She lived on a farm, learning to work, play, and love. She was devoted to animals of all sizes and kinds. Her mother was an intelligent woman who loved to read and told delightful stories. Her father taught her poems and readings. He delighted in her performances in the small country schoolhouse.

I'd like to walk a little closer to her along the way to school and nudge her to be a little more thoughtful of her parents, a little more unselfish. She should be kinder, more thoughtful when they are tired. She should help them more and try to cause them less worry. She should express appreciation for their work and sacrifices.

Then I'd tell her things that could make her marriage go

smoother. Perhaps how to raise her own children. I'd talk to her about taking her problems to God and sticking close to the good principles she was to learn.

It's awesome looking into an innocent little face and realizing that the future of this child is an open book to you. To know exactly all the mistakes she will make and still not be able to help her. I think that maybe God feels that way about each one of us. He knows exactly what will happen as a result of our every decision, be it good or bad. He knows, but because He has promised not to interfere with our free will, He won't do anything to stop us from making the choices we make. He won't keep us from suffering and paying the price for those mistakes. Maybe that is why Jesus wept, even as I feel like weeping now.

Why do I feel such emotion about this little girl? Because I can't turn back the clock. Why? Because this little girl is I, and I am she, and we are a grandma now. — FAITH KEENEY

May 14

Old and New

He said to them, "Therefore every teacher of the law who has been instructed about the kingdom of heaven is like the owner of a house who brings out of his storeroom new treasures as well as old." Matt. 13:52, NIV.

I like new things . . . perfectly white socks, sharp kitchen knives, tiny spring leaves. But I like old things, too, like butter molds, lace handkerchiefs, and antique cake plates.

While I was preparing the nursery for the arrival of our first baby, I discovered an antique rocking chair in my grandmother's attic. It was dusty and rickety, and had an ugly piece of plywood nailed over the seat. But when Grandma told me how this cherry wood rocker had come to Nebraska in a covered wagon at the turn of the century, I took it home, polished it, tightened the pegs, and sewed a soft cover for the seat.

As I rock our baby daughter now, I think of the pioneer women who sat in this chair before me to rock their many infants. What great hardships they endured! Stifling prairie heat, duststorms, failed crops, bitter winds, lonely winters. I marvel that they ever raised children without the aid of washing machines, disposable diapers, commercial baby food, pacifiers, or even running water!

Despite these modern conveniences, today's mothers have plenty of worries that most of our grandmothers didn't—such as the very real possibilities of our children being abducted or molested, abusing drugs, or contracting AIDS. For better or worse, raising a family "just isn't what it used to be"! Some things, however, never change. The mothers who rocked their babies in this chair nearly a century ago soothed their little cries, nursed them through sickness, loved them tenderly, and sacrificed so that they could have the best. And as I do the same, it gives me strength and comfort to have this link with generations past. — BRENDA DICKERSON

May 15

RECOGNIZED

Then the woman, seeing that she could not go unnoticed, came trembling and fell at his feet. Luke 8:47, NIV.

It's very easy to forget about the people. Considering the job, you wouldn't think that would be possible, but it is. After all, they do all look alike. They're all dressed in the same blah color that just matches the walls. They fade into the background sometimes because they are unable to communicate—to speak clearly or rationally. Sometimes they're forgotten because it's so much easier not to see them. They are not pretty, lovable people. At times they strike out with loud, angry words and waving fists. They are in pain, they are helpless, they are enraged.

Some of them are dying, and both they and you know it. It's easy to pretend you don't know, to go through the motions and draw blood from patient A, then patient B, and not really see Jane or Virginia or Billie.

She was used to fading into the background. She had been everywhere and to everyone to seek help, and all the medical professionals had given her case up. Nothing that we can do. After 12 years even her family was probably tired of her invalid condition. Probably at first people were supportive and sympathetic. They also probably expected her to die soon. Oh, yes, I imagine that she had learned to fade into the background very well.

Then one day there was a new healer. Purported in whispers of excitement to be the Messiah. Others considered Him to be a fraud and a fake. Yet she still had hope. She must have listened ever so carefully to the stories of His methods. It seemed He healed with a word or a touch. People who had been crippled and blind since birth were suddenly, miraculously whole. Perhaps there was healing for her in a touch. Maybe if He ever came this way she just might . . .

There was a great crowd of people. They pushed and jostled in the dusty street. Jesus was on His way to heal Jairus' daughter. She had probably seen Jairus fall to his knees and humbly ask if Jesus could come and see his dying child. Jairus was an important man. How could she speak? The crowd was so close, so noisy.

"But Jesus said, 'Someone touched me; I know that power has gone out from me.' Then the woman, seeing that she could not go unnoticed, came trembling and fell at his feet" (Luke 8:46, 47, NIV).

Recognized! Oh, the terror and the relief.

The gospels don't record that Jesus healed x number of lepers or y number of blind people. Every encounter in which Jesus healed was one of coming face-to-face. It was an interaction in which Jesus saw the individual, not just the disease.

"Good morning." I wait to see the eyes look at me, to get an acknowledgment of my presence. To see the person first, and to let them know they've been seen. To forget about the IV poles, the feeding tubes, the bandages, the disease. "Good morning, Virginia."

CHRISTINA ENNIS

May 16

QUILT JEWELS

And I pray that you, being rooted and established in love, may have power, together with all the saints, to grasp how wide and long and high and deep is the love of Christ, and to know this love that surpasses knowledge—that you may be filled to the measure of all the fullness of God. Eph. 3:17-19, NIV.

Those who know me best know that one of my favorite pastimes is quilting. I love the look of different fabrics and enjoy the process of sewing pieces together into interesting blocks. I eagerly await the moment I come to the last quilting stitch and proclaim the item "Done!"

One of my projects, a 24" x 24" wall hanging entitled "Columbus Scrap," proved to be more of a learning experience than I'd originally intended. I wanted to do a small project to help commemorate the 500th anniversary of Columbus landing in the New World. It had a mariner's compass (like a many-pointed star) in the center, surrounded by a variety of triangles and squares of fabric, some showing scenes of Columbus-related items such as ships, winds, people landing on dry ground, and even the year, 1492.

With needle in hand and thimble on finger, I set myself to sewing! Carefully I hand-sewed the center star so that all the pieces fit perfectly. This was the focus of the project, and I wanted to put my best effort into it. I wanted to use as many different fabrics as I could to surround it, giving it a truly "scrap bag" look. I started cutting triangles and squares, no two alike, from my fabric stash. Sometimes I said, "No, this is too wild," or "This doesn't look right," but eventually I found a place for it. I used the fabrics I had, and finally all the pieces were cut and sewed. The quilting was finished in two days (I was on vacation!).

Now I can stand back and gaze at the finished project. How wonderful it is to see the many colors, patterns, and prints of fabrics, each a bit different, each aiding the other in making the entire project look as if it has bits of brilliant jewels glistening in the sun with a radiant star in the center.

My quilt makes me think of how like those little bits of fabric we are, each different in some way. The central focus of our "quilt" is Jesus Christ and His abundant love. And no matter what piece we become, whether plain or fancy, we can reflect God's love to those around us and become brilliant jewels for our Lord!

My 24" x 24" project has 80 different fabrics in it. Each one I consider special, even those I hadn't originally planned to include. So let's all join together and become jewellike in celebrating our returning Saviour and His love! JANET STAUBACH BOTTROFF

MAY 17

BE STILL

Be still, and know that I am God. Ps. 46:10.

Not to be alone—ever—is one of my definitions of hell. I need daily private time to mend the holes in my soul no less than I require calories and exercise.

Being a melancholy married to a choleric/sanguine, I've repeatedly had to set boundary lines in the work/social/church clamor, recognizing that my husband's tolerance for involvement far outlasts mine.

I've often dreamed of having an out-of-house cocoon—perhaps an old caboose set on the back of our property, a snug tree aerie, or an abandoned one-room schoolhouse. There I would place a comfortable chair with a footstool, a small writing desk, crowded bookshelves, a strong reading lamp, and a few treasures. No telephone, radio, or TV—just blessed stillness!

Short of that, I seek privacy early in the morning in my den, driving in the car to appointments, or after work on a walk or the treadmill. Switching to meditative mode from fast forward takes a few minutes, but soon I'm on cruise control, opening my mind to impressions from God, sending back expressions of praise and petition.

I'm in good company, biblically, in the search for solitude. Four of my favorite writers went on retreat—two as shepherds (Moses and David) and two in exile (Daniel and John). Jesus positively hungered for time alone with His Father, and no hour of the day or night was off-limits for soul refreshment.

Do you want to step off the stress escalator and onto the mood elevator? Reserve a few minutes daily for spirit renewal—that quiet time when you can hear a thought drop, and perhaps receive news from a celestial corner of the universe. CAROLE BRECKENRIDGE

May 18

"Ask, and It Shall Be Given to You"

Ask, and it shall be given to you; seek, and you shall find; knock, and it shall be opened to you. Matt 7:7, NASB.

Many years ago as I complained to a friend in college about my waning spiritual fervor, she calmly assured me that it is necessary to fall away sometimes.

While I never quite agreed with her, I have discovered that it is impossible to stay hyperspiritual all the time. I have come to understand the meaning of the Negro spiritual "Sometimes I'm up and sometimes I'm down . . ." During my ups I maintain regular Bible study, pray often, enjoy witnessing and visitation. But when I am down, I am always tired: too tired for Bible study; too tired to pray at bedtime and mealtime; too tired to visit. Yes, sometimes even too tired to give a smile.

It doesn't take long in my downs to realize that I am spiritually vegetating. Several times I have struggled to stay up, but it makes being spiritual a burden I have to carry. I see Christ smiling down on me when I keep an appointment with Him. But then a real big problem comes my way when I don't keep my appointment. Somehow I have not been very comfortable with this kind of Christianity.

Lately, however, I have discovered an easy way to stay hyper for the Lord without much effort on my part. I simply tell the Lord when I notice myself slipping, "Here I go again, Lord. I don't feel like communing with You. I am weighed down with such and such a care. Please put me back where I belong and take away the tiredness."

If you feel as though you are down, don't struggle to come up; just tell it to the Lord. That is what Christ meant when He said, "Ask, and it shall be given to you." There is no prayer He answers more instantly than our desire to maintain a close walk with Him. He might answer yours differently from mine, but He certainly will answer. Just ask, and you shall receive.   HANNAH PRISCILLA SANDY

MAY 19

HE WILL DIRECT

In all thy ways acknowledge him, and he shall direct thy paths. Prov. 3:6.

One Friday afternoon as I was driving to town to pay some bills a strong impression came over me. It was as if a voice had said, "Go see Mrs. Jock *today*." The *today* was like a command.

I had been giving Mrs. Jock Bible studies. About halfway through the series her health failed, and her doctor told her she must not live alone. She then moved in with a sister and brother-in-law. A few weeks passed without any studies. Then came this silent command: "Go see Mrs. Jock *today*."

As I drove through town I saw a flower vendor near a parking space, so I stopped and bought a bouquet, then headed for her new address. But to my dismay, I found no one at home. What should I do now? There was a carton on the porch, so I put the bouquet in the carton with a note telling her I was sorry to have missed her.

As I drove away I wondered if my imagination had been working overtime when I thought I was directed by the Lord to go see Mrs. Jock that day. I did not have to think these thoughts long. The next day as I returned home from church the phone was ringing. It was Mrs. Jock's brother-in-law calling to tell me that she had died in the night, but that she had gotten the flowers and appreciated them so much and regretted not getting to see me.

I hope the flowers were enough to remind her of the decision she needed to make, and I thank the Lord that He urged me to do something for her that very day. I hope to see her in God's kingdom.

MARCEDENE V. WOOD

May 20

Washing Windows

Why do you look at the speck of sawdust in your brother's eye and pay no attention to the plank in your own eye? Matt. 7:3, NIV.

"I do windows, you know!" my friend jokes as she nods toward my rain-streaked panes. The spring sunshine is flooding in, showing every bit of dirt and grime left from winter weather.

"Here, let me help you wash them," she offers, brimming with her usual energy and caring.

So we set about to wash windows—she outside, I inside; scrubbing, rinsing, squeezing, drying.

"There!" she mouths as she points to a smudge. I rub and rub, but it does not disappear. "Your side!" I grin as I point to the stubborn spot. She rubs, smiling, and with a flourish makes the area shine. Encouraged, I see another speck and carefully show her. Her cloth is ineffective, so she taps the pane and indicates "Your side!" Oh! So it is! And so it goes.

Why are we so much like window washers? The flaws, the problems, and the faults so often appear to be "out there" on the other side. And we are so quick to point them out! When will we realize that too often they are actually on our side of the situation?

When I look at another's fault, Lord, help me to remember how it is with windows.

ALICE FAHRBACH

May 21

God's Mosaic

"For I know the plans I have for you," declares the Lord, "plans to prosper you and not to harm you, plans to give you hope and a future." Jer. 29:11, NIV.

Pick up almost any newspaper. Turn on the radio. Watch a TV newscast. The messages are distressingly familiar: wars, riots, famines, atrocities, disasters, shootings, corruption—an endless parade. And it's not just the news. Today scientists and ecologists are even more frightening doom-mongers than the most eloquent hellfire revivalists. The pace of life, with its pressures, perversions, paralyzing pessimism, and sometimes stark panic, swirls about us, and it's difficult not to be caught up in the frenzy.

But optimism, hope, and faith are not dead. They've just been lost by a bewildered, neglected generation born into a chaotic and violent world. Rather than infecting us with the restless anxiety of people about us, these awesome times can awaken us to a renewed understanding of and appreciation for our faith, and its relevance in coping with the present pandemonium.

God did not create this world and its people to let them end up suffocating into oblivion from their own follies. God has a master plan—the plan of redemption—and within it is a meaningful place, an important role, for every willing human being.

What a destiny! What a time to be alive! What a challenge to share with the world the hope and joy we know, the honor we feel at being needed and involved in the finishing of God's plans for our world.

One day God will pull back the curtain and show us the whole picture. We'll be able to see for ourselves how the differing parts and pieces of His plan fit in together, creating a great and wondrous mosaic that will stretch into eternity.   AILEEN LUDINGTON

May 22

Bad News and Good News

In whom are hid all the treasures of wisdom and knowledge. Col. 2:3.

Have you ever longed for a portion of King Solomon's wisdom? To have a mind that can quickly and efficiently understand a problem, evaluate the pros and cons, and come up with some brilliant suggestions? I have. Have you ever talked to someone and longed for a mind that can remember where a scripture is found and can quote it with confidence and ease?

If you are one of King Solomon's more distant relatives (like me), who often come up with all the good answers at night, long after the event has ended, and who often have to thumb through the whole Bible mumbling, "I know that the scripture I am looking for used to be around here someplace," then let me share some bad news with you, but also some good news. The bad news first.

Modern research has shown that 50 percent of our intelligence is formed before the age of 4 and 80 percent before the age of 7. Since both you and I are long past the tender age of 7, modern research leaves us with only 20 percent to develop. To me that is indeed bad news but I ask myself, "Can God do a miracle with the 20 percent left?" Yes, the good news is that He both can and will. Listen to this: "He who with sincere and teachable spirit studies God's Word, seeking to comprehend its truths, will be brought in touch with its Author; and, except by his own choice, there is no limit to the possibilities of his development" (*Education*, p. 125).

In this quotation we find the prescription for unlimited wisdom; it also opens our eyes to some conditions on God's part. Do we have the kind of teachable spirit He is looking for, or do we often rely only on the letters that we can add to our names and that make our wisdom known to the world? If we experience a lack of wisdom in coping with the problems of everyday life, is it because we, by choice, are cutting ourselves off from Him and His wisdom and knowledge? If we in our relationship with non-Christians are unable to open our Bibles and let scripture explain scripture, does the rust on our soul indicate heaps of dust on our Bibles?

King Solomon asked for wisdom once, and God opened up his mind and understanding in a way He has done with no other human. You and I may have to ask for wisdom every day and find that we get only enough for that day, but what more do we need? Wisdom was never meant to glorify ourselves, but to glorify its giver. If we are willing to be taught by God, to study His Word and try to comprehend its truth, we have God's promise that there is no limit to the possibilities of our development.   BIRTHE KENDEL

MAY 23

SAVED FROM EXTINCTION

The Son of man came to seek and to save the lost. Luke 19:10, RSV.

We had only one more day on the island of Mauritius in the Indian Ocean. We had asked, searched, driven on impossible roads in vain. Now my heart beat fast as I knocked on the gate set in a six-foot-high wall.

"Is Carl Jones here?" I asked the gatekeeper.

He nodded and disappeared into a low wooden building. I looked inside a courtyard ringed with aviaries and cages. The warm air was rich with sounds of flapping and cooing. Soon a tall man in his late 30s walked toward us.

"Come in," he smiled. "What can I do for you?"

"We're bird lovers from America. We've read of how you've saved the Mauritius kestrel, and we'd love to see one."

His smile broadened. "So Americans know of a Welshman who plays foster parent to these downy white chicks. In that big tree you'll see a monkey-proof, cyclone-proof nest box. Mama kestrel should be nearby."

Just then we heard a whir of wings. Above our heads sat a bird the size of a sparrow hawk with brown head and wings, mottled white breast and underparts, an impressive set of yellow talons, and a sharp curved beak.

"That rare falcon was once common in the forested mountain areas," Jones explained. "Doomed to extinction by misuse of chemical insecticides in the fifties and sixties, only four birds were known to survive in the remote Black River gorges of Mauritius in 1974. Two were a breeding pair.

"I felt it could be saved by captive breeding," he continued. "When I arrived on Mauritius we had to locate the breeding pair's nest and collect the eggs for captive rearing. Fortunately, wild birds will lay a second batch."

"Obviously you had a will to devote your life to keep this unique little falcon from the dodo's fate," I commented.

"I didn't do it alone. Hatching eggs in incubators and hand-rearing chicks is a 24-hour job. More than 120 young kestrels have been released to the wild. Many have survived and bred. By harvesting eggs from the wild nests, we hope to have 250 in the wild in a couple years."

"Is the sacrifice of years of your life worth the effort?"

"Absolutely!" he spoke with fervor. "To see these kestrels living and breeding again in their natural habitat is reward enough. How tragic it would be to have another beautiful Mauritius bird lost forever like the dodo."

I'm sure God smiles on Carl Jones, who, like His Son, delights to seek and save the lost. Is that also your desire?

EILEEN E. LANTRY

May 24

He Could Have—But He Didn't

You did not choose me, but I chose you and appointed you to go and bear fruit. John 15:16, NIV.

During World War I a recruiting poster was designed that was so successful it was used for many years. Picturing Uncle Sam dressed in his patriotic suit, with his finger pointing at whoever read the poster, the caption read "I want YOU for U.S. Army." The hope was that men and women would sense a feeling of patriotism and loyalty to their country and heed the call to serve. It was designed to make them feel no one else could do the job as well as they.

You and I have Someone who is calling us. He is not our uncle, but He is our Elder Brother. Jesus is calling you.

He could have called angels to do the work He is asking us to do, but He didn't. He is calling you and me to bear fruit. He wants us to experience the joy and privilege of working for Him.

Esther was brave when she said: "And so I will go to the king, which is against the law; and if I perish, I perish!" (Esther 4:16, NKJV). God could have sent an angel to the king to tell him what was happening and to put a stop to the proposed atrocities against the Jewish people. But He didn't—He chose a young woman who was prepared to plead the case of her people.

Today families are hungry and need shelter and food. People who are new to our country seek help to learn the language. There are many who live alone and spend their hours longing for friendship. Children listen for the story of Jesus and His love for them. He could call angels to care for these needs, but He doesn't.

God has given all people today special tasks to do for Him. Not all are called to be great leaders, because the little things in life also are important. The caring and loving concern we are able to give are needed and appreciated. The hug given to one who is grieving, time spent listening to one who is hurting, the visit to one who is ill or perhaps even in prison. These are little things that mean so much.

Have you discovered the very special task the Lord has given you? Do your work with joy and happiness, knowing He could have called an angel to do it but instead He chose YOU!   EVELYN GLASS

MAY 25

CAUGHT BETWEEN TWO OPINIONS

How long will you waver between two opinions? If the Lord is God, follow him; but if Baal is God, follow him. 1 Kings 18:21, NIV.

I was often asked to run errands for my parents both before and after school. One time one of these errands really put me in a troublesome position.

It was late afternoon, but the sun still shown bright and hot. My younger sister was sick, and my mother sent me to call for the family doctor, who lived on the other side of our village. He lived in a long white building that housed four tenants. His clinic was in the first part of the building, and my great-aunt lived in the last section. My aunt usually sat on the veranda in front chatting with friends or watching the traffic. At that time there was a strained relationship between my mother and my aunt, probably because my mother had recently become a Christian—in the Hindu country of India.

As I approached the building, my aunt saw me and became very angry. She shouted in a very harsh tone, "What do you want? The doctor is not there!" I turned around and went back home to tell my mother. She questioned the wisdom of my aunt. Mother told me to go back and make sure whether he was really there or not.

As I approached the building for the second time my aunt shouted, "I told you the doctor is not there! Go home!" Meekly I turned around and went back home. My mother was desperate to get help for her sick child and angry at my aunt for interrupting her plan. She then ordered me, "By all means, you must go for the doctor again." You can imagine my predicament and frustration! I was torn between two masters, two opinions.

With fear and trembling and legs that felt like rubber, I cautiously approached the building for the third time that day. The aunt was there as if expecting me to come again. Her face was flushed from her fury. She waved her finger and yelled at me for disobeying her and chased me back home. I ran home as fast as my tired, shaking legs would carry me and begged my mother not to send me again. Fortunately for me, she allowed me to stay home with my sister while she went to find the doctor herself.

That experience reminds me of a time in Bible history when the Israelites were in deep trouble at the time of Ahab's reign. His wife, Jezebel, had forced the nation into the worship of Baal. So God sent a drought for three and a half years. There was very little food and water. If they continued to worship Baal, they knew they would soon die of starvation. Yet if they turned to God, Jezebel was there ready to kill them. Wavering between two opinions, they lost faith in God.

Only one man dared to challenge the opposition and false opinion of Jezebel. Through Elijah, God proved His Lordship and brought the victory to those who were still faithful to Him. It was followed immediately by showers of blessing. The heavy downpour meant the assurance of food and water. Their true Master had come to their rescue.

It is so easy to enter into a conflict, even with family members, when there is a difference of opinion. At such times, let's follow Elijah's example and turn to God. He will bring peace to those who are willing to do His will.

BIRDIE PODDAR

MAY 26

"COME, SEE A MAN"

Come, see a man who told me everything I ever did. Could this be the Christ? John 4:29, NIV.

Jesus was passing through Samaria and stopped in Sychar. He was tired and thirsty, so He sat beside Jacob's well and waited. Soon a woman came to draw water, and Jesus did something extraordinary—He asked a Samaritan woman for a drink.

The interaction that followed was no mere social exchange of pleasantries. Jesus gently led a thirsty soul to an inexhaustible Fountain filled with purifying, invigorating water. The woman was thrilled! She left her water jar and ran to her village shouting, "Come, see a man . . ."

Today the invitation is still open to all. Come, see a Man who can inject vitality and effervescence into an otherwise listless Christian experience. See a Man who can bring joy to a life that has become disillusioned. This Man can give the power to love and forgive in the most challenging circumstances.

Come, see a Man who is equal to any emergency. He is our Brother (Mark 3:35). When we cry, He cries along with us. When we rejoice, He cheers with us. When we are at our lowest point, He is closer than ever. When we are overwhelmed with the challenges of a single status, the frustrations of parenting, the conflicts in marriage, the defeats in dieting, He reminds us that His grace is sufficient for us (2 Cor. 12:9).

He may not prevent us from being thrown into the fiery furnaces of life, but when we are in the flames, He jumps in with us to cool things down. When we are in the dens of despair, He is there to tame the lions that threaten to destroy us. He is with us when we feel alone and deserted. His eye sees us. His hand leads us. His mind reads us. His presence embraces us.

Come, see a Man who loves us with a love that is stronger than death (Rom. 8:35-39). This love gives us a feeling of security and self-worth that the nonbeliever does not understand.

This Man deserves our love and service as long as we have breath.

MARIA G. MCCLEAN

MAY 27

SIGHT HEALING

Therefore I counsel you to buy from me gold refined by fire, that you may be rich, and white garments to clothe you and to keep the shame of your nakedness from being seen, and salve to anoint your eyes, that you may see. Rev. 3:18, RSV.

I met Mrs. S while she was waiting for surgery. She readily acknowledged that anticipating this procedure made her "a bit nervous," yet she was eager. "I can't do much anymore," she said, "but I still enjoy reading. I have a cataract, and the words are getting too fuzzy."

I didn't tell her, but hearing of her frustration with poor sight and hope for future clarity reminded me of my own recent ordeal. Broken glasses on a holiday weekend had seemed catastrophic. My whole being felt stressed and on edge. Thinking was difficult; patience shortened. I was truly what some people call "out of sorts."

With the holiday past and glasses repaired, my life settled back into the usual. Once again I rarely thought of glasses. They were there on my face, assisting me to read and write. An entire day could easily pass without my conscious awareness of them.

Then, through conversation with Mrs. S I was reminded of how fuzzy the world can be without proper eyesight. Leaving her bedside that day, a scriptural reference came to my mind. Maybe you are thinking of the same one. It's in Revelation 3:18, where Jesus invites, "Buy from me . . . salve to put on your eyes, so you can see" (NIV).

Do you suppose that when we feel "out of sorts" emotionally it's because we need some of His eyesalve? Maybe when we feel edgy, when thinking is difficult and patience is short, we're experiencing symptoms of fuzzy spiritual vision. If so, we might do well to heed the invitation that follows this offer of soothing eyesalve.

Revelation 3:20: "I stand at the door and knock," He says. "If any one hears my voice and opens the door, I will come in" (RSV). He extends to us a solution for our fuzzy lives. We may be a bit nervous about trusting His procedure, but the outcome promises clarity and hope.

BEULAH FERN STEVENS

May 28

ROARING LIONS AND LAUGHING CLOWNS

Be self-controlled and alert. Your enemy the devil prowls around like a roaring lion looking for someone to devour. 1 Peter 5:8, NIV.

Yes, the devil would like to devour us, to snatch us away from Jesus. But he doesn't always roar. He has other methods of engaging us.

My husband and I went to the circus recently. We were in Donetsk in the Ukraine. The former Soviet Union is famous for its circuses, with its skilled acrobats and trained animals. The little gray poodle dogs amazed us as we saw them walking on their back legs, jumping through hoops and jumping over each other.

We likewise admired the skill of the trainers who had taught the horses to remain calm as acrobats performed on their backs. The horses stoically ran around and around while the acrobats juggled balls, formed pyramids, and defied gravity. No moment was wasted, for between acts the clowns captured the attention of children and adults alike.

Yes, the clowns entertained, but that wasn't their sole purpose. As they were leading us into mirth and laughter, the stagehands were busily setting up the next act. The workers came and went; they carried in props and then assembled the props. They carefully arranged, positioned, and secured the items that would be essential for the next act. And at the same time we laughed at the antics of the clowns until tears rolled down our faces.

The clowns' primary purpose was to divert our attention from the work of the stagehands.

No, Satan doesn't always roar. Many times the most effective weapon in his arsenal is diversion. He takes our minds off the real issues and engages us in pettiness. He cheers us on as we run from crisis to crisis; he keeps us too busy to plan and lay foundations. Most of us would run if we heard Satan roaring; there would be no temptation to embrace him.

But what are we doing and what are we going to do about the laughing clowns that divert our attention from the real issues of our day-to-day life? God's women have many good and noble diversions. Our lives are not crowded with sinful enterprises; we're smothered in righteous activities. We're called to do this virtuous deed, use our talents for that worthy cause, spend our time helping this deserving person, etc., etc.

Let's pray today that God will help us to look beyond the urgent and to discover the necessary. Let's pray today for the wisdom to recognize the roaring lions and the laughing clowns in our lives.

BARBARA HUFF

May 29

TREASURES

Do not lay up for yourselves treasures on earth, where moth and rust destroy and where thieves break in and steal; but lay up for yourselves treasures in heaven, where neither moth nor rust destroys and where thieves do not break in and steal. For where your treasure is, there your heart will be also. Matt. 6:19-21, NKJV.

The treasures that line the shelves and fill the drawers of my sons' room are treasures only in the eyes of little boys. There is an empty eggshell found in the yard this spring, stones from Mom-Mom's driveway before it was blacktopped, an odd-shaped lightbulb, and pieces of junk mail, rescued from the trash.

The other night they tried smuggling in lightning bugs (and judging from the occasional flickering at night when it is dark in the house, one of them was successful).

When we grow up, our treasures change. We want nice clothes, new cars, and big houses. All too often, though, it seems that something happens to our "treasures," and they become less valuable to us. I do not know how many times I have gotten a new dress or shirt or sweater that I really love and something happened to it.

Like the soft green sweater my mom gave me for Christmas one year. I followed the washing instructions carefully. It needed to dry flat, so I spread it out on top of the washing machine carefully. But there was a load of white clothes with bleach being washed in the machine. Suds came up around the edges of the lid and onto my sweater during one of the cycles. Now my sweater has a white outline of the lid on its back.

Matthew 6:19-21 tells us not to lay up treasures for ourselves on earth, because they will not last. But to lay up treasures in heaven, which will last forever.

What are treasures we can lay up for ourselves in heaven? Not clothes, cars, or houses. The only treasures we can take with us are our children, family, and friends, whom we love. As we lift up our prayers for them, love them unconditionally, witness to them through our words and lives of God's incredible greatness, we can trust the Holy Spirit to finish the work in them, so we can all be together in heaven. We can remember that we are all God's treasures.

Psalm 135:4 tells us that we are God's treasures. Isaiah 33:6 repeats this thought, telling us that those who fear God are His treasures. Can you imagine being a treasure to the King of the universe? The Almighty who could have anything, who has made everything?

Though sin has marred us, just as the suds with bleach marred my sweater, God still treasures us. He covers us with His glory, and the stain of sin is erased.

Isn't His love incredible?

TAMYRA HORST

MAY 30

LOVE'S FRAGRANCE

She hath done what she could: she is come aforehand to

anoint my body to the burying. Mark 14:8.

She creeps into the darkened room, unnoticed by the guests,
　　And finds the Saviour. From her garment lifts the costly chest—
Her alabaster box—for Him who makes her life worthwhile;
And with abandon born of love, she breaks the precious vial.

Then Mary pours the spikenard on His head; and on His feet
She empties it, and mingles with her tears her offering sweet.
Perhaps He isn't going to die! And she, with bursting heart,
Lets down her hair and wipes His feet, then hastens to depart.

But now, exquisite fragrance permeates the banquet hall,
And Mary's humble deed of love at once is known by all.
The shattered alabaster box lies empty on the floor—
A silent witness to an act that Christ does not ignore.

He tells a parable that only Simon understands;
　　And Simon yields his broken heart—the fragrance love demands.
A broken vial, a broken heart, affirm rebirth that day.
And Christ's forgiveness sweeps the sinful fragments all away.

Somewhere among your treasures is there something still concealed—
Within your alabaster box—too precious yet to yield?
Let go, and give the Master your whole heart—yes, every beat;
And in exchange, a heaven of joy awaits you at His feet!

　　　　　　　　　　　　　　　　　　　　Lorraine Hudgins

May 31

An Express Answer to Prayer

It shall come to pass that before they call, I will answer; and while they are still speaking, I will hear. Isa. 65:24, NKJV.

During the summer months it is sometimes very difficult to get a job assignment. As a result, I have to depend on my savings to take me through those dry months—paying bills and purchasing the basic necessities, such as food.

It was particularly difficult for me this summer because my brother and I, both full-time students, tried desperately to get jobs, but were unsuccessful. My resources were running low, and the bills were to be paid, and almost no food was in the cupboard. I awoke Thursday morning, August 19, feeling very discouraged. I was, however, inspired to play one of my favorite songs, "He'll Do It Again," by Shirley Caesar. Just listening to the song lifted me out of my despondency.

> "You may feel down and feel like God has somehow forgotten,
> That you are faced with circumstances you can't get through;
> Right now it seems there's no way out, you're going under;
> God's proven time and time again He'll take care of you."

Bible promises flooded my mind, and so I decided to kneel in my living room and pour out my soul to God. I started by telling Him that I believed in the biblical statement that I was of more value than the sparrow, but I was feeling low and needed some reassurance that He would provide for me. I told Him that there was no bread, milk, or juice, and that we were in desperate need for some food. I then thanked Him for the blessing He was going to send our way.

At 2:00 I went to check the mailbox. When I opened it, I saw a brown envelope. I said to myself, "Not another bill, Lord. I have no money." To my surprise, it was not a bill, but a letter from a dear friend, who had sent me $30 in cash.

Well, you can imagine how I thanked and praised God all day. My faith was renewed, and once again I saw God's act of love and mercy toward me. The letter had been mailed two days earlier. God, in His omniscience, knew that I would be calling, and He had already prepared the answer. — ANDREA A. BUSSUE

June 1

HIDDEN HARM

I will restore health unto thee, and I will heal thee of thy wounds, saith the Lord. Jer. 30:17.

The afternoon sun shone brightly as my children and I enjoyed an invigorating few hours at the beach. The children laughed and frolicked as they ran barefoot over the glistening sand dunes and played hide-and-seek behind clumps of sea oats. Periods of quiet working on a sand castle near the water's edge punctuated their activity. The restless waves rolled relentlessly onto the shore, filling the moat around their castle, much to their shouts of delight. Jaunty little sandpipers darted back and forth before the ebb and flow of the waves, which made interesting patterns on the dampened sands. The day was balmy, and life seemed good.

With the gentle breeze lightly tossing her curls, my youngest daughter ran lightheartedly across the sand. Suddenly, with a cry of pain, she clutched her left foot as the blood gushed forth. Some object hidden beneath the sand had cut and gouged her foot, causing a deep and penetrating wound.

Doctor's office, sutures, tetanus shot—all followed in quick succession. Thus ended our carefree day at the beach.

Hidden objects of harm! The devil is a master at placing these traps. The path ahead looks so smooth, and life is good. Plans, schemes, sand castles fill the mind with captivating thoughts. Suddenly there is a cry of pain as some object hidden in our pathway wounds us. We are hurt through no fault of our own. Perhaps it is undeserved criticism, loss of a job, disappointment, or emotional pain. We are angry. Our plans are interrupted. Why did this happen to me? Why me? Self-pity begins its infection of the wound and, like the tetanus germ, can be more deadly than the wound itself.

The Master Physician has promised to bind up the wound, and His treatment includes an anti-infective shot against the infection of self-pity and blame. "Vengeance is mine; I will repay, saith the Lord" (Rom. 12:19).

Today, if you are hurting, bruised, or bleeding through no fault of your own, I pray you will find healing and comfort from the Master Physician, who has promised, "I will heal thee of thy wounds."

JOAN MINCHIN NEALL

JUNE 2

FREEDOM TO SERVE

For he that is called in the Lord, being a servant, is the Lord's freeman: likewise also he that is called, being free, is Christ's servant. 1 Cor. 7:22.

I thank God for the freedom to serve. "To serve" means to work for, minister to, or attend to an employer or superior; to do manual or domestic labor for another; to be a servant to.

I can understand this, because I once had a servant—a necessity in Korea then. She lived in our home and willingly did anything we asked her to. She scrubbed our floors, sorted the rocks from our rice, cooked our meals from scratch. She changed our heaters' heavy, sooty coal briquettes; washed our clothes; ironed our baby's diapers during monsoons. She explained Korean culture to us, straightened our linguistic blunders, interpreted our good intentions to others.

With our big house and four children, she was overworked and underpaid, yet she often surprised us with hot drinks when we came home late on winter nights. She wept when we left Korea.

Freedom to serve may take many forms. It may be the freedom of good health and family circumstances that allows one to accept mission service. It may be the freedom to serve one's children at home during their formative years. Or it may be the freedom to serve at a routine, boring task with a smile.

We do not experience the freedom of service if we expect something in return, yet often there is reciprocity beyond any dreams. My husband once enjoyed a study quarter in Jerusalem, the gift of a former Korean student. Occasionally God wants us to grant others the blessing of service by receiving from them.

The freedom to serve cannot be taken from us easily. The face of a young man is etched in my mind by some home movies my husband took in a Korean prison years ago. This man had been drafted but refused to bear arms for conscientious reasons. Court-martialed, he was sent to military prison for three years. Upon release he was returned to the same officer; the same thing happened again. After his second three-year prison term, he was returned to the same officer once more. This time he was given five years in civilian prison; it was there my husband caught his picture in a long line of Voice of Prophecy Bible school graduates. The prisoner had helped prepare these men, and his whole shaven head beamed with joy. He had few other freedoms, but no one could take away his freedom to serve.

Freedom implies choice. We can serve when, where, and whom we choose. We can multiply our own buildings and conveniences, or we can help those who have none—or spread the gospel to those who know it not. We can even choose *not* to serve. Our freedom to serve others is inextricably tied to our freedom to serve Christ, our choice to be His people.   MADELINE S. JOHNSTON

June 3

Blossoming Desert

The wilderness and the wasteland shall be glad. . . . And the desert shall rejoice and blossom as the rose; it shall blossom abundantly and rejoice, even with joy and singing. Isa. 35:1, 2, NKJV.

One summer our family drove across Nevada. What a barren stretch of wasteland it was! Long stretches of highway with nothing but cactus, sagebrush, rocks, and dirt for company. Empty, quiet, parched, deserted, and depressing. Three or four miles felt like 30 or 40.

Every once in a while we'd come across a farm that was so beautiful one would almost want to stop and just stare at it, filling up the parched eyesight. Flowers of all colors and varieties would blossom before our eyes. Fruit trees produced in abundance and our mouths watered at the picture.

Then on we would go in the barren emptiness, hungrily waiting and watching for another one of those rare bursts of color.

After several such refreshments of beauty our family got to talking about the above Bible text in which Isaiah talks about the desert blossoming. We compared it to our own lives.

So many times we feel like a barren wasteland. Maybe you are a mother, at home by choice, but stuck in the rut of routine chores and tasks: depressed at not getting the recognition and perks a worldly career might offer; feeling empty and ugly and worn-out, like your life is a desert. God promises to make you blossom like a rose.

Maybe you are a student, in the last years of your education, feeling mentally exhausted, tired of the monotony of studying and eager to get on with your career. God promises to make your life desert blossom like a rose.

Maybe you're a single parent, doing a job you can't stand, just because it's your only source of income; feeling as though you've got no options and there's not enough of you to go around. God promises to make your life desert blossom like a rose.

We put a picture of a blossoming desert up in our house to remind us on those desert days that there will be brighter days with bursts of color when the desert will blossom into joy and singing. Maybe you'd like to do the same.

Shonna Dalusong

JUNE 4

GOD'S WORK OF ART

For you, O Lord, have made me glad by your work; at the works of your hands I sing for joy. How great are your works, O Lord! Your thoughts are very deep! Ps. 92:4, 5, NRSV.

When I look into the eyes of a kitten I see a part of God's creativity, a part of His wonderful works of art given for our enjoyment and for our comfort. Kittens' eyes are penetrating. They search the depths of my heart, almost as if they are seeking answers for questions they don't know how to ask.

Kittens are self-contained; they seem to own freedom itself. One moment purring in my ear, caressing my fingers; the next gone, slipped away.

They are at home with themselves. They don't need me for their ego or their livelihood. They trust me; I'm someone to purr to, meow at, or cuddle with on a cold evening. A kitten is a work of art. Round eyes, or slanted, or almond-shaped, as if the colors green, yellow, amber, smoke, or blue have been put together with a million tiny dots. Fur patterns run in bars, stripes, spots, patches, or solids, blended on the face in symmetrical lines or splotched over one eye. Yes, a kitten is a work of art—sensitive ears, delicate whiskers, soft, prickly paws, and perhaps a little nose with a spot of black. They think nothing of appropriating your pillow, your favorite chair, or a place by your plate.

One beautiful tiger cat I rescued as a kitten and named El Tigre Grande (the Great Tiger) had an opportunity to return the favor. When I injured my back and had to stay in bed for three months, he stayed beside me night and day. Then one night, when I felt I no longer could endure the lack of movement and pain, El Tigre Grande and two other cats, Mamma Kat and Bobi Spots, came to my bed. El Tigre lay down on my pillow, the second cat positioned her body touching my side, and the third lay touching my feet. It was as if they were giving me of their strength, and they stayed with me all the dark night. They had never done that before. They never did it again.

Another time, when I was missing a lost friendship, a kitten named Rinky Dink came to my room. She curled down beside me, putting one paw over my arm and her head on her paw. It was as if she could feel my tears.

Bo, a blond kitten, was one of my favorites. He was a tease. He followed me like a dog and loved to play ball, although I could never teach him to bring it back. Some mornings he'd be sure I was sleeping soundly, then around 6:00 he'd pounce on my feet and bury his claws into my toes. That was worse than an alarm clock!

Kittens tantalize me, humor me, tease me, and make me feel wanted. Kittens make me appreciate a Creator who fashioned such a work of art. EDNA MAYE GALLINGTON

JUNE 5

THE SHADOW BOX

Yea, though I walk through the valley of the shadow of death, I will fear no evil: for thou art with me. Ps. 23:4.

"Make a Quilt in a Weekend." The magazine header caught my eye as I stood in the grocery store checkout line. I'd heard of people who had attended quilt seminars. They claimed to have had no prior experience, yet they were excited about their finished product. Knowing I'd probably never work such an event into my schedule, I'd been intrigued but readily dismissed the thought.

Now, as I was standing in the checkout line, something clicked, and I purchased the magazine. Pictures and instructions claimed that even beginners could do this.

The featured quilt was called "Shadow Box," and the narrative said it was adapted from an Amish pattern. Carefully I followed the step-by-step instructions. I purchased fabric: one basic print and four coordinating colors. I cut squares, triangles, and strips as directed. Then I began sewing the pieces into blocks. Each step became more exciting as colors blended and complemented.

When I had enough blocks together to make the pattern emerge, I laid them out on my bed and stood back to admire. The arrangement of blocks gave the illusion of a box within a box. Standing there absorbed in the design, I became aware of an emerging truth.

Both light and dark fabrics were needed to create this special effect. Contrast gave depth to the design, character to the quilt. So in life. Some of us think that we would be happy with all light and sunny experiences. We shy away from "cloudy days" of life. Yet it is these very days that give us depth of being, that make our brighter days lighter. We can have peace and hope in both.

The psalmist wrote, "Yea, though I walk through the valley of the shadow of death, I will fear no evil: for thou art with me."

BEULAH FERN STEVENS

JUNE 6

"GOD WORKS FOR THE GOOD OF THOSE WHO LOVE HIM"

And we know that in all things God works for the good of those who love him, who have been called according to his purpose. Rom. 8:28, NIV.

This text became very real to me at the end of World War II. I was working for the Kindergarten Department of the city of Munich, Germany. Bombing went on day and night, and a lot of children died. To save the children, those in Munich evacuated them to small villages in the countryside near the Alps.

I was working in one of the homes and had only an occasional day off. Times were so uncertain that I planned to spend my next free day at home in Munich with my mother and brother. The journey by train was to be only one hour, and I started at 8:00 one evening. Soon after we started, the train came to a halt.

"Air raid, air raid!" shouted the conductor, and most people ran outside into the forest. I was too scared to run into the dark, and so I stayed in the coach, along with a very old man. All of a sudden there was a terrifying explosion, and then I didn't know anything more. After what seemed a long time, I woke up. The old man across from me said, "I am glad you are alive. I was sure you were dead."

We finally went on to Munich, arriving at 4:00 the next morning. The whole area was almost totally destroyed, but God spared the apartment house of my parents. My mother urged me to go for a checkup to find out if I had suffered any physical damage the night before. The doctor told me that the air pressure had damaged my heart, and he put me on unlimited lifeline.

Weeks later the war ended; with no government, there was total lawlessness and confusion for some time. There was no communication with any of our loved ones: my father was in one city in the Bavarian forest; my sister with her baby had been evacuated to the mountains, and we did not know if they were still alive or not. How thankful we were that at least we three were together.

Many terrible things happened to young girls alone, but I was safe with my mother and brother.

God can use even a bombing for the good of those who love Him. Today, almost 50 years later, when I read this text, I know God had a purpose for extending my life. — SOPHIE KAISER

JUNE 7

LOSING OR GAINING

What good is it . . . to gain the whole world, yet forfeit [your] soul? Mark 8:36, NIV.

At certain times of the year it seems we can't go to the mailbox without finding some correspondence promising a chance of great riches. Isn't it fortunate that "we" are one of the few who have made it through the selection process thus far!

Yes, I'm sure there are people who win these and other types of chance games. But personally I'm not enthused about spending my time putting all the right stickers into the correct spots, which necessitates going through a stack of about 10 inserts in order to get it done properly—what a maze! Then to cap things off, there's the last-pitch, "read-this-only-if-you've-decided-not-to-participate" message (which I usually read first)!

Anyway, as you can tell, I find these advertising tactics humorous and somewhat insulting to human intelligence. Yet after experiencing paradoxical curiosity and disdain of such letters, why is there always the lingering thought that these cards I'm throwing out might have been winners?

Winners! That's what we all want to be. And in the contest that really counts we need to be sure we're not ignoring or discarding the instructions outlining victory. Because when it comes to eternal life, the person in this world who ends up with the most toys doesn't necessarily win. But conversely, to invest everything you are and have in God's kingdom will eventually pay rich rewards. For truly, "where your treasure is, there your heart will be also" (Matt. 6:21, NIV).

> If I gained a world of wealth untold,
> Lands and houses, silver and gold,
> But I didn't know You, Lord,
> Didn't recognize the love into my life You've poured,

In the end what would it profit me
If the cares and toys of this life wouldn't let me see
The special gifts You have in store?
Oh, help me, Lord, to love You more and more.
When attractions of the world are strong,
Remind me of this question:
Is there anything in life
That is worth the slighting of Your precious sacrifice?
Take Your truth and burn it into my soul.
Help me see that You gave everything to make me whole.
That's what Calvary was for.
Oh, help me, Lord, to love You more and more.

You're every breath I take, You're every move I make.
In changing seasons of my life You're still the spring.
With every beat of my heart new life to me You impart.
To put it simply, You're my everything.   DEBBY GRAY WILMOT

JUNE 8

ALONE—NOT LONELY

I will guide thee with mine eye. Ps. 32:8.

"Just give me the six-pack." The clerk looked at the young man with the steel-blue-gray eyes and knew he meant what he said even though he was under 21.

Once outside, Edward opened a can and sipped it. His head was still spinning from the cocaine. Staggering over to the white Ford, he hoped traffic wouldn't be too heavy, because he had to drive all the way through Detroit.

He barely made it onto the freeway. Ten miles passed before he was startled into awareness by almost crashing into a bridge.

The car behind him honked, and he pulled back onto the road. Then a crashing jolt brought his mind to total awareness. He sat in his car surrounded by red, crunched metal. A woman's face appeared, blood dripping. "Have you seen my husband?" she demanded. "Where is he?"

Edward just sat and stared. The woman disappeared. He turned, and terror shot through him. A few feet away lay the body of a middle-aged man. "I've got to get out of here," he mumbled. "I've got to get out of this nightmare." His door wouldn't open, so he slid over to the other side. A young girl's face appeared. "Where's Daddy?" he heard her cry.

As Edward flung open the door he almost bumped into a little boy who stood staring down the road. Following the boy's gaze, he again saw the man's body. He turned, ran up the embankment, and disappeared into the night.

Behind him lay the horrible reality of four lives drastically changed. My three children and I were about to begin a new life, alone. Alone.

I wasn't sure my faith would survive. What helped me was to look back to times when there had been tangible evidence of God's having been with me. The psalmist had said, "I will guide thee with mine eye."

I remembered when soldiers took over the country in which we lived and we had no food. I'd knelt before an empty cupboard and prayed. A knock on the door. Two girls stood there with trays filled with food. God had started those girls on their way before my prayer for help. God would send help again now. He did.

A teacher who was going through a crisis became a friend to talk to. He shared a promise that became special: "His mercies never come to an end; they are new every morning" (Lam. 3:22, 23, NRSV). I had to accept that God allows us to be where we are. If we have a relationship with God, we can accept the promise that He will work whatever happens to our good. He goes with us. "When thou passest through the waters, I will be with thee" (Isa. 43:2).

If you feel as alone as I once did on a freeway in Detroit, if your faith hangs in the balance, look for evidence of God's love in the past. Then share with someone else how His strength helped you, and your faith will grow.   JEANETTE BRYSON

JUNE 9

GOD IS THERE

But all who find safety in you will rejoice; they can always sing for joy. Protect those who love you; because of you they are truly happy. Ps. 5:11, TEV.

Angel, a young person emotionally disturbed because of terrible maltreatment by her father, lives in a psychiatric hospital, suffering each day because of her thoughts. She has learned to hate herself. She breaks mirrors and uses the sharp edge to cut her wrists. Even when all sharp objects are carefully taken away, Angel manages to find something with which to harm herself. When allowed off the ward, she slips plastic ware from the cafeteria in her shirt sleeves to use on herself when she is allowed to shower.

She really wants to like herself. She simply does not know how! Every time she was abused by her father it made her feel that she was not worth anything, so she feels worthless. Her mother, dealing with problems from her own childhood, denies an awareness of the terrible things that happened to Angel. Angel felt she had no ally, no protection.

There is a bright side. Despite all the suffering, Angel has developed some of her many talents. She can sing, she plays several instruments, and she writes poetry. Her music and song are her outlets. When she is playing her recorder and creating beauty for others, she is developing strengths to find beauty in herself. And she is finding some, so there is hope.

Angel also believes in God. Prior to her hospitalization, she regularly attended Sunday school and church. And even now she continues to pray to God for deliverance. She was fortunate, for after years of living in her dysfunctional family, someone came to her rescue. Her Sunday school teacher assisted her by making appropriate referrals. Her parents were required to begin the painful process of psychotherapy.

Angel is not well yet, but she is on the road to recovery. Her music, her poetry, her friendships, and her therapists are helping her. And her trust in God is growing.

If you are experiencing traumas in your life, there is a way out. Request God's guidance as you seek help.   ELIZABETH WATSON

JUNE 10

WHEN YOU'RE DISCOURAGED

Then they cry out to the Lord in their trouble, And He brings them out of their distresses. He calms the storm, So that its waves are still. Then they are glad because they are quiet; So He guides them to their desired haven. Ps. 107:28-30, NKJV.

It was late summer 1984, and I was discouraged. For a year I had been planning to expand my weekly 15-minute radio program to a daily feature, and had spent every penny I had recording 60 sample shows, which was what the radio syndication agency said we had to have before it could start airing the program. And now I had just learned that the agency was no longer interested in syndicating the program!

For the previous two years I had operated this "family" ministry out of my living room. I had no office, no syndication agency, and no money. Feeling sorry for myself that Thursday morning, I sat down at my desk and opened a letter. Out tumbled a check for $25. When I noticed who the donor was, I couldn't believe it—Daryl, a 17-year-old student from Oklahoma Academy who had recently sat through all my camp meeting presentations! Then I read his letter. "Dear Dr. Kuzma: I know how hard it is in self-supporting work since I go to a self-supporting school myself, but just like the cattle on a thousand hills are the Lord's, so is your ministry. Hold on to Psalm 107:28-30."

I turned to the passage and found the promise that even though you are in troubled waters, the Lord will take you out of your distress and into your desired haven. I needed that hope, and began to pray, "Lord, I'm sinking. Please give me that desired haven."

Thursday night I received a call from a woman who had a building I could use as an office. Friday morning Ambassador Advertising Agency called and said that after a late Thursday night meeting it had decided to syndicate my program. Two wonderful miracles! But then I began wondering how I was going to pay for the expenses of a radio program.

Monday morning I received a letter from an unknown bank president in Washington, D.C., dated the Thursday before. "I heard you on a *Voice of Prophecy* program and feel your message for families is vital. If you ever decide to have a daily radio feature, I'd like to help support it."

I called him, and when he heard what I was planning to do, he offered to give $1,000 a month. Exactly the amount needed to cover the expenses!

Many times since then I've gone to bed worrying about finances concerning the Family Matters ministry. And then I remember the letter from Daryl that inspired the faith I needed to hold on to God's promise that He would rescue me from my troubles and bring me to my desired haven. And I have found again and again that God is faithful. — KAY KUZMA

June 11

Lord, Please Pass the Salt

Ye are the salt of the earth. Matt. 5:13.

Try as I might, I have not been able to find one redeeming feature about getting old. However, since I have not figured out how to stop the aging process, I will do the best I can with what I have.

You can imagine that when my doctor told me that I must try to manage my blood pressure problems through diet before trying other measures, I was not happy to hear that I had to give up fat and salt for a while. Giving up the fat did not bother me; but even though I have never used lots of salt, I do like a little because it enhances the flavor of food. In short, this news made me feel that I had been stabbed in a vital spot.

There are several different kinds of salt. There is plain table salt, iodized salt, and rock salt for ice-cream makers, roasting, and using on icy roads. There is kosher salt, and let's not forget Epsom salts. So it seems there is a salt for every occasion. I learned when I visited the Dead Sea that the salt content of the water was very good for skin diseases, but was lethal if you inhaled it while swimming with your face toward the water.

In Colossians 4:6 the apostle Paul says, "Let your speech always be with grace, seasoned with salt, that you may know how you ought to answer each one" (NKJV). Now, here is a kind of salt that I can use and not be afraid of the result. There can be no substitute for this kind of salt, either.

Both Old and New Testament Jews understood the importance of salt. It had been a part of the sacrificial system, and Jesus told His disciples that they were the salt of the earth. They were to flavor the lives of others with the good news of salvation. Then Jesus went on to tell the Jews about what happened to salt that had lost its flavor and become tasteless. Tasteless salt would be discarded and thrown out.

I can ask Jesus every day to help me be the right kind and the right amount of salt in the lives of those with whom I come in contact. I can also ask Jesus to help me avoid rubbing salt in the wounds of those who are hurting.

My daily goal is to help others taste and see that the Lord is good. I hope to recognize the needs of those I meet each day by taking the time to listen carefully. Then I hope to say the appropriate words to comfort, encourage, or strengthen the one to whom I am speaking. So, Lord, please pass me the salt. — SHEILA SANDERS

JUNE 12

UNCOMMON COURAGE

Be on your guard; stand firm in the faith; be [women] of courage. 1 Cor. 16:13, NIV.

What pictures come into your mind when you hear the word "courage"? Gallant knights with gleaming armor galloping full speed toward a formidable foe? A diminutive Dutch lad with his finger pushed deep into the dike? Or maybe you see the colorful form of Pocohontas as she bends over John Smith, defying her own people to save his life.

History books are scattered with stories of brave and courageous people. The Bible is full of stories of courage as well. When I think of courage such names as Esther, Joshua, Elijah, and Abigail leap to my mind. Maybe you know someone personally who epitomizes the word "courage" to you. My own husband risked his life for mine in an almost-fatal canoe accident not long ago. To me that speaks volumes of courage as well as love.

What made these people act as they did? What made them different or set them apart from the rest of the population? History and the Bible records make it easy for us to think that these people were never fearful—that courage was second nature for them. So we feel that courage should be second nature and come naturally to us. But one of the reasons these stories were recorded is that these events were out of the ordinary, not commonplace. All these people were human beings, and human beings have a rather long list of shortcomings and failures to their credit.

If we had the privilege of knowing the thoughts and emotions of some of these courageous people, we might be a bit surprised. I imagine that Esther had some last-minute thoughts about an uninvited audience with the king. Elijah probably had a few jitters about a test of beliefs with 450 knife-carrying leaders from the opposing religion. Abigail may have had a few choice words to say about the good-for-nothing husband she was trying to save. And Joshua may have even felt a little silly dressing up in his armor and marching around Jericho every day for a week (early-morning joggers were unheard-of back then—especially joggers who invite a few thousand of their friends along!).

God didn't use these people because they were perfect. He used them because they were willing and had learned to follow His biddings even though they didn't always understand His ways. When they put themselves in His hands, He supplied the courage.

Courage doesn't mean not being afraid, not ever questioning. Courage doesn't mean a feeling of self-assurance and bravery. Courage means knowing God can take care of things in His way and time and being willing to say yes when He asks us to do something. There may be some things in your life right now that you are dreading to do, or maybe you fear the future and what it will bring. But with God's help you can be a woman of uncommon courage.

JEANNE HARTWELL

June 13

A Wolf in Sheep's Clothing

Surely he shall deliver thee from the snare of the fowler. . . . He shall cover thee with his feathers, and under his wings shalt thou trust. Ps. 91:3, 4.

It wasn't easy working my way through college. As a full-time student it was necessary to work nights, but I was determined to get my degree. The hours between 10:00 p.m. and 6:00 a.m. were especially difficult when I had 8:00 classes.

During those years the bus was my only means of transportation. One night I got off the Bridge 60 bus about 9:30 and started the three-block walk to the John Hancock Building. A man got off the bus at the same time. After a casual glance at this well-dressed man with briefcase in hand, I felt less apprehensive. He remained a short distance behind me. The walk took several minutes. As I approached the descending driveway to the underground garage, there was suddenly the sound of someone running at full speed. I turned around. It was the man with the briefcase, and I was his target. It was impossible for me to build up enough speed to outrun him, but I had to try. Fear gripped me as I ran with all my might. Only God could deliver me now. As the perpetrator was bearing down on me, a car from the underground garage came up the driveway with headlights in high beam. The driver could see I was in trouble. He paused long enough for me to get away. When I did get inside the building I nearly collapsed.

Our omniscient heavenly Father knew my plight and had made provision for the emergency. Praise God for divine intervention! He had the driver of that car in the right place at exactly the right time, perhaps to save my life.

Thank God for the promise of Psalm 91:15: "When they call to me, I will answer them; I will be with them in trouble; I will rescue them and honor them" (NRSV). — LOIS MAGEE

June 14

TOO MANY FLOWERS

And the peace of God, which surpasses all understanding, will guard your hearts and minds through Christ Jesus. Phil. 4:7, NKJV.

I'm just browsing at the flower shop, looking at the plants, admiring, checking the prices. Anything marked down? Anything cheap? I've been here a long time searching, comparing. I want to buy some rose-pink impatiens to fill the bare spaces in my plant pots, but I know I don't really need any more plants; I just bought two hanging plants the week before.

My garden is blooming with flowers—the beds, patio planters, balcony planters, and hanging plants—they're all so beautiful, the product of many purchases and long hours of planting, arranging creatively, watering. For my small budget I've already spent too much.

Flowers. They stand there, suspended, adding brightness, color, variety, beauty, joy, satisfaction, restfulness, life—in contrast to my anxiety, discouragement, tears. Hands in the dirt digging, planting, transplanting, pruning, arranging, creating, watering, admiring, soothing my restlessness. It gives me peace, occupies my thoughts.

Browalia—three hanging pots not too healthy-looking—on sale, $9.99, $9.99, $5.99. Even the $5.99 one is still too much when I don't really need it. But I keep looking, holding them up, turning them around. Observing my interest, the owner says, "I'll give them to you for $3.99 each." I can't resist! I buy one! Excited at my new purchase, I quickly take it home.

I put the browalia with its little purple flowers out on the balcony; I set it nicely on an old chair in the corner. My other plants with their purple flowers are hanging attractively from a coat tree;

the planters are alive with color—yellow pansies, pink and purple petunias, red snapdragons, purple browalia, white and lilac lobelia. The atmosphere is beautiful up here on the balcony, and now this, my new bushy browalia hanging plant! Too many flowers—I know I don't need it.

I feel afraid, worried about myself. *Why did I buy it? Why do I keep buying? Is something wrong?* I sleep restlessly that night. I feel numb these days; I don't get at the many tasks I need to accomplish. I go out and buy. Not big things, not a lot of money—but I buy. I've tried to be strong through the rough times, to be strong for everyone.

My husband, observing my new purchase, voices my thoughts. "You're buying too many plants," he says.

"I know," I respond.

Lord, I'm searching for something—You, Lord; I need time with You. You are my strength; You are my peace. I fall to my knees and pour my heart out to the Lord, giving Him all my cares. He has promised: "Peace I leave with you, my peace I give unto you: not as the world giveth, give I unto you. Let not your heart be troubled, neither let it be afraid" (John 14:27). *Thank You, Lord, for Your promise, Your strength, Your peace.*

Luan Cadogan

June 15

A Shepherd in the Storm

He gently leads those that have young. Isa. 40:11, NIV.

I think we ought to turn back now," I said. "It sounds as if a storm is coming." It was lovely up in the mountains. We had come up the gentle way, for the children's sake, riding the ski lift, swinging up over the Alpine meadows, accompanied by the soft music of distant cow bells. It had been idyllic.

The children were happy to go back; they were young, and tiring of the walk. As we rounded the last bend, my heart sank with a sickening realization. The ski lift had closed for the day. We were stranded high in the Alps with no food, no raincoats, three small children, and an approaching storm.

There was a path down to the parking lot, but I had no idea how far it would be. We knew we had to get back down, but the children were already tired. Five minutes later the storm broke.

We found a locked hut and huddled against its walls, children screaming, rain pelting through our summer clothing, thunder crashing, and lightning ripping the air only feet away. It was a living nightmare. In minutes we were drenched, and then the hail came.

Baby Joel had sat in his backpack, smiling at the rain pouring over his face, but he began yelling as the hail dashed against his bare and hairless head. The ice chilled me to the bone as I tried to protect the terrified children. For a moment I had visions of us being stranded there all night—hypothermia, pneumonia, and absolute misery.

A text came into my mind: "He gently leads those that have young."

"Lord," I prayed, "we need some gentle leading now. Please help us! The children are tired and cold, scared and hungry, wet and miserable, and so am I. Please help the storm to stop. PS: Please make it stop within the next five minutes! Amen."

We began to sing to try to help ourselves feel more cheerful and confident. Suddenly we realized the storm had stopped. We yelled delightedly, and headed back to the path, which was now a torrent of water flooding down the mountainside. We couldn't walk on it, so we walked through deep fields of slithery hailstones, our feet numb with cold.

The rain held off as we picked our way slowly back to the main road and reached a small bus shelter. Bernie ran to fetch the car. We had been drenched in ice-cold water for more than an hour, but none of us got sick!

God "gently leads those that have young." He knows we are more vulnerable when we are caring for His little lambs. We may not be able to travel as far, as fast, or over such difficult terrain as before. So He leads us tenderly, softly, caring about our struggles and our needs, listening to our pleas for help, and answering our every call.

KAREN HOLFORD

JUNE 16

TAKE TIME

There is nothing better for a [woman], than that [she] should eat and drink, and that [she] should make [her] soul enjoy good in [her] labour. This also I saw, that it was from the hand of God. Eccl. 2:24.

"Look how late it is!" he calls after a glimpse at his watch. He seizes his teacup, but the tea is too hot, so he bites his sandwich twice and runs out to get his coat. "'Bye, darling . . ." A tiny smile, a hasty hug, and out he goes.

"I'm sorry, but I'm in a hurry," apologizes the lady to her neighbor, who called and wanted to chat for a while.

And the first grader tells his teacher: "My mother doesn't have time to study maths with me."

Is there anybody who has time today? Why? Each of us has the same amount of time: 24 hours a day. The old grandfather driving his wheelchair, the toddler in mom's kitchen, the manager of a worldwide association, and the beggar sleeping beneath the bridge have one thing in common: each day they have a whole day of lifetime.

How do we use this one day? Do we overload it with stress and activities? Or do we idle around till the sun goes down? Really, we should have plenty of spare time, because we have so many machines and technical things to help us work.

Cars, trains, and planes save precious time for us—imagine if you had to walk by foot, as our ancestors did! But there is no time left anyway, for we tend to invest our spare time in other undertakings.

It does not suffice; it is like a short blanket—if you pull it up to warm your arms and chest, your feet get cold. We press the hours, as if we had to squeeze the last drop of juice out of a tiny lemon. We want to win the world, but what do we lose? Maybe health, maybe happy relationships, maybe peace of mind. Those who try to exhaust the seconds will end up exhausted.

"For what hath [woman] of all [her] labour and of the vexation of [her] heart, wherein [she] hath laboured under the sun? For all [her] days are sorrows, and [her] travail grief; yea, [her] heart taketh not rest in the night. This is also vanity. There is nothing better for a [woman], than that [she] should eat and drink, and that [she] should make [her] soul enjoy good in [her] labour. This also I saw, that it was from the hand of God" (Eccl. 2:22-24). Solomon, the ancient philosopher, emphasized one point: Nobody can enjoy life's gifts without God. All our running around will come out as vanity. So why not allow yourself the luxury of a little pause? There are lots of daisies in your life meadow; learn to love them before you have to push them!

SYLVIA RENZ

JUNE 17

JESUS IS HERE!

Let the little children come to me, and do not hinder them, for the kingdom of God belongs to such as these. Mark 10:14, NIV.

Late one afternoon as I busily dusted the furniture in the living room the little girl I was baby-sitting came bouncing into the room and asked, in typical 2-year-old fashion, "What are you doing?" I stopped my work, took Megan on my lap, and tried to explain that the next day would be the Sabbath and that I was trying to make the house look nice because Jesus was our guest on the Sabbath day.

She nodded as if she understood perfectly, and then asked if she could help. I gave her a soft, clean cloth and showed her how to dust the chair legs very carefully. She smiled and continued with her work until the doorbell rang.

With a look of delight spreading across her face, Megan dropped her dustcloth and raced to the door. Dancing around on her tiptoes, she announced excitedly, "Jesus is here! Jesus is here!" When I opened the door and the only person standing there was Megan's mother, I had some explaining to do!

Later, as I reflected on the day's events, I couldn't help wondering what it would actually be like to entertain the Master. What would I do if He were *really* coming to my home? When He arrived, what would I say to Him? What would He say to me?

Perhaps He would remind me of His words in John 14:2, 3: "In my Father's house are many rooms; if it were not so, I would have told you. I am going there to prepare a place for you. And if I go and prepare a place for you, I will come back and take you to be with me that you also may be where I am" (NIV).

To be with Jesus—that's what I want. Today and every day!

BRENDA DICKERSON

JUNE 18

PAIN AND GOD'S GRACE

But he said to me, "My grace is sufficient for you, for my power is made perfect in weakness." 2 Cor. 12:9, RSV.

I've been singing today of my Saviour;
I love Him with all of my heart.
There seems no relief from the pain and the suffering,
But still there's a song in my heart.

Why, God, should there be so much suffering?
Why, Lord, should there be so much pain?
There's no escape from it, except by Thy grace.
When sleep comes in exhaustion,
In Thine arms of love I rest only briefly,
And awaken again and again.

I'm sure it is Satan's intention
To discourage and misdirect me.
By Thy grace I will not surrender
To the evil one's old, old game.
So hold me, dear Saviour, close to Thee.
Let my head on Thy bosom rest.
Hold me close to Thy heart of compassion;
Do not let me fail this hard test.

Thou hast promised us strength for the battle.
In Thee do I trust for the test.
When Thou comest in glory to take us home,
May the records show I loved Thee best.

I will not surrender to darkness,
But will, by Thy grace, hold on tight.
And I trust Thee to lead me forever
Into the land that is bright.

There's no pain in the beautiful land.
No tears to be shed in that place.
Because here Jesus brings comfort and solace;
There we will be—saved by His grace.

Whatever pain and suffering you or your loved ones may be going through, just remember that God had to allow His own Son, Jesus, to go through pain and suffering because of sin too. He does not cause or want us to suffer. Suffering is caused by Satan and sin. Someday soon Jesus will come and rescue us from this world under Satan's siege.

Hang on to Jesus, and He'll see you through.

DOROTHY MONTGOMERY

June 19

He Touched Me

And He said unto her, "Daughter, be of good cheer; your faith has made you well. Go in peace." Luke 8:48, NKJV.

I had been diagnosed with cancer of the larynx. It was the night before surgery, and visiting hours were over. One of the nurses had just asked me if I were certain I wanted to go through with this surgery. I didn't think I had a choice, for the tumor in my throat was golf-ball size and was slowly choking me.

The lady in the next bed to me had just received the good news that her breast biopsy was negative, and she had settled herself in for an evening of thrills with a murder mystery. It was obvious she didn't want to chat, and I felt alone and lonely. For comfort I decided to read the book of Luke, thinking that since Luke was a doctor, maybe I might find something special there—something just for me.

As I opened my Bible, these words seemed to sing out from the page: "Daughter [that was me!], be of good cheer; your faith has made you well. Go in peace." Jesus' tender words to this woman were a special promise to me as well.

The next morning when my husband arrived just before they took me into the operating room, I showed him my text. It was with peace that I went to surgery.

Later as I lay in the intensive-care unit—unable to talk, black stitches across my throat running from ear to ear, a trachea for breathing, a tube for feeding—my husband knew by the look in my eyes that I wanted to ask him something. He put a small pad of paper down by my hand; all I could manage was a crooked C, but he knew what I was asking. "Yes," he said, "they got it all."

Jesus had touched me and made me well.   PEGGY TOMPKINS

June 20

A Matter of Priorities

That you may become blameless and pure, children of God without fault in a crooked and depraved generation, in which you shine like stars in the universe as you hold out the word of life. Phil. 2:15, 16, NIV.

Our new car came with a little gizmo on the key ring that allows me to press a button and unlock the car door while several feet away. I'd never missed this particular "little wonder," mainly because I didn't know it existed.

But now this little gizmo is an integral part of my life. I find myself feeling irritated and impatient when I have to use the key to open our other car.

I thought of this recently when we were visiting a provincial city in Russia and becoming acquainted with our precious believers. In a superpower nation that has put people in space, why is it so difficult to get a telephone? In a country with enough modern weapons to wipe out the world, clothes are still washed in bathtubs, and there are long food lines.

But I detected no resentment and no complaining. What they had never had was not a big item to them. What *was* a big item in their lives was their religious faith. Many had been persecuted for that faith, some family members killed, nearly all denied higher education. Both men and women had accepted more menial work in order to have Sabbaths free.

Yet these people felt highly privileged. The disillusionment and despair of their atheistic compatriots did not touch them. While others chain-smoked through their days and drowned themselves in vodka at night, the Christians were busy building new churches for God.

I was greatly moved by their simple lives, unshakable faith, and great joy in their Lord. These people have their priorities straight.

As I go through my days pressing buttons—not just to open car doors, but to wash clothes, phone, get the news, clean dishes, cook food—am I in danger of being distracted by my "blessings"? Am I fervently building up *my* church, or am I just hoping to get around to it someday?

Aileen Ludington

June 21

Role Model

See how very much our heavenly Father loves us, for he allows us to be called his children—think of it—and we really are! . . . And we can't even imagine what it is going to be like later on. But we do know this, that when he comes we will be like him, as a result of seeing him as he really is. 1 John 3:1, 2, TLB.

In one of 1984's newspapers amid all the reports of ugliness, greed, disaster, and dissoluteness, a gem stood out—a centenary in commemoration of Eleanor Roosevelt. Her past history is remarkable: Rejected by her mother, an unstable father, orphaned at age 9, housewife until nearly 40, a marriage that never fully recovered from her husband's affair with Lucy Mercer, a life overshadowed by the Depression and World War II. Yet her greatness came not from seeing herself with her limitations, but from transcending that self.

She became a role model of what a woman could do in public life. She transformed the job of first lady, and became an advocate taking up one beleaguered group after another. She had a sense of character that inspired.

In one incident in 1939 she placed her chair between Black and White sections of a segregated Southern meeting. Adlai Stevenson asked, "What other single human being has touched and transformed the existence of so many? She walked in the slums . . . of the world, not on a tour of inspection . . . but as one who could not feel contentment when others were hungry."

Eleanor Roosevelt transcended her unfortunate parentage with a vision of a world of loving potential, and the courage and discipline to make it happen.

We each struggle with our own inadequacies—as friends, wives, career women, as loving people with solid self-worth. We find it impossible to see ourselves as all that we would like to be. Christ meant to free us from humdrum ruts in our lives and make all the beauty of the universe ours. Our Creator sees our potential as higher than the highest human thought. We are daughters of royalty. We role-model after God, our heavenly parent.

As we appreciate God more and more as we get acquainted, we become more and more like God. We transcend our earthly role models, faulty parenting is healed, and we make the world a better place. We cannot even imagine how much we will transcend ourselves when we no longer see God from a distance, but in person. But we know we're going to love the experience!

SHARI CHAMBERLAIN

JUNE 22

HALF-PINT HOSANNAS

But when the chief priests and the teachers of the law saw the wonderful things he did and the children shouting in the temple area, "Hosanna to the Son of David," they were indignant. "Do you hear what these children are saying?" they asked him. "Yes," replied Jesus, "have you never read, 'From the lips of children and infants you have ordained praise'?" Matt. 21:15, 16, NIV.

We were singing the closing hymn for church one day with a certain lackluster when my ears picked up a voice loudly off-key. Others had raised their eyebrows and were casting sidelong glances at the musical offender.

My husband spotted him before I did and nudged me. A sturdy little boy, maybe 3 years old, with chubby hands, had his generous hymnal propped up on the pew ahead of him. In blaring dissonance he was delivering his praise, in his own words, to his own tune.

More and more heads turned his way. He looked up, and I saw his eyes widen with concern because he was being watched. We ducked back into our songbooks, and he resumed his loud and unaffected worship.

What I liked almost as much as the off-key singer was his mother's attitude. Not once did she lean over and try to tone down the cacophony. Although she was aware of people staring, she didn't shush him for fear of embarrassment, but solemnly sang out of her own songbook. Her unconcern affirmed his right to worship.

There was a visible difference in our congregation as amusement changed to admiration. Heads lifted, and voices blended in rich harmony and heartfelt praise swelled and enfolded that priceless noise of innocence.

I thought about how we spend our time trying to persuade others that we have grown beyond the simple and uncomplicated. Yet Jesus gave us an example of how different His kingdom is. He stared down the smooth-talking gatekeepers of the Temple, and ousted their lowing and bleating merchandise. Then He gathered a group of little children that day, put babies on His lap, accepted their watery kisses, and taught them to sing hosannas. Off to one side lay a discarded pile of crutches, dirty bandages, and lumpy mats. All around the marbled court now cleansed of the haggling and cow manure, the pure, simple lisps of praise ascended because the children were rejoicing in their new Friend Jesus.

Our church service was a memorable one because our modern-day little praise singer was not afraid to belt out his joyous worship. With a mature flourish he closed his hymnal and bowed his head. Hovering close by must have been a guardian angel cherishing a touch of holy pride. His young charge had taught us by contrast that "God has deliberately chosen to use ideas the world considers foolish and of little worth in order to shame those people considered by the world as wise and great" (1 Cor. 1:27, TLB).

MARILYN APPLEGATE

JUNE 23

GOOD AND FAITHFUL SERVANTS

Well done, thou good and faithful servant: thou hast been faithful over a few things, I will make thee ruler over many things: enter thou into the joy of thy lord. Matt. 25:21.

We awakened early to see the sun streaming through our bedroom window. What a glorious day to be out in the bush surrounded by nature!

After breakfast we called some friends. "How would you like to join us for a day out with a picnic lunch beside the river?" An hour later we were on our way, up through forested trails lined with palms and green ferns.

We had no definite destination in mind when we set out except to reach the river at some point for lunch, but as we traveled a plan formed. About 10 years earlier my husband had purchased 1,000 acres of timbered land near the river and had divided it into blocks for sale. We had not seen the area for many years. We wondered if the acreages had been cleared, built on, or what.

Driving along with the sun and wind on us, we took note of the blocks of land. Several had partly built sheds or houses. One had been cleared and dozens of tropical fruit trees had been planted.

Another had been cleared and a few banana trees planted. Some were still heavily timbered with tall, straight trees.

But it appeared that one family had made maximum use of their land. We stopped to talk with them. First they had selectively logged the area, then built a workshop and house. They had installed solar power for heating and electricity. Fruit trees had been planted, and an organic garden flourished with rows of peas, lettuce, cabbage, and spinach. All looked neat and productive.

One couldn't help comparing this neat, well-ordered area with some of the other blocks. It made me think of the stewards in the Bible story in Matthew 25. They all had an opportunity to increase their assets, but all did not invest wisely. Here in this subdivision all the owners had the same size block of land and all had equal potential, but only one had taken maximum advantage of the resources available. Some had done a certain amount of improvement, but others had left untidy sheds, neglected gates, and fences overgrown with weeds. What a contrast to the well-ordered garden and neat home of the owner we visited!

So it is with life. If we are good stewards, we must make the best of our opportunities and talents so that one day we will hear that "well done, thou good and faithful servant: thou hast been faithful over a few things, I will make thee ruler over many things: enter thou into the joy of thy lord." ALMA ATCHESON

JUNE 24

THE LESSON FROM THE BUTTERFLIES

A wise woman builds her house, while a foolish woman tears hers down by her own efforts. Prov. 14:1, TLB.

I enjoy watching the beautiful and elegant butterflies, and sometimes I connect the various phases of their lives with the different stages of the life of a Christian woman who has a family.

Butterflies are hatched from tiny eggs as small voracious creatures that eat much, which results in rapid growth into strong caterpillars. At the end of the growth period they go in search of an adequate place for the metamorphosis.

During the cocoon stage the slow process of metamorphosis takes place, and when the days are finished, the beautiful and colorful butterfly emerges and begins its flight.

I like to compare the phase of childhood and youth with the period of the growing caterpillar in the stages of the butterfly. This is the time for growth—physical, intellectual, and moral preparation.

The cocoon, I think, we can compare to a married woman with children. In that period the woman is linked to the home, fulfilling God's purpose in modeling, shaping, and carving the character of the defenseless youngsters or the capricious and insecure adolescents.

An author on the Christian family has written that "the mother is God's agent to Christianize her family" (*The Adventist Home*, p. 235). She notes that "especially does responsibility rest upon the mother. She, by whose lifeblood the child is nourished and its physical frame built up, imparts to it also mental and spiritual influences that tend to the shaping of mind and character" (*ibid.*, p. 242).

The butterfly, flying gracefully, helping to set in motion the process of pollination of flowers, reminds me of a mature woman who has already fulfilled her duties as mother and now goes about showing the world the beautiful colors of her profession, which was latent during the educating years. With experience and power she can now share her wise counsel.

Butterflies fulfill faithfully the purposes of God in the various phases of life. Women have different phases in life, and every one is of great value to God.

Am I wise or foolish?

May God give me assistance to be wise.

MIRIAM BERG

JUNE 25

HIS PERFECT STRENGTH

And He said unto me, "My grace is sufficient for you, for My strength is made perfect in weakness." 2 Cor. 12:9, NKJV.

Life broke my heart
And wrecked my path,
With rocks and pitfalls, too.
I sat and wept and then I asked,
"Whatever shall I do?"
A gentle whisper deep within
I had to strain to hear
Said, "Hold My hand and take a step
And don't give way to fear."

And so I stood
And, reaching out,
I felt His presence strong;
Tentatively, a step I took—
The pathway seemed so long.
The boulders huge and pitfalls deep
Were agony supreme,
But then I heard His voice again,
"Don't be afraid to lean."

I leaned on Him,
My precious Lord,
And felt my feet grow light,
And sunshine seemed to fill the sky
Where once it had been night.
My weakness is His perfect strength,
His eyes the way will guide,
And though the path be rough at times,
We'll walk it—side by side.

ALICE COVEY

JUNE 26

GOD'S TIMETABLE

He who began a good work in you will carry it on to completion until the day of Christ Jesus. Phil. 1:6, NIV.

Sitting in the darkened auditorium, I slowly relaxed and unwound from the day's events. The music soothed my spirit as I recounted all that God had done that day. My husband had had an appointment with the surgeon. His arms were healing. The accident had been three months previous, and Tim had regained most of the use of his hands and wrists. But God had not done all that I had hoped for. I was sure He was going to work out something new with Tim's job. But He had not. I was also sure that when we left the doctor's office that morning, Tim would be released to go back to work.

Our pastor and his wife knew my concerns regarding the visit and had called us that morning to pray with us before we left. And God had shown me that He was still in control. When we left the doctor's office, Tim was not sent back to work and would not be for three more months.

Now we sat in the auditorium listening to one of my favorite Christian singers. I smiled as I thought of how hard I had tried to get tickets to this concert. This night's performance had been sold out. Another concert had been scheduled for the next night. I had tried to get tickets, but everywhere I went they were sold out. I had given up.

Then our neighbors called Tim while I was out and asked if we would like two tickets. They were a busy pastor's family that we had rarely seen or spoken to in all the years we had lived there. The tickets had been a gift from a source I would never have expected.

The music quieted and brought me back to the present from the thoughts that had crept in. The quiet song began, "He who began a good work in you, He who began a good work in you, will be faithful to complete it; He'll be faithful to complete it; He who started the work will be faithful to complete it in you . . ."

I heard no more. Tears filled my eyes as I realized that God was speaking directly to my heart. He had placed me at this moment in time to remind me that He was in control. He was not finished with us yet, but He promised to finish the work He had started in our lives. He is a faithful God.

All these years later I can still remember that night, sitting in the quiet darkness of the auditorium, on the end of the back row, hearing God speaking to my heart, to the concerns I had.

The memory still brings tears to my eyes and reminds me that He *will* complete the good work He has begun in my life.

TAMYRA HORST

JUNE 27

WAITING

God made the . . . animals according to their kinds. . . . And God saw that it was good. Gen. 1:25, NIV.

I walked to our little country post office this morning. There was just time to mail my letters before my bus arrived.

Hiking back from the post office toward the bus stop, I noticed a beautiful German shepherd standing stock still by the roadside. As I neared him, he seemed frozen to the spot, his head cocked to one side. As I came alongside him, I wondered if he were ill. "Is something the matter, doggy?" I sympathized softly.

With that he began to walk slowly along with me toward the bus stop. I checked my watch—still five minutes until the bus was due. I decided to get a bit more exercise by boarding the bus at the next stop down the road. The dog was not interested in proceeding further.

After a bit I glanced back and saw that the bus was pulling to a stop where I had left the German shepherd. I knew the driver would not leave that station for several minutes, so I hurried on to the next stop.

Arriving there, I looked back up the road toward the bus. To my surprise, the driver was outside throwing a stick, the shepherd chasing and retrieving it. The dog even caught the stick in midair! Over and over the game went on. It was hard to tell who enjoyed it most—the dog, the driver, or the spectators.

Boarding the bus a minute later, I remarked to the driver, "I enjoyed your dog show!"

The driver grinned. "That fellow waits for me there every morning. I don't know who his owner is, but he's a faithful friend," he said.

Now the dog's peculiar behavior became apparent. He had been listening for the bus. He'd been waiting for his friend.

I also await the coming of my Friend. May I be as earnestly attentive to be ready as was that German shepherd.

"Even so, come, Lord Jesus" (Rev. 22:20).   ROBERTA SHARLEY

JUNE 28

I TOUCHED THE HEM OF HIS CLOAK

Yea, though I walk through the valley of the shadow of death, I will fear no evil: for thou art with me. Ps. 23:4.

Never in all my life did I think that I would pass through the valley of the shadow of death, and that the words of my favorite psalm would fit so well those moments of suffering.

Death always seems distant while we are alive.

In 1990 I had surgery, apparently minor, to take out my appendix. Everything went well during the operation, but because the appendix had been hot and infected, the incision broke open one week later.

Precautions were taken for the cut to heal properly, but all in vain. Twenty days later the picture changed completely. A fever took hold of me. Nothing would bring the fever down.

On the day that this happened, my husband was traveling. He was contacted and came at once.

When he arrived at the hospital, he found me very ill. He went to talk to the doctor. The physician informed him that I had little chance to live in view of the generalized infection. He was desolate, not knowing what to do. With much anguish in his heart he went to a dark corner of the hospital and prayed to God, asking that my life be traded for his.

On my deathbed that very night I could sense that in the valley of the shadow of death Jesus, the Good Shepherd, was by my side. I could see only His clothes, and in that instant I asked Him to let me touch Him and I would be healed.

I felt the soft touch of His garment.

Peace and a feeling of relief took hold of my heart. With a tender voice He said to me, "You will not die, dear. I love you very much."

The next morning I felt completely well. The doctor reexamined me, and the miracle was verified. The medical team couldn't believe what they were seeing.

God provided the way for me to be totally cured.

I don't know if I was dreaming, but it seemed very real to me, and tears still run down my face when I remember that I touched the cloak of my beloved Shepherd.

Today, looking back, I feel that God loves me in a very special way, permitting me to live in order to share His love with my family, my friends, and my acquaintances. — MARILISA FOFFA STINA

JUNE 29

WAITING FOR THE LORD

You must understand that in the last days scoffers will come, scoffing and following their own evil desires. They will say, "Where is this 'coming' he promised? Ever since our fathers died, everything goes on as it has since the beginning of creation." 2 Peter 3:3, 4, NIV.

My husband and I were preparing to travel from Bangalore, in southern India, to Jullundur, in the north, to conduct some church meetings. But when we arrived at the railroad station to begin our trip we were told that the trains to Jullundur had been canceled because of floods. We could go back home or travel to Bombay and try from there.

After prayer for God's direction, we decided to try Bombay.

However, on arriving at the stop after Bombay, we found that there was only one train going to Jullundur and that tickets would be issued only an hour before the departure. I waited on the platform with our luggage while my husband stood in the long line for nearly five hours for tickets. Although we were without food or water, we were most concerned about getting the tickets.

We got the tickets, but the wait did not end there. We went to another platform for the Jullundur train, only to find hundreds of passengers waiting for the same train and more people arriving all the time. The only place we had to sit was on our luggage.

Then they announced that the train would be an hour late. We waited. Another delay. We waited.

It was while we were waiting, uncomfortable and weary, that I thought about the second coming of Jesus. That can be difficult and unpleasant too. It brings anxiety, tension, irritation, and disappointment. But Jesus has promised, "Behold, I come quickly" (Rev. 22:7). From our infancy we have heard our parents, teachers, and preachers say, "Jesus is coming soon." But the question arises, "How soon?" Often when troubles, perplexities, sickness, natural calamities, and death become unbearable we cry out, "How long, Lord, how long?"

Our train did arrive nearly three hours later. The moment we heard the train, we were ready to board. As we go on our heavenly journey, may we not become discouraged and go back. Instead, "let us run with patience the race that is set before us, looking unto Jesus the author and finisher of our faith" (Heb. 12:1, 2).

HEPZIBAH G. KORE

JUNE 30

THE RIPPLE

For if they fall, one will lift up the other; but woe to one who is alone and falls and does not have another to help. Eccl. 4:10, NRSV.

The crowd in the cafeteria had thinned out. A few mothers with small children were still finishing up their evening meal, and a few small clusters of people chatted as they made their way to the workers' meeting in the girls' dormitory chapel.

We were at camp pitch on the campus of Bass Memorial Academy. My husband was always part of the crew to help set up for camp meeting. I loved going to camp pitch and having the week away from the kitchen and housework, renewing friendships, and making new ones with other ministers' wives before the camp meeting with its busy schedule began.

"What? You don't *really* want to take my kids for a day! You must be out of your mind! Why would you want to do that? Are you *sure*?"

My dear friend Maxine Center, the conference treasurer's wife, had come over to our table in the academy cafeteria and made an offer I had never had before. I was speechless—in total shock and disbelief! No one had *ever* offered to give me a day off from my four sons and one foster son before. I didn't know how to handle it!

"You need a break, and my daughter and I have discussed it and decided to give you a whole day off. We'll come to your room right after breakfast tomorrow and get the boys and their things. You spend the day doing whatever you want."

After recovering from my shock, I went to our room in the boys' dormitory and organized the clothes, toys, diapers, and bottles for the next day. The boys ranged in age from 7 years to 9 months old, so I made a list of feeding and nap schedules for the younger ones. My thoughts were racing. *What will I do with myself? Will the boys behave? Will they miss me? How will they manage without Mama? How will Maxine manage?*

The next morning Maxine took the boys, who acted as though it was the adventure of a lifetime. I felt alone, abandoned. They hadn't even cried! I went walking, worried about the kids, felt guilty, read for a while, took a nap, sewed, skipped some smooth stones into a puddle, and spent some time reflecting on the ripple in the puddle. The action of one small, insignificant stone reached out to the very ends of the puddle. Every drop of water was affected. We can have a similar effect upon the lives of every person we come in contact with if we just reach out a helping hand and encouragement.

I'll never forget what Maxine did for me that day. Through the years I've looked for other mothers who need a break, and I try to encourage them. Sometimes I've offered to take their children for a day or a weekend so they can get away alone or with their husbands. Reach out today and make a ripple!
CELIA CRUZ

July 1

It Was Good

In the beginning God created the heavens and the earth. . . . God saw that all that he had made, and it was very good. Gen. 1:1-31, NIV.

Today in America quiltmaking has become a refined work of art. My local fabric shop is filled with beautiful shades of calico prints. Nearby templates, cutters, and racks of aids for perfect measure stand ready for an excited quilter to purchase and use. Rolls of washable batting are available in precut packages or on bulk spindles. Pattern books abound.

The early mothers of America did not have such ready conveniences. Often their quilts were pieced from scraps of fabric; perhaps even the shirttail of a worn garment or other bits they collected. Work space was limited, and each piece was carefully stitched by hand. Even so, these frontier women had a way of bringing beauty into their creations. Patterns were designed and shared. Color was used to every advantage, and quilting parties provided friendship and socialization.

Whether the quilter is a modern person enjoying the advantage of today's technologies or was an early frontier settler, I have a feeling that the joy in the finished product, the satisfaction of creating something beautiful, has not changed.

There is something rewarding in viewing a finished project into which one has invested time, energy, and yes, self. As one craftswoman said, "I just fall in love with each project so that when I finish I have to leave it out where I can enjoy looking at it for a while."

Is it possible that in using our creative abilities with whatever gifts God has given, we might, in an infinitesimal way, understand Him just a little more completely? How must He have felt when He finished creating this world from chaos, stood back, surveyed the beauty, and declared, "It is good"? He loves us.

Beulah Fern Stevens

July 2

The Miracle of Forgiveness

Forgive us our debts, as we forgive our debtors. Matt. 6:12.

It was a beautiful July day. We had just returned from a four-day Radke family reunion at the Oregon coast and were looking forward to having all the family members who were staying in the Portland area at our home for dinner the next day.

My cousin and her husband from Saskatchewan were staying over with us, and she had decided she would make her mother's spectacular doughnuts for Sabbath dessert. While she was getting the doughnuts ready to fry, I took a quick trip to a local raspberry patch for some fresh berries. Then I continued on to the grocery store to make sure we had plenty of other goodies for the weekend, since my daughter and her three sons were also staying with us.

My stop at the grocery store took longer than I intended, but I hurried home to get the final preparations made. When I turned the corner that led to the hill on which our home stood, I saw a great pillar of black smoke rising into the air, and immediately I knew our home was on fire.

When I approached the road to go up our hill, it was blocked, but I convinced the sheriff I needed to go to my family, and he let me through. Never will I forget the look of devastation on my cousin's face as I walked into the driveway. She threw her arms around me and sobbed, and told me how sorry she was. The oil she was going to fry the doughnuts in had ignited while she was out of the room. I knew there was absolutely nothing I could do about the house. It was gone; all the mementos and keepsakes of 40 years of marriage had been destroyed.

At that very moment the Lord gave me the greatest gift He could ever give: He showed me that people are more important than things. No one had died in the fire, but someone's heart was broken because she didn't mean to do it—it was totally an accident, something I might have done myself. He filled my heart with forgiveness and love and compassion even before I asked Him to, and today after many other miracles connected with the fire, I thank Him most of all for the miracle of forgiveness, and that my cousin and I are even closer than we were before.

Anna May Radke Waters

JULY 3

THINKING CRITICALLY

Only a simpleton believes what [she] is told! A prudent [woman] checks to see where [she] is going. Prov. 14:15, TLB.

Recently I took a class titled "Critical Thinking." The first day the professor walked into class and told us that this was not a critical thinking class but a class in thinking critically. *Oh, great,* I thought, *now I'm in for some modern philosophical babbling!* I went home after class and thought a lot about the result of reversing those words.

I am already a first-class critical thinker—critical of the preacher's sermon, the actions of a fellow church member. You can imagine how critical I can be about my husband's and children's actions. I use critical thinking even on myself.

But until I got involved in this class, I was not thinking critically. At last I'm catching on. I must contemplate both sides of an issue before I can come to an intelligent decision. The pastor can come up with some real "meat to chew on" if I just give some thought to what he is saying. And before I write off the church member who grates on my nerves because she's so set in her ways, I need to take a look at her side of the issue. My husband and children also have points of view that need to be considered before I fly off the handle.

Even politics and current world events must be examined from all angles. It is imperative that I train myself to think critically. The day is coming when I will need to support my beliefs in a factual manner that cannot be refuted. The claims of the opponent need to be studied carefully in order to present my case properly.

My walk with God has even taken a new dimension. I'm much slower in reading through a scripture during my devotional time. The passage often says more than what's written there. God speaks through so many avenues that unless I take the time to think critically about both sides of what's happening, I sometimes miss the point of what's being said.

Try thinking critically just once, and you too will be hooked. Instead of critically thinking about the next person or problem you face, think critically about it. Dissect the fine points and contemplate them. Think about how they affect you from one side and then from the other. God is the master of thinking critically.

SUSAN CLARK

JULY 4

GOD'S MONUMENTS

Come unto me, all ye that labour and are heavy laden, and I will give you rest. Matt. 11:28.

When my husband and I worked in the New York City area, we often took guests to visit some of Manhattan's landmarks. From the highest point of the Empire State Building one can view the mighty ships anchored in the harbor far below, the United Nations building, St. Patrick's Cathedral, Times Square, Central Park, and robotlike pedestrians marching briskly along streets jammed with cars and yellow cabs. In the distance is the famous Statue of Liberty—symbol of freedom.

But because this is no ordinary landmark, we often want a closer view, so we join the traffic, and turn down Fifth Avenue toward Washington Square and the Arch, where the rich and poor live side by side; past Wall Street and the Stock Exchange; the Bowery, whose song has made it famous, and Canal Street, where filth can be felt. We love our nation for its principles and its beauty, but this is not a spot of which we can be proud. Beggars wait at stoplights to wipe our windshields with rags from the streets. We pass broken and boarded windows, buildings hidden under accumulated soot; small businesses where merchants swing back iron gates to push their trivial wares onto the sidewalks. Vagrants roam freely, and some in drunken stupor lie shivering against buildings.

At the Battery we're pushed with the crowd onto the boat and look over the rail at souvenir booths, hamburger stands, and trash cans where hungry victims—God's precious children—search eagerly for discarded food to ease their pain. Now, as we approach the peaceful little island, we see her—the tall and benevolent copper lady, Mother of Exiles, symbol of America and freedom.

She holds her scroll for all to see, and lifts her lighted torch high above her head. We read the words of hope she speaks with silent lips: "Give me your tired, your poor, your huddled masses yearning to breathe free, the wretched refuse of your teeming shore. Send these, the homeless, tempest-tost to me . . ."

But there is another happier land, "whose builder and maker is God," and our thoughts turn to its Ambassador who became one of us. His invitation is strangely similar: "Come unto me, all ye that labour and are heavy laden. . . . Ye shall find rest unto your souls"

(Matt. 11:28, 29). Rest from the burdens we carry, comfort from heartache and pain, relief from vice, hunger, and disaster, freedom from tyrants—and from the archenemy who has caused it all!

He bids us become His living monuments, an invitation to freedom, to hold high His lighted torch of love! A blessing beyond measure awaits us.

"Hold high the torch!
You did not light its glow—
'Twas given you by other hands, you know. . . .
And He once said, who hung on Calvary's tree:
'Ye are the light of the world. Go—shine for Me.'"
—*Anonymous*

LORRAINE HUDGINS

JULY 5

BEATING BURNOUT—1

Come to me, all you who are weary and burdened, and I will give you rest. Take my yoke upon you and learn from me, for I am gentle and humble in heart, and you will find rest for your souls. For my yoke is easy and my burden is light. Matt. 11:28-30, NIV.

Illinois, Florida, Puerto Rico, St. Croix, Oregon, and Idaho—back-to-back seminars. In six weeks I hadn't eaten one home-cooked meal, slept in my own bed, been able to discuss anything above a whisper, or spend one evening at home. My days were crammed with teaching seminars and counseling, a radio show and counseling, an afternoon seminar and counseling, supper and more counseling. After I'd retired to my room a knock at the door signaled more counseling. Then off to the next state to begin again.

Finally I was home after all the pressure. So why couldn't I shake the depression and enjoy being home? Usually I coped well with my traveling lifestyle. I tried to follow my daily plan for Bible study and exercise. I had no energy for either. I wasn't sleeping well. Tension mounted between Harry and me. My writing came to a virtual halt.

I sought answers. Did I need vitamins? Perhaps sleeping medication. Maybe we needed to move. Perhaps a new church or new friends. The more I searched for solutions the more confused and listless I became. What was the matter?

In a nutshell, I was on the verge of burnout. Burnout is the lessening of caring energies following an extended period of stress. Burnout can result when we are constantly confronted with a set or series of circumstances that cannot be changed. That was me. If one more person called with a problem . . .

Burnout has several identifiable symptoms displayed in both the physical and emotional arena. Depression often tops the list. The burned-out person may also suffer from sleeplessness, an exhaustive tiredness, constant irritability, or seething and erupting anger.

Are you caught in a downward spiral of events that could lead to burnout? If so, you can halt its progression by recognizing its symptoms and acting quickly to reverse the trend.

You need to feed yourself—not physical food, but emotional and spiritual food. No woman can constantly give to others without replenishing herself. I was invited to a family life workshop at Andrews University to give a one-hour presentation. I offered to teach a seminar, too. "No," said Drs. John and Millie Youngberg. "We want you to relax and enjoy an entire week with no responsibilities." Caregivers themselves, they recognized before I did the importance of the caregiver being on the receiving end once in a while.

I recently attended a women's conference *as a spectator*, a new experience for me. I've been to many women's conferences, but always as a presenter. I am still soaring from the spiritual food I received.

Christ recognized the need for time alone, to stop His labor and regroup. He was healing and teaching so many people that He and His disciples didn't even have a chance to eat. "Come with me by yourselves," He said, "to a quiet place and get some rest" (Mark 6:31, NIV). Another time He dismissed the crowd and went up on a mountainside to pray (verses 45, 46).

Let us resolve today to feast upon some spiritual food and find rest in Him.

NANCY VAN PELT

JULY 6

BEATING BURNOUT—2

The apostles gathered around Jesus and reported to him all they had done and taught. Then, because so many people were coming and going that they did not even have a chance to eat, he said to them, "Come with me by yourselves to a quiet place and get some rest." Mark 6:30, 31, NIV.

The woman suffering from burnout is often an ambitious overachiever who possesses high ideals and is constantly pushing herself. Exhaustion from the unswerving pressure eventually triumphs over even the most stable woman. This exhaustion depletes the energies, and symptoms of depression appear. The ambitious overachiever begins questioning her values, goals, commitments, and worth.

The burned-out woman may find even her prayer life sagging or entirely nonexistent. This is what happened to me. I prayed but mechanically, forcing myself to repeat trite phrases. "Thank You, Lord, for the birds and trees . . ." "Forgive me for . . ." "Bless . . ." "And . . ." Mechanically I went through my routine. I was handling it all wrong!

When you are feeling this low and don't have the faith or energy to say a prayer, say so. "Lord, I don't feel like praying today. I am exhausted, lonely, and depressed." Then comes the clincher: "Lord, send Your Holy Spirit to change my attitude. I trust You to do this for me."

This is not the time to pray for the missionaries overseas, or the earthquake victims in the Far East, or your local church. Now is the time to ask for strength to make it through the next hour. Keep your prayers simple and specific. Repeat the Lord's Prayer, the twenty-third psalm, or Isaiah 26:3: "Thou wilt keep [her] in perfect peace, whose mind is stayed on thee: because [she] trusteth in thee." Writing your prayer requests in a prayer notebook also helps you focus on real needs.

Remember, if you are suffering from burnout, it means you were once on fire! At one time you were consumed with excitement, zeal, and determination. This fire can be rekindled. The lessons you are now learning in the management of your priorities can become a pacesetting example for others and greatly enhance your capacity to share from your own personal experience.

I had one more lesson to learn. I had to learn to say no. When someone asked for a seminar I'd turn my schedule upside down trying to accommodate all requests. I tried to please everyone—an impossible task.

To be in constant demand, to feel the burdens, to feel affirmation of others, feeds the high achiever to the point where judgment is clouded. You push yourself beyond reasonable endurance. Why? Because you feel it is required of you.

Instead, learn to say no. You cannot be all things to all people all the time. Accept this. It may mean giving up important things you even love to do.

Yes, the fire in you can burn again, but all fires require careful tending or they burn themselves out all over again. Only you can de-

termine if there is a need to go to a "quiet place and get some rest."
Nancy Van Pelt

July 7

Miracle Leftovers

Therefore I say to you, whatever things you ask when you pray, believe that you receive them, and you will have them. Mark 11:24, NKJV.

It was the summer of 1931. The Great Depression had begun, and many in the little town of Healdsburg, California, had lost their jobs and were joining bread lines. In order to increase income, Mother rented rooms to several of Dad's employees and provided meals.

One evening after supper Mother and I were cleaning the kitchen. "Bertha, look at all this food left over. I misjudged tonight! Too bad we don't have one of those new refrigerators I have read about. Why don't we take this food to the Russell family?"

As the sun was setting we packed two large baskets of food, adding cans of beans, corn, and fruit, and started down the hill. As we walked into their driveway we noticed that the Russell family was having worship. All were kneeling in prayer. We slipped politely behind a tree. As the windows were open we could hear their prayers.

Eleven-year-old Charles was pleading earnestly, "Jesus, please send us food. We are so hungry."

Mr. Russell continued, and ended by saying, ". . . and Lord, You know how hard I've tried to get work. So far I've not had to join the bread lines. But tonight we have no food. Help me to get work so we can feed these three children. We thank Thee for hearing."

Mother and I waited before going to the door. I was 15 years old at the time, but in all the years that have gone by I will never forget what happened next.

At the first knock Charles jumped up, raised his hands, gave a big clap, and shouted, "God is sending us food already!"

Mr. Russell opened the door. "It's so good to see you, Sister Sullberg and Bertha. Come in."

Charles, ignoring his father's warning looks, announced, "Our food, Dad!" My mother confirmed his confidence, explaining that we had cooked too much and maybe they wouldn't mind leftovers.

Ready for the occasion, Charles was at the table. "Let's just start right in, Dad. I'm hungry."

Mother and I walked back up the hill in silence. "'Before they call I will answer'" (Isa. 65:24). With tears in her voice Mother spoke the text softly and with confidence. I nodded in wonder.

BERTHA APPLETON GLANZER

JULY 8

THE TWO BIKES

Train up a child in the way he should go: and when he is old, he will not depart from it. Prov. 22:6.

Lance had made up his mind. After a week of intense searching, he'd settled on a bright-red Yamaha Enduro dirt bike. He had gone to the bank and withdrawn the exact amount of money he needed from his savings account. Now I watched him from across the room as he made the purchase. Every muscle in his 13-year-old body was tense with excitement, anticipation, and pride as he counted out the money, so diligently earned, and watched the sale being written up. Then with shining eyes he approached his motorcycle, the salesman following with final instructions.

"Watching that son of yours has warmed my heart," another salesman commented to me. "You know, last week a father and son came in here. The boy was about 15. They picked out a beautiful bike, one of our most expensive. As the father was paying for it, the son walked over to look at some accessories. I said to him, 'You must feel really thankful for a dad who'll buy you such a nice bike.'

"But all he did was glance scornfully at his father and ask, 'Why should I? He's loaded. The money's nothing to him.'"

My mind jumped to some familiar words in the Bible regarding the last days:

"For men shall be lovers of their own selves, covetous, boasters . . . disobedient to parents, unthankful, unholy" (2 Tim. 3:2).

Lord, my son has been quite a witness today. Thank You for teaching me that careful attention and training in childhood will pay off in later years. Thirteen is not very old, but already I'm beginning to enjoy the rewards.

AILEEN LUDINGTON

July 9

To Be Like Him

Wash me, and I shall be whiter than snow. Ps. 51:7.

I had just filled my car with gas when my eye fell on the sign "Free Car Wash With a Fill-up." I decided to surprise my husband and get the car washed. I pulled around to the car wash, rolled my window down, and put the token into the slot. I pulled forward to where the machine grabs onto the car, and waited.

I am always fascinated by those giant brushes that twirl and swirl and swab and scrub with no effort on my part. So I was watching the approach of blue bristles at least a foot and a half long. The brushes hit the windshield along with a torrent of water, and in the next moment I was receiving the worst face washing of my life. The big blue brushes along the side reached in and pounded my cheek, swabbing out my ear clear down to the drum. Of course I had no idea what was happening, so I turned to look—just in time for the second set of brushes to complete the job!

Yes, I finally got the window rolled up. And as I peered out through the soapsuds running down from my eyebrows I vowed I would tell no one about this super-shower situation. But of course I went straight home and told my husband.

God tells us in Isaiah 1:16: "Wash yourselves, make yourselves clean" (NKJV). And again in Jeremiah 4:14: "O Jerusalem, wash your heart from wickedness, that you may be saved" (NKJV).

I don't know how it is with you, but I can tell you that I struggle to be like Jesus. That is my greatest desire. To be like Him. My heart is willing, but my habits hang on. I'd like to be scrubbed up and squeaky clean spiritually. But when I wash myself I'm pretty gentle. I don't seem to do what needs to be done. I understand why David asked God to do the job for him. In Psalm 51:2 he invites God to "wash me thoroughly from my iniquity, and cleanse me from my sin" (NKJV). In verse 7 he continues, "Wash me, and I shall be whiter than snow."

When we ask, that is exactly what God does. When we finally say, "Lord, will You do whatever needs to be done? I just want to be thoroughly clean. Use the soap. Use the brushes. Throw in a little bleach if necessary. I just want to be clean!" He will do it. In fact, Titus 3:5 tells us it is "not by works of righteousness which we have done, but according to His mercy He saved us, through the washing of regeneration and renewing of the Holy Spirit" (NKJV). That's good news. God is in the super-shower business. And it's free. He's already paid for it. He's offering free tokens. Have you picked one up lately?

GINNY ALLEN

July 10

Miraculous Marketing

For we walk by faith, not by sight. 2 Cor. 5:7.

Mathematics is not my thing. I have a daily reminder of that fact—my 9-year-old son, Brandon. I tried to help him with his third-grade math, later to be informed by both Brandon and his father that I was wrong and Brandon was right. How embarrassing! And how I dread to take college math.

Math is definitely not one of my strong points; it gives me a headache. Anything pertaining to numbers or mathematical problem solving causes me stress. That is why the weekly grocery shopping with my Lord is so miraculous.

Shopping on a fixed income and trying to buy all the necessities at today's prices is a real challenge! I buy only what's on sale. I rarely buy off-sale items. A pile of coupons always matches my sale—items list. I spend a long time with my shopping preparation ritual.

However, that is not the miracle I am talking about. The miracle happens after I finish at the checkout. Before entering the market, I talk to God first. I say, "OK, Lord, You know how much I have to spend. You know the best buys, the most nutritious foods, the coupons I have, so I pray that You will lead me in this adventure of shopping, and help me to be wise, so I don't go over my budget."

I place all my items into the cart, without even attempting to strain my brain calculating the cost. Sometimes a voice will say, "Now, do you really need that?" and I usually put it back. (When I ignore the voice, I often go over my budget!) Going to the checkout, I pray again, a little nervously. My grocery bill has been within pennies of the set limit too many times to be coincidental. My God is an awesome God! He cares even about my staying within my budget when grocery shopping.

In the third chapter of Malachi is a promise that I often claim when funds are low and there is a struggle as to whether to tithe in full. Malachi 3:8-10, NKJV, tells us of God's promises to pour out blessings in abundance to those who do not rob Him. Many times we have been so blessed that I have given food to others after my shopping excursions. He is faithful to bless when we are faithful to give. And His mathematics is wonderful. — LAURA LEE SWANEY

JULY 11

MY FATHER'S LOVE LETTERS

I have loved you with an everlasting love. Jer. 31:3, RSV.

It was a devastating blow! For the second time in six years my dad lay the helpless victim of a shattered hip. After the first break, my husband and I had invited my parents, then 82 years of age, to make their home with us. They were not relegated to "their own quarters" in our home. We lived as one happy family throughout the house. Their keen sense of humor delighted us. Their enthusiasm was contagious.

Now, again, he lay on his bedroom floor in pain. The ambulance was called, and soon Dad was undergoing surgery. He got along famously, but the shock was too much for Mother. A few days later she suffered a stroke and was obliged to enter the same hospital for surgery.

Life was never again the same. Mother's arthritis soon rendered her bedfast, and Dad was now in a full-care facility, where the six months of physical therapy seemed endless. How time dragged for each of them! Only on rare occasions was either strong enough to visit the other. Talking on the telephone was not enough. Loneliness was destroying their lives. One of us would visit Dad daily while the other stayed at home with Mother.

Then Dad's first tiny love note—written on a sheet from his little three-ring notebook—was penned. "I think about you with prayers all the time." "If I didn't love you so much I wouldn't be so lonesome." More love notes. "I keep thinking of us together in heaven. We'll be well then." "Your sweet face never grows old; it's always young and beautiful." "We'll have new names in heaven." "Lots of love. You'll have to take a rain check on the kisses." Mother saved them all.

That little red notebook is now my prize possession—filled with love letters my father wrote from the deep painful turmoil of his heart. Tears roll down my cheeks as I read.

I have another book—one that comforted Dad daily, just as his love letters comforted Mother. Dad's name is on the cover, but my heavenly Father's name is on every page. They are His love letters to me. "I will come to you" (John 14:18). "I have loved thee with an everlasting love" (Jer. 31:3). "Continue ye in my love" (John 15:9). "I have graven thee upon the palms of my hands" (Isa. 49:16). "I will never leave thee, nor forsake thee" (Heb. 13:5). "Behold, I come quickly" (Rev. 22:7). "For I the Lord thy God will hold thy right hand" (Isa. 41:13). "Fear not; I will help thee" (verse 13). "Surely I come quickly" (Rev. 22:20). Filled with pathos, they express my heavenly Father's love, His longing, His intense desire to come and take me home.

Again the tears course down my cheeks—tears of love, and of hope, and of gratitude. What a wonderful heavenly Father! I can hardly wait to see His beautiful face. LORRAINE HUDGINS

JULY 12

THE TALE OF TWO GRAVESTONES

For God so loved the world, that he gave his only begotten Son, that whosoever believeth in him should not perish, but have everlasting life. John 3:16.

The raspy breathing of baby Joel woke me from my shallow sleep. I recognized the symptoms of croup, dragged myself wearily out of bed, and gathered Joel up in his shawl. First I went to the open window and let him breathe a few breaths of the chilly night. Then downstairs to boil the kettle.

A half hour of steam, and his breathing was easier. He was sleeping, and wearily we climbed the stairs again to bed. Tucking him into his cot, I thanked God for his recovery.

On the Isle of Wight, England, is a village church in an ancient churchyard. In the heart of that cemetery, filled with mossy, time-eroded stones, I found a tragic story of a mother's struggle. A tiny grave with one headstone. Four little girls, ages 1 to 8, died within 10 days. The stone said that they all died from croup.

My vivid imagination pictured the agony of a mother watching her children die, helpless, holding them in her arms as their breathing became more labored, praying, crying, desperate, more desperate with the loss of each beautiful daughter. I could only imagine the depth of her sorrow, her despair, a heart broken four times in two handfuls of days. As I stood by that headstone, worn by 150 years of sea breezes, my own heart ached for that long-ago mother.

Finally I pulled myself away and went on to the next stone, a young woman, not even 30. Another tragedy. And then I noticed something else. This stone was a sequel to the first.

This was the grave of the young mother, with a broken heart. Three months of profound grief was all she could bear, and then she joined her four little girls under the island sod.

The tragedy seemed to be amplified because such a simple solution could have prevented such intense sorrow. A steamy kettle in the middle of the night. Maybe she didn't realize how easily she could ease the suffering of her little ones.

Today many people are tragically dying, unaware of the simple solution that could save their lives, bringing them forgiveness, acceptance, peace and comfort, hope and joy. Jesus is waiting, knocking on the door, with all the help they need. The solution is so close, so simple, but they just don't realize it.

If I had lived 150 years ago I would have wanted more than anything else to share the simple treatment for croup with a young mother. If I hadn't, I'd have felt responsible in some way for the loss of those little lives. But maybe today there are people I'll meet in need of simple remedies to save their souls for eternity. Do I feel the same urgency to help them? Karen Holford

JULY 13

FALCON FAMILY

Are not sparrows two a penny? Yet without your Father's leave not one of them can fall to the ground. As for you, even the hairs of your head have all been counted. So have no fear; you are worth more than any number of sparrows. Matt. 10:29-31, NEB.

Walking in downtown Salt Lake City some years ago, my husband and I noticed a knot of people around a telescope trained on the elegant Westin Hotel. Uniformed officials offered passersby a look. We learned they were watching an endangered peregrine falcon family.

The pair had come before, but this was the first year the female was old enough to lay eggs. Officials and volunteers made the birds' safety their primary focus for several weeks.

Four eggs, laid in a precarious spot, were soon broken. Hotel personnel let wildlife officials attach a nesting box to the building 15 stories high. The pair moved in and laid three more eggs. The hotel listed "Mr. and Mrs. P. Falcon" in the registry and forbade employees to enter that suite.

Guests watched via a TV monitor in the lobby. Newspapers, TV, and even a BBC cinematographer covered developments. The whole city followed.

All three eggs hatched. Officials later examined and banded the chicks after distracting their parents. An assistant, with a rope around her waist, removed the family's garbage.

Five or six official observers watched daily. One even watched nights. As the chicks began flying, these people kept minute-by-minute track. With binoculars, walkie-talkies, and trained eyes, they usually knew where the birds were.

Employees in the Kennecott Building across South Temple Street kept logs of sightings and gave observers full access to the 18-floor building.

Inexperienced falcon wings could not muster the power to clear downtown buildings. Once two chicks landed on ledges too low for the parents to risk feeding them. Eventually one volunteer climbed up and took one to the rooftop. The other then flew, crashing into the Kennecott Building. He was immediately captured, X-rayed, and taken to the roof.

Observers thought nothing of dashing into four-lane traffic to rescue a fallen falcon. City officials became more worried about the bird-watchers than the birds. Downtown traffic was slowed for three baby birds.

The all-consuming dedication, effort, and concern had impressed me. However, the rescued showed little gratitude. They squawked, wailed, and clawed.

I was reminded of One who observed even a sparrow's fall. He knows when and where to look for us. He knows our exact measurement, the hairs on our heads. He bands us with His own name. He observes with concern our first attempts at flight, glad for our yearnings for independence but cognizant of our lack of strength and experience, aware of the obstacles we could crash against. We are never lost from His sight. But He stands by, ready to pick us up out of the traffic of life, hold us tight, fix up our injuries, and return us to the heights to soar again. MADELINE S. JOHNSTON

July 14

REASONABLY UNREASONABLE

For God's foolishness is wiser than human wisdom, and God's weakness is stronger than human strength. 1 Cor. 1:25, NRSV.

We often say, "God is good and kind and just." I feel we must also say, "God is unreasonable." Although this may shock some, reading the next several paragraphs might persuade them to agree with me.

When I first joined the mission work, I was paid only Rs 76 a month. In 1952 this amount was not even $10. It seemed unreasonable that more than one tenth of this puny salary should go to the church as tithe and offerings. I continued to give for the rest of my 38 years of service and even now as a retiree. I could have saved much had I not been so foolish in giving. God owns the whole universe; why does He want my money?

In spite of all the pressure and mad rush to work, we are to spend time in prayer and meditation. We read our Bibles daily, and study other religious and spiritual materials. We have not only our private worship, but family worship, office worship, and church worship, too. Why so much time for religious exercises?

I also think it's very unreasonable for us as mission workers to work so hard. After all, we are paid far less than government workers. We must even work overtime without getting paid for it. Some people make up for this small amount of pay by sneaking away during office hours. Sometimes they see us working overtime and mock us. We can't blame them, can we?

Jesus said that if someone should slap me on one cheek, I should allow that person to slap the other cheek, too. Even if it were my husband, the only reasonable thing is to fight back. Yet Jesus went on to say, "Love your enemies." If my enemies are hungry, I am supposed to feed them, bless them, and pray for them. If thieves steal my coat, I am supposed to give them my shawl, too.

But through the years I have discovered that God has richly blessed. Food, money, and clothes lasted longer. There was always enough to share. Daily devotions made the days go better. The overtime work was even enjoyable. I have seen "enemies" and thieves become friends because of kindness.

To accuse God as being unreasonable is not so wise after all. In fact, it shows only human foolishness. First Corinthians 3:19 says,

"The wisdom of this world is foolishness with God" (NRSV).

Through my own experience I have discovered that God has been very reasonable in asking me to follow His ways. As Samuel says: "As for God, his way is perfect" (2 Sam. 22:31, NIV).   BIRDIE PODDAR

JULY 15

PROMISE YOURSELF

So we do not lose heart. Though our outer nature is wasting away, our inner nature is being renewed every day. 2 Cor. 4:16, RSV.

I'm getting older—and I don't mind! You don't believe me? It's true. I'll tell you why.

Knowing the inevitable aging process would soon catch up with me, I've been studying and getting prepared. I can give you my secret of how to age joyfully and gracefully in just seven words. Do I have your attention? OK. Say these words daily. Post them where you can read them often. They're yours. Make them come true.

"You're not getting older—you're getting better!"

Why do these few words make a difference? Because it's really what's inside you that counts. Let me share some texts with you. Psalm 89:15: "Blessed are the people who know the joyful sound! They walk, O Lord, in the light of Your countenance" (NKJV). Psalm 90:17: "And let the beauty of the Lord our God be upon us, and establish the work of our hands for us; yes, establish the work of our hands" (NKJV). Second Corinthians 3:18: "But we all, with unveiled face, beholding as in a mirror the glory of the Lord, are being transformed into the same image from glory to glory, just as by the Spirit of the Lord" (NKJV). Second Corinthians 5:17: "So if anyone is in Christ, there is a new creation; everything old has passed away; see, everything has become new" (NRSV).

Here's a goal for today, this week, this month, this year. You'll need God's help to reach it. Just claim Matthew 19:26: "With God all things are possible." Beauty can be yours. The lines of the following poem remind me of God's ideal for His children.

Promise Yourself
Promise yourself to be so strong that nothing can disturb

your peace of mind.
To talk health, happiness, and prosperity to every person you meet.
To make all your friends feel that there is something in them.
To look at the sunny side of everything and make your optimism come true.
To think only of the best. . . .
To be just as enthusiastic about the success of others as you are about your own.
To forget the mistakes of the past and press on to the greater achievements of the future.
To wear a cheerful countenance at all times and give every living creature you meet a smile.
To give so much time to the improvement of yourself that you have no time to criticize others.
To be too large for worry, too noble for anger, too strong for fear, and too happy to permit the presence of trouble.

—Christian D. Larson

Make this your prayer today: "Jesus, we want to grow more and more like You. We want family, friends, or even strangers to see CHRIST in us as CHRISTians. Then we can all go home."

GINGER MOSTERT CHURCH

JULY 16

HAIKU PROVERBS

A word fitly spoken is like apples of gold in pictures of silver. Prov. 25:11.

I have loved poetry for as long as I can remember. Many times as a child I thrilled to the sounds of my mother's voice as she read poems to me. Joyce Kilmer's "I think that I shall never see a poem lovely as a tree" was a particular favorite.

As I grew older I was happy to discover that God too loves poetry. The Bible—especially the book of Proverbs—is full of poems. When I discovered haiku, a form of poetry practiced by the Japanese for centuries, the similarities enriched my understanding of Bible Hebrew poetry even more. Since haiku is traditionally written in the Japanese language, most of us in our society are exposed only to the English translations. Translations often lose something from the original, and yet they can still enrich our lives through their explosive simplicity.

Classic haiku is characterized by very specific rules of writing: 17 Japanese syllables arranged in a five-seven-five sequence, and a reference to nature other than human nature. Unlike Western poetry, which often contains much detail, haiku is more like a skeleton, offered so that the readers can interpret the meaning based on their own experience. It omits all unnecessary words; sometimes there are no verbs in an entire poem. The sentence can even be left unfinished. Here is a haiku that I created:

> Loneliness. Like dark
> Before the dawn, it passes.
> Give it a moment.

There is another quality of haiku: the quality of growth. That is, there is an ability to convey more emotion and more content than a person might feel just by reading the poem one time. Reading the lines again and again allows the readers to think new thoughts and to compare the ideas contained in the verse more deeply with their own experiences.

Solomon may well have been creating something very much like haiku when he wrote many of the proverbs. Perhaps one of his Eastern wives influenced some of his writing. The 17-syllable format is not necessarily followed, but the overall flavor is similar. Take these two verses, for example:

> "Where no wood is, there the fire goeth out:
> so where there is no talebearer, the strife ceaseth"
> (Prov. 26:20).

> "As a ring of gold in a swine's snout,
> so is a lovely woman who lacks discretion
> (Prov. 11:22, NKJV).

Since I've started reading the Proverbs as one does haiku, slowly, one at a time, trying to create a picture around the skeleton of the verse based on personal experience, I see a depth and a beauty in them that I never recognized before. Delve into the book of Proverbs and see something that you have never seen before. Read the verses from a haiku perspective and see God in a new way—the God who loves poetry and color and emotional word pictures.　　　　Arlene Taylor

July 17

Singing Unto the Lord

I will sing to the Lord as long as I live; I will sing praise to my God while I have being. Ps. 104:33, RSV.

Most of us have at least one song that brings comfort and cheer to our souls, much like the assurance that minstrel singers brought to prophets of old who needed to hear an immediate word from the Lord.

Such a song, "Anywhere With Jesus," was echoing within my soul the very day I journeyed by plane from Douala to Yaounde, Cameroon. Having long since lost contact with my French guide, I didn't have the slightest idea what would happen to me next. Between the severe headache that I had acquired during my week in Nairobi, and the noise and confusion of passengers scurrying hither and yon, it had been necessary for me to call "time out" from vocational matters to deal with the physical.

It was clearly time too for the spiritual. Suddenly these appropriate words from the hymn seemed to soothe my throbbing head, winning for me some calm and respite, at least for the Sabbath hours:

"Though His hand may lead me over dreary ways,
  Anywhere with Jesus is a house of praise."

The course of events began to transpire too rapidly to recount. One thing was clear, however: I was all on my own, with no friendly face in sight. Frightening thoughts kept pouring through my mind, adding fuel to the pain that still burned inside my head. Again words of solace from that hymn of faith and trust rang in my ears:

"Anywhere without Him, dearest joys would fade;
  Anywhere with Jesus I am not afraid."

These words assured me that I had no reason to be afraid!

Providence then led me to a seat on the plane near one of Yaounde's musical ensembles that was returning from Paris. My seatmate, the director, and I began to communicate, and, upon learning of my dilemma, "adopted" me as a member of the company. With their aid I was able to get through customs without questions and baggage inspection, locate a reputable hotel without delay, and obtain guides to assist me throughout my stay. God had clearly provided for me through this small group of musicians.

That night, finally alone in my hotel room, I pondered the events of the day, feeling certain that I did not need to know what would transpire on tomorrow. Filled with the confidence that Jesus would take care of my needs day by day, I knelt beside my bed and prayed this prayer of confidence before retiring for the night:

"Anywhere with Jesus I can go to sleep,
When the gloomy shadows round about me creep;
Knowing I shall waken nevermore to roam,
Anywhere with Jesus will be home sweet home."

"I will sing to the Lord as long as I live; I will sing praise to my God while I have being." ROSA TAYLOR BANKS

JULY 18

JUST DO IT!

But be doers of the word, and not merely hearers who deceive themselves. For if any are hearers of the word and not doers, they are like those who look at themselves in a mirror; for they look at themselves and, on going away, immediately forget what they were like. But those who look into the perfect law, the law of liberty, and persevere, being not hearers who forget but doers who act—they will be blessed in their doing. James 1:22-25, NRSV.

Proverbs 20:1. Jane had read it before. Many times. But this time it seemed so unclear. Would it really be so bad to have just one? In the past Jane had been so positive it was wrong. She even remembered telling her best friend why she had quit. She had been convincing, too.

They were sitting on Agnes's back porch enjoying the warm afternoon. "Want a beer?" Agnes had queried. She had held out one can while slurping the foam off the top of the other one. Her eyes hooked into Jane's, not letting go. When Jane didn't say anything, Agnes set the can down on the porch. Jane could almost see an imaginary line dividing the space between them . . . and the can was on *her* side.

Jane looked at Agnes's shoes. She loved those shoes. Why

couldn't she dress more like Agnes? Why couldn't she be more like Agnes? Maybe she should just drink the beer. It didn't mean she would have to start drinking again. Just one beer. No big deal.

As Jane reached for the can, she fought desperately to erase the memory of Proverbs 20:1: "Wine is a mocker and beer a brawler; whoever is led astray by them is not wise" (NIV).

Yeah. So maybe I'm still too young to be wise, Jane thought. She opened the can. Then she remembered: "Everyone who hears these words of mine and puts them into practice is like a wise man who built his house on the rock. The rain came down, the streams rose, and the winds blew and beat against that house; yet it did not fall, because it had its foundation on the rock" (Matt. 7:24, 25).

Jane looked at the can in her hand, the beads of condensation making her palms cold and damp. *Why ask why?* she thought. *Why not just do it? Why not stop worrying about things and live to gratify self? Party on!*

Suddenly she began to get a really disgusted feeling in the pit of her stomach—the same feeling she had gotten in fifth grade when Fred had kissed her right in the middle of English class and the teacher had seen it. "Why?" Jane said it aloud.

"What?" Agnes asked. "Hey, you going to drink that or what? It's probably warm now."

Forget about Agnes, Jane thought. *Forget about being like her. Do what the Word says.* Jane set the beer down on the other side of the imaginary line and got up. "See you around, Agnes. Gotta go."

WENDY PINER TAYLOR

JULY 19

CALL ME BITTER

Call me Mara [bitter], because the Almighty has made my life very bitter. Ruth 1:20, NIV.

Naomi was angry. Bitter. And she had reason to be. She had once been a happy, contented, stay-at-home mother. Then she had to leave that home in Bethlehem, which means house of bread, because there was no more bread. In a foreign land her husband was taken from her. And then one son. Then the other son. Now she was left with only two foreign daughters-in-law. One of them then decided to leave.

It was all God's fault, and she didn't mind saying so. "Don't call me Naomi [which means pleasant]," she said. "Call me [bitter], because the Almighty has made my life very bitter. I went away full, but the Lord has brought me back empty. Why call me [pleasant]? The Lord has afflicted me; the Almighty has brought misfortune upon me" (Ruth 1:20, 21, NIV).

And you can't blame her. It was more than most of us would want to bear. But the wonderful thing is that God didn't get upset at her anger at all. He knew she needed to voice it and get it out. We know He felt that way because He inspired someone to write about it in the beautiful book of Ruth.

One of the marvelous motifs that weaves through the book of Ruth is that of empty to full. Naomi was once full; she became totally empty. And then gradually, chapter by chapter, we see her being filled, until in the last chapter, when Ruth gives birth to a son, the women of the village say, "Praise be to the Lord, who this day has not left you without a kinsman-redeemer. . . . For your daughter-in-law, who loves you and who is better to you than seven sons, has given him birth" (Ruth 4:14, 15, NIV). No one could ask for more than seven sons. She was truly full now.

But along the way it was not always easy to see how God was working. One of the most interesting passages is found in the second chapter. Naomi was still empty and bitter, but she did what she could to help herself. She sent her daughter-in-law Ruth out to glean in the fields. Verse 3 says that Ruth "went out and began to glean in the fields behind the harvesters. As it turned out, she found herself working in a field belonging to Boaz" (NIV). Probably you remember how the story turned out: Boaz, the kinsman-redeemer, married Ruth. But did you notice? When everything was going wrong, God got the blame. But when things started to go right, it was "as it turned out." It just sort of happened. Luck.

Isn't that the way it often is with us? We ask, "God, why did You let this happen to me?" We call it an act of God when disaster strikes. But when things go right? Do we recognize His quiet hand behind the affairs of our lives in the good as well as in the bad? "Loving Jesus, thank You for every good thing in my life, and help me to bear the bad. Help me remember how You patiently worked with and through Naomi, from bitterness to fullness in You."

ARDIS DICK STENBAKKEN

JULY 20

GO TELL!

The Lord declares, You are my witnesses, you are my servants chosen by me to know me and put your trust in me and understand that I am the Lord. Isa. 43:10, REB.

Last year I told a member of my church's nominating committee that I was exhausted and did not want to be elected to any church office that year. Instead of doing church work, I wanted to become involved in the work of the church—active witnessing.

I prayed about the whole matter and asked the Lord for the opportunity to tell someone of His wondrous love to me and the entire human family. I was gently reminded by a friend that I must be careful about what I pray for, because God will surely answer, and I must be prepared to do whatever He asks me to do.

Since I have made that commitment to witness, I have become more aware of the people around me, and every time I speak to someone, be it a friend, relative, or a complete stranger, a little voice whispers to me, "Tell that person about Me, and how real I have been to you. Tell him/her that I am coming back again soon, very soon."

Sometimes I have heeded that small voice, and sometimes I must admit that I have turned a deaf ear to it. Needless to say, I have always felt guilty when I failed to obey the voice.

Recently I met a young man who seems to be searching for a true understanding of God. I immediately developed MIS—Moses' inadequate syndrome. I said, "Lord, this one is beyond me intellectually and professionally. What am I going to say to him? Who says he would be interested in what I have to say? What about ———? He's in a better position to witness to him!"

I must admit that I am quite capable of inventing excuses if I don't want to do a particular thing. God knows that too, but we made a promise, and He is keeping His promise while I am reneging on mine.

Like a highway neon sign our verse for today flashes into my mind. "You are My witness, the one I have chosen." I recognized His answer to my doubting and quietly said, "OK, Lord, please help me to do this gigantic job. I need Your help." Again His word came to me as with Moses—"I will be with you."

May God help me to surrender to His will at all times, even when the task seems insurmountable. ANDREA A. BUSSUE

July 21

Are You Homesick?

And if I go and prepare a place for you, I will come again and receive you to Myself; that where I am, there you may be also. John 14:3, NKJV.

I remember when my children first went away to boarding school. I felt like a mother wren pushing her babies out of the nest. During the first month of their exile (as they called it) their weekly letters and phone calls centered on one theme, homesickness.

Of course, after four to six weeks my "birds" learned to use their own wings and became quite contented in their new surroundings. Bouts of homesickness were less frequent, but never totally extinct. Home leave still created a quiver of excitement and anticipation.

When I knew they were coming home, I'd prepare their favorite foods, clean their rooms, and then sit by the window watching. As soon as the car entered the driveway, I'd fling open the door and run to meet them with open arms. The walls vibrated with laughter.

Years have passed; one child married and now lives in a different state. The other moved closer to a university, where she works full-time and attends classes. I deal with the empty-nest syndrome, and I wonder if coming home means as much to them as it does to me. I still go through the same rituals when they visit. I prepare their favorite foods, fluff their pillows, and place a few childhood treasures in sight. The house is cleaned from top to bottom. Then I sit by the window and watch for the familiar car bearing the most precious cargo in the world. When it arrives, I fling open the door and run to meet them in the yard. Are they as excited as I am? Do they notice how much time I've spent preparing the house, the food? Do they realize how much I long to squeeze them, touch them, hear their joyous laughter?

Now I can partly understand the yearning in the heart of our heavenly Father, who has already waited thousands of years to be relinked with His children. From the very beginning of the work of redemption it has been the all-consuming desire of God to bring His children home. He emptied all of heaven in the gift of His Son, Jesus Christ, to die for our sins.

Our Father has been patiently waiting for this permanent reunion. He longs to touch us, to hug us, to hear our joyous laughter. He's arranged our rooms. He's prepared our favorite foods. He's coming with a royal retinue of angels to greet us. He'll fling open the gates of heaven and exclaim, "Welcome home, children!"

Are you as excited about the homecoming as He is?

CRYSTAL EARNHARDT

JULY 22

FALLING APART AND BEING MADE SOUND

May God himself, the God of peace, make you holy in every part, and keep you sound in spirit, soul, and body, without fault when our Lord Jesus Christ comes. He who calls you is to be trusted; he will do it. 1 Thess. 5:23, 24, NEB.

Falling apart!

I don't like to write those two words. I don't like the emotions they evoke in me.

For most of my life I have envied people who never seemed to fall apart. I wanted to be together, like them.

Ironically, while I was feeling disintegrated, or at least fragmented, others perceived me as being together! After having heard several people identify me as "together," I had to conclude that many, if not all, of us feel as if we are falling apart, while others perceive us as being together.

The process of falling apart, of learning to let ourselves be fragile and fragmented, actually has great benefits. We can more deeply sense our need of God's ability to create us anew, bringing order out of chaos.

When I feel together, I tend not to ask for help, and God honors me by not forcing help upon me.

The process of falling apart can get me in touch with deep needs that were not met in my childhood years. Because unmet needs can drive me to compulsive behaviors designed to fill those needs, the process of falling apart is also a process of becoming conscious of the aspects of myself that I don't particularly like, and therefore I have the ability to thank God for forgiveness of specific things rather than uttering such a prayer as "If I have done or said anything that has displeased You today, Lord, please forgive me."

In the midst of falling apart I discovered the precious promise quoted above.

I choose. God performs. We are a team, interactive, invincible.

KATIE TONN-OLIVER

July 23

Birth of Confidence

A woman, when she is in labor, has sorrow because her hour has come; but as soon as she has given birth to the child, she no longer remembers the anguish, for joy that a human being has been born into the world. John 16:21, NKJV.

The stories are intense, dramatic, vivid, and each storyteller has her own twist to the saga. You've heard them too, those stories echoed for centuries. There's a sameness about them all—first, gripping pain, followed by horrendous pain, followed by nearly unendurable pain, followed by a baby. Thus it was that I entered pregnancy with an unhealthy dose of apprehension regarding childbirth.

As parents do the world around, my husband and I prepared for our newcomer. The borrowed crib soon filled with soft blankets and furry stuffed animals. I lined little dresser drawers with pretty wallpaper and neatly stacked tiny garments in them. We also attended a local Lamaze class. As we viewed a video of three women giving birth, determination filled me. This silent conception of courage convinced me that I would weather whatever travail lay ahead.

Thus it was that I awoke in pain. Hot, hard fingers seemed to stretch around my protruding body and clasp in my back, squeezing, tightening. Then my body would relax and I would doze off again, only to be reawakened by another truly laborious embrace. After a couple hours I initiated the deep breathing techniques we'd rehearsed. As we dressed for the trip to the hospital, every last fragment of fear fled.

Hours later I was exhausted, still pushing, but with no baby. But a short time later the nurses were beckoned, and it was only minutes until the warmer was wheeled out, the doctor was ready, and our baby son was born and in my arms. Instantly the pain vanished. We had done it! Celebration!

Sometimes when I think of the second coming of Jesus, all I can see are the labor pains: friends betraying me, no family supporting me, the uncertain fate of my children, my own weakness and sins. An unholy dread smothers my soul. Rather than longing for the Second Coming, I fear it. And Satan rejoices.

Yet Jesus calls me to remember my labor and delivery. I experienced intense, gripping pain, sickness, exhaustion. Yet I gladly endured it all for the joy of receiving my little son. And so I'm reminded that though troublesome times are ahead and though all should forsake me, my Deliverer will never leave me. And after the moments of travail, I'll spend eternity with Jesus, the one who bore my sins so that I might be born again. — COLLENE KELLY

JULY 24

ONE BLUE RIBBON WILL DO

God opposes the proud but gives grace to the humble. James 4:6, NIV.

My husband was Jewish, and very proud of the fact. While he basically accepted only the first five books of the Bible, he read all the Old Testament and was well acquainted with the New Testament. One day he asked me if I had ever read Matthew 23:5, and whether I knew what the phrase "enlarge the borders of their garments" meant. (He was convinced that the King James Version of the Bible was the only reliable translation outside of his own Hebrew Bible, so I will use it as our reference here.) I told him that I had no idea what it meant, and he was pleased to refer me to Numbers 15, where the priests were instructed to put on the borders of their garments "a ribband of blue" (verse 38). "And it shall be unto you for a fringe, that ye may look upon it, and remember all the commandments of the Lord, and do them. . . . That ye may remember, and do all my commandments, and be holy unto your God" (verses 39, 40).

Now, the priests turned out to be very human, and soon figured out that if one ribbon of blue was good, another ribbon of blue would make them better. So by the time the New Testament came along, the priests had added many ribbons of blue to make them appear to be more holy than ever. Hence the reference in Matthew about enlarging the borders of their garments.

The Lord, in His infinite wisdom, anticipated all our weaknesses, and tried to arrange forms and services to point away from ourselves and toward Him. However, too often we hang on to the forms simply to make us look as though we are serving Him, while losing their real meaning. Doing those works for the eyes of others is just another way of adding a blue ribbon on our garments.

One of my favorite verses, one that my husband loved to quote, is found in Micah 6:8: "He hath shewed thee, O man, what is good; and what doth the Lord require of thee, but to do justly, and to love mercy, and to walk humbly with thy God?" He makes it sound so simple. Just three little requirements. I try to be honest and merciful, but since I am sometimes tempted to sew a few ribbons of blue on my garment, I must ask the Lord daily to show me the way to go, and then let Him lead.   SHEILA SANDERS

JULY 25

MY TEARS SHALL BE WIPED AWAY

And God will wipe away every tear from their eyes; there shall be no more death, nor sorrow, nor crying; and there shall be no more pain, for the former things have passed away. Rev. 21:4, NKJV.

The new bathinette leaned desolately against the living room wall. There had been no money for the bathinette I had so desired for our first child. Now, by the courtesy of my stepmother and friends, I had my bathinette, but I had no baby to place in it.

Our tiny boy, in my eighth month of pregnancy, was stillborn. I was lucky—if you could call it that. At least I had not died, as the doctors had predicted; I was still alive to raise our 5-year-old daughter. But my arms ached to hold the little boy I had carried for eight long months—to see him grow, to see him take that first step, to hear him talk.

"Why, God, why?" I was a Christian; I had tried to live a good life.

Eventually the new bathinette was sold to someone who did have a baby to place in it. Through church meetings and Bible studies I learned the story of the great controversy in heaven and why, sometimes, such pain exists in our lives.

A few years ago at the Howard County Fair in Maryland, while doing health screening and counseling, I met a young girl with a 3-year-old boy. She too had lost a baby. "My mother doesn't understand, my husband doesn't understand, why I still grieve for my baby," she said.

"I do understand," I assured her. "I too lost a baby, years ago. Find a support group for parents who have lost an infant, because you will understand how others feel. When you begin to help them, you too will begin to heal." I wish I could say I quoted our Bible text for today to her, but I was too emotionally involved even to think of it. I know that God, who gave His own Son to die for us, is waiting to wipe away our tears and give us back our loved ones.

I often think of a statement I once read: "As the little infants come forth immortal from their dusty beds, they immediately wing their way to their mother's arms. They meet again nevermore to part" (*Selected Messages*, book 2, p. 260). I too wait for that day when there will be no more tears, and I will hold again our little baby boy. If some of you have lost an infant, I pray that this will be an encouragement to you to look forward to the Second Coming and to your baby winging its way to your arms. — LORAINE SWEETLAND

JULY 26

GOD-GIVEN INSTINCTS

Do not be conformed to this world, but be transformed by the renewing of your mind, that you may prove what is that good and acceptable and perfect will of God. Rom. 12:2, NKJV.

Our home borders the wilderness where squirrels, bobcats, deer, and coyotes live. I love both the wilderness and domestic cats, but the two do not mix. Poodles, our 15-year-old tortoiseshell cat, lives in our garage at night. Just before closing the garage door at dusk we feed her, so her hunger guarantees obedience to the nighttime curfew.

One evening Poodles did not come running up to the garage to be fed. I felt guilty because I was a little late, and wondered if the coyotes had beaten me. After rattling the food in her bowl without result, I felt a sense of panic creeping over me. "O Lord, please don't let my kitty suffer because of my neglect."

I dropped to my hands and knees to look under the car in the dim light. The inside of the back tire looked rather furry. But Poodles would not move or acknowledge me. I caught one leg and pulled her out, while she clawed the concrete frantically. Normally she does not like to be held, but now she clung to my chest like plaster. "Are you hurt, Poodles? Why are you disobeying me?" I was torn between concern and irritation with her stubborn behavior.

Crunch, crunch. I heard steps that sounded like the crackling of dry oak leaves. What could that be? In just a few seconds whatever it was would be around the corner of the garage. I crouched behind the car, and to my amazement a big brown bear came lumbering slowly along.

I instantly forgave my cat's "disobedience." "Lord, You gave Poodles the instinct to hide quietly, and now I have put us both in danger. Please tell me what to do." My thoughts raced ahead of my frozen feet. Perhaps I should run into the garage and close the door. No, the noise might startle the bear. Maybe I should get out of range of the bear before being seen and run down to the house? Yes, much better idea. "Dear Lord, be with me. I don't want to tangle with this bear!"

I backed up slowly, hidden by the profile of the car. When I was close enough to make a dash for the front door, I started running. Once inside, I hustled to a window and watched the bear slowly plod around the back of the house, quite oblivious to us.

Even though Poodles did not come to me when I called her, she had done the proper thing. She had obeyed her natural protective instincts given by God.

How I would love to respond as naturally to God's will in my life's challenging dilemmas.

The key is our connection to Christ. "Teach me, Lord, to hear Your quiet voice and tune out everything that entices me from Your plan. I want to react spontaneously with God-given inspiration to my daily struggles as confidently as my cat obeyed her wild instincts. We have more than instincts: we have You, Lord."

LINDA HYDER FERRY

July 27

Pray for Your Children

Then Samuel said, "Speak, for your servant is listening." 1 Sam. 3:10, NIV.

That still small voice came so urgently: "Pray for your children." I'd heard that voice before and often prayed for my children during the day, but this time the message was more specific: "Pray out loud for your children."

For six months I had been part of a very special prayer group that met every Wednesday morning. For three hours we studied a Bible text and prayed for each other. It was a time of closeness with our Lord, and I treasured these times. After our study I headed home on the freeway; it was about 12:30 p.m. when I was impressed to pray. Not knowing what to pray for, I began to pray for their health, their relationships, schooling, anything that came to mind—

and I prayed out loud.

A short time after I arrived home, the phone rang. It was Jason, our oldest son. "Mom, there's been an accident." My heart raced as I tried to remain calm. "I'm OK, but my car isn't." Then he told me that he had been driving down the winding mountain road from camp and that as he'd entered a curve, a large delivery truck had suddenly appeared on his side of the road.

On one side was a 30-foot drop-off; on the other side was a dirt bank. Somehow (he still doesn't know how) he managed to go behind the truck and land in a ditch next to the dirt bank. He was uninjured, but his car was the recipient of a very flat tire. He was shaken, but praised God for his narrow escape. It was then that I realized that the accident had occurred at the moment that I had been impressed to pray for my children.

As I pondered this, I realized that I had no answers for why some accidents happen and some are prevented. All I know is that when God calls, I want to be like Samuel and say, "Speak, for Your servant is listening," and then to listen to His instructions, even when I don't know what I am praying for.   JANIS VANCE

JULY 28

FAR FROM PERFECT

I in them, and thou in me, that they may be made perfect in one. John 17:23.

My first project in woodshop class was a cutting board in the shape of an onion. It was a pretty simple project, really. All I had to do was glue together strips of pine and oak and then cut it out with a jigsaw.

My onion turned out rather lopsided. I was so discouraged that I had no desire to start on the next project. The teacher noticed my lack of enthusiasm.

"I want to show you something," he said, unlocking a cabinet. It was full of metal boxes. "These boxes were made by my students. They were told to make them exactly three inches high and five inches long." He measured several boxes for me. They were all different sizes! "You could measure every box here without finding a perfect box," he told me. "Not one of my students followed my instructions exactly. I don't expect anybody's projects to be perfect, but I do expect you to keep trying."

We should never be discouraged because we are so far from perfect. Rather, we should strive to follow God's instructions more precisely so that we can get closer to our goals.   GINA LEE

JULY 29

GOD NEEDS LOVE TOO

We love Him because He first loved us. 1 John 4:19, NKJV.

Through the years I've often heard of God's love for me. And the concept that I would love Him in return seemed a logical response. But it never crossed my mind that the One who has everything could really need *my* imperfect gift of love. Only through the maturity of years and the varied circumstances of life have I been reminded of the positive impact that appreciation, kind words, and expressions of love and support can have.

Because I want to become more comfortable in the receiving and giving of love, there is a mental visualization I practice in the morning that helps to make Jesus the close, personal friend I desire Him to be. I imagine going with God to one of my favorite sites of nature. We hold a conversation: I, sharing my concerns, successes, failures; He, listening, encouraging, supporting me with a warm hug, a bit of advice, or the mere strength of His presence. We have walked arm-in-arm through pine-scented forests, splashed in the ocean waves as they broke around our feet, or felt the cool breeze on our faces as we cycled on a vineyard-bordered country lane. Sometimes I invite someone else along on our excursions (someone I know needs to have Jesus especially near at that particular time) and extend an invitation to join in saying to the Lord, "I'm so glad we're friends. Thanks for loving me."

> When my life gets busy and the world is crowding in,
> I'm thankful for the times of quietness
> When I talk to You, Lord, and listen for Your voice.
> Grateful praise to You I must express.
> You thought of me, Lord; I was in Your plan.
> Thanks for accepting me the way I am.
> You will supply all my need. By Your Spirit You will lead.
> Take my life today.

Thanks for loving me.

Then I hear Him gently say, "I'm glad you took the time
To read My Word and talk to Me in prayer.
When we walk together I'll keep you in My love.
Believe the promise of My special care.
I thought of you, child; you were in My plan.
Loving, accepting, is the way I am.
I will supply all your need. By My Spirit I will lead.
I gave My life for you.
Thanks for loving Me."

DEBBY GRAY WILMOT

JULY 30

THE FALL OF GIANTS

I destroyed the Amorite before them, though he was tall as the cedars and strong as the oaks. I destroyed his fruit above and his roots below. Amos 2:9, NIV.

One of California's more celebrated natural attractions is Sequoia National Park. In some ways the huge sequoias outshine even their taller cousins in the magnificent redwood forests. Once there, visitors always gravitate to the General Sherman Tree, standing 272 feet tall in its grove of only slightly less ancient sequoias. Standing in the presence of one of the oldest and most massive living forms on earth is likely to slow down even the most flippant tourist. General Sherman was hundreds of years old when Jesus was born, and today the forest rangers regard him and his nearby elderly companions as the venerable gentlemen they are.

Wearing a coat of bark as much as two feet thick, a giant sequoia tree is impervious to brushfires. No disease can destroy it. It grows, reproduces, and appears strong and alive!

But, like the judgment described so poetically by Amos, even this tree can fall. It is vulnerable. It has one fatal, tragic flaw. Its root system is very shallow. Although the General's roots spread out over an acre of land, they lie no more than five feet deep in the ground. So he has spent more than 2,000 years doing a delicate balancing act. The force of the wind or the weight of snow in his top branches could easily bring him down.

Jesus' parable of the handsome-but-fruitless fig tree points up the discrepancy between what is seen and what lies within or below. Sad as it may be, looking at a diseased or dying tree is not as heart-wrenching as witnessing the fall of a giant. Death by toppling over is the way the great sequoias go. The pastor whose influential ministry ends in scandal. The "ideal" parents who abuse their children. The prosperous (and perhaps generous) businessman who turns out to be corrupt. The devoted and apparently compatible couple who turn up in the divorce court. The esteemed doctor who is a drug addict. The trusted friend who betrays our confidence. We have all watched the giants fall, crashing to the earth with their spreading roots ignominiously turned up toward the sky.

Outward appearances may be what they will, but the key to survival still lies in the homely and invisible root system. It has to be nurtured so that the roots can reach down and tap into the deepest source of spiritual life. Here—and nowhere else—can we find security.

DOROTHY MINCHIN-COMM

July 31

FROLICKING IN EDEN

No eye has seen, no ear has heard, no mind has conceived what God has prepared for those who love him. 1 Cor. 2:9, NIV.

Now and again in life we discover delightful surprises, things we never dreamed of. Such an experience was mine on my first trip to Hawaii.

"Oh, it's nothing like it used to be," helpful friends commented. "We don't go to Hawaii anymore. It's too commercial."

But John and I had never been to Hawaii, and we longed to go. Besides, dear friends had moved there and were urging us to visit.

"There must be *something* natural to see," we told each other. "How can people completely spoil the beaches and the ocean?" So we set off into the unknown.

I liked Hawaii from the moment we arrived.

Oh, how I loved the beaches! I would have enjoyed my stay if we had done nothing but soak in the ocean all day every day. The warm, soft ripples of the waves bore me in their arms like a cradle. Soon my heat-dried California skin was soft and supple.

But the surprise came early one morning.

"Let's go to Hanauma Bay," our friends suggested. "It's a spawning place for all kinds of tropical fish. We'll take fish food, and you'll enjoy feeding the fish." We piled snorkeling gear into the car and took off early. "Before the tourists get there" was the explanation.

We parked at the top of the cliff and hiked down to a horseshoe-shaped cove formed in the basin of an ancient volcanic crater. One side had been washed away by the sea, and waves had washed in sand which formed a beach. Lava covered part of the floor of the bay, and coral had formed on the rocks. As we walked out into the water I could hardly believe my eyes or senses. Hundreds of colorful fish darted this way and that and gathered around us as we scattered fish food. It was exactly as if I had walked into an aquarium at Sea World.

I was not prepared for the depth of feeling this experience brought to me. No one had told me about it. I was overwhelmed. It was as though I had either joined Eve in Eden's waters or been transported into the earth made new. I was breathless and thrilled as entire schools of fish eddied around me as I fed them.

For the rest of our vacation I begged to go to Hanauma Bay each morning before we began the rest of the sightseeing day. I came to know many of the fish by species name and a few individually by human names. Every morning I experienced the presence of God among the fish. The day we left Hawaii we spent the early morning at Hanauma Bay.

"Goodbye," I told the fish, feeding them for the last time. "I love you."

We needn't wait for heaven. God has prepared His delightful surprises for us here and now.   — CARROL JOHNSON SHEWMAKE

AUGUST 1

DUSTY—1

In the same way your Father in heaven is not willing that any of these little ones should be lost. Matt. 18:14, NIV.

Noelle was almost 9 years old when she decided she wanted a hamster for her birthday.

Naturally I said no.

I have no idea where she even got the idea. Must have seen the little creatures in a pet store. At any rate, I didn't think a whole lot about it until she stood before me in her blue-and-white-checked sunsuit, knobby knees bruised as usual, and confided that she was praying for a hamster. I told her we'd think about it.

She chose a honey-colored ball of fluff known as a teddy-bear hamster and bore him home in a cardboard box as if she were carrying the crown jewels. He bit her finger when she tried to pet him, and the finger bled. Noelle said he didn't mean to do it.

She named him Dusty.

Dusty lived in a luxurious plastic hamster haven floored with sweet-scented shavings. He had an exercise wheel plus other assorted toys. He soon made himself at home, delegating corners of his box for different activities—a kitchen, a bedroom, a sanitary station. It was fun to watch him fill his cheeks till they couldn't hold another seed and then run to the "kitchen" and spit the seeds out one at a time for storage there.

One would have thought Dusty had everything he could need or want right at his toetips. But for some reason known only to him, he wasn't content. Dusty just had to travel.

The first time he escaped we all panicked. But in due time someone found him—in a closet, as I remember—and returned him safely to his box. It seemed that he'd flattened his furry little body and squeezed through an incredibly narrow opening in the box, cutting his foot in the process. I hoped that would slow him down. I was wrong.

We began to call him Houdini.

Thinking Dusty might be unhappy with such a small home, we added a connecting tube and another room to his dwelling. He'd visit the new apartment occasionally, but he still preferred the challenge of escape and the wide-open spaces of the whole house. We added a second traveling tube that led to an enclosed exercise wheel. He used it now and then, short legs churning violently, but after we turned out the lights and covered his cage for the night, he'd begin to sniff around for a new way out. He often found it.

We piled books and other heavy debris on the cage. Somehow he still managed to lift up the lid just enough to make his getaway. Finally we screwed the lid down. That worked for a couple days.

Despite all the fear and extra work that his wandering feet and inquisitive little mind brought us, we grew to love him. And Noelle? She adored him.

How like us. We wander. We hurt ourselves. But God is always ready to guide us back home. And He continues to love us unconditionally.
PENNY ESTES WHEELER

August 2

Dusty—2

The last enemy to be destroyed is death. 1 Cor. 15:26, NIV.

A few months after Dusty, the hamster, joined our family we moved to Michigan. I drove all the way from Tennessee to Berrien Springs with my elbow resting on Dusty's home while Noelle kept a constant vigil. We didn't want any chance of his escaping in the car.

The move didn't seem to slow him down, though by now we'd grown almost as clever as he, making it more difficult for him to break out than before. He was a source of delight, using his tiny paws like little hands to hold a sunflower seed for careful nibbling. He wasn't particularly friendly; he never wanted to be held or cuddled. But that didn't matter to Noelle. She loved him.

Then Dusty got sick. We noticed he wasn't eating and just rested in a corner of his box. So we went off to the pet store for medicine—drops to put in his drinking water in case he had pneumonia. Keep him warm, the man at the pet store told us. Hamsters are subject to all kinds of problems. With care, he might recover.

I sat up with him the next night. My little boy was sick that night too, and I worked between child and hamster through the long, dark hours. I kept the heating pad at just the right temperature under Dusty, tried to help him take a few drops of medicine, and by daylight he seemed to be improved.

Noelle crept fearfully to his box the next morning, afraid to look, yet compelled. "He seems a little better," I told her. "Maybe he'll be OK."

"I'm praying for him," she whispered.

I worked with him off and on all day long. He didn't fight my hands, didn't try to bite, and didn't try to escape. He just buried himself in the sweet scented shavings, tucked his head against his dusky chest, and slept.

When I checked on him again that evening, he didn't stir. He hadn't moved in some time. With one tentative finger I stroked his head. It was cold.

Noelle sat on my lap in the rocking chair that night, her long legs dangling to the floor, her head against my chest, sobbing. "I loved him," she repeated over and over. "I loved him."

I cried with her.

"Why is it," I demanded of God, "that a little girl can't even keep a pet that she loves? It isn't fair. It isn't right."

The answer came. It wasn't fair and it wasn't right. But that's the way life on this earth is.

A million years from now someone from a far-flung planet may kindly question, "What was sin like? What was it like to live on a whole planet that obeyed its own rules and sometimes God didn't even intervene?" And I'll have an answer for that curious questioner. Noelle will have an answer.

Sin hurts. That's why God gave His life to remove it from the universe. Sin separates. Sin caused a little girl to lose a honey-colored hamster that, despite its antisocial ways, she loved with all her heart. Sin's results are no respecter of persons—rich or poor, strong or weak, parent or child, flower or pet. All are touched—inevitably all are hurt—by sin.

I held Noelle long after the tears stopped flowing down her cheeks. We rocked together in the dark, quiet house.

She's never wanted another hamster.   PENNY ESTES WHEELER

AUGUST 3

JOY

In thy presence is fulness of joy. Ps. 16:11.

The dictionary says an acrostic is one or more sets of letters that, when taken in order, form words. You can make an acrostic with the word "joy."

>J is for Jesus
>O is for others
>Y is for yourself

J is for Jesus, whom joyful or joyous people put first in their lives. So many times in our hurry and flurry, hustle and bustle, Jesus does not rate number one. Some mornings we oversleep, so we neglect to take time to read the Bible. We do not offer a prayer of thanksgiving and praise or ask for protection through the day. We rush to work. The hours of the day go rushing by, and Jesus is forgotten. I like the words of the gospel hymn "Take time to be holy; the world rushes on." The sad thing is we seem to rush right along with the world.

O stands for others. While we are rushing, we may step on or over someone as we are trying to climb up the ladder of success. We are thoughtless and often heedless of the needs and concerns of others. They too would appreciate a smile, a cheery greeting, a helping hand.

When we do this we are last. Yes, Y stands for yourself. This does not mean we are not important—we are. Jesus died for us, and we should regard ourselves as highly as He does. But neither are we better or more important than others. It brings us joy when we seek to serve others for Him. Christianity is spelled out in this little three-letter word—joy. We are not trying to outdo or outsmart our companions, our neighbors, our coworkers. We are to show forth the fruit of the Spirit in our daily living. And the second fruit listed in the Good Book is joy!

Here it is for your study: "The fruit of the Spirit is love, joy, peace, longsuffering, gentleness, goodness, faith, meekness, temperance: against such there is no law" (Gal. 5:22, 23).   MARION SIMMONS

AUGUST 4

THE HEARING EAR AND THE SEEING EYE

The hearing ear, and the seeing eye, the Lord hath made even both of them. Prov. 20:12.

The first time I remember hearing this verse was at Loma Linda University church when H.M.S. Richards, a famous radio speaker, was going to preach, but the offering was for *Faith for Today*, a Christian television series. You could sense the discomfort of the congregation because this seemed awkward, even inappropriate. However, the man appointed to call for the offering walked over to the microphone and promptly read this verse. The entire congregation gave a sigh of relief, and the moment of discomfort passed.

In the ongoing struggle to learn God's direction for my own life, I have considered this verse and others, wondering if I really could see and hear what is important. Proverbs is so full of commentary: "The heart of the prudent getteth knowledge; and the ear of the wise seeketh knowledge" (Prov. 18:15).

In Matthew 13 Jesus said, "Who hath ears to hear, let him hear. . . . Therefore speak I to them in parables: because they seeing see not; and hearing they hear not, neither do they understand. And in them is fulfilled the prophecy of Esaias, which saith, By hearing ye shall hear, and shall not understand; and seeing ye shall see, and shall not perceive: for this people's heart is waxed gross, and their ears are dull of hearing, and their eyes they have closed; lest at any time they should see with their eyes, and hear with their ears, and should understand with their heart, and should be converted, and I should heal them. But blessed are your eyes, for they see: and your ears, for they hear" (verses 9-16). "But he that received seed into the good ground is he that heareth the word, and understandeth it" (verse 23).

When we really search and ask for the gifts of hearing and of sight and perception, we can hope God will answer us. If we are hearing and seeing, we should be bearing the fruit also. Proverbs 8:1 says, "Can't you hear the voice of wisdom?" (TLB).

In Hebrews 5:11 we read, "There is much more I would like to say along these lines, but you don't seem to listen, so it's hard to make you understand" (TLB). So where does all of this leave us? Are we listening to God's wisdom? Do we learn when we read and study? Are we just repeating words we have heard over and over, not putting them in our hearts? Looking for God's guidance is not a superficial, instant action. In our current society of fast food, instant replay, and 24-hour access to money at the bank, we want our guidance quick and easy! If ever there was a time for us to take time to listen, it must be now. Here are my ears, God; help me to listen.

JULIA L. PEARCE

AUGUST 5

SAFE AT LAST!

There is no fear in love; but perfect love casteth out fear.
1 John 4:18.

The womb must have felt far safer to me than being out here does. My mother tells me I nearly killed her when I was being born.

Sometimes, being out here scares me so much I expend all my energy in an attempt to get the safety back. So I make nests for myself—homes, rooms, places in the mind, relationships, affiliations. Sometimes, being out here feels so large and menacing that I seek safe beliefs. I ask no questions. I propound or entertain no uneasy concepts. I avoid all changes.

When I find myself in this safety-at-expense-of-all-else frame of mind, I have the idea that life should not be difficult. Rain should fall only at night while I sleep, as it does in mythical Camelot. Snow should fall on slopes designed for skis and sleds. I deny that life is difficult, and hope for ease because I want to be safe and sure once more. Unborn.

The irony exists: safety comes only when I live with the fear—taste it in my mouth, smell it in the room, look at its reasons, touch it with my heart, hear it emerge from my mouth in prayer. When fear becomes more than ideological, when fear is visceral, I attend to fear. Only then can I learn from it, let it go. Only after I fully experience fear can I begin to realize that God's love casts it out.

After I pay attention to the fear and find its roots, I can explore the possibilities—creative and vibrant—that emerge when the need to feel safe no longer controls me. And I learn that despite the fear I can find safe places hidden in my heart by the touch of God.

"And we have known and believed the love that God hath to us.
God is love;
and [she] that dwelleth in love dwelleth in God, and God in [her].
Herein is our love made perfect,
that we may have boldness in the day of judgment:
because as [God] is, so are we in this world.
There is no fear in love;
but perfect love casteth out fear; because fear hath torment.
[She] that feareth is not made perfect in love.
We love [God], because [God] first loved us" (1 John 4:16-19).

Today, Lord, I am willing to be out here, alive, with all my senses, reborn. Help me to let the fears be fears. Help me to know what I fear most, and why. Help me to accept that life isn't safe. Then help me to trust that You are out here, with me, where it is scary. And Lord, thank You for the promise!   KATIE TONN-OLIVER

AUGUST 6

POSITIVE PICTURES

Fix your minds on whatever is true and honourable and just and pure and lovely and admirable. Phil. 4:8, Phillips.

A drop of perspiration rolled lazily down my nose and spattered on the wooden handle of the dandelion digger. Adjusting my broad-brimmed hat, I determinedly thought about the projected loveliness of the lawn without a single dandelion in sight—a reverie broken by the sound of squealing tires next door. Paul had zoomed through his gate and screeched his 10-speed to a stop on the patio. "Hey, don't drop those batons," he called to his younger sisters, who were practicing their latest routines.

As if on cue, both batons fell to the ground. "You did it again. You made us mess up!" the twins yelled in unison. Crestfallen, Paul jammed his hands into his pockets and headed for his house.

Deciding that intervention might be the better part of valor, I sang out, "Hi, neighbors. How about coming over here for some popsicles?" Their faces brightened, and all three kids scrambled toward my patio. We sat together companionably, tempers cooled by the icy refreshment. "I believe you meant to help your sisters," I said, looking at Paul, "and I also understand [glancing at the twins] that sometimes it seems as though Paul's help doesn't help." They nodded vigorously. "Do you recall what you were thinking the first time you tried to ride your bike through the gate, Paul?" I asked.

He smiled wryly. "I was thinking I didn't want to hit the gatepost—and I ran into it anyway."

"What goes through your mind now?" I persisted.

After a moment of reflection he said in his best age-10 voice, "Now I tell myself to aim for the middle, and it always works!"

I explained how our minds create pictures from our thoughts. How when Sheena and Sheila heard the words "Don't drop your batons," their minds had first created a picture of failure and then tried to imagine the reverse—unsuccessfully. How much better to create the positive picture initially.

"Why not grab your batons and have Paul talk to you with positive comments right now?" I suggested.

The girls began twirling their batons, and Paul said, "Catch those batons, girls!"—and they did without a hitch. They all got the point; Paul actually got a bit excited. "This is cool," he said enthusiastically. "It's like magic." I recalled the many times that I had sabotaged my own behavior by creating mental pictures of failure, temporarily forgetting that as we think in our hearts so are we (Prov. 23:7).

A few days later I again heard the familiar squeal of tires and heard Paul's voice cut the air. This time he called out "Nab those batons" as he ran into the house.

"Lord, make me more like a little child," I prayed. "Help me to learn lessons as quickly as they do. May I fix my mind on positive mental pictures—today and forever."   ARLENE TAYLOR

August 7

"Help Me!"

Call upon Me in the day of trouble; I will deliver you, and you shall glorify Me. Ps. 50:15, NKJV.

Through the open windows of our bedroom we heard a female voice crying in anguish: "Help me! Help me!" Jumping out of bed, we rushed to the window and, looking out, saw a dark form lying on our front lawn. Immediately we wondered who would be out here, seven miles from the nearest town, at 3:00 a.m. calling for help? Was this a ruse someone was using to gain entrance to our home? Was she a victim of an abduction and fleeing her abductor? All these thoughts and more ran through our minds.

Feeling she would be more comfortable if she heard a female voice, my husband asked me to talk to her. I called to her and asked her what her needs were. She cried, "I've had an accident. Help me!"

As we brought her into our home her cry was: "I want my mommy! I want my mommy!" Through her tears we were able to learn who her parents were and called them. Choosing to sit on the floor, she rocked back and forth and insisted that we not call an ambulance. Repeatedly this woman in her late 30s continued to plead, "I want my mommy! I want my mommy!" (Later her mother reported that a physician had examined her and found she had no major injuries, but was badly bruised.)

Suddenly she cried, "My car! It's ruined!" As we talked to her we learned what had happened. Her prize possession was a BMW that she had just had restored. Driving it home to Minnesota from California, she had become tired. As she'd reached down into a cooler to get something to drink she'd lost control of the car, and it had rolled over and over. Still, she had been able to get out of the car and walk. Not knowing in which direction to go, she'd wandered for about two miles, in the dark, before reaching our house.

Sometimes I feel that I have had a wreck with my life and I want the comfort and assurance that only Jesus can give. I then cry out to Him, "Help me!"

His answer is quick and sure: "Here I am; what do you want, My child?" He is always there, ready to give me peace.

As our "woman in the night" needed the comfort of her mother's arms, so I need to feel His comforting arms around me. I am so glad He is always there, ready to give me the love I need. He provides the healing required for all my bumps and bruises. Will you also reach out to Him for the love and healing He wants to give you?

EVELYN GLASS

AUGUST 8

GOD ANSWERS PRAYER

Therefore I tell you, whatever you ask for in prayer, believe that you have received it, and it will be yours. Mark 11:24, NIV.

My 5-year-old granddaughter, Lauren, recently learned to read, and now spends hours every day reading her storybooks. Sometimes I read her a story, but recently what she really wants me to do is tell her a "real" story. So, bit by bit, I've been telling her experiences family members have had in the past, especially those of her mother when she was a little girl. She seems to like these stories in a special way.

The other day Lauren asked again, "Grandma, tell me a real story, please!" I paused for a moment, thinking I'd told her all the stories, but then I remembered one from when I was just her age.

My parents were missionaries teaching at a Christian college in São Paulo, Brazil. I have very happy childhood memories of our years there. But this memory was different, and very special.

While playing outside, we children saw the doctor, with his black bag, saying goodbye to our mother. He looked very serious. Mother looked worried and sad too. She called us in and briefly told us that our daddy was very sick and might die. "But," she said, "let's go to his bedside, and we're going to pray together to Jesus to help Daddy."

I clearly remember how she told our heavenly Father what was wrong with Daddy; he had bruised and cut a leg on a ladder while he was doing repairs in the boys' dormitory, where he was dean. He was young and strong and had paid no attention to his leg; it had gotten worse and was now gangrenous. She also told the Lord that the doctor couldn't do anything. (This was in the days before penicillin and other antibiotics.) She asked for wisdom for how to care for Daddy, and that if it was His will, to please heal him. "Don't leave us alone," she pleaded.

Though I was so young, I felt that I might lose my father, who was so dear to me; yet at the same time Mother filled us with confidence that God could heal him.

Minutes later two young men from the dormitory arrived at the house, offering to treat my father with hydrotherapy. A wood stove, huge pots of hot water, ice, sheets and white towels, others chopping wood, small groups praying. . . . A long day full of worry for Mother! But when the doctor came the next day, he was very surprised to see Mother with a big smile.

Yes, I learned that God always answers prayers—and this time it was with a yes. In my little-girl mind I realized that beyond my good earthly father was a heavenly Father who cared and watched over us.

As I finished the story my little granddaughter Lauren said to me, "Jesus always takes care of us, and I know He can hear me, just as He heard your mother's prayer." EUNICE PEVERINI

AUGUST 9

LOVING IN DEED

Let us not love in word, neither in tongue; but in deed. 1 John 3:18.

Judy's eyes were red and itchy. According to the doctor, it was a mild inflammatory infection. In spite of Mary's careful application of medication the condition in her 8-year-old daughter's eyes persisted.

One morning as Mary was rushing to get breakfast ready and children off to school, she heard, "Mama, I can't open my eyes. Come take me to the bathroom."

After Mary had helped Judy to the bathroom and Judy had washed her face, she could see again. But during breakfast she began negotiating to be allowed to stay home from school, using her eye condition as a basis for her argument. Mary was firm, however, and Judy reluctantly and sullenly joined the group waiting for the bus.

Later that morning Mary received a scrawled message from her daughter. Judy said she was feeling tired and weak; her eyes hurt, and she didn't feel like doing schoolwork. Mary was amused as she pictured the pathetic scene at school.

Trying to think how to encourage Judy, Mary finally remembered a forgotten candy bar. She carefully wrapped it with a note saying how sorry she was that Judy wasn't feeling well, and suggested that maybe this reminder of her love would help.

When the school bus arrived home in the afternoon a happy,

bubbling Judy came bounding off and straight into her mother's arms.

"Oh, Mama, do you know how I felt when I got your note? I was so happy! When my friends saw what you sent me, they said, 'I wish I had a mama like yours!'"

When Mary told me of this incident several days later, I sat listening with a lump in my throat as she described what joy it was to her to make her daughter so happy. How much more convincing we are in our expressions of love and support to others by the little things we do for them than just by the words we express. Often these deliberate acts of kindness involve a sacrifice of time and effort, but if like Mary we can keep the larger perspective in mind, the love we give will heal, comfort, and encourage—and come back to us again.

RAE LEE COOPER

AUGUST 10

ALL THINGS WORK TOGETHER

And we know that in all things God works for the good of those who love him, who have been called according to his purpose. Rom. 8:28, NIV.

I have always loved children. Since I was a little girl I have been associated with babies and children. At church I would "borrow" a baby to care for or play with. During my teen years I baby-sat and worked in a day-care center. In college I specialized in early childhood education, building on my natural interests and God-given talents with children. When I married I eagerly looked forward to having a family.

When Matthew, our first child, was born, it was a period of great joy. But that joy was short-lived, because a few weeks after the birth I realized something was wrong. A visit to his pediatrician confirmed our worst fears. A yet-unknown something was drastically wrong with our firstborn. His eyes could not track a penlight in a dark room.

Then began a stream of seemingly unending visits to specialists in many fields. It was like being on an emotional roller coaster. Within six months I was told that my firstborn was legally blind and mentally retarded. Somehow I remember stumbling out of the doctor's office. I was crushed. So many hopes and dreams for my child vanished that day.

Would he ever run and play like others? Would he be able to go to school? Would he date and marry? What did a blind and mentally retarded child do for a lifework?

I don't remember being as concerned with how or why it happened. I was more concerned with how I would mother a child with disabilities. Was I equipped with the specialized skills necessary to parent a child with special needs?

During my pregnancy my husband and I had prayed for this child—a three-part specific prayer: that he would love the Lord; that he would be healthy; and that he would have a temperament that I could handle. I now recognize that God answered my prayer and continues to work in Matthew's life.

Matthew, who is now a teenager, does love the Lord and has testified verbally to it. He was baptized in a special ceremony last year by his grandfather in front of the entire church family. And he is a healthy child, even though he has functional limitations. Furthermore, he has a quiet, pliable, and adaptable temperament. He is the easiest of the four boys to discipline.

The burden of caring for a child with disabilities is heavy. It isn't something that's dealt with once and then forgotten. It's something that I live with daily. Sometimes I am overwhelmed. It's comforting to be able to turn to God in prayer and ask Him to lift this burden from me.

God is good; He answered my prayer, though not the way I would have chosen. And God began preparing me for this task as a youngster with an overwhelming love for children and through special education courses.

A promise that I claim is that God will not bring upon me more than I am able to bear (see 1 Cor. 10:13). I look forward to heaven, where my firstborn son will be made perfect—along with his mother.

CARLENE WILL

August 11

"Sing Unto the Lord a New Song"

Praise ye the Lord. Sing unto the Lord a new song, and his praise in the congregation of saints. Let Israel rejoice in him that made him: let the children of Zion be joyful in their King. Ps. 149:1, 2.

Just a few days ago I attended a two-day prayer retreat. I had been there only a few minutes when I was asked to sing for Friday morning worship. On Thursday night I prayed that God would give me a song.

I awoke at 3:30 a.m. Taking my Bible lesson guide, Bible, and hymnbook, I walked up the hill to the lodge. After thumbing through the quarterly for several minutes, I decided to read something from the Bible. Turning to the Psalms, I read the first four. As I began reading Psalm 5, "All Hail the Power of Jesus' Name" came to mind. I can remember thinking that I liked that song, but the words didn't fit the theme of our prayer retreat. It was then that my eyes fell upon verse 11, and I began singing it to "All Hail the Power of Jesus' Name":

"But let all those that put their trust in thee rejoice.
Let them ever shout for joy,
Because thou defendest them.
Let them also that love thy name
Be joyful [joyful] in thee."

The words fit the tune perfectly. Try it! BARBARA HALES

AUGUST 12

TAKING WHAT IS GIVEN

Now we have received, not the spirit of the world, but the spirit which is of God; that we might know the things that are freely given to us of God. 1 Cor. 2:12.

As our Sonshine group from the boarding school entered the hospital room we could tell by her eyes that something was not quite right with the patient. She was an elegant, elderly woman; by her recently permed and colored hair it was obvious that someone was taking good care of her. But there was something wrong besides broken bones. Her eyes and responses told us that either the medication or an illness had brought about some mental misconnections; but she was attentive, so we proceeded.

We introduced ourselves. Then, when the students started to sing, the woman started to ask for Shirley, then for Francis. We kindly told her we didn't know who they were or where they might be. She was polite but incessant, so the students decided to stop singing and motioned for me to have prayer. I walked over closer to the bed and asked her, "Would you like for me to pray for you?" She looked straight at me, clutched her robe at the neck, and said loudly, "I already had a bath." Later I commended the teenage girls for keeping a straight face. I know I blinked in surprise. It took me a moment to gain composure and state my offer again, in case she hadn't heard. This time she really got excited. After calming her down with assurances that I wasn't going to bathe her, we said our farewell and left without the prayer.

I've given some thought to that visit. I've wondered how many times God has sent me a "Sonshine" person to cheer me and instead of rejoicing in the ones He has sent, I am discontent because the ones I want are not there. I have wondered how many times God has spoken to me and I have not understood because my mind has been chemically influenced by too much medication or food or by poor habits of choice, such as what I view, listen to, or read. I've wondered how many days I have gone around clutching my own robe, saying "I am clean; I don't need what You are offering" when what He was offering was a cleansing at a depth I could not do myself. I've wondered how His robe of righteousness would have changed me. Or how much more I might have accomplished had I not been using one hand to clutch my old garment.

I've wondered if the angels and the Trinity have held back their chuckles when my answer to God was on a different topic than He had spoken of. Or if the angels have turned away in sadness because I didn't take what they were giving. I wonder how much I've missed because I've been focusing on what I've wanted instead of on what was being given to me. I wonder. —EVELIN HARPER GILKESON

August 13

"In the Secret Place of the Most High"

He that dwelleth in the secret place of the most High shall abide under the shadow of the Almighty. Ps. 91:1.

I saw a dim light shine on the inside of the study window. Was it my imagination? Perhaps it was only a reflection from a passing car's headlights. In the autumn-chilled night air I turned and looked around. The street was dark, and no moving cars were in sight. Our cat came softly out to greet me. She looked up at me, but made none of her usual purrs and meows in greeting. Something was wrong!

Seldom ill, I had taken that day to stay in bed and nurse a cold. My husband, Jim, was out of town, and I had the house to myself. In the evening I forced myself out of bed, dressed, and went to the nearby Burbank airport to pick up a friend who would be visiting with us a few days. At the ticket desk I was told that because of fog her flight would land at the downtown airport. She would arrive by bus later that evening.

Having a couple free hours, I planned to go back to our warm home to wait. But as I was about to turn the car into our street, I suddenly remembered that I needed to buy some wrapping paper for a baby gift. A half hour later I arrived in front of the house.

Nothing had seemed amiss as I walked up to the front door until I saw the light in the window. Fighting fear, I prayed, "Lord, help me to keep calm and do the right thing!" I had to be sure I wasn't just imagining things. I walked as quietly as I could to the side door of the house. The window had been broken!

As fast as I could, and without attracting attention from those inside the house, I walked back out to the car, got in, and drove away.

Later, after the police had searched the house, they told me it was safe to enter. "Yes," the police officer told me, "it's a typical break-in." Things were strewn around the rooms in the search for valuables. A quick check proved that the intruders got very little. The officer said that it looked as though they had been interrupted. "It's a good thing that you weren't in the house when they came and that you didn't go into the house while they were there. You might have been raped or killed."

There is no doubt in my mind that God's hand was protecting me. I praise and thank Him for taking me out of the house and keeping me away while the intruders broke in. He allowed me to see the searching flashlight, which prevented me from getting caught in a burglary in progress.

God protects each of us every day, although only occasionally are we made aware of a specific incident in which God has saved us from harm. He preserves us from a thousand unseen dangers and guards us from the subtle attacks of Satan, lest we should be destroyed. He is so great and so good! Let us thank Him daily for His love and protection as He keeps us in His secret place. Certainly we can put all our trust in Him!   JOYCE NEERGAARD

AUGUST 14

SOAPS ON CALL

Do not be afraid. I am the First and the Last. I am the Living One; I was dead, and behold I am alive for ever and ever! And

I hold the keys of death. Rev. 1:17, 18, NIV.

I was relaxing with the newspaper one Sunday morning when my eyes fell on a column entitled Soaps on Call. I was amused as I read, "The Washington *Post* provides daily updates of soap operas on PostHaste, its free telephone information service. Call 202-334-9000, from a touch-tone phone, and then enter the category code of the soap opera you want: *All My Children* (8201); *Another World* (8202); *As the World Turns* (8203); *The Bold and the Beautiful* (8204); *Days of Our Lives* (8205); *General Hospital* (8206); *Guiding Light* (8207); *Loving* (8208); *One Life to Live* (8209); *The Young and the Restless* (8210)."

Many women live out their fantasies in the world of soaps. They look on as men and women glamorize love triangles and other immoral entanglements. I decided to rewrite the notice of the soap opera update, and here's what I came up with:

"Jesus is coming soon, and I want ALL MY CHILDREN ready to leave this sinful earth for ANOTHER WORLD. AS THE WORLD TURNS, it's plain to see that the BOLD AND BEAUTIFUL children of God must live the DAYS OF THEIR LIVES in readiness to meet their King! Soon we won't need GENERAL HOSPITAL, or any other hospital, because Jesus Christ, our GUIDING LIGHT, will put an end to all suffering. Our LOVING Lord reminds us that we have only ONE LIFE TO LIVE, whether we're 'over the hill' or among THE YOUNG AND THE RESTLESS.

"Someday soon we'll all stand before the judgment bar. But to those who believe in the saving blood of Jesus, this is not a day to be feared! God promises strength to those who choose to live a victorious life. Dial 1-800-HEAVEN for help. You'll get not an answering machine but immediate access to the King of kings! This resource is available to all our readers, and the call is free!" — Rose Otis

---

August 15

Reflections on a Harbor

Come out of her, my people, so that you will not share in her sins, so that you will not receive any of her plagues. Rev. 18:4, NIV.

We stood at the railing, looking down on Aberdeen harbor, one of the commercial ports on the south side of Hong Kong Island. It was our first visit, and I had much to see. New sounds, new sights, new smells. Oh, the smells! How could anything so close to the beautiful South China Sea smell so absolutely putrid!

The harbor was crowded with sampans, each owner vying for space. So closely were they jammed in that the children were hopping from one boat to the other. In the meantime mothers were cooking, tending their babies, and trying to dry their clothes. Fathers were preparing their fish for market.

Along the wharf street people had devised crude shelters of cardboard boxes. The stench of garbage and human waste reeked. "How can people stand to live like this?" we pondered. "Why don't they do something?"

On the short side of the harbor a large crumbling warehouse served as a day school for any families that wanted their children to learn to read. For two hours a day someone came to teach the few children who responded. It was a pitiful, wretched sight—all these teeming people living in this stinking, polluted harbor, and the countless others who claimed only a squalid square of sidewalk for their home.

My daughter and I looked at each other, tears in our eyes, pain in our hearts. "How will they ever hear about Jesus?" she asked. But that was two decades ago.

Another trip to Hong Kong, and this time I returned with my wonderful new husband. Anxious to share with him all the special places I had remembered on my first visit, I could hardly wait until we could see Aberdeen. "It's a sight you'll never forget, Lou. Your life just won't be the same," I promised.

We stood at the railing. Looking down on Aberdeen harbor, still one of the commercial ports on the south side of Hong Kong Island. New sounds, new sights, new smells. How could anything so vile become so changed!

The sampans were gone. In their place lay a magnificent yacht basin full of posh crafts from the most splendid marinas in the world. The wharf was clean, the cardboard shacks removed. Replacing this were neat rows of benches interspersed with plantings of subtropical splendor.

The crumbling warehouse? In its spot stood an imposing, elegant three-story building faced with white tile, trimmed in gleaming glass and chrome. This yacht club complemented the basin handsomely. There seemed to be nothing left that reminded me of the former depravity. Even the stench of the old harbor had given way to a faint whiff of incense—two joss sticks burning in petition of a loved one.

Louis and I looked at each other, tears in our eyes, pain in our hearts. "How will they ever hear about Jesus?" he asked. "Will the fragrant power of the Holy Spirit ever replace the aroma of Buddha's joss sticks?"

LORABEL HERSCH

AUGUST 16

DRIED BONES

A cheerful heart is good medicine, but a crushed spirit dries up the bones. Prov. 17:22, NIV.

This was ridiculous. Here it was only 6:00 in the evening, and I was ready to crawl into bed and call it a day. A very long, exhausting day. I couldn't figure it out. It wasn't as if my job involved a lot of physical exertion. Sometimes it was a lot of walking back and forth, but nothing that would account for this state of exhaustion. Slumped on the couch, I pushed the replay button in my memory to try to figure out where the day had gone downhill.

Beep! Beep! Beep! Oh, no, not Monday again. I have to hurry and get ready. So much to do.

Great. Three people have called in sick. Right. I really believe that. If I weren't so dedicated I'd call in too. It isn't fair for us to have to work extra-hard just so they can get a day off.

One thing after another has gone wrong. Doctors keep calling up and yelling for their results. It's not my fault this machine picked today to break down. Will this day never end?

Stop. The replay of the day faded out. Where had all that come from? I'd sounded so grumpy, irritated. Ever since I'd gotten out of bed I'd had absolutely nothing good to say about anything. I'd woke up this morning prepared to resent the entire world. I didn't really hate my job. The day hadn't been all that bad.

"A cheerful heart is good medicine, but a crushed spirit dries up the bones." Yes, I remembered that verse. But what did it have to do with sitting here ready to sleep for the next two days? Oh. My heart hadn't been very—

Beep! Beep! Beep! Oh, no, not Tuesday. Wait a minute. I'm not going to repeat yesterday. A cheerful heart, huh, Lord? Thank You for Tuesday.

"Oh, no, we're just going to be swamped today!" a coworker mourned. "It's going to be even worse than yesterday."

"Oh, we'll be busy, but we usually are on Tuesdays," I replied.

That's how it went the whole morning. Someone would say something negative about how much work we had to do, and I'd reply that it wasn't quite that bad.

"Are you always so positive?" one coworker finally asked in exasperation.

That's when I figured it out. They enjoyed complaining. They liked being miserable, and didn't appreciate my positive comebacks. They had been grousing all morning, and they had also been complaining about how tired they were. They all felt so worn out. Not me. Not anymore. It's sometimes hard to cultivate a cheerful heart, but the day goes much better. I don't come home ready to collapse anymore. Maybe it'll catch on. CHRISTINA ENNIS

AUGUST 17

EMPTY CHAIRS

Children are a gift from God; they are his reward. Ps. 127:3, TLB.

And look at all those children! There they sit around the dinner table as vigorous and healthy as young olive trees. That is God's reward to those who reverence and trust him. May the Lord continually bless you with heaven's blessings as well as with human joys. May you live to enjoy your grandchildren! Ps. 128:3-6, TLB.

As Ed and I sat around our dinner table we were very grateful for our 5-year-old firstborn son, with whom God had blessed us. Even though we loved each other deeply, we saw the three empty chairs around our table! Young Ed, named after his father, saw the other neighbor children with brothers and sisters and longed for a brother and sister of his very own.

Unknown to us, there was a family down the river a few towns away that had suffered brokenness. The father was sent to another state, while the mother fell in love with her old schoolmate. That union left her children on the outside, needing to be a part of someone else's family.

For three months this 3-year-old boy and 1-year-old girl were placed with an elderly baby-sitter. In time the kids proved to be too much for her to handle.

She called us to see if we were home, and came to visit us. She knew that we had only a son, and thought that perhaps we would like the little girl.

When we saw the little boy with the big smile and the little girl with the bright eyes, we knew we couldn't separate the children, so we decided to open our arms and welcome these little ones into our family. It took three long years for John Stephen, whom we named after my dad and Ed's dad, and Shari Lee, given a name close to mine, to become part of our family legally. Young Ed was thrilled, and John and Shari blended very well with us. Now our dining room table had only one empty chair.

Six weeks after John and Shari became part of our family, I began to get sick in the mornings. The doctor confirmed what we suspected. "A little girl would be so nice, Father," I whispered. He gave us the desire of our hearts.

Our baby girl, Melinda Rae, named after my sister, was soon born. Our family was now complete. God in His wisdom knew the end from the beginning and filled those six chairs in His own way. Thirty-five years ago we began life together as a family that only God knew how to place together. Children are indeed a true gift from God.

Our children are now all grown and married, and as our text states: "May you live to enjoy your grandchildren!" God has granted us our heart's desire once again, as our family, so far, has four granddaughters who have their own special place at Papop's and Grandma's table.

Sandy Lee Dancek

August 18

Four Years Too Late

An anxious heart is dispiriting; a kind word brings cheerfulness. Prov. 12:25, REB.

The twilight was quickly fading as I walked across campus with a friend. Seeing the outline of a person walking ahead of us, I squinted to read the writing on his letterman's jacket. Though the figure was rapidly getting farther away, I was able to make out the name of a young man I had attended boarding school with. My heart beat excitedly. I hadn't seen him since graduation, and I was eager to do some catching up and find out what he had been doing since we last saw each other.

He was almost out of earshot, but I hesitated before yelling his name. Suddenly shyness overcame me; I was never good when it came to making small talk, and I felt especially uncomfortable when there were long pauses when the small talk ran out. What if I said something stupid, or stuttered over my words? As he turned toward the men's dorm I told myself I'd talk to him later. After all, there were nine months of the school year ahead of us.

The chat I had put off never came. The day after I saw him, my friend, driven by desperation to pay his bills, attempted a bank robbery and ended up taking the life of a woman.

Four years later I sat beside him in a prison visiting room. Again I felt afraid of making small talk, wondering what we would talk about for an hour. This time I also felt regret. I wished I had taken the time to speak with him that night four years before. Maybe he was feeling alone, heavyhearted, and anxious. I too had struggled to make ends meet during college; perhaps I could have shared some words of encouragement. I don't know if it would have made a difference when he made that fateful decision, but I can't help wondering if it might have.

How many times have you avoided someone when you were in a hurry, didn't feel like talking, or just felt shy? We don't know the hidden griefs in the hearts and minds of those around us. For those that are weighed down with sorrows, our words of strength and encouragement may mean all the difference in the world.

I urge you to take the time to share a kind word with someone today. You never know when it may be too late, and the cheerfulness it brings may be just the help they need to calm their anxious heart. —Kathryn M. Gordon

August 19

He Still Heals

Immediately her bleeding stopped and she felt in her body that she was freed from her suffering. Mark 5:29, NIV.

Concern overwhelmed me as I grasped the seriousness of Myrtle's condition. She was nauseated, disoriented, unable to focus, colorless, and very weak. The attending physician advised that she should be taken immediately to the hospital.

Leaving her in the care of the doctor, I hurried off to my appointment. This was the last morning of the women's retreat that I was coordinating, and I needed to make sure everything was in place for the closing exercise. Yet Myrtle's illness was paramount on my mind.

When I arrived at the retreat, I met Juanita, one of the main speakers, and explained Myrtle's condition. Immediately she responded, "May I go and pray for her?"

Our prayer for healing included our desire for God's will to be done. When we opened our eyes we noticed a pink flush on Myrtle's face. Almost immediately Myrtle sat up and announced that she felt better and wanted to return to the meeting. The doctor reentered the room and urged her to lie down. But Myrtle insisted that all her symptoms had left. With tears in her eyes the doctor commented, "Today I have documented a miracle."

That afternoon, on the advice of the doctor, Myrtle returned to the hospital and was readmitted. The attending specialist determined that a large duodenal ulcer had ruptured late Saturday night and had hemorrhaged until the time of special prayer. The physician also stated that if the hemorrhaging had not ceased at the time it did, Myrtle's life would have been in danger.

Myrtle experienced God's healing touch. I too experienced God's touch. With awe I witnessed His power and eagerness for each of us to realize His personal care.

He healed me of lingering doubts I tended to harbor when during rough times I would sometimes wonder if He heard or cared for me. My wavering faith was now strengthened, fulfilling the promise that if I have faith the size of a mustard seed He will honor it.

God has become a personal God to me, one who in this country of accessible modern medical facilities is still willing, as recorded in Mark 5:29, to touch a woman whose lifeblood is ebbing away.

NORMA JEAN PARCHMENT

AUGUST 20

GOD'S LOVE SENT VIA OTHER PEOPLE

Beloved, let us love one another, because love is from God; everyone who loves is born of God and knows God. Whoever does not love does not know God, for God is love. 1 John 4:7, 8, NRSV.

It was late evening, and I wasn't ready for the message that flashed on the copy machine. "Clear paper path in 2, 3, 4, and 5."

Wouldn't you know it, I thought. And I was reminded of a sign I'd once seen:

"Warning: This copy machine knows when you're in a hurry!"

"More truth than fiction," I grumbled.

I opened the front door of the copier and methodically pulled paper from slots and curvatures labeled 2, 3, and 4. At number 5 I found the problem. One page, stubbornly twisted around a hot cylinder, refused to come free.

"Oh, Lord," I sighed as I poked and pulled, "I need help." The paper remained stuck. Thoughts of giving up became enticing, but knowing I needed the handout for class the next morning kept me contending.

Accomplishing nothing alone, I went in search of help. Two respiratory therapists from the department next door came to my rescue. Their previous experience and current perseverance soon put me back in business. With handouts copied I could finish the project and be on my way.

Why do I tell you this experience? Because I was reminded that God sends His help—His love—to us in many ways. Sometimes His interventions are direct. Other times He works through people and circumstances. This time He sent help through willing fellow employees.

You've heard it said, "God moves in a mysterious way His wonders to perform." Part of that way is loving and helping us through others. I thank Him, and I thank those benefactors who helped me with that stubborn machine. BEULAH FERN STEVENS

AUGUST 21

JUST SITTING AND LISTENING

Be still, and know that I am God. Ps. 46:10.

Life seems to go in cycles. When I was a girl in the forties, my mom made crocheted doilies and lace-bordered hankies by the mile. My generation was the beginning of the plastic, double-knit generation. No more embroidered dresser scarfs on our "blond" furniture; no more cotton dresses to iron. We were liberated women, back in the workforce. At least that is where we were told we should be.

Now that my little girl is a young married, it's doilies again, only this time they may be in a hoop on the wall or a cover on a pillow. Homemade quilts are popular too, and silk flowers have replaced the plastic variety. If you aren't "doing a craft," you just aren't with it. So now it's a career and a craft, or so we are told.

What happened to sitting and listening? Or maybe just sitting? I've often heard the expression "Oh, I couldn't just sit." I wonder if God told the story of Mary and Martha because He knew women would always feel they were on a guilt trip if they "just sat." I find that even if I do "just sit," my mind is working. If I didn't sit sometimes, I might miss that still small voice.

You can learn a lot by just sitting, especially outside in nature. Sometimes we sit conversing with a friend or listening to a sermon or good music, but maybe at times we need just to "sit" and let God talk to us. There is a possibility that we might be surprised at what He has to tell us.

I love a thought I read recently from *The Ministry of Healing*: "We must individually hear Him speaking to the heart. When every other voice is hushed, and in quietness we wait before Him, the silence of the soul makes more distinct the voice of God" (p. 58).

From doilies to plastic and back to doilies again—what will it be next to keep our hands and minds occupied until He comes?

PEGGY TOMPKINS

AUGUST 22

SHE LAYS OUT HIS CLOTHES

She does him good and not evil all the days of her life. Prov. 31:12, NASB.

The nursing supervisor burst into our busy intensive-care unit one morning, her face reflecting indignation and disgust. As things were relatively calm at that moment, several of the nurses gathered about her, curious as to the cause of her agitation. I joined the group in time to hear her relating her discovery, only moments before, that one of the doctor's wives made a practice of laying out her husband's clothes every morning.

The women's liberation movement, then in its heyday, had made a strong impact upon these nurses. To the revelation of apparent servitude on the part of a fellow woman they responded with comments echoing the feelings of the nursing supervisor.

Without thinking, I commented, "Well, I lay out my husband's clothes too!" As a group they turned to me, surprise and puzzlement reflected on their faces. Feeling a bit on the defensive, I thought, *Have I put my foot in my mouth this time?* But these were my friends as well as my coworkers. They knew both my husband and me well. After a moment someone said, "Maybe that's why Marilyn has such a good marriage!" With that we scattered back to our work, and the matter was laid aside.

Marriage for me these past 40 years has been filled with the joys and delights of give and take. Early in my marriage I observed my husband's faithfulness, kindness, gentlemanliness, and willingness to work hard and long for his family. As a busy contractor, he returned home each evening with the effects of concrete work and general construction evident. It seemed only natural to have a hot bath ready and his clothes for the evening laid out. Even when I went back to work after 17 years as a homemaker, it was no problem to continue the practice. Now in retirement that habit continues.

Our relationships are joyous and various as we experience the fun of doing little acts of kindness for others, especially for family members. I praise God that over the years I've had the privilege of "laying out his clothes"!

MARILYN KING

AUGUST 23

PUDDLES OR POSSIBILITIES?

Search me, O God, and know my heart; test me and know my anxious thoughts. See if there is any offensive way in me, and lead me in thy way everlasting. Ps. 139:23, 24, NIV.

Rain pelted against the windows. It blew in sheets across the front lawn and poured from the eaves of the house. Small rivers of water streamed across the patio, ending in a giant puddle at the driveway edge.

I eyed with satisfaction my freshly waxed kitchen floor. At least one thing had been accomplished on this soggy day. I'd even managed to keep two pairs of small feet out of the way while the wax dried—no small task when they belonged to two energetic housebound little boys.

Now Steve stood, his nose pressed against the patio door. "It isn't raining anymore; it's stopped."

"It's stopped," echoed Mark.

"May we go outside?" The question was asked in unison with the same degree of intensity.

I paused and looked past my shining kitchen floor to the soggy world outside. The rain had ceased, and the sun was attempting to break through the gray sky. I imagined what the mud puddles would do to clean sneakers and clothes, not to mention my kitchen floor.

"Please, Mommy," pleaded Mark while clutching in his hands the toy sailboat he had spent so much time constructing out of scrap lumber.

Reluctantly, stifling the urge to say "Stay away from the mud puddles," I nodded my approval. They bounded for the door with a shriek of delight.

As I watched my children play that afternoon I realized that they and I viewed mud puddles in a completely different light. To me they were a problem: dirty shoes, soiled clothes, tracked-up kitchen floors, and more work.

To my children they were not puddles but possibilities. A puddle was an obstacle course to ride your bike through or an ocean from which to launch a new boat. There were bridges to be built and dams to be made—the prospects were limitless.

What about the puddles in my life? I thought.

So often the trial ends, the struggle ceases, the gray clouds lift, and God's love shines through, but the puddles remain—puddles of remembered hurts, fears and failures.

Am I viewing them in the correct way, Lord? Am I guilty of allowing puddles to muddy my relationship with You? Have they become pools in which resentment, bitterness, and disbelief breed?

Perhaps a bridge to a better relationship with a family member or friend can be built over a puddle in my life. Maybe a puddle can be an obstacle course in which my faith grows stronger or a spot from which to launch a new beginning and let You guide the sails.

I know that Your light shining through will soon cause the puddles to disappear, but until then, give me wisdom to see all the possibilities.

REBECCA J. GRICE

August 24

Worry Over Nothing

Don't worry over anything whatever; whenever you pray tell

God every detail of your needs in thankful prayer, and the peace of God, which surpasses human understanding, will keep constant guard over your hearts and minds as they rest in Christ Jesus. Phil. 4:6, 7, Phillips.

Some years ago God allowed a great "earthquake" to shake my existence. My marriage ended. For 10 years I lived with a very gentle, loving, and understanding man. They had been years of happiness. In just a few months his behavior changed to the point that I thought I was living with a stranger; and without even allowing the possibility of a settlement, he left home.

I felt that my life had turned into absolute darkness. It felt as though I was suspended in the air, in a nightmare from which I could not awaken, never touching the soil. I felt thoroughly disoriented and lost.

In my desperate search for something to attach myself to, I found two verses in Philippians. I understood that I could ask and also claim God's promises; but I must believe that I would receive them, regardless of how I felt previously. Moreover, I should be thankful even before results were visible.

Even though most of us are grateful, generally we show gratitude after receiving something. I must confess it was very difficult for me to have to be thankful for what I was living, for the peace and joy that were absent. Nevertheless, in spite of all, I obeyed, and after having presented God all my pleadings, I thanked Him for the blessings He would give even when the occasion was obscure. Today, after many years, I can say that God blessed beyond my wildest expectations.

A woman author I admire once said, "Whatever your anxieties and trials, spread out your case before the Lord. Your spirit will be braced for endurance. The way will be open for you to disentangle yourself from embarrassment and difficulty. The weaker and more helpless you know yourself to be, the stronger will you become in His strength. The heavier your burdens, the more blessed the rest in casting them upon your Burden Bearer" (*The Ministry of Healing*, p. 72).

God wants every child of His to be tranquil, quiet, and at peace, regardless of the circumstances of life. It sounds like a contradiction: how can we enjoy this quietness in the middle of problems! But it is God who promises, and it is our duty to claim the blessings. Do not waste the opportunity of having today this sweet and blessed rest.

CRISTINA FERNANDEZ

August 25

Jesus Helps Me Grow

Grow in grace, and in the knowledge of our Lord and Saviour Jesus Christ. 2 Peter 3:18.

Years ago I began wearing a pair of glasses, half glasses, like Ben Franklin's. But I didn't have to wear them all the time, so when my husband would call, I'd answer and lay my glasses down anywhere close by: on a chair, on the piano, behind something, on the steps, next to the wall, in the garage, on one of the shelves of tools, on top of one of the files, etc. I'd almost always forget where I'd left them.

I continued this pattern for some years. I'd pray, and God would always answer my prayers almost instantly and help me find them. Finally a feeling came over me that I was terribly careless, and needed to change. I decided to stop praying and make myself find them on my own. This didn't work.

One day I decided I would never find them without God's help, and I prayed with tears, "Lord, I'm ashamed of my carelessness, I've been trying to overcome it, but it seems I can't find my glasses without Your help. I don't know anything else to do. Would You please help me find my glasses once more?" And He did—instantly.

One day I was ready to go to church, and looked for my purse everywhere. Then I felt that I needed to go back to the living room again. This time I looked on the other side of the organ bench, and there was my purse. I praise God that He continues to help me; I think I have grown through His help.

Growth is a gradual process, and I will use the story of a mirror to explain how it works. I used to have a small mirror in our closet. There was a light there, and I would turn it on to take a last look at my hair. One day I happened to take the mirror to a window through which the light of the sun was shining. I was shocked at what I saw. It was not OK!

Ever since then I have thought of the Sun of righteousness, and the Light of the world. As we look at Him, we will always see some area in which we need to change, to grow. He doesn't show us everything at once; we would be so discouraged that we would give up. Step by step we will grow if we follow Him; we will grow in grace and in the knowledge of our Lord and Saviour Jesus Christ.

Margaret Mondics Gibbs

August 26

A Child's Prayer

Even though I walk through the valley of the shadow of death, I will fear no evil, for you are with me. Ps. 23:4, NIV.

My home is in São Paulo, Brazil. One summer afternoon as my husband was visiting some church schools where he worked, a big thunderstorm broke. My 4-year-old daughter asked me, "Mama, where is Papa?"

I replied that he was working.

Again she asked me, "But Mama, is he at the office now?"

Then I told her that he had left to visit some schools that afternoon. I could tell that she was very worried. My daughter insisted, "Mama, let's kneel and ask Jesus to take care of Papa."

I had already prayed silently, but I promptly knelt down and we prayed together. A few minutes passed; again she asked to pray, and the scene repeated itself. I thought it strange that she was so worried about Papa that rainy afternoon.

When my husband returned home, I didn't have a chance to tell him how worried our daughter had been, for he immediately began telling us what had happened to him that afternoon. As he was driving down a steep hill he found he had no brakes. The road was wet and slippery; the car began gaining momentum, and at the bottom of the hill it entered, at a high rate of speed, what is normally a busy intersection. My husband braced himself for the almost certain crash, but at that exact moment there were no other cars around! Shortly afterward he was able to bring the car to a stop.

Then our daughter exclaimed, "Papa, it was Jesus who kept you safe! I prayed to Him."

In that moment I realized that God really had listened to the prayer of a child.

These simple happenings in our day-to-day lives become great victories when we put them in the hands of Jesus.

Our life can be compared to that car. The agitation of modern life drives us with an almost uncontrollable speed. The steep decline can represent everything that impedes our communion with Christ. How are our brakes when we need them?

ELLEN ROCKEL DOS REIS

August 27

Our Hands for God

Ye shall be a blessing: fear not, but let your hands be strong.
Zech. 8:13.

After several months of illness I lost the ability to manipulate my fingers on the piano keys. This became a sore trial for me, as I enjoyed playing the piano.

A day or two after my discovered loss of finger function, my best friend, Millie, came for her weekly visit. I confided my difficulty, and she insisted I go immediately to the piano and try to play just one measure. Before leaving my home she prescribed therapy: one measure daily, adding one more each time until I could play an entire song.

In time, with prayer, patience, and painful persistence, I regained the use of all my fingers. But until this experience, I had never considered the importance of my hands.

In battle Moses' upraised hands signaled victory for the Israelites in their conquest against the Amalekites (Ex. 17:8-12). When his hands grew tired, Aaron and Hur upheld them. Even so, we are to uphold vicariously the hands of our leaders through prayer, cooperation, respect, and financial support.

The virtuous woman of Proverbs 31 used her hands to plant, sew, weave fabric, and cook for her family. She also took time to assist the poor and needy.

Dorcas, an esteemed member of the early Christian church, sewed garments for the poor with her skillful fingers.

While Jesus was on earth His hands were kept busy in His father's carpenter shop. In His short adult life His hands were outstretched in compassion and sympathy to suffering people. With His hands He broke bread and fed the hungry multitude. He healed the sick, gave sight to the blind, and raised the dead.

Our hands are extensions of the Master's. God expects us in His strength to lift, pray, strengthen, help, and encourage one another by word and deed.

May our hands move at the impulse of His love.

Mabel Rollins Norman

August 28

Surrender, Healing

When thou passest through the waters, I will be with thee. Isa. 43:2.

Let's pray!" Judy was beckoning me to the corner of the little emergency room.

"Oh, no!" my mind screamed. "I can't! I can't! Lord, You *know* I can't!" Since dear friends had been killed on the battlefields of France, I knew I couldn't pray. Nice polite prayers, yes. But not for real heart-wrenching desperate needs like this: the very life of my 12-year-old daughter. She had not taken a breath since the explosion more than 20 minutes ago. It was obvious that we needed a miracle. But I didn't feel I could pray. I'd often declared fearfully in my inmost soul that if anything ever happened to my kids, I would curse God and die.

"Judy, you pray!" I begged. She did. Beautifully.

CPR continued under the strong hand of my husband. His silent prayer, in contrast, was one of simple faith. "Lord, I don't believe You brought us out here to the mission field to lose Jan." Makeshift positive pressure continued with Bishara gulping oxygen from a tank and blowing it into a tube in Jan's throat. But Jan's mottled chest and nonreacting pupils indicated impending death.

Now it was my turn. What was I saying? I couldn't believe it. "Lord, it's OK. She loves you. She told me so just yesterday. I'd rather lose her now than eternally. It's all right. I know You can save her if You want to. If it's best. And if not—it's OK, Lord. It really is! Just please help me with the other three children."

Peace. Heavenly peace flooded my soul. A gift. Purely a gift.

Then we heard it. Crying! Louder and louder. Jan was crying! "She's alive! She has a chance!" Joyous emotion exploded in the emergency room. But my prayer had already been answered. I knew, without a shadow of a doubt, that God would see us through. *That* is what prayer is all about!

"So, Lord, You too want her to live. Thank You! Thank You!"

Alice Fahrbach

August 29

A Right Spirit

And do not be conformed to this world, but be transformed by the renewing of your mind, that you may prove what is that good and acceptable and perfect will of God. Rom. 12:2, NKJV.

It had been "one of those days" all week long. It was Friday, and my list of things to do was long. Many of the things I normally did on Thursday had gone undone. While I was running errands my car's muffler had fallen half off, and I had been stranded for three hours waiting for my husband to come "rescue" me.

Now driving in my very loud, mufflerless car, I tried gathering my thoughts. But my 5-year-old son, Zachary, who rarely stops talking, kept asking me questions. I was irritated. I wanted to be left alone, to wallow in my discouraging thoughts.

"You know what, Mama?" Zachary asked.

Only half listening, I responded, "What?" It was a routine we repeated several times an hour.

"Every day I ask Jesus to take all the bad thoughts out of my mind." He went on to tell me about one thought that had stayed in his mind. Something scary he had seen in a store as part of their Halloween display. But he went on to say that he was going to ask Jesus to take away that one, too.

His statement spoke to my heart. Did I ask Jesus to take all the bad thoughts out of my mind? the negative attitudes? the discouragement? Or more often than not, did I allow myself to think on these thoughts and feel worse and worse (just as I was doing then)? Was I allowing Jesus to renew my mind so I could think good and acceptable thoughts, and to know God's perfect will?

Too often I allow myself to wallow in self-pity or discouragement, not turning to the only Source of help. Unlike my son, I did not ask God to take away the bad thoughts of my mind.

I prayed silently in my heart, *O Lord, forgive my discouragement and all negative attitudes that hinder my walk with You. Cleanse my heart and mind, and renew a right spirit and right thoughts within me. And thanks for speaking to me through my son. Amen.* Tamyra Horst

August 30

It's Really Good

Your word is a lamp to my feet and a light for my path. Ps. 119:105, NIV.

I have just recently entered a university as a (very) mature student. The first few weeks have been a bit of a nightmare, as I have realized the great gaps in my knowledge. Some of the lectures have been almost incomprehensible, others have been interesting, and some have even been exciting!

One such was the lecture on the Bible as a cultural source. I have been very heartened by the way in which the Bible has been presented as essential to our study of English literature, and during this particular presentation I was able to follow everything perfectly. I came out of the lecture feeling that even if I didn't know all I should about Greek mythology, at least I had a good working knowledge of the Book that was considered the most important.

As we stood around discussing the lecture, one of the young girls asked me, "Have you read the Bible?"

When I replied that I had, she asked with a very serious look on her face, "Is it any good?"

Of course I said yes, and since she did not own a Bible, I gave her one of mine the next day.

At first the question seemed amusing, but after a while it began to haunt me. I found myself wondering if I value the Word of God as I ought. When was the last time I read it as avidly as I do some other books? Do I ever say to my friends, "This is really good; you ought to read it," as I do with popular articles and books?

The Bible has been a lamp for us for so long and its words are so familiar that perhaps we do not appreciate what a treasure-house it really is. Since my encounter with that young student I have been reading my Bible with new eyes and praying for the Spirit to illumine the pages. Each day I find something new and exciting, making it easy for me to say with conviction, "It's really good!"

Audrey Balderstone

August 31

Angels on Overtime

The righteous cry, and the Lord heareth, and delivereth them out of all their troubles. Ps. 34:17.

Take a trunkload of health journals, a dark night 70 miles from home, and three elementary-age sons. Add a dash of mystery and heartthrobbing danger. Yield: eight hours of angel overtime.

Summer vacation had nearly ended. We were bone-weary of promoting health magazines for the upcoming school year's tuition. A good project, but we were tired.

We planned to camp overnight at Maryland's Ocean City and head home the next day. But after calling my husband and discovering that company was coming for dinner in my disheveled house, we headed home that night.

We loaded the car, locked all four doors, and headed into the blackness of night. The young salesmen collapsed into the seats.

A long stoplight; 1:00 a.m. The night air echoed a toot from the neighboring car. And another. The young driver motioned for me to roll down my window! The light still held. The stranger leaped out of his car toward my door! "Oh—I thought you were alone!" I heard him exclaim. He jumped back into his car.

Shaken, I gunned the intersection and made a quick right at the next light. Much later a road sign shocked my weary mind: "Welcome to Virginia." I had been searching for a welcome to Delaware! Nothing to do but retrace the weary miles.

Suddenly two glaring lights blinded my mirror; then the car began tailgating me. When I sped up, it did too. When I did a quick U-turn, it did the same. Then it pulled up alongside. "Dear Lord, O Lord, please help! Deliver us from evil this night!"

Finally the car spun ahead. I noticed several wide-shouldered, dark-coated men as they sped off into the night.

At the next truck stop I stopped. Trembling, sobbing, I babbled that "someone" was following me.

"Tell you what," the attendant explained. "That trucker there is hauling tomatoes to a plant right in your little town. Just follow him, and if you need help, blink your light."

As the sun rose, three sleepy boys tumbled into their beds, and I shared the story with my husband. But how eager I am to hear "the rest of the story" in heaven from our guardian angels!

Janice Chamberlain

SEPTEMBER 1

BUGS RESIST TOO

Resist the devil, and he will flee from you. James 4:17.

My three children and I were playing along the sandy beach of the Atlantic Ocean. As the waves washed ashore, small shell animals were left lying on the beach as the waves receded. Some of these small animals would quickly hide in the sand. Others lay on the beach until carried back to sea by the next wave.

After playing in the waves for a while, we ran along the beach. We noticed a large black bug sitting on the wet sand. When a wave came in and receded, the bug remained on the sand, closer to the ocean, yet not carried out to sea. My sunglasses, a man's hat, shell animals, and other things had been easily carried away by the waves, and so we waited to watch the bug get carried away too.

Whenever the wave receded, the bug simply crawled a little farther ashore or else remained where it was. Wave after wave came, and the bug was always left not too far from where it had been originally. The children pushed the bug closer so that the incoming wave could wash it away. As the waves approached, the children sang, "Bye-bye, bug," but it remained steadfast.

Since the bug seemed to have no intention of going out to sea, we finally decided to leave it alone.

Satan relentlessly sends temptations our way, trying to carry us away into sin. Sometimes there are even persons who try to lead us into sin. But although we are often surrounded by temptation and almost swallowed up by sin, God says, "Resist the devil, and he will flee from you."

When Jesus was tempted in the wilderness, He quoted Scripture to support His decision not to fall into temptation. After a time Satan left, realizing that tempting Jesus was useless. JOY CAVINS

SEPTEMBER 2

THE CIRCLE

Now that I, your Lord and Teacher, have washed your feet, you also should wash one another's feet. I have set you an example

that you should do as I have done for you. John 13:14, 15, NIV.

It was Communion. Seven pairs of feet had been washed. Seven pairs of hands were joined in a circle of prayer before returning to the sanctuary. One began the prayer.

"Lord, bless each family that is represented here. Thank You for Your presence with us . . . thank You for this fellowship . . ."

We had shared that fellowship as one knelt before the other with a basin of water and a towel. A squeeze of the hand said, "Thank you . . ." Another began to pray.

"Lord, I need to talk to You." The strained voice revealed a burdened heart. "All of us here are women, wives, mothers, grandmothers." There were three generations of women in that circle.

"Women are special to You. Mothers are special to You, Lord. You know the burdens we carry for our children." The minds of those mothers must each have pictured her own, little or grown. Some saw children in the first years of life, all the learning and new experiences . . . the sibling rivalry, the new world of school, learning about Jesus, about life and death, learning to obey or daring not to . . . their futures all untold, ready to be molded.

"Lord, bless us as mothers. Give us strength and wisdom to guide and encourage our children." Others saw teens facing the challenges and consequences of making their own choices, knowing the frustration and fear they face, but unable as a parent to make an escape for them from the realities of responsibility and mistakes.

Still others saw adult children struggling with grown-up problems . . . raising families, perhaps alone; walking away from the faith that was taught them; struggling with finances, careers, substance addiction. Adult children with broken dreams, broken hearts, broken lives.

"Lord, help each of us in the days and weeks and months ahead." My mind followed the voice around the circle of women and the burdens of each, some of them shared, others kept within the heart, untold, perhaps deeply painful, but now being lifted to God in that circle of prayer.

"Lord, bless us as women . . ." There were personal difficulties in that circle. A troubled marriage, advancing age, not enough money, not enough time, too little energy, illness, loneliness, spiritual doubts, sickly, aging parents, change . . . too little or too much. Stress. Fear. Pain. Grief.

At the amen another squeeze of the hand said, "Thank you for your friendship." Tears of some said, "Thank you for that prayer."

We started slowly, quietly back into the sanctuary to continue our service, but two remained, sharing an embrace that meant "I know what you are going through. I've been there."

"Lord, help us as women. Give us strength and wisdom to encourage not only our families but each other. Teach us to carry one another's burdens and to recognize pain in the heart. May we learn true communion with You and others." — MARY JOHNSON

SEPTEMBER 3

SUPERWOMEN

Come with me by yourselves to a quiet place and get some rest. Mark 6:31, NIV.

As women we often experience conflict in our lives because we are trying to juggle the way we were brought up (what is expected of us) and the reality of life (who we are as individuals). Many daily stresses and pressures are placed upon us, some subtle and some blatant. The confusion that women often experience as they attempt to cope with the exhaustion (both from excessive responsibilities and the conflict between trying to juggle two different expectations) often drives them into becoming Superwomen.

Superwomen are those who attempt to perform perfectly conflicting roles as wife, mother, volunteer, paid worker, and homemaker—with all the attendant ramifications. These can cause psychological symptoms, interpersonal symptoms, and physiological manifestations.

Religion often puts the sincere Christian woman at the highest risk of all for developing this syndrome. "Christianity" begins with "God first, others second, and yourself last"; continues with "It is more blessed to give than to receive"; and adds the description of a "virtuous woman" in Proverbs 31. It is no wonder that the Christian woman can get so "busy" taking care of everyone and everything that she forgets how Christ commended Mary for choosing to spend time nurturing her own personal growth and spiritual connection with God (Luke 10:38-42).

Sometimes women become confused about the difference between "caring" and "caretaking." Caretaking involves doing for others what they are capable of doing for themselves. It can wear out the caretaker (often causing fatigue, resentment, and burnout). It can deprive others of the chance to take responsibility for their own personal growth and from learning to take healthy risks. In a larger sense, caretaking is not a "Christian" virtue, because self-neglect does not help anyone in the long run—an empty cup has nothing of value to give. Caring, on the other hand, involves the healthy, balanced nurturing of ourselves as well as others, with a goal of supporting everyone to become as actualized (real) and differentiated (reaching our individual potential) as possible.

Christ, our egalitarian model, regularly took time to "fill His own cup." It must have looked somewhat "selfish" (in the eyes of some) for Jesus to get into a boat and leave crowds of people who wanted and needed help. Christ regularly took time, however, to withdraw to a quiet place to rest and to obtain a change of environment. He did this to set us an example of balance (Mark 6:31, 32).

Part of role-modeling true Christianity involves developing balance in personal everyday living. To do otherwise leaves us vulnerable to become distracted and encumbered by the myriad tasks in life and to neglect the one thing that is "necessary" (Luke 10:42, NEB). Women must give themselves permission and instruction to withdraw "to a quiet place" to find refreshment and to get some rest. God understands that need and calls us to go to Him (Matt. 11:28-30), to take His yoke upon us—for it is light and we will find rest unto our souls.

ARLENE TAYLOR

SEPTEMBER 4

IS YOUR GOD ALL-POWERFUL?

Among the nations I will raise a psalm to thee; for thy unfailing love is wider than the heavens and thy truth reaches to the skies. Ps. 108:3, 4, NEB.

One evening when our youngest daughter was 7, I sat by her bed ready to listen to her evening prayer. Finally she settled down, folded her hands, closed her eyes, and began to pray. I listened to her usual prayers for Mom, Dad, Grandmom, Granddad, the neighbor's dog, etc., but suddenly she began to pray for the children in Africa that she had seen on television, who were suffering from lack of proper clothes and food. Snuggling down in her own warm bed, she said: "Please, Jesus, send each child in Africa a blanket, a pillow with a pillowcase, and a bedsheet." She paused for a long time before she finally added, "If that is too much, could You send them sleeping bags?"

I must admit that I smiled. She was only 7 and didn't understand the implications of an all-powerful God, a God for whom nothing is impossible. She evidently felt sure that she had asked God for more than He could handle, and wanted to help. She believed He could solve the problem, but at the same time she unknowingly transferred her own limitations to God.

I do not smile at her prayer anymore or at her lack of understanding, for her prayer opened my eyes to the many times I as an adult have made the same mistake. I cannot count the times I have suggested to God how He could best solve my problems, nor the many times I in lack of faith have transferred my own limitations to a God I knew ruled the universe. I always trusted Him, but at the same time often made additional plans just in case something should go wrong.

When God called Abraham and asked him, "Do you trust Me enough to leave your country, your father's home, the security of your extended family, and go to a land that I am going to show you?" we know that Abraham answered, "Yes, Lord, I do." At the same time God gave to Abraham a promise that was especially precious to the people in those days: many descendants and national greatness. It is easy to visualize Abraham running home to Sarah with the good news that God was going to bless them with children after all, and Abraham's unquestioning obedience is one of the most striking evidences of faith to be found in all the Bible.

Sometimes we do forget that the God we worship is all-powerful, a God who knows the beginning from the end, a God who does not ask us to believe in Him without giving us sufficient evidence for our faith. BIRTHE KENDEL

SEPTEMBER 5

I AM "THE CALLED"

And we know that all things work together for good to them that love God, to them who are the called according to his purpose. Rom. 8:28.

Nearly four years have passed since our daughter, her husband, and their little Kari were killed in a tragic automobile accident (see *The Listening Heart,* Oct. 20). Years of pain, personal, throbbing, haunting, sometimes seemingly endless pain. Sessions with grief recovery groups and compassionate friends helped to ease and release the deep chilling pain of such a loss. A loving mother, who listened compassionately and without judgment of me as I poured anger all over her and God, helped to release the pain.

Anger is very much a part of grieving; ironically, so is laughter. Embarrassment at unexpected laughter when the pain is so intense is also part of grieving. But laughter and tears live in the same body, and today, four years later, laughter is finally more evident than is the pain.

The path of grief is very dark; sometimes it is a long, dark tunnel, but there *are* lights along the way . . . eventually. Faith, love, caring, understanding, another's tears with me—all were lights through the tunnel of my grief. Eventually the greater light of acceptance was seen, and I realized the end of the dark tunnel was in sight. Often I felt desperately alone in that darkness, and I kept groping for Jesus' hand. I could not always feel His presence, but somehow I *knew* He was always there. His promise in the scripture for today assured me over and over that I was one of "the called" and that even in this tragedy, "all things work together . . ."

Four years have passed. Our children are gone, and I am still here; even my own existence has at times been painful. But Jesus is also present in my life, day by day, hour by hour. I long to be more like Him, yet I fail so miserably. He never leaves me nor forsakes me, though I must at times bring Him deep sadness by my actions, or lack of action. You see, He has promised never to leave me or forsake me (Joshua 1:5), and He hasn't! He's been with me through the darkness of grief, the sunlight of laughter, the throbbing of pain, and the elation of happiness. He is my "very present help" (Ps. 46:1). I praise God that I am never alone though I may be lonely, for He is "touched with the feeling of [my] infirmities (Heb. 4:15).

Thank You, Father, that "all things," even the trauma of death, can work together for good to those who love You, who are "the called" according to Your purpose. BETTY R. BURNETT

SEPTEMBER 6

TO HIS GLORY

Whatsoever ye do, do all to the glory of God. 1 Cor. 10:31.

Today I watched a huge mama turtle digging a hole in the gravel by the roadside. She was preparing to lay her eggs. I was awed by her zeal and persistence. Even our close proximity didn't sway her from the project at hand. First one leg went down, down into the hole. Slowly it came back up, pushing with it a little sand and shoving it to one side. Then the other leg—the whole shell caving downward as if suctioned—carried on the task.

"Isn't she ugly?" my friend asked. I agreed. But the turtle was oblivious to that fact. It didn't bother her a bit. Only one thing occupied her mind—the need to dig a hole in which to lay her eggs. That her own life might be in danger did not seem to affect her. She had determination.

In more human terms we might say she had ambition. She had a goal and she set out to reach it. I recently read this quote on a calendar: "Ambition is like hunger; it obeys no law but its appetite" (Josh Billings). That's true for determination as well. The old turtle proved it.

But what appetite is driving the mama turtle's ambition? It can't be motherly love. Once the eggs are laid and covered, she never gives them another moment's attention. Surely it must be pure instinct.

And so the question I must continually ask myself is "What appetite is driving my ambition; my determination?" Is it service to God? to others? to self? Or is it just blind compulsion?

Nothing is so dangerous as ambition underwritten by a craving appetite for self-glory. Nothing is so glorious as determination fed by the self-sacrificing spirit of Jesus Christ. We aren't turtles, bound by blind instincts. I have a choice. You have a choice.

Let's determine to feed our appetites on the love of Jesus, so that our ambitions may blossom into humble service to His glory.

DAWNA BEAUSOLEIL

SEPTEMBER 7

GOD ANSWERS SIMPLE PRAYERS, TOO

Since you are my rock and my fortress, for the sake of your name lead and guide me. Ps. 31:3, NIV.

The weather report the day before had forecast snow and winds up to 70 mph; yet we were still planning to ski that morning at Sugar Bowl in the California Sierra Nevadas before heading home to Idaho.

I felt uneasy as I awoke, but not wanting to disturb the others, I just sat up in bed and started praying. *I don't know why I feel so uneasy, Lord, but I need Your divine guidance. Should we really go skiing today, or should we just head on home?* Though Jesus and I have been friends for years, I felt a little silly asking Him whether or not we should go skiing. He has so many more important things to worry about! Yet I continued praying: *Lord, I need something very tangible, something very clear that will show me Your will.*

Just then a blast of wind hit the 35-foot trailer home we were sleeping in and rocked it on its settings. *That seems like a pretty dramatic answer!* I thought! We were at an elevation of 1,234 feet; we were planning to ski at nearly 7,000 feet! *If the wind is that strong down here, what must it be like at Sugar Bowl?* I had my answer, but would it be enough to convince the rest of those planning to ski?

When I went into my sister's house for breakfast, she said that her married daughter who had planned to go with us had called and said there was no way she would go with winds that high. Another clear sign.

We tuned in to the morning news and learned that snow had already begun to fall over Donner Pass (it was raining where we were), and there was a travel advisory that chains were required from Nyack to Reno. By now the others in the ski party were also convinced that we simply ought to load up the car and head home.

Only about an hour after we crossed the pass, it was closed to all motor traffic. In fact, it took us four and a half hours to reach Reno, a trip that usually takes only one and a half to two hours. We plowed through six inches of snow and would never have made it without our car chains.

There was an avalanche at one of the ski resorts in the Sierra Nevadas that day, and one person died. Some trucks and cars were held up there in the snow for more than a day.

I had asked God to lead and guide me. Not only had He done so, but He had impressed all of us similarly. We arrived home safely, praising God for His protection. LOIS MOORE

SEPTEMBER 8

DO IT NOW!

Behold, now is the accepted time; behold, now is the day of salvation. 2 Cor. 6:2.

Twilight. Soon evening would come. The rush-hour traffic swirled past me as I walked rapidly to the home of a piano student. As I approached his home I stopped short. I noticed a commotion, as though something terrible was about to happen.

Children gathered quickly around the house just ahead of me. As I came nearer I could see many people on the front porch. On the walk just in front of the house sat a middle-aged woman in a chair with her feet propped up on the bottom step. People were all around her. Suddenly someone darted from the crowd, bounded down the walk, and ran out into the street with arms waving wildly. "Down here! Down here!" he shouted. As I looked toward the direction in which he was waving I could see the flashing, circling lights of an emergency van in the next block.

Quickly the driver made his way to the house and immediately set to work. Everyone looked on in petrified silence. I stood motionless, unable to take my eyes away from the scene—from the woman in the chair.

The last rays of the setting sun reflected in the deepening shadows fell over the quiet neighborhood. The ambulance attendant raised himself up, shook his head, and said he had done all he could do. She was gone. The flurry of excitement was electric. The words "Somebody do something!" rang out in the air. A niece, watching from nearby, ran screaming toward her aunt, flinging her arms around the dead woman. Her sobs racked my frame as I felt her grief. Unable to endure more, I finally went into the house of my student to teach the piano lesson.

Later, upon leaving, I looked in the direction of the former commotion and was shocked to see the lifeless form of the woman unchanged, and the niece still clutching the dead body, as if to say "I will not let you go." She remained there, grieving quietly but unrelentingly—she and her aunt in the gathering darkness. The finality of the scene was painful. No strings could be pulled; no miracles performed by medical science—nothing. It was night. Death—so quick. So sudden. So sure.

Indelibly those scenes have been embedded in my thinking. The finality and quickness of death, the movement of human emotion, the futility of humans, and the finality of God's timetable. Again and again I have been impressed with the necessity of doing what must be done *now*! "Behold, now is the accepted time; behold, now is the day of salvation."

AUDRE B. TAYLOR

SEPTEMBER 9

ABOUT TRANSLATORS

You show that you are a letter from Christ, . . . written not with ink but with the Spirit of the living God, not on tablets of stone but on tablets of human hearts. 2 Cor. 3:3, NIV.

My lifeline had a kink in it. No, I wasn't on a respirator, nor was I deep-sea diving. I was trying to communicate via a translator. I could tell by the body language of the woman I was talking with that the message she received from my translator was not the message that I had given my translator. I tried to smooth away her troubled expressions with smiles and kindness in my voice. But I have no idea how the situation was settled.

Natasha represented me—my thoughts, my words, my actions. I wanted to communicate a kind, loving Saviour, but she couldn't be bothered with people she felt were unworthy. Once I told her that Jesus died for people with foolish questions just as He had died for her and for me. It didn't seem to sink in.

She told me that I was a prominent person in town and that I should rest. She said I shouldn't talk to anyone without that person's having a previous appointment. I told her that I had come to serve and that I wasn't tired.

I could never trust what she said. I was never positive that my words had been accurately translated. Instead of being my lifeline, as faithful translators always are, she became a barrier, a hindrance.

You take the name of Christ—Christian. Do you truly speak the words that He would speak? Do you represent Him? Can He trust you? Do you speak as He would speak? Are you like a letter from Christ?

Natasha had to be dismissed, and another took her place. Oh, how safe I felt with the new translator. If initially we didn't understand each other's intent, we talked it over until everything was clear. Then I could trust her as my voice and as my messenger. She understood where I was coming from and where I wanted to end up. And even if at times she didn't have a complete picture, she understood my style and my motives, and she never let me down.

What a solemn yet joyful experience it is to take the name of Jesus and to be His voice or His letter. How accurately are you and I translating His words, His actions, His motives? BARBARA HUFF

SEPTEMBER 10

FRIENDSHIP A PATH TO GOD

Dear friends, let us love one another, for love comes from God. Everyone who loves has been born of God and knows God. 1 John 4:7, NIV.

Madge is 20 years older than I am. When we first met, it was a big age gap for a child of 12, but we became firm friends and have remained so to this day, more than 30 years later. I have always been conscious of the huge debt I owe to my friend, for she helped to mold and shape my character and the characters of other young people in the church.

Madge never married. Her life was spent caring, first for her invalid mother and later for her father. She was blessed with many talents, and these she used unstintingly in the service of the church. She was the young people's leader and trained us with firm but loving discipline. Most of her former young people are now leaders in churches in all parts of the world, and all remember her with deep affection and respect. She taught us that service and loyalty are all-important, but she made our participation in church life full of fun and excitement.

She shared in our hopes and aspirations. She listened to our agonizing about boyfriends and girlfriends, and her advice was always Christ-centered. Knowing how difficult it was for me in a non-Christian family, she and her sister and brother-in-law would often invite me home for lunch after church. In the winter their home was always open on Friday evenings. Their Christianity was always practical, and they were the optimum of loving and lovable Christians.

When I moved from Ireland to England, we kept in touch by letter and eagerly looked forward to seeing each other during the holidays. Then we would talk endlessly about all that had happened in the intervening months.

Madge is ill now. Her vitality and strength have gone, and her long illness has tested my own faith at times. Hers has never wavered. She continues to be cheerful, to hold firm, and to trust in her loving Friend.

Just as I have so often poured out my heart to her, so she pours out her heart to Him, knowing that the "gentlest of hands will take what is worth keeping and, with a breath of kindness, blow the rest away."

To have a friend means being a friend. To have Jesus as a dear, treasured, and much-loved friend means learning from Him, keeping in touch with Him, and looking forward eagerly to seeing Him again. I am still learning from my friend, and through her I am constantly reminded of the parallels between our earthly friendships and the friendship of the One who teaches us to know God as our friend.

AUDREY BALDERSTONE

SEPTEMBER 11

SPIRIT LEAVES

They are like trees planted by streams of water, which yield their fruit in its season, and their leaves do not wither. In all that they do, they prosper. Ps. 1:3, NRSV.

As the Master of the seasons
effects changes in the leaves,
so the Master of all sinners
causes changes within me.

The leaves swish to the earth
as the wind rustles trees,
and my sins drop quickly also
by the Spirit's rustling breeze.

A snowy-white soft blanket
blots out brown decaying leaves,
and Jesus' cleansing blood applied
covers my filthy, now dead, deeds.

As warm springtime showers
water well the leafless trees,
so Jesus tenderly allows
trials and pain to water me.

And today as tiny twigs
pop out on the trees,
so I realize I am growing
real-life Spirit leaves.

So I thank God for the seasons
and thank Him for the trees.
He now lives deep within me—
The evidence is leaves.

COLLENE KELLY

SEPTEMBER 12

LISTEN TO ME, LORD

Hear my prayer, O Lord, and let my cry come unto thee. Hide not thy face from me in the day when I am in trouble; incline thine ear unto me: in the day when I call answer me speedily. Ps. 102:1, 2.

I sat in the doctor's office waiting for the test results. Finally he came; the test was positive. Our second child would be born around the middle of the next April. That was just what we wanted. Our son would be 2. We had planned for this baby; so why was I suddenly feeling as though I didn't want to have this child?

By the time I arrived home the feeling was overwhelming. My husband was thrilled. I was depressed; but I didn't tell anyone. I felt that the child I was carrying was not going to be perfect, and I didn't want to have it! I prayed that something would happen so that I would lose the baby. I hated being pregnant! I hated the baby! I even wished that I believed in abortion! "So, Lord," I'd pray, "why don't You do something?" He didn't seem to be hearing or answering my prayer the way I wanted.

During my sixth month I finally told the doctor that I felt something was wrong. He checked everything; the heartbeat was normal, growth was normal, everything looked perfect. So what was wrong with me?

What was wrong? I was praying and telling God what to do instead of praying for His will to be done. When I finally sat down and asked Him what He wanted me to do, the answer came right away. "I'll be here for you, to help you when things are tough." The peace I felt was incredible. I finally was able to love the child I was carrying. That love became so complete that I didn't even think about what would be wrong the rest of my pregnancy. When the doctor said, "You have a little girl, and she has a few problems," I wasn't surprised. My first thought was *Thanks, Lord, for the peace of mind; now I'm really going to need Your help!*

We often pray for things and then tell God what we want Him to do, how we want Him to do it, and when we want it done. Then when it doesn't happen our way we say God didn't hear our prayer. He doesn't promise to make our lives perfect, but He does promise to give us the strength to get through anything that comes our way. He is always there listening to our prayers and ready to answer. We just need to listen to Him. — LINDA REYNOLDS

SEPTEMBER 13

THE DISCARDED TEAPOT—1

In a large house there are articles not only of gold and silver, but also of wood and clay; some are for noble purposes and some for ignoble. If a [woman] cleanses [herself] from the latter, [she] will be an instrument for noble purposes, made holy, useful to the Master and prepared to do any good work. 2 Tim. 2:20, NIV.

I would love to tell you I found the old metal teapot at a neighborhood garage sale or at a secondhand store, or better yet, in a dusty antique shop in Portland's Old Town, but that would be a lie. I found the container at an illegal dump site, surrounded by bald automobile tires, naked bedsprings, and the rusted skins from outdated appliances.

My discovery cannot be credited to either a sharp eye or skilled sleuthing. The pot was buried beneath tin cans and plastic milk cartons until the toe of my sneaker bumped against it. Even after I uncovered my "find" I questioned whether the battered little container was worth the time and energy it would take for me to remove the filth.

However, since I possess a conscience perpetually time-warped between the Great Depression and the age of programmed obsolescence, I gingerly picked up the pitcher with two fingers and held it at arm's length for a quick appraisal. With my free hand I scraped at the thick brown clay coating until my nail scratched against a dull metal surface. "Probably 1957 vintage aluminum!"

Upon reaching home, I tossed the teapot onto a shelf in the garage to await a more "convenient season." Weeks passed. One day, as I was searching for a vase to hold the first spring blossoms from our apple trees, I spied the teapot.

It's the right size, the right shape, I thought, *and just rustic enough to*

show the delicate blossoms off to their best advantage. I grabbed the container from the shelf and returned to my kitchen. *If I hurry, my centerpiece will be ready for the supper table.*

Within a few minutes I stood at the kitchen sink, up to my armpits in sludge. Dish detergent and hot water removed the mud coating, but not the layers of tarnish and corrosion still clinging to the pot's original surface. I scrubbed until the steel wool pads chipped my nails and disintegrated in my hands. As the black residue oozed through my fingers and down the drain, I mumbled, "This had better be worth it."

As I scrubbed, I thought too about being a finder. Whether in a downtown street, an illegal garbage dump, or right in my own home, human treasures are everywhere, waiting to be found. At first glance their value might not be evident, but somewhere beneath the layers of sin a treasure awaits discovery. They may look like junk, but the Master Finder always sees the potential for beauty. The potential can be uncovered by love and care or destroyed by careless or overzealous scouring.

"And the whole world will know we are Christians by our matchless love for one another" (see John 13:35).   KAY D. RIZZO

SEPTEMBER 14

THE DISCARDED TEAPOT—2

For [she] is a chosen vessel unto me, to bear my name before the Gentiles, and kings, and the children of Israel. Acts 9:15.

As I scrubbed the teapot I had salvaged from the dump, I turned the vessel upside down and worked on the base. As I scrubbed, I noticed an engraved design emerging. One by one, letters appeared beneath the persistence of my steel wool. *Revere—Sterling Silver.* Try as I might, I couldn't make out the date that followed.

Horrified, I dropped the teapot into the sink. I had been scrubbing an expensive silver teapot with a common, everyday scouring pad! While I knew very little about cleaning and restoring silver, I did know that I shouldn't attack the malleable metal with steel wool and scouring powder. I couldn't believe someone had purposely thrown this beautiful piece of artistry away.

I picked up the container and studied the designer's imprint once more. Gone was the careless touch I'd previously given the pot.

Gone were the abrasive cleansers and harsh steel wool. I had discovered a treasure of undetermined value, but of value nonetheless. A few days later I took the teapot to an antique dealer and gasped with delight at his appraisal. The silversmith's signature had added incredible value to the silver container. I knew I would never again toss the vessel back onto the storage shelf in the garage. Instead, after the expert had restored the silver to its former beauty, I cleared a spot in my breakfront for the teapot where it could be seen and admired by family and friends alike.

Like the teapot, regardless of my age or the extent of the corrosion of my sin, I bear the Saviour's signature—the signature of the cross. The Saviour's signature changes even the filthiest, mud-encrusted scion of society into a royal vessel. His signature changes me into a masterpiece of infinite worth. — KAY D. RIZZO

SEPTEMBER 15

THE TOUCH OF FAITH

And he said unto her, Daughter, thy faith hath made thee whole; go in peace. Mark 5:34.

Beside the road she sits and scans the masses hurrying by;
Twelve years she's suffered; now physicians give her up to die.
But people passing tell her of the Saviour's wondrous cure;
And once again her hope springs forth. His touch she must secure!

She follows to the seashore, but the crowds obstruct her way.
She presses on in painful search day after weary day
Until at last despair and anguish overwhelm her soul.
In grief she prays to find the Healer who can make her whole!

The Great Physician nears! Despite the multitude's rude glance,
She presses on with confidence. She cannot lose her chance.
The jostling throngs surround the Lord. This is her only hour.
He is so near! Contend she must for His transforming power.

She follows on, and faith grows strong. If she can only touch
The Saviour's robe she will be healed! Then reaching out to clutch
The border of His garment billowing in the gentle breeze,
She fingers it, and straightway she is healed of her disease.

With glowing health she turns to leave the curious multitude
Whose careless contact cannot sense her heartfelt gratitude.
Abruptly Jesus turns and asks, "Who touched Me?" Terrified,
She shrinks away, but meets His gaze with joy she cannot hide.

Then Jesus, knowing, sees her tears of happy, sweet release,
And says, "My child, your faith has made you whole; go now, in peace."
The touch of faith! What will you have Christ do for you today?
What heavy burden at His feet do you desire to lay?

His gentle, kind compassion can relieve your aching heart
And bring you peace and comfort when the bitter teardrops start.
What will you have Christ do for you? His feet for you have trod
The path you tread. Reach out! And you will touch the heart of God!
—Lorraine Hudgins

September 16

But Lord!

Always keep on praying. 1 Thess. 5:17, TLB.

Dear Lord, the preacher says we are to "pray without ceasing" and to take time to know You. I don't have time to spend hours holed up somewhere reading and praying. Take today, for instance: I did two weeks' washing and then washed the outside windows in my apartment; I made an appointment for an oil change for the car; I paid bills; I went grocery shopping, emptied the trash, and bought tickets for a Shakespeare play on Sunday. (It's a really good play, Lord . . .) All this in addition to my full-time job. And I got a hole in my panty hose.

What do You mean, "Be still"? I sit and listen in church. Huh? But I told You I don't have time—I hardly have time to kneel and pray once a day. How can I possibly be constantly "in the attitude of prayer"? Isn't that a little unrealistic? After all, this is almost the twenty-first century.

Of course I am Your disciple! But do You have any idea how busy we are down here? People run marathons, jump hurdles, go to concerts, attend lectures, play soccer, go to school, go to work, clean house, take care of children, look after parents, and help out at church.

There are even some young people who are married, have children, work 40 hours a week, and go to college full-time. That's busy, Lord.

What? "Be still"?

But—are You telling me that if I'd just spend some time with You my day would go smoother? I'd get more done?

Pray more? But—oh, yes, I guess I am praying right now, aren't I? OK, I'll try it—but will You give me little reminders along the way that You are with me?

What's that? Oh, thanks, Lord. I love You, too. — SANDY ZAUGG

SEPTEMBER 17

THE HONOR GUARD

The mountains and the hills shall break forth before you into singing, and all the trees of the field shall clap their hands.
Isa. 55:12.

It was a bright, clear September day in Anchorage, Alaska. The drive up the winding mountain road was breathtaking. Against a backdrop of dark-green firs and snowcapped mountain peaks yellow-leafed alders stood sentinel along both sides of the road.

I thought of the flaming trees as an honor guard placed there especially for me. I drove my Subaru slowly along the gold-lined highway and could almost hear "Pomp and Circumstance" heralding my approach!

A slight breeze ruffled their leaves, making them seem to be waving at me. Or could they be clapping their hands? In those few moments I felt really important. God loved me so much that He put those shimmering golden trees in place to tell me how special I was to Him, how very much He loved me!

"Thank You, Lord," I sang out. "Thank You for this reminder that in Your eyes I *am* special and important."

The feeling of being a woman of some importance stayed with me through the day and brought a smile to my lips as I lay in bed that night savoring the memory.

The words of Isaiah 55:12 came to mind: "The mountains and the hills shall break forth before you into singing, and all the trees of the field shall clap their hands."

This had been my afternoon experience. On the mountain road I had caught a glimpse of how God values me. Because I am God's daughter, I can hold my head high and walk up life's path with joy. I can hear the mountains singing and the trees clapping their hands for what He is able to do through me. I am a woman of high worth. I am a woman of destiny, a woman of importance. I am a daughter of the King of kings. I am special to Him.   DOROTHY EATON WATTS

SEPTEMBER 18

JUST A DREAM?

Verily I say unto you, Inasmuch as ye did it not to one of the least of these, ye did it not to me. Matt. 25:45.

I am dreaming of the judgment day. Ladies and gentlemen, farmers and beggars, priests and atheists are standing in a long line waiting for their turn. When some are finished, they go to the right side, smiling. Others have to turn left, and they look discouraged and sad.

The line in front of me is melting away. I feel the sweat running down my forehead, burning in my eyes. Now it's the turn of the man before me, and I prick up my ears. The Judge asks him: "Did you feed Me when I was hungry? Did you hand Me a glass of water when I was almost dying of thirst?"

The man shrugs his shoulders and does not know what to say, but the Judge continues: "Did you get Me some clothes when I rang your doorbell, half naked and chilled as I was?"

The man tries to protest, but the Judge does not listen. "You did not comfort Me when I was down. You didn't care when I was sick and lonely."

"But Lord," the man gasps, "how could I have known? Nobody told me. I would have sent You a check, or told my secretary to help You. Really, I didn't have the slightest idea of Your troubles. To be honest, this is the first time I have ever met You."

"We met daily. Any man, woman, or child who was needy—that was Me," the Judge says, and His voice rolls like thunder above the earth and awakes me. I sit upright in my bed, trembling, and take a deep breath: "Praise the Lord, it was just a dream!"

Just a dream? "And the King shall answer them, saying: Verily I say unto you, Inasmuch as ye did it not to one of the least of these, ye did it not to me" (Matt. 25:45). Lord, help me to recognize You in any needy person. Fill my heart with charity and make me a loving woman—a living reflection of Thy grace! SYLVIA RENZ

SEPTEMBER 19

FRIEND

No longer do I call you servants, for the servant does not know what his master is doing; but I have called you friends, for all that I have heard from my Father I have made known to you. John 15:15, RSV.

Her pastor had visited a few days earlier, but that day she couldn't respond very well. Today she was more lucid. Her family thought she might enjoy a visit from the chaplain. I was the fortunate one on call.

When I first entered the room, a daughter and granddaughter met me. After a few words of introduction, I stepped close to Laura's bed.

"Laura, I'm one of the chaplains here at the hospital," I began. Her quizzical look told me I'd better start over. "I'm one of the pastors for the hospital." Laura's thin, tired face broke into a grin. Wisps of gray hair and a few "age spots" only emphasized her loveliness.

I learned that Laura was the mother of nine children and so many grandchildren that she'd lost count. I also learned that she was 103 years old and that God was her very good friend. "He'll be with me when the time comes," she told me confidently.

When I asked if she would like prayer, her eyes lit up. "I'd like that," she said.

"Is there anything special you'd like us to pray about?"

Laura was quiet for a moment, and then the smile and sparkle flashed again. "My family."

I held Laura's hand and prayed aloud. When we finished, Laura thanked me, but I felt the true ministry may have gone the other direction. I almost felt as though I'd held the hand of Enoch, the man who walked with God. And I was reminded that He is there for each of us; not just for "when the time comes," but as our Friend in every situation, whether we're 23, 43, or 103.

I held her hand a moment longer. "Thank you, Laura, for sharing this time with me. I've been blessed." Laura flashed one of those precious smiles and nodded her head. BEULAH FERN STEVENS

SEPTEMBER 20

TRUSTING IN HIM

Blessed are all those who put their trust in Him. Ps. 2:12, NKJV.
O Lord my God, in You I put my trust. Ps. 7:1, NKJV.

I was leaving the next day for an overseas trip. Since I was not used to air travel at that time, I was quite concerned about traveling alone on the first part of the trip. It was the day of the week I normally meet with my prayer group, but I had many errands to run and last-minute things to do.

I thought about skipping this prayer time, until I realized that I needed this time of prayer and the prayers of others. I shared with the other ladies my anxieties about the trip, and they prayed that the Lord would calm me and give me safe travel.

I had asked the driver to pick me up at 7:00 that morning, but the evening before, for one reason or another, I had called him and upped the time for departure to the airport by 15 minutes. When I arrived at the airport I saw Fred Knopper, at that time an employee at Christian Record Services. He introduced me to his mother, who was visiting from the Northwest, and then they left for her gate.

I had to stand in line for several more minutes, so by the time I got to the gate waiting area, Fred had already left to go to work. His mother called me over to sit with her.

The departure of our plane was going to be more than an hour late, and my anxieties began to mount with the fear that I would miss my connection in Denver. I shared my anxieties with Mrs. Knopper, and she shared with me how she had come to grips with fear of air travel. The text she shared was "Blessed are those who put their trust in Him." That is what I needed—trust. Trust in a God who was already answering the prayers of my friends in our prayer group.

If I had not rescheduled my time to leave home 15 minutes earlier, I would not have been at the airport when Fred was there, and I probably would not have met his mother. She would not have known me. As it turned out, we were able to sit together all the way to Denver. It was a trip that changed my feelings about air travel and trust in a God who is so concerned about us that He impressed me to arrive at the airport earlier so that this dear lady could minister to me.

Thank You, Lord, for Your ways of caring for my every need!

PEGGY TOMPKINS

SEPTEMBER 21

USED BY GOD

"Very well," Deborah said, "I will go with you. But because of the way you are going about this, the honor will not be yours, for the Lord will hand Sisera over to a woman." Judges 4:9, NIV.

There she was, sitting under the tree, holding court. This court must have been well established and accepted, because the tree bore her name: the Palm of Deborah. No one seemed to mind that the judge was a woman. Her husband, Lappidoth, didn't seem to mind. Israel didn't seem to mind—they came to her to have their disputes settled. And God didn't seem to mind that a woman was leading His nation, His church. He was glad to speak through her.

So Israel recognized her as a prophet as well as a judge. In fact, she was the only judge said to have been a prophet too. And the commander of the army, Barak, didn't seem to mind that she was a woman. When she called, he came.

When Deborah told Barak that the Lord, the God of Israel, wanted him to go against Sisera, the commander of the enemy's army, he wanted her to go with him. If she didn't go, he wouldn't either. He seemed to have more faith in her than in God, so God said, "Because of the way you are going about this, the honor will not be yours, for the Lord will hand Sisera over to a woman."

In that time and culture that was a great disgrace. In another story in Judges Abimelech was storming a city, and a woman dropped a millstone on his head and cracked his skull. He immediately begged his armor-bearer to draw his sword to kill him so that no one could say, "A woman killed him" (Judges 9:50-55).

If you have not recently read the story of how Jael drove the tent peg through Sisera's temple and won the war, read it in Judges 4.

The part of the story that has struck me so, however, is found in the Song of Deborah in the next chapter. The story of the battle is told in poetic form, lauding the Israelite participants.

Then in verse 28 the picture switches to Sisera's mother in the enemy's distant palace. She is peering through the window lattice, wondering why Sisera has not come home. "Why is his chariot so long in coming? Why is the clatter of his chariots delayed?" she cries (NIV). Then the wisest of her ladies-in-waiting answers her, hoping to reassure Sisera's mother and herself.

"Are they not finding and dividing the spoils:
a girl or two for each man,
colorful garments as plunder for Sisera,
colorful garments embroidered . . . all this as plunder?"
(verse 30, NIV).

God had highly honored women, giving them respect and honor, using them to lead His people in peace and war. But to those who didn't know and love God, women were just plunder, part of the spoils of war to be divided up and used, a girl and a garment or two for each man. No wonder Deborah sang,
"I will sing to the Lord, I will sing;
I will make music to the Lord, the God of Israel" (verse 3, NIV).

ARDIS DICK STENBAKKEN

SEPTEMBER 22

ATTITUDE

A joyful heart is good medicine, but a broken spirit dries up the bones. Prov. 17:22, NASB.

We all love to be in the presence of people whose happy, contented attitude gives us a lift. A tiny plaque hangs in our kitchen with the picture of a rabbit doubled up in laughter because it sees a ladybug sitting on a leaf. The caption reads "A giggle a day keeps the glums away." When we can laugh about what is happening around us and to us, life ceases to be depressing or boring.

While in concentration camp Victor Frank was stripped of everything he owned, including the very hair on his body. He said he learned that everything can be taken from a person except the attitude one chooses to have in any given set of circumstances.

Attitude—how far-reaching it can be in affecting not only our emotional and physical lives but the lives of those around us.

We can choose to be disgruntled, critical, and sorry for ourselves, or we can avoid much distress, weariness, and ill health if we decide to be optimistic and full of courage. Experience and science have proved that a person's health can be improved by altering attitude.

As humans we have the tendency to moan about our trials and problems as if life should be easy, but nowhere have we been promised this. Scott Peck begins his book *The Road Less Traveled* with the words "Life is difficult," and he conveys the idea that once we willingly face this fact, life becomes less difficult. Paul tells us, "We can rejoice, too, when we run into problems and trials for we know that they are good for us—they help us learn to be patient" (Rom. 5:3, TLB).

Choose to have a "joyful heart" today. MARIE SPANGLER

SEPTEMBER 23

VIEW FROM THE TOP

Our steps are made firm by the Lord, when he delights in our way. . . . I have been young, and now am old, yet I have not seen the righteous forsaken, or their children begging bread. Ps. 37:23-25, NRSV.

Twenty years ago I stood overlooking Geneva, Switzerland, the city in the valley. I was a summer school student at the seminary in Collonges, France, and just for the fun of it I agreed to go rock climbing one afternoon. My companions were an experienced climber, Patrick, and another friend, Loida, but I felt completely vulnerable. I found myself in tears as I looked down hundreds of feet to the rocks below. Climbing without any protective gear and ropeless, we could have fallen to our death at any moment.

Throughout the trip Patrick continued to be supportive, to walk us through every detail and to assure us that we were almost at the top, where we would rest. I had never been so frightened or felt so helpless in all my life. Hours later, when we reached the top of the Saleve Mountain, I learned of students who had literally fallen to their death or severe injury on this same climb.

The view from the top was breathtaking! As far as the eye could see, there were mountains and lush, green valleys, with highways winding through the countryside. The air was clear and refreshing.

The trials and fears of the climb were forgotten as we rested and looked out over the valley. We had reached the summit!

I still have pleasant memories of precious lessons from that experience. I have experienced many mountains and valleys: highs and lows of everyday life. My most devastating valley experience was the adjustment to life after the death of my dearest friend, my mother.

Now, at the top of the hill, I am able to see that I will always get through the valleys. I see that valleys offer more options than I could see during my youthful days.

Patrick, our guide, was nicknamed "Cat Man" at Collonges because he could safely climb the Saleve Mountain and return in record time. With so much climbing experience, he was able to walk us through any difficulties that we faced. We had complete trust in him.

Just as Patrick was able to encourage us during that climb, it is clear to me now that God does the same. Whatever challenges we face, He has made provision for us to get to the top. He can be fully trusted to provide options, even when we cannot see the top.

If you are facing a valley of discouragement, brace yourself, pace yourself, and keep climbing. You can do all and accomplish all with our Guide, our precious heavenly Father (Phil. 4:13). The view from the top is worth the climb.

Lynn Marie Davis

September 24

Confidence in God

The Lord is my light and my salvation—whom shall I fear? The Lord is the stronghold of my life—of whom shall I be afraid? Ps. 27:1, NIV.

It was the end of summer when I arrived home to our apartment with the results of my medical exam. My husband, my little girl, and I were anxious to know the results. As we read, we were surprised. We almost couldn't believe what we were reading! Only one kidney, and it was compromised? Yes, it was reality.

In that moment we three embraced and prayed. A living faith and a certainty that God would not abandon us sprouted within. There followed days of exams; finally the medical team decided that an operation was necessary to make some corrections in the ureter. The kidney was hydronephrotic and already very damaged.

The surgery took seven hours. Afterward the kidney stopped

functioning, the drains and sounds were not working, and the medical team met and confirmed the need for a new emergency surgery. I was very debilitated. That night relatives and friends united in prayer.

The team was ready for surgery; the chief surgeon was waiting for me in the surgical suite. The aide was already in my room to transport me to the operating room. In the blink of an eye everything started working again!

The chief surgeon came to the room and stayed a few hours, observing everything. At that moment I weakly stuttered a few words to the doctor. I said that I was praying to God and that many friends and relatives were too. The doctor didn't say a word, but I was able to see tears roll down his face.

Already 12 years have passed. I live with this physical problem. I have had many limitations, but at no time have I lost my confidence in God, or that His presence is real in my life. God continues to strengthen and use me in new ways.

I hope that in this day you can have the certainty that Christ is the light and force of your life, and because of this, follow Him into battle bravely and without fear.   MEIBEL MELLO GUEDES

SEPTEMBER 25

PEARLS

The kingdom of heaven is like a merchant looking for fine pearls. Matt. 13:45, NIV.

I had been through a very stressful month: my grandmother had died, and I had just two days to make the transcontinental trip and prepare her funeral service in the midst of my family's and my own grief. When I returned home after all this, I found I had lost my job. Then I became seriously ill myself and couldn't seem to regain my health for several months.

About this time a friend gave me a gift of a beautiful pearl barrette. As I treasured its beauty, it was a reminder to me that pearls are not the product of pleasure, but of painful stress. The stress is caused by a tiny worm or a parasite that bores its way through the shell of an oyster to the tender membrane inside. Immediately all the resources of the oyster rush to the spot where the breach has been made. The oyster secretes a substance that closes the breach and saves its life. The intruder is covered by the precious secretion, and the wound is healed by a pearl. Perhaps no other gem has so fascinating an origin as the pearl: the pearl is a healed wound; it is a reminder of a tiny creature's struggle to survive. If there were no stressful wounds, there would be no pearls. Some oysters never get wounded, and those that seek pearls throw those unwounded oysters aside.

What can we do when difficulties seem to surround us on every side? We can choose to be bitter or we can choose to get better, to contemplate that a sovereign God may have a grand, ultimate universal outcome to our human stress. We can choose to trust the grand scheme of things to the hand of God, not with a blind trust, but on the basis of past experiences with the loving character of God.

God is the great pearl maker covering our hurts with the blood of Jesus Christ, making gems out of our groaning and pearls out of our pains. SHARI CHAMBERLAIN

SEPTEMBER 26

FOOD FOR THOUGHT

Go to the street corners and invite to the banquet anyone you find. Matt. 22:9, NIV.

Our landlord in the walled city of Harer in Ethiopia was a wealthy truck owner. One day he visited our home with an invitation. "Come to my house for dinner tomorrow, and I will tell you about something you will not want to miss," said Ato Takele with a mischievous twinkle in his eyes.

Our family happily accepted the offer, and the next day we were seated on the wooden benches at the long tables hired for the occasion. Maids in their long white traditional dress served the tasty meal to 100 dignitaries.

Talking to the other guests, we learned that this celebration occurred annually. Ato Takele took Christ's words in Matthew 22 literally, and held a feast for his friends. As we were leaving, the host leaned over and whispered in my husband's ear, "Look over your fence tomorrow!"

Tomorrow came, and my children, husband, and I could hardly believe our eyes!

Cripples, lepers, beggars, widows, and street urchins came streaming down the street, making their way to our neighbor's home. They were warmly greeted and taken to the same tables we had been seated at the day before.

Oblivious to our watchful eyes, the bedraggled group now being waited upon began to enjoy themselves. Eyes that had been hollow and empty now twinkled. Faces that were full of concern now relaxed. Bodies that were hunched up in their drab coverings began to take on a happier aspect. Eager hands stuffed the delicious food into empty mouths.

But the vignette forever engraved in my mind's eye came later, when the well-fed and happy group gathered together and left the party. Cripples waved their sticks in farewell, and scruffy friends waved and called out to each other as they waddled off down the road, to spend yet another night huddled together out in the cold, empty streets.

It didn't take much to realize which of the two groups had really enjoyed themselves. It certainly gave me food for thought. Dare we take Christ's word seriously? How many of us, instead of throwing a party just for our friends and relatives, would be willing to include the neighbor who just lost her job, the singles living down the street, the old man whose wife recently died, or those rowdy college kids renting the house across the road?

Think it over today. Whom are you going to invite to your party?

Go out into the streets and invite the lonely, the sick, the homeless, and the suffering into your home. Make it a day Christ will remember!   JEAN SEQUEIRA

SEPTEMBER 27

EMPTY-NEST SYNDROME

How often I have longed to gather your children together, as a hen gathers her chicks under her wings, but you were not willing. Matt. 23:37, NIV.

My son started school this year. He is my youngest—my baby. For a whole year I anticipated this great milestone. He was so excited he could hardly wait! And I felt proud of him, but in my heart I grieved. No more babies. No more nursing. And all those "firsts." First outing, first bath, first smile, first tooth.

Once those days had seemed so never-ending. Late nights of fussing with earaches or tummy pains, all the dirty diapers and laundry and messes he was always getting into. But now . . .

My mind seemed to race wildly on ahead to graduation day, moving out on his own, college, marriage, career, etc.

Where had all the time gone? I felt a sense of panic as I realized how few precious years I really had left to mold and shape and prepare my son for his future. Now that his days were full of school and friends it seemed as though there was precious little time left for me. I felt left out! Tears rolled down my cheeks as I carefully pondered that thought. It frightened me to realize that my task was over and that motherhood and all that it entails must also go through "growing pains." So much of my job was finished.

Then I snapped back to reality and thought about all the precious moments that are still before me. I know that I do not want to miss out on a single one. There really is a lot of time until he graduates and leaves home. After all, he is only in kindergarten! But a little voice inside me whispered, "Time goes quickly; don't let those precious moments just slip away."

Picking up my Bible to search for words of comfort, I read John 16:21. Here Jesus is talking about grief being turned into joy. "A woman giving birth to a child has pain . . . but when her baby is born she forgets the anguish because of her joy that a child is born into the world" (NIV). How true that was. All those difficult times when he was a toddler were faded memories. How happily I remembered and cherished all his little baby moments.

Jesus went on in verses 6-26 of John 17 to share with His disciples His desire for each one of us, that we might be a part of Him and His kingdom. He prayed a prayer for *us*. A prayer that you and I would each come to know Him and be His children. He saw no end for us and our relationship with Him. He saw only a glorious future. "Thank You, Lord," I prayed.

And now, with Jesus' example, I pray for my son and my daughter, too. I pray for their future, that it will be bright and full and happy, and that I will be there to cherish each moment. With a certainty that I did not have before, I realize that I have many precious moments yet to spend with my children and my Saviour. I don't want to miss out on even one. In fact, I can start right now!

KATHY JO DUTERROW YERGEN

SEPTEMBER 28

MY REFUGE

For wherever I am, though far away at the ends of the earth, I will cry to you for help. When my heart is faint and overwhelmed, lead me to the mighty, towering Rock of safety. For you are my refuge. Ps. 61:2, 3, TLB.

The salty breeze playfully twisted my long brunet hair as I walked along the beach searching for treasured shells and agates. Cool sand clinging to my bare feet felt nice as I interrupted my search to try stepping inside some footprints made by others who had passed that way earlier in the day. As I recall, I was a young girl, nearly 5 years of age, on this occasion. The ocean fascinated me then as it does today, and I was enjoying the special time with my family at the Oregon coast.

After a while my family and I came upon a man battling to reclaim his four-door sedan from the sea. He had driven dangerously close to the water's edge and become a captive of the elements. The surf mercilessly lapped at the vehicle even as a tow truck joined in the rescue efforts. Sadly, the aid was too late, and we watched as the car continued to sink, being swallowed by sand and saltwater.

Consulting the tide schedule, Dad and Mom determined we could resume our walk. Dad, being familiar with that section of the coast, noticed that more of the beach was covered with water than he remembered from past visits, but guessed that the tide simply hadn't gone out much yet. Not wanting to be an alarmist, he cautiously walked on while keeping his eyes trained alternately on us and the tide flow. Clint toddled beside Mom, while Judi, Cliff, and I eagerly raced along toward the large rock formation on the shoreline ahead. We were eager to explore what lay beyond. As we finally began to walk alongside the towering rock wall and gaze at its magnitude, Dad yelled in an authoritative tone, "Climb! And don't look back!" Immediately all six of us began climbing as fast as we could, with Cliff and Judi in the lead and Mom carrying Clint. After climbing as high as possible, I felt my father shield me as he grasped the rock on either side of my trembling frame. Suddenly powerful waves slammed against us. Sufficiently wet and scared, we realized that the tide was coming in instead of going out, as recorded in the schedule.

The rock had been my refuge, safe in the protection of my father's strong arms. Through the years that experience has helped me recognize and treasure our heavenly Father as my towering Rock of salvation. —SHERYL WALTER-SHEWMAKE

SEPTEMBER 29

BATTERIES, BUNNIES, AND BLESSINGS

Therefore go. . . . And surely I am with you always. Matt. 28:19, 20, NIV.

Out across the barren wasteland he parades stalwartly to the beat of his drum, past wilted palms and sun-bleached bones, past exhausted oases and windswept sand dunes. Vultures circle lazily above his head, waiting for him to stumble, to fall, to perish. On he marches as his adversaries plummet to their deaths. Yet he marches on . . . and on . . . and on . . .

I don't know which of the Energizer™ battery ads is your favorite, but this one's mine. Since the day of his birth on some illustrator's sketch pad, the pink bunny has tramped across dining tables and shower stalls, ocean floors and crime-ridden city streets, without faltering. The indomitable bunny beats his drum and keeps on going . . . and going . . . and going.

Recently, when Donna, my Bible study teacher, asked a provocative question, I thought of the Energizer™ bunny. Donna read two lists of hymn titles to the class. One consisted of songs about taking refuge in Jesus and receiving blessings from Him, while the other contained a list of more strident, military hymns of service. Then she asked, "Which do you favor?"

I didn't need to think about my answer. I much preferred the sentiment of "Leaning on the Everlasting Arms" to that of "Soldiers of Christ, Arise." In an instant I would choose the security of "Softly and Tenderly Jesus Is Calling" to "Sound the Battle Cry" or "Onward, Christian Soldiers!"

Now, Donna's purpose wasn't to present a moral dilemma, to compare evil with good, or negative with positive. All she intended was to remind us that healthy Christians, in order to grow, need to give and to go forth for the Master, as well as to receive and to "lean."

At first it seems like a dichotomy of purposes. Jesus lived His life on this earth to show me how to lean on Him, not how to stand like the brave; how to resist the urge to "do it myself" and depend on His strength; how to align my will with that of the Father's.

But before the Saviour returned to heaven, He gave me, one of His disciples, the commission to "go and tell." He also supplies me with the Power to do so—the power of the Holy Spirit. To fulfill His purpose successfully, these two contrasting principles must develop side by side within me. If I don't learn to lean, I will falter as a soldier of Christ. If I refuse to "sound the battle cry," my trust in Jesus will remain untested and weak.

This is where the pink bunny comes back into the story. I love this ad, not for the long life of the batteries, but for the indomitable spirit of the bunny. Despite his enemies, despite the adversity, despite the confusion around him, the pink bunny beats his drum and keeps going . . . and going . . . and going. As a child of God, can I do less?

KAY D. RIZZO

SEPTEMBER 30

DEDICATED HANDS

Mine elect shall long enjoy the work of their hands. They shall not labour in vain. Isa. 65:22, 23.

I had been a farmer's wife for a number of years when my mother, looking at my hands, exclaimed, "Oh, Katie! You are ruining your pretty hands."

My mother believed in taking care of the natural beauty God gave her. She often reprimanded me for my lack of vanity concerning my hands and face. My working in the sun without protection from its rays grieved her.

As I ran about the farm in jeans and ungloved hands, it wasn't beauty I was concerned with, just the multitude of chores of a farmer's wife.

But it was Mama who had taught me from Ecclesiastes 9:10, "Whatsoever thy hand findeth to do, do it with thy might." My earliest memory of Mama was being buried deep in the feather bed with my two sisters and brother. Mama was reading to us from her Bible. As the youngest, I couldn't tell you what she read, but I knew she was sharing "something special" with us.

It was only after the serious results of a home accident that I realized I was applying some of Mama's legacy while neglecting the most important matter.

I was not giving praise to God for His mighty power in my life. My industry was carried beyond the "six days shalt thou labour." I had not incorporated "set-aside time" into my work plan.

One evening my husband asked me to go to the city with him the next day. Grandmother would care for our children.

I decided to wash the baby's diapers before the trip. It was 1948, before we had electricity on our farm, but we had a gasoline-powered washing machine. As I threw diaper after diaper into the rolling pressure wringer I noticed too late the pile of accumulated cloth as one of the diapers wrapped around the roller.

Hitting the release button, I grabbed the rotating cloth. I screamed as my entangled fingers were drawn into the metal beneath the rollers. Crushed fingers, broken bones, and months of treatment followed. Sulfa was the new miracle drug, but the constant use of my hands when diapering an active baby prolonged the healing.

Finally Mama insisted that I see a specialist in the city. The doctor reported that I had gangrene in a finger. For five days I was hospitalized with round-the-clock treatment.

One morning the doctor told my husband, "I'm afraid we'll have to amputate the end of her finger little by little until we reach the seat of infection."

My husband wept as he thought of my losing a finger, while I boldly protested, "You're not going to cut my finger off!"

The doctor looked surprised, but when he X-rayed my hand later in the day, we both knew that the Great Physician had given a gift I hadn't even asked to receive. I had spoken in faith, believing, and God had blessed, with the help of many "dedicated hands."   MARY KAY MILAM

OCTOBER 1

PRAY FOR ONE ANOTHER

If anyone sees [her sister] commit a sin that does not lead to death, [she] should pray and God will give [her] life. 1 John 5:16, NIV.

Karen was waiting for me as I rushed in to work about five minutes late. This was her first appointment with me, so we had never met. I apologized for being late, saying, "I just came from teaching a young women's Bible study group."

"Bible study? What do you do?" Karen asked.

For the next half hour as I cut her hair, I explained to her what we did in the Bible study. She showed so much interest that I said,

"Karen, someday you may want to be in one of the Bible study groups I teach."

"No, not me!" she countered in surprise. "I could never do that. I would be scared to death!"

She liked her haircut and made an appointment for the following month. I put Karen on my prayer list. Each time she came we got better acquainted. The years passed, and every fall when we organized new study groups I invited her to join one of them. Her answer was always no. I kept praying for her.

Four years went by. As September rolled around and I was thinking about new groups, Karen came in for her usual haircut. She started the conversation by saying, "Hazel, are you still teaching Bible study?"

"Yes, Karen. Can you come?"

She said, "Well, I just enrolled my youngest child in school, so I have no excuse. I'll make a deal with you. If you promise that you won't ask me to pray or read, I'll come."

I said, "It's a deal. I won't ask until you're ready!"

About the sixth week of our study I went through all the steps of how to accept Christ into you life as Lord and Father, and Karen prayed to receive Christ! There were tears running down her cheeks and mine. She was like a little blossom opening up to the warm spring sunshine. Each week after that she volunteered to read Scripture and to pray!

At the end of 12 weeks she asked if we could have the next series of lessons at her house because she had already told her neighbors how much fun it was to study the Bible. One of my groups met at Karen's house with nine of her neighbors attending faithfully, and more lives were changed.

The scripture just before our text today says, "If we ask anything according to his will . . ." We are certainly in His will to ask for eternal life for the people God puts in our life. Eternal life is like the sunshine—it is not to be kept from anyone. It is freely given to all. Like the sunshine, it warms our hearts, and we blossom and bear fruit. What good news!

Let's be intercessors and pray for the people God puts in our lives, and we will discover that there is no power greater than the power of prayer. "Greater is he that is in you, than he that is in the world" (1 John 4:4).

HAZEL BURNS

OCTOBER 2

PERSPECTIVE

He has made everything beautiful in its time. Eccl. 3:11, NIV.

Some years ago, when we first came to the prairies, I wrote this one October afternoon. At first I was feeling sorry for myself, but by the time I had finished I knew I was where I ought to be. Perhaps some of you who have just moved to the prairies or have often longed for warmer climes can empathize with my feelings. At any rate, it is for all who might be missing another place right now.

> Cup in hand, I gaze through newly washed windows,
> wishing—no, longing—to see trees with graceful
> fall branches spreading toward the blue of prairie skies.
> Unbidden, my mind recalls gentler scenes from windows
> of the past—hills, mountains, sparkling lakes.
> Even a country garden.
>
> What twist of fate brings me to this place of early winters?
> Gazing still (the cup now cold), instead of much-loved trees
> my eyes define the straight, clean lines of rooftops.
> Chimneys, some brick, some shining metal, send little
> waves of warmth into the endless cold.
>
> One lone streetlamp, curving skyward, yet bending earthward
> like a silent, faithful guardian angel, keeps vigil.
> This watching cherub, disconnected from his base by
> intervening structure, seems, from my window, to spring
> from no place in particular.
>
> Three small planes, soundless in my insulated room, fly
> like well-fed birds across the horizon.
> Each tips its wings as, one by one, they establish patterns
> of flight that will take them to some other place—
> perhaps a spot where fall leaves still lend golden hue to
>   landscape.
>
> A half hour of seeing and feeling the beauty of symmetry,
> the beauty of cold, blue skies, of sun shining on friendly

rooftops, of skies deepening as late afternoon adds streaks of rose and pink, of shadows cast by neighboring fences.

Beauty? Yes, there is beauty here.
It dwells not only in the past.
It is here. It is now. ELLEN MACIVOR

OCTOBER 3

MEASURE OF FAITH

Ask, and ye shall receive, that your joy may be full. John 16:24.

After a morning in the strawberry field, I visited an elderly friend. I planned to give him as many berries as he would take. "How many can I give you?" I asked somewhat teasingly. "And what shall I put them in?" Purposely I left the choices to him.

He seemed pleased, and brought a medium-sized mixing bowl. I heaped the field-warm fruit into it, happy to share with him. But somehow I felt disappointed that he had not asked for more. I would have filled all his mixing bowls if he'd had the faith to bring them.

Many times we do the same thing with God. While the wealth of heaven can be ours, we hesitate to claim boldly as much as we desire, as much as God would willingly give us.

He demonstrated His love for us with His best gift—His only Son! For the more we ask of God, the more He delights to bestow upon us.

"Ask, and ye shall receive, that your joy may be full."

Let us never doubt God's love and readiness to grant greater blessings than we could ever dream of asking. FANNIE L. HOUCK

OCTOBER 4

HOMEWARD BOUND

Let not your heart be troubled: ye believe in God, believe also in me. In my Father's house are many mansions: if it were not so, I would have told you. I go to prepare a place for you. And if I go and prepare a place for you, I will come again, and receive you unto myself; that where I am, there

ye may be also. John 14:1-3.

One day as my husband, Dennis, was doing his pigeon chores he noticed something unusual in the yard. Looking closer, he found a severely injured homing pigeon of his, working its way to the loft by moving its wings on the ground to propel itself forward. An encounter with an unseen wire had broken both legs. Somehow the pitiful bird had managed to fly home, but now it was on the ground and was still having to rely on its wings for the last 100 feet. Dennis picked it up and brought it into the house. He felt that a pigeon with dedication like that was worth keeping. He handed the bird to me, and I cradled it as carefully as I could. Tears stung my eyes while Dennis fashioned splints from short lengths of copper wire, gauze, and bandage tape. I gently placed it in an unused carrying basket and put food and water within easy reach. A few weeks later Dennis declared the bird healed and ready to fly again.

Dennis's favorite hobby is racing homing pigeons. He has always loved birds and is very committed to the work and training that homing pigeons require. The longest race his birds are involved in is 600 miles. The birds are released in the early daylight hours on race day, and fly feverishly with single-minded vision toward home. Thirst and hunger are repressed as they journey without stopping for food or water. An exceptional bird will fly home from that lengthy race by nightfall and is considered a "daybird."

During one particular 600-mile race less than ideal weather conditions existed, with 15-mph headwinds. Dennis did not anticipate any daybirds, and so was not anxiously waiting and watching the skies, as he usually did after a race. However, at dusk he thought he'd check the loft just in case. To his delight with his bird and chagrin at himself, a daybird was waiting for him. What time had it arrived? Sadly, its master was not there to welcome it home when it arrived.

How unlike our heavenly Master! Christ will be waiting for us at journey's end with a "Welcome home, children."

Is our desire to make the heavenly home our only goal? and not to let anything sidetrack us from reaching it? If it isn't, let's purpose in our hearts to make it our goal to be there to occupy the mansions that He has prepared for us. — MARGE LYBERG MCNEILUS

October 5

Beautiful Eyes

But the eyes of the Lord are on those who fear him, on those whose hope is in his unfailing love. Ps. 33:18, NIV.

Eyes are one of the most delicate and beautiful creations God has given us. I often look at girls with beautiful eyes and admire them. Some even have long curly eyelashes enhancing the beauty of their eyes. As children we used to play a game to see whose eyelashes could hold a matchstick. We discovered that only a very few could win this game.

Many Indian women use Kajal, a mixture of soot and oil to put around their eyes. They say this keeps their eyes cool and makes them look beautiful. At a modern beauty parlor much attention is paid to the eyelashes and eyebrows. Shaping the eyebrows and applying eye shadow are supposed to make eyes look beautiful.

We all recognize, of course, that eyes mean much more to us than just their beauty. But often it is only when we begin to have eye problems that we realize the value of our eyes. Fortunately there are eye specialists to help us with almost any kind of eye problem. With the help of our eyes we can do our work more effectively, enjoy our life more, and communicate better with one another.

As a mother I often laughed when my children played hide-and-seek. Usually the older ones would hide where they could not be seen at all, but the little one would cover only his eyes. Now I play hide-and-seek with my little grandson, and he does the same.

To a child, eyes mean a person. Quite often a baby will reach for its mother's eyes with its little fingers. Much of its communication with the mother is through the eyes. If the mother covers her eyes, the baby feels lost. How often we as God's children feel lost and lonely with God out of sight. At such a time we can comfort ourselves with the assurance found in 2 Chronicles 16:9: "The eyes of the Lord run to and fro throughout the whole earth, to shew himself strong in the behalf of them whose heart is perfect toward him." King David assures us that as long as we fear God and hope in His mercy, God's eyes are upon us.

Children often look at their teachers and parents for a look of approval. But when they do wrong they cannot face the look of rebuke. When erring children see love and tears in their mother's eyes, their hearts will melt and change far more than if they see rebuke. We can remember what Jesus' loving and forgiving eyes did to Peter.

How fitting it is for us Christians to keep looking up as we tend to our temporal duties. King David says, "Mine eyes are ever toward the Lord" (Ps. 25:15). If this is our motto, and we keep our eyes always toward the Lord, we shall be blessed with truly beautiful eyes.

BIRDIE PODDAR

OCTOBER 6

NO, NOT YET

Wait on the Lord. Ps. 27:14.

My husband travels a lot. His work takes him to different parts of the country and sometimes overseas. So whenever he calls me, I savor the time I spend with him on the phone. Sometimes, at the end of our conversation, he'll say, "Well, sweetheart, I'd better go now." Then I'll plead, "No, not yet." I really have nothing more to say, but I want just a few more seconds with him. When he laughs his easy laugh and spends those last few seconds on the line with me, I'm satisfied. By his willing attitude to stay a little longer, he has shown me his love.

I sometimes wonder if perhaps God could feel a little bit the same way at times. When we hurriedly run through our prayers in the morning and then rush off to work or other appointments, we may be unconsciously showing an attitude that other things are more important than our time spent with Him.

My favorite author, commenting on this problem, wrote:

"Many, even in their seasons of devotion, fail of receiving the blessing of real communion with God. They are in too great haste. With hurried steps they pass through the circle of Christ's loving presence, pausing perhaps a moment within the sacred precincts, but not waiting for counsel. They have no time to remain with the divine Teacher. With their burdens they return to their work" (*Education*, p. 260).

Perhaps if at the end of our devotional prayers we would linger in silence a few seconds, we may not only demonstrate our reluctance to leave God's presence but also receive from Him the assurance of His everlasting love. The irony is that the more time we spend in God's presence now, the more likely we'll be of spending an eternity with Him.

NANCY CACHERO VASQUEZ

OCTOBER 7

RULES, RULES, RULES

And I will delight myself in Your commandments, which I love. Ps. 119:47, NKJV.

Several years ago I volunteered to go as a student missionary to the atoll of Majuro in the Marshall Islands. I taught 26 wiggling, squirming, and very active 5- to 7-year-olds in the kindergarten classroom. One of our classroom rules was that the children had to keep all four legs of their chairs on the floor. This rule was especially annoying to the children, and they pushed the boundary frequently.

One day as I wrote out an alphabet lesson on the chalkboard I heard a thump and then a loud, anguished cry. I turned to see one of my 5-year-olds, Enoch, his chair tipped backward on the cement floor. He was rubbing the back of his head as tears streamed down his brown cheeks.

I ran to him and pulled him onto my lap as I righted his chair and cuddled him close, all the while whispering in his ear, "See, Enoch, that's why I made the rule. I was only trying to protect you from getting hurt."

The day continued on without much thought. I sat down to rest my weary legs and watched the little heads bent forward at their tables struggling over an assignment. Suddenly God spoke. It was as clear as if my aide had been speaking to me. He said, "See, Shonna, that is why I made rules." I jumped to attention. For the first time in my life I saw the Ten Commandments from a different perspective. My Father God, Teacher, making rules to keep me from hurting myself. How often do I push those boundaries with little white lies or "Christian" slang words? Do I covet, just a little bit? Do I dislike someone, or worse yet, do I hate anybody? What does pushing those boundaries do to my spiritual life? to my emotional life? to my relationships? It was so much to think about!

What an incredible God of love I have! My heavenly parent, setting boundaries, making rules, protecting me—because He loves me so very much.

SHONNA DALUSONG

October 8

Covered by His Wings

When thou passest through the waters, I will be with thee; and through the rivers, they shall not overflow thee: when thou walkest through the fire, thou shalt not be burned; neither shall the flame kindle upon thee. Isa. 43:2.

It had been a clear, seasonably warm October day—perfect weather for a class trip. I could sense my daughter's excitement build as the day drew nearer. Finally, when the day arrived she hurried feverishly, taking care of a typical 12-year-old's last-minute details—calling friends to find out what they were wearing, who was bringing cameras, and most important, where the cute guys would be sitting on the bus. I gave one final "Hurry up or you'll be late!" as I went out to start the car to drive her to school.

"Mom, can I have some money for the trip?" she asked as we drove into the school parking lot. Reaching into my purse, I handed her a few dollars and told her to have fun. "Don't forget to pick me up at 5:00 tonight," she said.

My eyes followed her as she walked briskly toward the crowd of kids who were waiting to board the bus. I couldn't help getting caught up in their excitement. In my imagination I reviewed what her day would be like and wondered what she'd take snapshots of.

At 4:30 p.m I received a telephone call from a nurse from the local hospital. She informed me that the bus had been returning from the field trip when an object was thrown through the window where my daughter was sitting, sending flying glass into her face. I was stunned. The nurse assured me that my daughter was all right but that she had scratches on her face and possibly some glass fragments in her left eye. I immediately drove to the hospital, where I found that the doctor had already washed and bandaged her eye. He said that he didn't think there were any fragments, but that since splinters of glass are hard to detect, she should be seen by an ophthalmologist the next day, just to be sure.

The following day we were in the ophthalmologist's office. After an examination and a few simple tests, the doctor informed me that she had only a small scratch underneath her eyelid and that there was no glass in her eye. No glass splinters, no corneal abrasions. I thanked God.

I praise my Father for protecting her that day, and for His endless love toward His children. We may never know until that day when the earth is made new how many times we were covered by His wings.

JAMISEN MATTHEWS

OCTOBER 9

REAL VALUE

What are [human beings], that thou art mindful of [them]? or the [sons and daughters], that thou visitest [them]? Heb. 2:6.

My friend found herself lying on a California freeway in the midnight darkness, thrown from her husband's motorcycle when it blew a tire. As her husband struggled to gain control of the raging mechanical beast, Charon was too petrified to move. She watched the lights of the oncoming cars race toward her and wondered what it was like to die. Cars sped toward her, saw her in their headlights, and at the last moment swerved around her. Three cars did this before her husband dragged her to the side of the freeway. Neither was hurt, other than being very stiff the next day. This experience brought her closer to God as she realized how near she had been to death.

Sometimes illness or a broken relationship puts a barrier between us and God, and it takes faith and courage to hang on, as with Job we cry out, "I go forward, but he is not there; and backward, but I cannot perceive him" (Job 23:8).

When I took astronomy during my senior year in college, I thrilled with learning of the magnitude of the universe. Yes, I already knew about the planets, stars, and galaxies, but the largeness of it all, and the trillions of light-years away, and the stillness of time—somehow I never again viewed my small world quite the same, nor the God who created, cares for, and loves this universe. He's quite a God!

That this powerful, intelligent-beyond-all-imagination Being loves and cares for one world, among the possibility of many systems, would be enough, but to care also for the minute details (even as seeing the sparrow fall) and to put care and precision into the smallest of creation boggles my mind.

But this wonderful Being has gone even further—He has given His life that we might be with Him forever, with complete emotional, intellectual, and physical healing from all that has marred and hurt in the world. He would love and save us if we were the only ones on earth.

How this teaches us to value each life that is so valuable to Him!

He is not only the Creator God of the universe—a world beyond that we know so little of—but is present in our hurt, damaged world. But we know that our lives and world will be wholly beautiful again. James Russell Lowell said it so well: "Standeth God within the shadows, keeping watch above his own."

EDNA MAYE GALLINGTON

OCTOBER 10

CRADLED IN HIS ARMS

Lo, I am with you alway, even unto the end of the world. Matt. 28:20.

The terrible words hung in the air and echoed in my ears. "Your husband is dying. Call your family."

Removing the stethoscope, the doctor put his arm across my shoulder, said "I'm sorry," and left the room. Time stood still. I felt perched on the edge of eternity. The echo faded away, and I was surrounded by silence. "Lord, please help me," I prayed. "What do I do now?"

The family had come to be with me, but had returned to their own homes out of state, for we'd been told that their dad was better and would likely be going home soon. Our pastor was on vacation. Our family doctor had gone for the Labor Day holiday weekend. I was alone.

"Lord, I have only one phone number with me."

A soft voice broke through the silence. I hadn't noticed a hospital employee in a blue uniform dusting nearby. "Is there someone I can call for you?" she asked. I gave her the number and explained that I didn't know if she could reach anyone, as my granddaughters had returned to college. Their mother and father had gone back to their camp.

The lady dialed the number, then handed the phone to me. I took it, not expecting anyone to answer. Then I heard a familiar voice. "Gram? How's Grandpa?"

I told her why I had called and asked her to please call her aunts and uncles. "Oh, Gram, I'm so sorry; I'll be with you as soon as I make the calls."

Standing beside my husband's bed, I felt the presence of the Holy Spirit and was at peace. A deep feeling of warm love filled me. How quickly the years had sped by. Exactly 50 years ago that Labor Day weekend we had gone on our first date.

My granddaughter arrived, and together we praised and thanked God for one of His many revelations of His help and nearness. If I'd called five minutes sooner or five minutes later I would have missed her. She'd left for college but come back for a book she needed, and was unlocking the door when the phone rang. A moment later she would have picked up her book and been gone.

A minister I'd served with as a deaconess was filling in for our pastor. If given a choice, I'd have chosen him to minister to us, for he always represented the gentleness of Jesus to me. He was there. He came and prayed with us.

A brother and his wife and daughter whom I hadn't seen for years appeared on my doorstep while we were making funeral arrangements. They were on vacation, so they hadn't received the phone call. But they'd felt impressed to take a side trip and call on us.

The next few hours in the hospital that first day and several days afterward were a blur, but I was always conscious of Christ's comforting arms holding me and whispering to me, "I will never leave thee, nor forsake thee" (Heb. 13:5). DORIS JENNER EVERETT

OCTOBER 11

EISEGESIS

They hardly hear with their ears, and they have closed their eyes. Otherwise they might see with their eyes, hear with their ears, understand with their hearts and turn, and I would heal them. Matt. 13:15, NIV.

The postman had filled my mailbox to overflowing. How I enjoyed reading the communications from my family and friends! The last envelope contained only one sheet of paper, but the words "Help! Help!" were written across the top in bold letters.

"Dear Leona, Last weekend, during a question-and-answer period at the end of one of my seminars, a man waved his hand in the air. Honestly, you will not believe what he said: 'My Bible tells me that women should remain silent in the churches. How is it that you are going against the Word of the Lord by not only speaking aloud in churches but doing it from the pulpit? You need to go home and study 1 Corinthians 14:34!'

"Leona, please tell me what that text really says in the original. I did not argue with the man—but he really expected me to sit down and shut up!"

Sitting down in front of the typewriter, I chuckled—not at my friend Arlene's plight, but at her way with words. I could just imagine the scene. Although I was glad that she had completed her seminar without arguing (Phil. 2:14, NIV), I knew that questions of that nature can be very wearing.

The typewriter keys fairly flew: "My dear friend," I began, "I always cringe when I hear exegesis of texts turned into eisegesis (reading things into them instead of just bringing out their full meaning)."

I continued typing, explaining. "The original Greek word for 'remain silent in the churches' means not to talk or chatter. The apostle does not want the women of the Corinthian church chattering—talking among themselves if they do not understand the sermon.

"The next verse tells women to ask their husbands at home rather than speaking out—breaking in with questions—during the church services. We must remember that women did not have the same opportunities for education then as men did, and Christianity had brought in a feeling of equality that could not be allowed to turn into license for irreverence in worship."

I concluded my reply with "This should fortify you with ammunition." Before sealing the letter, I added a postscript. "Do not feel bad if, after you explain the original meaning of this text, it is not accepted by everyone. Remember that Isaiah talked about people who have closed minds so they cannot understand (Isa. 44:18). And of course, don't sit down and don't shut up!"

"Thank You, Lord," I breathed as I hurried to mail the letter. "Thank You for preserving some of the early Hebrew and Greek manuscripts so that we can more clearly understand what You really meant." LEONA GLIDDEN RUNNING AND ARLENE TAYLOR

OCTOBER 12

DRIFTING NEAR THE ROCKS

He shall call upon me, and I will answer him: I will be with him in trouble; I will deliver him, and honour him. Ps. 91:15.

Several years ago I, with a group of volunteers from Coffs Harbour, Australia, flew out to the New Hebrides on a fly-and-build project. That meant not only air travel but also sea travel to a small island in the group. We left Aore about midnight on a mission boat bound for a small island where some of the group were working on an airstrip. The moon shone down, the sea was calm, and the native crew sang. What a treat to listen to their splendid harmony and songs of praise!

As we left the sheltered waters and rode out into the open sea the restless waves caused some of the volunteers to become seasick. We were glad to welcome the dawn and to find we were only a few hours from our destination. Then just as we were approaching a small rocky island the engine stopped. The engineer tried every trick he knew to coax the temperamental engine into action. Our boat started to drift toward the rocks—so close, in fact, that one of the leaders ordered, "Out with the life raft." It looked as though we would hit the rocks any moment. Crew and passengers alike were quiet, silently praying that something good would happen. The life raft was inflated and dropped over the side. Meanwhile two of the volunteers were down in the engine room doing their utmost to help the engineer. The leader was trying to persuade the ladies to get into the life raft, but they decided they would take their chances on the ship rather than trust their lives on the flimsy raft.

Only a few feet away from the rocks the engine gave a splutter, then a trusty *throb! throb!* God had heard the prayers of His people. We continued on our way rejoicing, profoundly thankful to reach land again.

During this experience a very expensive piece of life raft equipment had fallen overboard, and so the next day the boat and crew returned to the place of near disaster to try to salvage it. We as volunteers marveled when the divers returned some hours later with the piece, recovered from the depths of the wide blue ocean. We are sure that God had a hand in that, too.

I believe that when Christ sends us, He always goes with us.

ALMA ATCHESON

OCTOBER 13

GOOD MISTAKES

Whatsoever ye do, do it heartily, as to the Lord, and not unto men; knowing that of the Lord ye shall receive the reward of the inheritance: for ye serve the Lord Christ. Col. 3:23, 24.

While teaching American students in the country of Japan, I was invited to sing contralto solos with the Japanese Voice of Prophecy Quartet. As we sang for church services and evangelistic meetings, the quartet members encouraged me to take up the challenge of singing some songs in the Japanese language.

I was reluctant to do this, though I had learned one of the three Japanese alphabets and had studied enough to feel confident in shopping, travel, and asking directions should I become lost. But to read songs required knowledge of all three alphabets.

I began this endeavor with much prayer for God's help. The inevitable happened one Sabbath afternoon at a youth rally in Tokyo. I mispronounced one syllable in a song about the crucifixion of our Lord Jesus.

Later I asked the quartet members what I had said. The Oriental custom of saving face was extended to me as they assured me it was no problem and nothing terrible had been said.

Not satisfied with their response, I continued asking until I found someone who knew the Western culture well enough to realize that it would be more beneficial for me to learn from mistakes, rather than just save face.

With continued Oriental courtesy I was assured that my mistake was of greater benefit to them and had made the song more meaningful. Instead of saying that Jesus was crucified, I had sung that He was 10 times tortured. "It was," I was assured again, "a good mistake!"

How often throughout our lives do we blunder and feel devastated by what we believe have been irreversible mistakes? Something has occurred that made us feel less than perfect. A happenstance has left us feeling inadequate and a failure to family, friends, and the Lord.

Romans 8:28 assures us that "all things work together for good to them that love God." When we wholeheartedly give all our actions to God, our mistakes may teach us more than our successes.

Today, live heartily as unto the Lord. If need be, He is able to turn around your blunders—to turn them into good, meaningful mistakes!

LORNA LAWRENCE

OCTOBER 14

A TEACHER

Teach me your way, O Lord; lead me in a straight path. Ps. 27:11, NIV.

Today is my birthday, and I have just been handed a special gift. It is a hand-drawn picture of a large pink birthday cake decorated with red flowers and topped with yellow candles. It has been colored with crayons and is done on a sheet of white construction paper. Printed across the bottom of the picture is the message: "Happy Birthday, Teacher. Thank you for being my special friend. Love, Tim." And it's made me cry.

Tim has tried *so* hard to please me and his classmates this year. He wants to "fit in" with my primary Sabbath school class, and to be able to do things as they do. He studies his lessons faithfully every week at home, but he just can't seem to remember them on Sabbath, in spite of all his efforts. We have to have many lesson repetitions each week to keep Tim current with the class.

Slowly but steadily resentment has set in toward Tim and his learning disability. Several of the primary children have given me their opinion that Tim should be in another class, as he is slowing their progress. The joy of learning has been quickly diminishing. Recently it has not been a happy time for any of us.

Until today.

As I read the words that Tim has printed, I wonder, *Have I really been his friend these past several weeks? Have I always shown patience and love to him when his lack of understanding irritated me? Have I been a friend to him when he's needed one?*

Tim wants to be like us and to be one of us very much. He accepts us as we are with our faults and mistakes. Why can't we accept him as he is, with his imperfections? For even as we were repeating his Bible lessons to him so that he could learn, he was unknowingly teaching us valuable lessons about love and tolerance that we hadn't learned.

So who really has had the learning disability? O God, help me always to be acceptive to the needs of other people, and to love Your children as You do. And above all, I ask that You show me how to be as good a teacher as Tim is!

ROSEMARY BAKER

OCTOBER 15

THE SUN WILL SHINE AGAIN

Then the righteous will shine like the sun in the kingdom of their Father. Let anyone who has ears listen! Matt. 13:43, NRSV.

I live in Erie, Pennsylvania, sometimes said to be the second-cloudiest city in the world. Some refer to it as the city that sits under a cloud; others describe it as dreary. I don't know if there are any substantial statistics or facts to verify this, but I have to admit there seem to be more cloudy days than sunny.

Originally coming from a state in which the sun usually shines, I often find myself feeling just a little depressed on these extremely dark days.

They tell me studies have revealed that people living in these conditions are more likely to become depressed. I believe this is true, because I've met people elsewhere who could not adapt to the lack of sunshine here and have moved.

One day while sitting in my kitchen looking out the window at the dark and dismal sky, I felt as though I was in a fog. I began to slip into a state of despair, when suddenly a beautiful thought entered my mind: *The sky may be gray, but behind those clouds the sun continues to shine. So focus on the fact that the clouds are only temporary. The sun will shine again.*

Life is like that. Sometimes darkness hides the Son of God from us, and the clouds of circumstance brought on by Satan come between God and us. Though we cannot see Him, He is still there. Just as the sun will break through the clouds and shine again, so the Son of God will again illuminate our lives. Clouds of discouragement will roll back like a scroll, and we will again see His face.

Now I have no trouble coping with the overcast days, for God has put sunshine within me. When I think of Jesus and His love and recall the promises He gave, even cloudy days seem sunny.

Also, there is something to be said for clouds. Remember Matthew 24:30: "And then shall appear the sign of the Son of man in heaven: and then shall all the tribes of the earth mourn, and they shall see the Son of man coming in the clouds of heaven with power and great glory."

JESSIE BEARD

October 16

God's Special Person

Now the word of the Lord came to me saying, "Before I formed you in the womb I knew you, and before you were born I consecrated you; I have appointed you a prophet to the nations." Jer. 1:4, 5, NASB.

While I was grading English papers in our air-conditioned bedroom away from Singapore's oppressive heat, a feeling of apprehension and uneasiness suddenly fell over me. Propelled to the door, I heard excited voices and came upon a scene I shall never forget. I saw our younger daughter, Linda, lying limp in my husband's arms, with Patricia, our older daughter, bending over her. You can imagine the myriad of questions racing through my mind.

I ran closer to investigate, and noticed Linda's eyes flickering. "She was knocked out by the electricity," my husband explained.

Many houses in Singapore are built on pillars anchored to a cement slab so that air can circulate under the house. Patricia and Linda were sweeping and hosing down this cement slab in preparation for Patricia's school graduation party. As Linda lifted a poorly insulated electrical cord, 220 volts of electricity coursed through her body. Through God's providence my husband had just come home from the office to see how things were going when he heard Patricia cry out, "Linda is being electrocuted!"

My husband quickly yanked the wire from the socket, and Linda was freed from the immobilizing electrical current. Only a burn in the palm of her hand gave evidence of this terrible experience.

When Jeremiah stood unflinchingly in proclaiming the devastating prediction of Jerusalem's collapse, he experienced the anger of His whole nation and even his family. But he remembered the words of the Lord as found in our text today. Jeremiah knew he had been selected by God for a specific purpose and work, and he tenaciously hung on under all odds to perform the work God had for him to do.

Our text today applies to all God's children. He protected baby Moses in the wicker basket on the Nile, where Pharaoh's daughter found and adopted him as her son. Esther's belief that God had a plan for her life compelled her to let Him use her in saving her people.

God had each of us in mind before we were born. Each of us is special to Him. Each of us is "God's special person," and He has a plan for every life.

Your circumstance may not be as dramatic as saving a nation or being spared death, but whoever you are or wherever you are, remember that you too are God's special person and that He has a plan for your life. When times get rough and life seems futile, remember that you are "more precious than fine gold" (Isa. 13:12).

Hold to the conviction "I am here for a reason, I have a work to do given me by divine appointment, and by God's grace I will do my best to honor His investment in my life." MARIE SPANGLER

OCTOBER 17

RELIANCE

Thou wilt keep him in perfect peace, whose mind is stayed on thee: because he trusteth in thee. Isa. 26:3.

"Mommy, I can't do it!" Cassandra said as she fought back tears of fear. She stood in three and a half feet of water, her body trembling. Though the sun shone brilliantly, warming the air into the 90s, her body shook with fear.

Cassandra desperately wanted to learn how to swim. "But I'm too scared, Mommy. Just let me play instead. Please!" I longed to help her, so I asked her if she trusted me. "Yes," she said, "but . . ."

As a swimming instructor I'd encountered only two others as afraid of water as my 11-year-old daughter: one was a young boy; the other, my mother.

Watching from a poolside lounge chair, Grandma (my mother) watched Cassandra's struggle. She couldn't help reliving her own regret that her fear of water had deprived her of the pleasure that swimming provides. Silently she ached for her granddaughter and prayed that the Lord would be able to use her to help Cassandra overcome her fear.

The next day Grandma surprised us all as she entered the pool along with us! While Grandma Loweta persuaded herself to learn to swim and began by putting her face in the water, Cassandra quietly watched. *Since Grandma is afraid and is swimming now, with Jesus' help so can I*, Cassandra determined. After praying about her fear, she took courage, began to relax, and eagerly exercised her trust in me to help her in learning safe water skills. Before the remaining two weeks of our California vacation had passed, both Cassandra and her grandmother had overcome much of their fear—and were swimming.

My heart rejoiced as my oldest daughter fulfilled her beginner's swimming requirements.

"What made the difference?" I asked the Lord. "Was it just a matter of them needing more encouragement? Was it a lack of trust? Was I not sympathetic enough to their fear? Or perhaps what they needed most was the assurance that someone else suffering the same fears was able to overcome them."

Then the Lord impressed me that what I needed was the revelation that I've often allowed my fears and worry to deprive me of the joy of trusting Him. He assured me that He too had endured trials as I do and that within His strength I too could be victorious. My heart filled with peace as on my knees I surrendered my anxieties to God.

SHERYL WALTER-SHEWMAKE

OCTOBER 18

WILL YOU TRUST ME?

Trust in the Lord with all thine heart; and lean not unto thine own understanding. In all thy ways acknowledge him, and he shall direct thy paths. Prov. 3:5, 6.

I've often wondered what it must really have been like for Abraham to make the choice to follow God fully—all the way to Mount Moriah. And until April of 1991 I could only speculate. At that time God provided me an opportunity to find out "personally" by similarly testing me. No, it wasn't my child's life at stake. But it was something (or actually someone) I loved and wanted more than anything this world could offer.

In short, because of circumstances I did not choose, I was placed in a state of "singleness," during which I reencountered a man I had known and loved from my past. A man I would have married back then in a heartbeat had the circumstance been different and the request forthcoming (neither of which was the case).

Now the circumstances were right—or so they seemed. Our paths recrossed, the sparks rekindled, and he asked me to marry him. I was so excited! so happy! so amazed at God's providence! It was a miracle, a dream come true. And we made short-term arrangements for a wedding to be held at once. The only problem was that I had become a Christian since we last knew each other. I felt that he was a Christian, but was concerned that he showed little interest in seriously investigating my beliefs, little interest in my trust and friendship with God.

In the ensuing few weeks before the "big date," the Holy Spirit began to work on my heart, both through circumstances and the Christian concerns of others. Gradually I had an unwelcome and profound uneasiness regarding my decision. Echoing in my ears were the words of Proverbs 14:12: "There is a way that seems right to a person, but its end is the way to death" (NRSV). I could find no peace until I laid *all* on the altar of God.

I loved this man. I wanted more than anything to be his wife. Still, God failed to answer my anguished earnest prayers with an affirmative peace of mind. Yet I simply could not make the decision not to marry him! I wanted it! But somehow the one thing I wanted even more was to be right with God and serve Him faithfully. All I was capable of was surrendering my will to His and leaving the rest up to Him. He'd have to give me the strength, the wisdom, "the very words in my mouth" to stop the marriage. For *I* would not, indeed, *could* not! To do so would betray in me all that I'd ever longed for, hoped for, and had lost so long ago. To lose it again, to give it up now, was unthinkable.

But I so loved my Lord. And I truly wanted whatever He knew was best for me. Two weeks before the wedding, by the sheer grace of God, I called it off. It was the hardest and most painful thing I'd ever done in my life. But God, in His goodness, gave me peace in my decision. And He never left me through the hurt and loneliness that followed. He was and is my comfort and hope.

Since then, God has blessed me with a fulfilling and even more compatible relationship with an attractive Christian man who shares my same beliefs.

I thank the Lord for my "Abraham experience," for through it I have been drawn closer to God. I have learned to trust Him and not myself. He knows what's best for me even more than I. There have been many confirmations since that time to affirm my decision and strengthen my confidence in Him.   ROSEMARY BRUCKEN

OCTOBER 19

IF I CAN HELP SOMEONE

Inasmuch as ye have done it unto one of the least of these my brethren, ye have done it unto me. Matt. 25:40.

"You owe me 50 cents' change. Now be quick about it. I don't have all day!" I could not help hearing the irate voice as I walked up to the produce stand to complete my purchases for our camping trip. It is always embarrassing to hear a person being "chewed out," but the object of all this wrath was a small girl, perhaps 11 years old, who was helping in the family business. She almost burst into tears as she gave the angry woman her change. My heart hurt for her as she walked away from the cash register to a more private place.

How can anyone be so thoughtless and inconsiderate as to direct such anger at a petite, sweet-looking child who must have become confused and frustrated? I wondered as I started to fill some bags with produce. I could empathize totally with the young girl, having been in the same situation myself. I too had helped sell small vegetables and flowering plants by the dozen. Several times adults took advantage of my diminutive size, thinking that a child might not know or care about the difference 10 or 25 cents made in the total of the whole purchase.

Pulling my thoughts back to the present situation, I tried to think of something I could do to help her wounded self-esteem. As I was choosing the corn, a plan grew in my mind. I finished my selections, paid for the produce, and walked over to where the girl was standing. I said hello to her, offered her some coins, and asked if she could please help me carry my bags to my car. She gladly accepted my offer, picked up two bags in each hand, and got to the car almost before I could open it.

"Thank you so much," I told her. "You have been a big help to me! Have a very happy day." I drove away with the positive thought that I had left her a happier child, feeling much better about herself and hopefully about some of the people around her.

Lillian Musgrave

October 20

God Said I Could

Thy word is a lamp unto my feet, and a light unto my path. Ps. 119:105.

Teaching a feisty second-grader how to carry numerals in subtraction was proving to be a larger challenge than I'd anticipated. The determined little lad insisted on taking the smaller number from the larger, regardless of which one was on top. Then his pudgy fingers would quickly smudge in an answer.

He presented his notebook to me, a slight look of defiance playing in his usually innocent brown eyes.

"All done, Miss B!" he announced.

"But Joey, how many times must I tell you? You can't do it that way!" Exasperation edged my voice.

His reply was swift and sure. "But my mommy said I could!"

Ah! Such loyalty. If Mommy but says the word, it's gospel truth. No room for misunderstanding or argument. That's just the way it is.

Joey eventually learned to carry in subtraction.

And I learned a lesson in devotion.

If only we could have such loyalty to the words of our heavenly Father. If God said it in His Word, it must be true. We can follow it unconditionally—no questions asked.

Why did I take a mighty leap in faith and accept Jesus as my Saviour? Because God said I could.

Why do I confess my sins and leave them behind me in the deepest ocean? Because God said I could.

Why do I walk in assurance each day, holding on to the hand of my Best Friend? Because God said I could.

How am I able to love my enemies? Because God said I could.

The world may ridicule us for following God's words. We may be told that we misunderstand, that what God said isn't important anymore.

But like Joey, our devotion to our heavenly Parent should be such that if God said it, we do it. We know He loves us more than any earthly parent and He tells us to do only what is for our own good.

I choose to give my life in total surrender today to the leading of the Holy Spirit. God said I could. DAWNA BEAUSOLEIL

OCTOBER 21

SING THE CLOUDS AWAY

Therefore the redeemed of the Lord shall . . . come with singing; . . . and sorrow and mourning shall flee away. Isa. 51:11.

I heard my baby's shrill scream and rushed into the dining room in time to see 9-month-old Vernon standing beside the table with his hand in the bowl of hot oatmeal.

I snatched him up into my arms, quickly wiped the hot oatmeal off his hand, and hurried to apply medication. He continued to whimper, so I sat on a nearby chair and cuddled him close to me.

Joy, our 2-year-old, leaned against my knees and gently patted Vernon's back. Leaning over him, she lisped, "Sing c'ouds away, Bernon. Sing c'ouds away."

Of course Vernon didn't sing, but he smiled, and slid from my lap to the floor, soothed.

Later, reflecting on the incident, I thought, *How fitting if in times of pain, distress, and discouragement, we would sing.*

Should we lift our voices in song, burdens and cares will grow lighter and our faith in God stronger.

According to medical authorities, singing helps clear the sinuses, and relaxes the entire body. The relation affects the respiratory and muscular systems, automatically elevating the mood.

When a child is angry, song can be a blessing. An authority on child raising once wrote that soft tunes will have a quieting influence. We should sing them these subdued tunes in regard to Christ and His love (*Child Guidance*, p. 93).

As a boy, Jesus sang psalms and heavenly songs. When His companions complained of tiredness, He sang sweet melodies.

The Lord wants us to lighten our cares by singing songs of faith, hope, and courage. Song also subdues rude and uncultivated natures. It quickens thought and awakens sympathy and banishes gloom.

Come, let us "sing the clouds away."   MABEL ROLLINS NORMAN

OCTOBER 22

SHOE CLIPS SHOW GOD'S LOVE

Therefore I tell you, do not worry about your life, what you will eat; or about your body, what you will wear. . . . Consider the ravens: They do not sow or reap, they have no storeroom or barn; yet God feeds them. And how much more valuable you are than birds! Luke 12:22-24, NIV.

Recently I had been worrying about life in general, and although I had opened my Bible several times to Luke 12:22-31 and Matthew 10:29-31, I still did not feel the full assurance that God would take care of everything.

One morning I carefully dressed for church. To add the final touch to my outfit, I clipped on my gold shoe clips to dress up my otherwise plain patent leather pumps.

I was taking the bus to church that particular day, and as I stepped out my door, I saw that it was coming. I started to run and was able to catch the bus.

After a short ride, I had to change to a second bus, which would take me directly to the church. As I was waiting, I glanced down at my shoes and noticed to my dismay that both my gold shoe clips were gone. I realized that they must have fallen off during my run for the bus. My first reaction was to feel upset, but almost immediately a calming force, which could only be the Holy Spirit, came over me. I prayed to God, asking Him to allow me to go to church and gain a blessing, and to keep my clips safe wherever they were so that I could pick them up on my return trip home. I continued on to church without worrying about the clips and thoroughly enjoyed and was blessed by the service.

On the way home I again prayed that I would find the clips. As I stepped off the bus and started my walk home, I kept my eyes to the ground. As I crossed the street, there in the middle of the road lay one of my clips. Picking it up, I noticed that a car seemed to have run over the back of it, but it was not damaged. A few inches from where I had found the first clip I found the second one just lying on the sidewalk. I thanked God again and again.

Then it came to me that if God could hear and answer my prayer about such a trivial thing as my gold shoe clips, why was I worrying about the big things in my life? I have since then placed them all in His hands, because I *know* He cares.

KAREN BIRKETT

OCTOBER 23

THE TABLECLOTH

He will wipe every tear from their eyes. There will be no more death or mourning or crying or pain, for the old order of things has passed away. Rev. 21:4, NIV.

Tonight I took a scrub brush to the brown-and-white picnic tablecloth. I found my strokes softening to a caress as I let the memories flood over me. My tears mixed with the soapsuds. Now the cloth is ready for another picnic—another memory.

The brown-and-white picnic cloth was purchased for the after-church picnic the day before our daughter's wedding. We sat under the trees in Grandma's backyard, swatting bugs and eating a tasty homemade meal, talking, laughing, dreaming. Both families were there. How we enjoyed that day!

We also had the brown-and-white picnic cloth at the snorkeling trip when the whole family visited us in our mission home in the Philippines. In fact, after lunch 10-month-old grandson Alex slept on it. That was the day Father enjoyed his first glimpse of the underwater wonderland. That was also the day of the lobster legs. The picnic cloth stands for all those happy times.

Yesterday we also used the brown-and-white cloth at our daughter's birthday picnic, the first family gathering after her husband's death. Actually, the celebration was only partly a birthday party. It was a celebration of the 10 years we had Dennis with us. Ten years rich with interest and joy, touched here and there with a few shadows, but basically good years. It's been terribly hard to say "Until the morning." We miss Dennis. But we will cherish the memory of his puns and clever sayings, of his multiple acts of gentle kindness, of his love to all of us. And we look forward to the land where death does not separate.

I don't suppose the brown-and-white tablecloth will make the final journey with us. But as we sit around the heavenly table, an unbroken family once more—perhaps an expanded family—I'm not sure but that my eyes will see it on that golden table. In any case, the tears will be of joy. There will be no more pain or sighing. No more goodbyes.

"Amen. Even so, come, Lord Jesus." NANCY JEAN VYHMEISTER

OCTOBER 24

GOSPEL SURGERY

There is neither Jew nor Greek, there is neither bond nor free, there is neither male nor female: for ye are all one in Christ Jesus. Gal. 3:28.

Prejudice is peculiar. Few of us want to have it, but most of us do and deny it.

Like imperceptible cataracts, prejudice lays a film across our eyes, dimming our vision. Because we cannot see well, we cannot examine our own condition. This makes self-diagnosis difficult—even among God-fearing people.

Take the example of two apostles who collided because of the cataracts of prejudice. Their difference of opinion nearly split the early church. Even today, nearly 2,000 years later, their arguments send tremors through our equanimity.

Both apostles wanted to do God's will and unite people who were badly divided by social, racial, and religious tensions. But Paul exclaimed in Galatians 2:11, "When Peter came to Antioch, I opposed him to his face, because he was clearly in the wrong" (NIV). Two spiritual giants had come to opposite conclusions.

Paul's words must have cut Peter deeply. After all, Peter had pioneered the gospel to the Gentiles (Acts 10; 11). Peter had insisted to his Jewish critics that God regarded no person as common or unclean—and neither should they.

Both believed in the same thing: equality. But they behaved very differently. Paul was eating with the Gentiles; Peter had stopped eating with them. With influential Jews present, Peter decided to favor his friends over the Gentiles. He saw it as a small concession to gain a larger peace.

Paul was aghast. It was the ancient version of the "equal but different" argument. He believed that Peter's well-meaning decision emasculated the gospel. If the gospel doesn't change our attitudes and our choices, we're not listening to it.

Paul believed prejudice was a moral issue. "You are a Jew, yet you live like a Gentile and not like a Jew. How is it, then, that you force Gentiles to follow Jewish customs?" he asked Peter in Galatians 2:14 (NIV).

Peter's eyes, still partially scaled over with prejudice, needed theological surgery. He needed the healing eyesalve of the Spirit.

In words that have not lost their currency down through the centuries, Paul then articulated this new understanding: "For ye are all the children of God by faith in Christ Jesus. . . . There is neither bond nor free, there is neither male nor female: for ye are all one in Christ Jesus" (Gal. 3:26-28).

For us to see *all* other human beings as children of the same God and to accept them as members of the same family is God's ideal.

Most of us still struggle with it. Fortunately, people of the vision rise up to check our spiritual eyesight. We must become like Christ, who recognized no distinction of nationality or rank or creed and who came to break down every wall of partition.

Prejudice is stubborn stuff and painful to peel away. But by the grace of Christ it is possible. Let's ask for gospel surgery. Let's ask the Spirit to come into our lives so that we will truly relate to each other with "love, joy, peace, patience, kindness, goodness, faithfulness, gentleness, and self-control" (Gal. 5:22, 23, NIV).   KIT WATTS

October 25

STRENGTHENING THE WEAK

Encourage the exhausted, and strengthen the feeble. Say to those with palpitating heart, "Take courage, fear not." Isa. 35:3, 4, NASB.

The tropical seeds came through the mail in one of those numerous solicitations to "send money to save the world." Curious about what sort of tree they would produce, my husband planted them. Three sprouted, but only one survived the early days of spindly growth. As it stretched fragile fronds toward the light from the window, its stalk grew top-heavy, and I tied it loosely to a small stake. By spring it needed a larger pot and a longer stake to support its pencil-thin trunk.

I pruned the top, hoping it would branch out. It did. During the summer the tree grew outdoors, and I trimmed it back occasionally. When the weather turned cold, we brought it in. By the third summer the trunk no longer leaned or pulled against the stake. It had developed its own strength, so I removed the support. The tree flourished, blossomed, and produced several long seed pods, which showed transparent against the light. We watched new seeds develop and grow within the pods. "We're making babies," my husband announced, proud of his young sapling.

At Christmas, instead of an evergreen, we strung lights on our living tree. We've left them there, partly to provide light to the tree on gloomy days, but mostly for the pleasure of looking at this plant, which grew able to bear fruit and give back to the surroundings that nurtured it.

People are like trees. It's easy to draw the analogy with children: nurturing, guiding, pruning—and rejoicing in what they become. But adults also experience times of need emotionally or spiritually.

Blessed are those who serve as "stakes" for persons newly growing in Christ or who are suffering damage from life's cruel winds. People who are "there"—trustworthy, strong, nurturing; people who understand the importance of "strengthening the feeble" while maintaining their own identity. Such persons know how to nurture and leave room for growth. They know when it's time to pull out, and how to enjoy the specter of someone else's blossoming.

Dear Lord, make me an instrument of Your healing and nurturing in the lives of others. Help me not to facilitate dependencies, but to help others discover their strength in You. Where they have felt brokenness or weakness, may I see Your ability to produce blossoms. May my own life flower and bear fruit to Your glory. Amen. LOIS PECCE

OCTOBER 26

MARY MAGDALENE: THE BETTER WAY

Mary has chosen what is better, and it will not be taken away from her. Luke 10:42, NIV.

Mary Magdalene was special. At least twice Jesus commended her publicly for some good thing she had done. One occasion was in front of her family, which, as far as we know, consisted of her, her sister Martha, and her brother Lazarus. Jesus praised Mary for choosing not to remain in the rut of dishwashing and serving tables.

The other time Jesus approved of Mary was when she poured perfume on His feet. You may read Jesus' words about her in Mark 14:6-9. But beyond all the words Jesus spoke in her favor, nothing could match the special privilege given to Mary on Resurrection morning. It was to her that Jesus appeared first.

Now, what kind of person was Mary to receive such distinction? I suggest that she liked to go and do beyond what the ordinary person would do. I might have thought of washing Jesus' feet with water and wiping them with a washcloth. Not Mary. It had to be perfume. And not an inexpensive brand, but "very expensive . . . , made of pure nard" (Mark 14:3).

Unhappily, this trait of not doing things in an ordinary way carried itself even to the negative side. Mary was not an ordinary sinner. Jesus had to cast out of her seven demons. Nothing short of divine love could point out even from this situation a rich lesson of love: "Her many sins have been forgiven—for she loved much. But he who has been forgiven little loves little" (Luke 7:47, NIV).

Then that Sunday morning following Jesus' crucifixion, the followers of Jesus went to the tomb. After they found it empty, what more could they do but leave? Not Mary. It was not enough to know that the tomb was empty. She had to know where its precious contents had gone. She was going to do something about it once she received the needed information. Then she noticed the gardener. "Sir," she speaks through tears, ". . . tell me where you have put him." But it is not the gardener. It is the very One she is seeking.

What if Mary hadn't lingered a few moments longer? What if she hadn't asked the gardener a favor? Think of the privilege she would have missed—that of being the first to see Jesus, the first to talk with Him, to be addressed by Him after His death.

Just a few extra moments to do a few extra gestures! Some of life's greatest deeds are done within those moments.

BIENVISA LADION-NEBRES

OCTOBER 27

THE PORTRAIT

Let us lay aside every weight, and the sin which doth so easily beset us. Heb. 12:1.

"You have been selected . . ." the cheery voice on the other end of my telephone line announces. Another gimmick! For an optimist, I take a surprisingly pessimistic view of this sort of phone call. ". . . to receive one beautiful natural portrait in full color . . . free!" it squeals. "Absolutely free!"

Of course. I know their game. They know I'll buy the whole package—8 x 10s, 4 x 6s, wallets, ad infinitum. So I listen to the details. "No obligation, ma'am. All you have to do is agree to a sitting within two months."

But in spite of the negative vibes, I'm convinced I can't lose. I've been wanting to have a portrait made for Christmas gifts. Why not now! It's already September, so I make the appointment for October 15. This gives me time to lose those extra five pounds I've intended to shed.

Portrait day dawns. I've had a sleepless night, a bad week, and it's raining. I look in the mirror. *Not exactly a candidate for a portrait,* I muse. My hair is unruly, and those five pounds now look more like 10. So I call the studio and ask for an extension of time. They give me two more weeks, and I go to work on my diet.

I turn the pages of my favorite Book, and my eyes fall upon a familiar "offer." It too is fascinating. It too has a deadline. It too is in full color, and free. It's already paid for at an overwhelming cost. But on this offer there is no extension of time. I have to be ready.

I look into my "Exodus 20" mirror. I have to lose weight—lots of it! All those sins that "so easily beset." And the blemishes—those little annoyances, bouts with self, impatience, wasted moments . . .

It seems like an impossible task, and discouragement creeps over me. I'm ready to give up. Then I read further. "Looking unto Jesus"! Suddenly I remember something I had read by a Christian author that said that Christ is sitting for His portrait in every follower. That's my problem—and my solution! I've been looking at the wrong image. I've been "looking unto self"! I must take my eyes off the image in the mirror, and fix them on the perfect Image I want to pattern. I don't even have to work at it! By staying close to Him, that excess "baggage" begins to melt away, and the blemishes in my character lessen. It's a moment-by-moment, day-by-day experience.

Sometimes I slip back, but with His help the progress is forward. If I stay close to Christ, then when the Father comes with His reward He will see not my imperfections, but the lovely character of the precious Saviour I reflect—in full and living color. And He will accept me.

LORRAINE HUDGINS

OCTOBER 28

GOD'S INSTRUMENTS

Love the Lord your God with all your heart and with all your soul and with all your strength. Deut. 6:5, NIV.

During the days of wavering faith that occurred in my 20s, the Holy Spirit led in my life by the simple action of taking me on a visit to a different church. It had not been my custom for a long time, but I went early to attend Sabbath school and found it a great blessing. I sat in with a class that met at the back of the church. The faith-filled teacher, Dr. W. Arouca, so impressed my heart with the presentation of the day's lesson that I went back the next week to hear him speak again on the Word of God.

Dr. Arouca gave such an attractive presentation of the love of God that again I started reading the Bible every day to find what he had pointed to. From that experience grew a new beginning, for which I still praise God. Not only was my return to church a fact, but I also married someone from that church.

God has used many ways to make Himself known to me, and that one, so many years ago, was the beginning of a joyful journey through the Word. Since then, others have contributed to make the Scriptures a river of life. That experience caused me to see many of Bible characters as examples of faithfulness, and Moses is not the least of them. Now I can understand how he arrived at the point of making the above statement to the people of Israel. He had spent much time learning, and to learn, he needed to become acquainted with God.

God used different methods for teaching Moses at different stages of his life. His early life in Egypt taught him principles of leadership and organization. His 40 years tending sheep in Midian helped him become acquainted with God. Moses' willingness to be taught led him to walk so close to God that after his death, God raised him back to life and took him to heaven.

There is no better way for me to know what God wants for me than to learn about Him from His Word. Since that long-ago Sabbath morning in a special teacher's class, all Scripture has been a means of uplifting me toward God. I thank God for that teacher, one of God's instruments. I would like to be such an instrument in the hands of the Master, today and every day. WILMA HERTLEIN

OCTOBER 29

DON'T ALWAYS SING IN THE RAIN

Singing to a person who is depressed is like taking off a person's clothes on a cold day or like rubbing salt in a wound. Prov. 25:20, TEV.

There's a disreputable old green bowl in my cupboard. It's a disgraceful thing, really—chipped and cracked as it is. But it's a one-of-a-kind item, and there is a story there. More than 60 years ago our family had a whole new set of them, and they were a rare luxury.

I was blessed with an exuberant dad who enjoyed life. When it was time for him to come home, my sister and I waited eagerly for our happy, always-singing daddy to burst through the door. Often he would jump in and dance a jig right there in the entry before saying a word. Sometimes the door would open a crack, and his hat would come sailing in. "To test," he said, "whether it was safe to follow." If his hat didn't come sailing back out, he allowed it was safe.

At the same time as this exuberant dad loomed large in my life, there was a quiet, tidy little lady who was my mother. She was his complete opposite, but I loved them both.

It was cold outside on this particular winter day. But inside a fire glowed in the Home Comfort range, and supper filled the kitchen with good smells. Mother had been working hard, as she always did. The table was set with the new green dishes. Green was Daddy's favorite color.

Suddenly Daddy burst through the door, scooped my little mother up in his arms, and chortled, "Hello, Mama!" Now, that would have been tolerable, but Daddy never did anything by halves. Bending to lift her from the knees so she would be almost sitting on his shoulder when he stood up, he caught the corner of the tablecloth in his grasp. Our squeals of delight turned to screams of horror as the tablecloth swooped across the table, scattering new green dishes in every direction. Mama, who mostly tolerated these unseemly outbursts from her totally unpredictable husband, ran out of tolerance.

My recollections of the rest of the evening are vague of necessity. It was not a time for song. Knowing when to sing and when to echo the plaintive tune of another's heart is a gift rarely cultivated. It's true, a leopard cannot change its spots, and my father never did. When he was dying, his eyes glistened with laughter as he told a joke on himself. The next day he was gone. Mother died shortly afterward, as if life without her exuberant "singer" was too much for her to tackle alone. His efforts were a priceless gift to her and his "girls."

NELMA DRAKE

OCTOBER 30

AUTUMN LEAVES

For God has said, "I will never leave you or desert you." Heb. 13:5, REB.

A tree in autumn is
   slow-motion fire
that creeps over
first the leaf
then the branch
flaming to the tip of the tree and
sending sparks spinning away
until at last
the shadow of the flame

>   lies cold on the ground.
>
>   I shuffle through the embers
>   to take home a glowing coal.
>   It will heat my memory
>   through the whitest landscapes of winter
>   like the glow of God's regard for me
>   through the worst chill of despair.
>
>   Jo Habada

OCTOBER 31

GOD'S DWELLING PLACE

If you make the Most High your dwelling—even the Lord, who is my refuge—then no harm will befall you, no disaster will come near your tent. Ps. 91:9, NIV.

Psalm 91 was read many times to me while I was growing up. I heard it during worships on Friday evening, or at the beginning of the week. We read it during tornado warnings as we waited and wondered what might happen next. I even memorized it in school, and loved it so that it became one of the psalms I claimed as I traveled in foreign lands.

On one particular journey I was headed home after a long day in meetings, two hours from the campus where I lived. As I drove along, a friend riding with me commented that there were more people walking along the side of the road than we usually saw. Because of that, I decided to try a new route around the city rather than go down to the middle of the town. But that didn't help. The crowds just seemed to get bigger. Suddenly I heard a loud cry from the people around us and the sickening sound of a huge rock hitting my car. Thoroughly frightened, I just kept going, not daring to stop to check for damage.

Over the next few days the country was shaken by rioting and burning of buildings. There were shootings of people, sometimes aimed at those who were foreign to the country. It was a difficult time for all of us on the mission compound, as we sat helplessly listening to gunfire and watching shops burning around us. Of course, we prayed throughout it all. The Lord heard our cries for peace, and the unsettling events quieted down.

About six months later my friend's husband greeted me, saying, "Surely the Lord is with you." When I inquired just what he meant, he told me that the day after I had come through the area where my car had been hit with a rock, he had traveled the same road. He had seen at least six cars overturned and burned. In addition, a shop had been burned, and a foreigner was dead.

I still read and treasure Psalm 91, and I know that God is covering His believers with His "feathers" and loving care (Ps. 91:4, NIV).

Rita Van Horn

November 1

The Bread of Life

But Martha was distracted by all the preparations that had to be made. Luke 10:40, NIV.

There are times when I slip into the Martha role. A few years ago we were excited to learn that my brother Joe and sister-in-law Patsy would be visiting us from Africa. We looked forward to their coming. It was always a spiritual feast to listen to their stories of conversions, answered prayer in work situations, and God's protection.

I started planning my menu for the meals I needed to have while they would be visiting us. It was fun to plan. I would make lemon pie (Joe's favorite), three-day buns (a family tradition), homemade bread, and gluten (a must!). There were so many things I couldn't prepare ahead of time that I still had plenty to do while Joe and Patsy were in our home.

Joe watched me work and prepare all this food while the weekend rapidly slipped away. Not only had there been very little time to visit, but little opportunity for us to get our spiritual batteries charged! Finally he said, "Hazel, we appreciate all that you want to do for us. The food has been wonderful, but I would rather eat a sandwich and have you sit down so we can talk. I came to see *you!*"

I have often thought about my brother's love for me. He came to see *me!* He will never know how many times while preparing for company I have thought about what he said and crossed some of the items off my menu because of all the preparations that had to be made.

I think this is what Jesus was saying to Martha. "There is a time and a place for the table to be covered with goodies, but Martha, I will not be with you long. Mary is sitting at My feet because she is hungry for the Bread of Life. Martha, today it would have been better to have fixed a sandwich!"

Because we want to prepare our best menu for those we love, we sometimes neglect the more nourishing food: the Bread of Life. We are too tired to pray, read, talk, or listen, and it is easy to grumble because we have so much work to do.

Mary came to Jesus because she needed help. She was encouraged by every word He spoke. She was learning to depend on Him—the kind of dependence that would help her for the rest of her life. She knew she needed the Bread of Life.

"Lord, help me remember that the more uncluttered and simple my life is, the more time I will have to sit at Your feet and eat the Bread of Life."

HAZEL BURNS

NOVEMBER 2

ON EAGLE'S WINGS

As an eagle stirreth up her nest, fluttereth over her young, spreadeth abroad her wings, taketh them, beareth them on her wings: so the Lord alone did lead [Jacob]. Deut. 32:11, 12.

Three tall trees and a birdbath in our front garden, plus the mild climate of Cape Town, ensure an abundance of bird song and movement all year round. I try a bit of amateur identification, but despite the reams of ornithological studies in existence, birds remain creatures of mystery and delight to me. God seems to take great joy in this early part of His creation, and certainly has special uses for His feathered servants.

Doves from the ark brought the first message of hope for Noah and his family, plucking an olive leaf from a newly budding tree after the devastation of the Flood. And birds will be the last creatures alive on earth, according to Revelation, supping on God's enemies after an even greater devastation. Ravens fed faithful Elijah while he was hiding in the wilderness, and quails fed the rebellious Israelite nation in another wilderness, to their doom. God uses the sparrow to illustrate our weakness and insignificance, and the eagle to show the power of His response to our need.

Biblical birds carry yet another message of great significance to each of us as God uses the image of the mother eagle to assure us that among His characteristics are the tender, nurturing graces usually attributed to women. How our mother's hearts are touched with God's grief for children loved and lost, as He wept in lament over Jerusalem. What picture could be more graphic than that of a mother hen wishing to protect her chickens from calamity with her own body?

God also gives us examples of His great love for us when He identifies with the women in labor in Isaiah 42 and 54, and breastfeeding in Isaiah 49.

What depths of empathy and care God offers all women. What a source of comfort is His compassion and love. May we bask in the warmth and strength of His loving arms today and always.

IVY M. PETERSEN

NOVEMBER 3

AN ENCOUNTER WITH DESTINY

Peter . . . kneeled down, and prayed; and . . . said, Tabitha, arise. And she opened her eyes: and when she saw Peter, she sat up. Acts 9:40.

The minutes ticked by and became hours as I watched the hands on the big clock in the operating room of a small hospital. I was undergoing surgery with a spinal anesthesia. I seemed to feel the touch of the scalpel on my flesh, but it didn't hurt.

This was my birthday. My husband had promised to come in after work and bring a treat to celebrate my successful surgery. I reached out my hand to take it. Many days later I learned what happened next.

I had hemorrhaged and gone into postoperative shock. This was before blood banks, and when someone needed blood, family, friends, neighbors, and coworkers lined up to be tested to donate blood. My blood type is rare, and prayers were said round the clock as specialists searched for the right donor. At last one donor was found. I needed another. Days went by. I remained unconscious in spite of the excellent care and 24-hour vigilance of special nurses.

There were times when I could hear people calling my name over and over. The voices seemed far, far away. I tried to respond, but could not lift myself above the thick veil of fog that seemed to encase me. Later I was told the following events.

My sister, a nurse, was sitting with me when a man in a black suit with a clerical collar entered my room. He asked to pray for me, and my sister consented gratefully. She wasn't unduly surprised at his visit, for my pastor and ministers from area churches had prayed for me. They all knew my sister from their hospital visits with other patients and loved her for her dedication to her profession and her compassionate care of her patients. She didn't recognize this man, but assumed he was from a nearby parish.

He knelt down amid the various jugs, tubes, and bottles surrounding my bed and prayed. Arising from his knees, he said, "She will waken soon and recover. The Lord has need of her." My sister thanked him, and he left. He had barely left the room when I opened my eyes and said, "I'm hungry." Nurses and hospital personnel began praising and thanking God for His tender mercy.

The questions were inevitable. "Who was the minister?"
"What parish is he from?"
"Did anyone speak to him?"
"Did anyone see him come in?"
"Did anyone see him leave?"

Many questions with no answers. No one had seen him until he stepped through the door into my room. No one saw him leave my room. Everyone agreed that he must have been my guardian angel.

I recovered quickly and was soon able to be home. I felt God's hand on me to follow wherever He leads. I have the blessed hope of Jesus' second coming. I look forward to that day when I will see Jesus face-to-face and meet my guardian angel.

I want to thank him for the many times he saved my life.

DORIS JENNER EVERETT

NOVEMBER 4

THE CUSHION

A furious squall came up, and the waves broke over the boat, so that it was nearly swamped. Jesus was in the stern, sleeping on a cushion. Mark 4:37, 38, NIV.

The pastor was vividly describing the stormy weather on the Sea of Galilee, one of my favorite stories. You could almost taste the salty air and feel the heaving of the boat. Once the waves started crashing in, I took myself out of the picture. Continuing the story, the pastor highlighted a small detail that only Mark recorded in the Gospels. Jesus was sleeping "on a cushion." Who provided Jesus with a cushion? Probably not common furnishings for a fishing boat. Ropes, oars, and nets, yes, but a cushion? Interestingly, the pastor suggested that the disciples must have brought it for Jesus.

I frowned. The disciples bringing a cushion? They didn't even remember to bring bread along on some of the trips. I mused that it was probably the women who followed Jesus that were so thoughtful to provide Him with a cushion to rest on.

Actually, as I later studied this verse in several commentaries, I learned that the cushion was probably a regular part of the boat's equipment. A carpet or coarse leather cushion was placed in the back of a boat for the one steering to sit on or for any special guests.

Nonetheless, this cushion prompted my thinking about the women who followed Jesus. Luke records that as Jesus preached from town to town the 12 disciples and many women were with Him. These women not only followed Jesus, but helped to support Him and the disciples from their own resources (see Luke 8). Matthew also mentions that there were many women at the cross. "They had followed Jesus from Galilee to care for his needs" (Matt. 27:55, NIV).

Caring, giving, serving—these were wonderful traits of Christian women of the first century. These qualities are still the goal for Christian women of today as we share our "cushion" with our family, friends, and neighbors as they go through the storms of life.

HEIDE FORD

NOVEMBER 5

PRECIOUS MOMENTS

And when he putteth forth his own sheep, he goeth before them, and the sheep follow him: for they know his voice. John 10:4.

The mighty power of prayer
Lies beyond the realm of human thought;
Yet still it reaches the holy throne of God.
It tenderly soothes and heals my wounds
And enables me to endure.
It gives me strength for today
And peace of mind concerning tomorrow.

With faith I believe that God's in control
And what will be is meant to be;
As I earnestly desire to follow Him,

Wisdom He imparts unto me.
Through the pain I silently bear
An unknown price seems paid.
And from the depths of my surrendered soul
Come spiritual pearls, perfectly formed,
Their majestic beauty inwardly and graciously adorns.
They are truly cherished and humbly worn
While I patiently await the coming of my Lord.

Spiritual pearls are formed through pain. Each of us will experience the process differently, in relation to the circumstances surrounding us.

The greatest pearl of all, for me, is very painful and hard for me to share. Two and a half years ago I buckled under. For two weeks the Lord placed me on the psychiatric floor in a hospital. The Lord promises that if we knew the end from the beginning, we'd not change a thing. I must believe this. The Lord gave me a "time-out." I was still the best witness ever on the fifth floor, and from that experience my precious husband began to think and has come back to the church. I've seen such tremendous spiritual growth in my entire family. I also realize that I am limited. I must avoid high-stress situations causing anxiety. My life must be kept simple. Therefore, in order to survive, I must leave it all at Jesus' feet. I see myself as a shattered vessel, broken and pieced together. With time and patience my Lord has miraculously bonded the fragments of my life together with His love. I see Him still at work through what I'm inspired to write. I am now fitted for one cargo, the lightest of all.

DEBORAH SANDERS

NOVEMBER 6

FRAGRANCE

But thanks be to God, who always leads us in triumphal procession in Christ and through us spreads everywhere the fragrance of the knowledge of him. 2 Cor. 2:14, NIV.

At my vantage spot at the international gate at an airport, I was able to observe arriving passengers at the custom desk.

A young passenger caught my attention. She had on her arm a large, well-packed flight bag. The customs officer inquired if she had any alcohol, and she responded that she did not. The officer, taking her word at face value, gave her clearance. The young traveler flashed a smile to the customs officer and waved to her waiting relatives. She proceeded to pick up her suitcase. As she stooped, her flight bag slipped from her shoulder and crashed to the floor. The sound of shattering glass was unmistakable, and almost instantaneously a stream of liquid flowed from the bag. Within seconds the smell of alcohol permeated the air.

She had been successful (she thought) in avoiding paying duty, but she paid in other ways. She paid the price of embarrassment, deceitfulness, and now total loss. She might have lamented, "What a waste!"

When Mary broke her expensive bottle of perfume and used it to massage Jesus' feet (Matt. 26:6-13), someone else through deceit condemned her and called it a waste. To Judas this broken bottle represented a waste of time, of effort, of money, and of attention.

But to Jesus what Judas called waste was love portrayed. The sweet fragrance of the broken bottle filled the air, symbolizing the sweetness of her surrendered life to her Master. She had to surrender her fears of being misunderstood, being criticized, being rejected, being vulnerable. And by surrendering, she put herself at risk. If her act of love to Jesus was not accepted, what would this rejection do for her self-esteem? What would it do to her already-damaged reputation?

Her zeal to ensure that her Saviour realized her love for Him was stronger than her fear. And 2,000 years later the fragrance of her perfume of love continues to permeate the Christian's meaning of total surrender, devotion, and hope.

I must request the Holy Spirit to search me and help me to know if, like Mary's perfume, my life exudes a fragrance of love. Have I been encouraging? Have I been kind and sensitive to someone's needs even at the expense of my time, my effort, and my money? Am I willing to risk my reputation in order to show love for my God through service for my fellow humans? Only God and I can measure this. I pray, "Lord, help me today to be a fragrance of Your love."

NORMA JEAN PARCHMENT

NOVEMBER 7

OUR FATHER'S THOUGHTFULNESS

Thine ears shall hear a word behind thee, saying, This is the way, walk ye in it, when ye turn to the right hand, and when ye turn to the left. Isa. 30:21.

As my oldest son was driving home from work a few months ago, a sudden whim made him turn onto a road he had not traveled in some time. He soon saw a pickup truck ahead of him go out of control, finally landing in a smashed-up heap. He stopped his car, hurried to the badly damaged vehicle, and was shocked to hear a familiar voice call, "Dad." Horrified, he saw his daughter in the wreckage.

The woman with Cindy was unconscious and at first was thought to be the more severely injured. The emergency crew worked quickly to put her into the ambulance, but they were unable to get Cindy out of the truck. There was another wait for the firefighters with the necessary equipment to cut the twisted metal and remove her from the collapsed vehicle.

Cindy remained conscious through the whole ordeal. But when the metal was cut away and the EMT crew could get to her, it was obvious that her injuries were extensive and serious. She was rushed to the nearest hospital, where personnel called for a mercy helicopter to carry her to a larger, better equipped facility.

Many hours of waiting followed as doctors called upon all their skills to patch her broken body. She had a compound fracture of her right leg, and both ankles and her pelvis were broken, but her internal injuries were the most frightening. Part of her liver, several inches of small intestine, and part of her colon had to be removed.

Miraculously, she has recovered as much as possible. I just received a cheerful letter from her in which she thanks the Lord for sparing her life.

I praise God she is still alive, and I stand in awe at the fact that the Lord was so thoughtful to send Cindy's father to stay by her through that long and fearful time of waiting for medical treatment.

LILLIAN LAWRENCE

NOVEMBER 8

THE SAVIOUR'S HAND

And immediately Jesus stretched forth his hand, and caught him, and said unto him, O thou of little faith, wherefore didst thou doubt? And when they were come into the ship, the wind ceased. Matt. 14:31, 32.

Our daughter Amy was born with many problems. Some were visible, such as a cleft lip and palate; some were not. A couple hours after her birth the doctor discovered that she had a diaphragmatic hernia. By the time she was 16 hours old she'd been transferred to another hospital and was having her first surgery.

The hospital was an hour away from us, but every day we made the long trip to see her. In time Amy recovered from her surgery, and the hospital staff asked us to come learn how to feed her so she could eventually be released to come home.

When the happy day came, it was a surprise. I had to call home to have someone bring some clothes so that I could dress Amy for her homecoming. Her doctor asked to see us before we left. He sat at his desk and told us that Amy was trisomy 13, just a couple steps down from trisomy 21, Down's syndrome. "Her prognosis is not good," he continued. "She has a 20 percent chance of living four months, and a 2 percent chance of surviving two years. The rest of the children with her condition die by age 4 or 5," he said. Only two children had been known to live longer.

For the next several months it was like living in the midst of a storm. Amy cried most of the time. Her two weeks in the hospital had taught her that touch meant pain. If we hugged or kissed her, she cried. Feeding gave her gas, so she cried! And she didn't trust us. It took months and many hours of careful, loving care to break through.

It was easy to get so wrapped up in Amy's care that I'd forget to take time out for God. So many times I found myself sinking in a sea of despair. One terrible day it all seemed to be pulling me down. I felt like the water was closing up over my head and I was going to drown. I finally sat down and told God I couldn't do it by myself anymore. Like Peter, I reached out and took the Saviour's hand. With that a peace settled over me that I will never forget.

How often we forget the Saviour's hand is there waiting for us. All we need to do is reach out to Him. He'll never force it on us. The storm around us will not always go away. But He will always be there to get us over the rough waves and into the calm. I wish I could say that I always hold His hand, but I often let go. *But thank You, God, for always being there. You remind me of Your love every time I think of Amy. She will soon be 18 years old!*   LINDA REYNOLDS

NOVEMBER 9

THE LORD WORE OLD CLOTHES

Then the righteous will answer him, "Lord, when was it that we saw you hungry and gave you food, or thirsty and gave you something to drink? And when was it that we saw you a stranger and welcomed you, or naked and gave you clothing? And when was it that we saw you sick or in prison and visited you?" And the king will answer them, "Truly I tell you, just as you did it to one of the least of these who are members of my family, you did it to me." Matt. 25:37-40, NRSV.

My 41-year-old husband, Wayne, had lost his yearlong battle with colon cancer. Now he was sleeping in painless peace, waiting for the Lord to come. I felt so alone. All I seemed to be able to say to the Lord was "Help me!" How was I to be both mother and father to my two children? How could I go on without my beloved husband? I remember desperately praying, "Lord, I need You *now*. I need Your comfort, support, and strength."

And He came. No, not in white robes. Not even in a vision. He came disguised as my neighbors, my church friends, my husband's colleagues from the Christian college at which he had been a chemistry professor for 12 years.

On the day Wayne went to the hospital for the last time, the Lord came in the form of four ladies in old clothes, who cleaned my house from top to bottom. (I hadn't done much cleaning since my husband had become ill.) They had arranged for another friend, a motherly lady who had seen a lot of sadness and knew how to listen, to take me out for a long lunch.

When we returned, these four dust-covered representatives of my Lord were gone. My house was spotless (even my 8-year-old daughter's closet!). In the main bedroom, where my husband had spent most of his last six months, the furniture was rearranged, and on the bed were brand-new sheets and a matching bedspread, all in a colorful, happy print!

The love that reached out from them to me was overwhelming. I remember lying facedown on the bed and sobbing. Later I found a note in the kitchen telling me what had been prepared for supper. All I had to do was follow the simple directions they'd left for me.

After I became a widow, the Lord came in old jeans to move my household belongings to a smaller house, closer to the school at which I taught and the children attended. He also came bearded, in sixties' caftan, and worked in the yard, doing whatever Wayne would have done had he still been alive.

Later He stopped in after work to cut boards to the right size for bookshelves. I had thought we didn't need help, but neither I nor my 13-year-old son knew how to use the circular saw, and we were both afraid to try it.

To recount all the ways the Lord came that year would take pages. All those dear people who were His arms and His hands to me—how could I ever repay them?

It took awhile before I realized that I could repay them only by being the Lord's arms and hands to someone else in need. I didn't deserve His (and their) goodness to me, but I received it in full measure, running over.

Lord, make me aware of the pain and suffering around me, and let me be Your arms and Your hands to someone in need. Amen.

SANDY ZAUGG

NOVEMBER 10

WHEN FERVENT PRAYER AVAILED MUCH

Thus saith the Lord, the God of David thy father, I have heard thy prayer, I have seen thy tears: behold, I will heal thee. 2 Kings 20:5.

King Hezekiah was sick unto death. The prophet Isaiah came and told him, "Set thine house in order; for thou shalt die." Not wanting to die, the king turned his face to the wall and prayed and "wept sore." The Lord heard, and the message of today's text came back to Hezekiah. What a wonderful answer to prayer! I know just how Hezekiah felt!

My husband, our 7-year-old son, Carlyle, and I had gone to an all-day church youth festival in the park. After lunch Carlyle was left playing with his friend while his father and I went to view the crafts. Suddenly a girl rushed up to us. "Are you Mr. Were?" gasped the out-of-breath girl. "Your son has had an accident. Come!"

We followed, totally frightened, arriving at the scene at the same time as an ambulance. Carlyle was lying unconscious, receiving first aid from an attendant. One eye was protruding, and the position of his legs told us they were broken. His breathing was labored, and numerous cuts and abrasions covered his body. He had been hit by a passing car and tossed into the air before landing on the side of the road.

Hospital doctors told us that his condition was critical. He had sustained a depressed fracture of the skull, his right side was paralyzed, and both femurs were broken.

As soon as possible he was taken to the operating room, where surgeons elevated his depressed skull; but there was little hope for his survival. In his critical condition his legs were not even touched. Placed in the intensive-care unit, he was put on life support and remained unconscious for 48 hours, hovering between life and death.

Back at the park the youth and other friends had special prayer for Carlyle. Soon we began to receive messages from all over the state and even other states assuring us that caring and concerned individuals and churches were upholding us and our son in earnest prayer.

Gradually Carlyle began to respond. After five weeks, several surgeries, and much tender, loving care, he was discharged from the hospital, encased in a plaster cast from his toes to above his waist. Four weeks later the cast came off and he was handed a pair of crutches. In due time Carlyle went back to school. Some six months after the accident, he and his father climbed the notorious Ayers Rock in Australia's red center. Doctors and hospital staff were amazed at his recovery.

Today Carlyle is a healthy, tall young man, a lover of God's great outdoors, with one semester to go to complete his Bachelor of Education degree. He is a living testimony to the power of prayer.

We feel sure that the Lord heard our cry as He did Hezekiah's so many years ago. We shall always be grateful to a wonderful church family who stood by us with their prayers in our darkest hours.

VERYL DAWN WERE

NOVEMBER 11

BETWEEN THE MOUNTAIN AND THE MULTITUDE

When he came down from the mountainside, large crowds followed him. Matt. 8:1, NIV.

I had a couple hours to kill in London's Gatwick Airport recently. In preparation for my flight home to the United States I sauntered among the shops, getting rid of my last small change—those fragments of foreign currency that never interest the money changers.

The attractive display in the Body Shop arrested my attention—a glass reflecting soft lights, pastels, and lace. One step across the threshold, and I was transported from the colorless, matter-of-fact airport world into a feminine fantasyland, a dream of luxury and relaxation. The great array of perfumes and powders, creams and lotions, exuded a delicious blend of fragrances.

Indeed, the store reached out almost irresistibly toward its customers, inviting them to linger and, hopefully, to buy. Being conditioned (as we all are) to the blandishments of the cosmetics industry, however, I was familiar with the great assortment of "pamper yourself" slogans. In fact, the invitation to "do something nice for yourself" is almost overwhelming to those of us who are work-weary and tired beyond all reason. Without doubt the potentials of the Body Shop must charm us even more than it would the "idle rich" and those who have the time and wherewithal actually to live their lives in this exclusive atmosphere of beauty.

Then, above a row of cut-glass perfume bottles, a large placard caught my eye. Actually, it grated on my soul like a harsh abrasive. *If it doesn't feel good, don't do it.* Now, this *had* to be the ultimate seduction. In the context of the Body Shop, the double entendre of "doing it" became highly suggestive. What, then, happens to our old ideals of duty and service? Suddenly I felt myself looking down into the great empty chasm of self-interest.

So I inhaled the dainty airs of the Body Shop one more time and stepped back into the realities of the airport concourse. I would keep on buying my economy "cosmetics" at the local supermarket. And every day, for the rest of my life, I would have to be doing things that didn't "feel good."

But too many Christians are workaholics, and herein lies the quandary. On the one hand, the Body Shop has many good and legitimate features, for loveliness, relaxation, and privacy are all divine gifts. At the same time, self-discipline and industry have wondrously rich rewards.

Finding the balance between the "mountain and the multitude," then, is a daily task for us as Christian women.

Dorothy Minchin-Comm

NOVEMBER 12

THE PEACE THAT PASSETH ALL UNDERSTANDING

"For I know the plans I have for you," declares the Lord, "plans to prosper you and not to harm you, plans to give you hope and a future." Jer. 29:11, NIV.

There are instances in all our lives when we begin to doubt God—not His existence (at least not for me), but His love. Let me explain.

God has always been a presence in my life: as a child I knew Him as my heavenly Father who protected me. I did not understand the relationship between the Trinity at that time. I just understood that Jesus was my heavenly Brother (the brother I never had!), the one who interceded for me when I prayed. It wasn't until much later in life that I truly began to comprehend and appreciate what Jesus Christ really meant to me.

Three years in a row adversity struck our family. But it wasn't until the third catastrophe, the death of our son from a fatal asthma attack, that I began to see the significance of Calvary. Because I failed to see the Lord working in my life, and instead began to concentrate on my losses, my faith wavered, and I wondered if this journey was worth it. I failed to remember the promise of our text, Jeremiah 29:11.

The morning of my son's death were the darkest hours of my life. The pain, I felt, was unbearable, and my whole being wanted to scream out to God, "Why, Lord, why?"

Satan and his hosts were also there, probably gloating in the knowledge that they had won this battle—I was defeated. But the Lord was there to hold and to comfort me. And through the darkness and depths of despair, instead of being overwhelmed by death, I looked up and saw Christ on the cross of Calvary—for me. My heavenly Father and Brother reached out to say, "Come unto me, all ye that labour and are heavy laden, and I will give you rest" (Matt. 11:28). Rest and peace.

Finally, I understood. He's there; God is there. He has always been there. He knows every pain and sorrow we experience. I still do not understand why my son had to die when he did, but I have been able to accept God's will.

Thank You, Lord, for helping me to understand, and for giving me "the peace . . . which passeth all understanding" (Phil. 4:7).

MARCIA A. KELLER

NOVEMBER 13

BAG LADY

I delight greatly in the Lord; my soul rejoices in my God. For he has clothed me with garments of salvation and arrayed me in a robe of righteousness. Isa. 61:10, NIV.

"Come on, get the lead out," my husband called as he pushed through the crowded street. "We need to get out of here before the evening rush hour."

Our family had packed a lot into this day of sightseeing in Philadelphia. So now with aching feet and weary bodies we hustled toward the car.

"A shortcut down this side street, and we'll be there."

That's when I collided with her, at least her shopping cart. The cart tipped, and things tumbled across the sidewalk.

"Oh, I'm so sorry. Let me help," I offered as I bent to right the cart.

She mumbled something, and I looked at her. Stringy, dirty hair fell across her gaunt face. Tattered, filthy clothes hung from her bony body. I was repulsed, but then—for a moment—her eyes met mine, and it was as if I looked into her soul. Despair, confusion, and hopelessness confronted me.

My heart was torn, and I wanted to reach out to her. But it happened so quickly. A heartbeat later she was gone, pushed along, lost in the crowd.

That night I could not stop thinking about her. Where was she? What would it be like living on those dark, lonely streets? Was she hungry? cold? sick?

I looked around me. I loved my home. Though it was not elegant, it was comfortable. I enjoyed sitting by our wood stove on cold nights and soaking up its warmth. I liked the way the lamplight shone on the woodwork. I enjoyed the ticking of the clock on the mantle and the soft voices of my boys upstairs as they talked about the day's events. All around me were mementos of the people and things that I cherished.

How would it feel to give it all up? to bid my family goodbye and go back out into the dark, cold night? to drive into the city? to search every alley, every street, until I found her? and when I found her, to put my arms around her and with love and compassion offer her the life that was mine in exchange for the fate that was hers? How would I feel as I placed upon her cold, frail body my warm, clean clothes and put on her filthy rags? I shuddered to think of the shame, humiliation, and death that would be mine.

As I thought of her, I thought of Someone Else—Someone who had left His heavenly home for us all. And though I cannot understand it, He would have come for just me. He searched until He found me. He encircled me with His love. He took my despair and gave me hope, took my fear and gave me peace. He covered my filthy, sin-stained garments with His pure, clean robe of righteousness. He suffered the shame and death that should have been mine so that I could have the life that was His, and someday I shall live in His home for eternity.

REBECCA J. GRICE

NOVEMBER 14

MITTENS, WHISKERS, RAINBOWS, AND PRAYER

Pray without ceasing. 1 Thess. 5:17.

I am a raindrops-on-roses, whiskers-on-kittens person; rainbows make me smile. So when Laneta gave me the tiny crystal butterfly with many facets to each wing, I hung it with a nylon thread in my kitchen window. Every sunny day brilliant, dark rainbows dance all over my kitchen—rainbow-colored bread dough and milk and cupboards and floors—and I smile every time, as if I'd never seen them before.

The rainbows make me smile because they make me think of special things that I can't see the same way I see the rainbows. They bring a picture of Laneta, who cared for me enough to make me the gift—and in celebration of no particular holiday, too. They cause wonder about light refraction and the light spectrum, but mostly it's just plain beauty that makes me smile. I see an infinitesimal part of God peeking through my window finding a small way around the estrangement that we have caused Him and feel His finger lifting my heart through Laneta's love and through the light's little miracle of physics.

But rainbows and romance isn't all of me. I also see things in the more down-to-earth bright copper kettles and warm woolen mittens—miracles are everywhere. I am amazed at the sucking instinct of a newborn baby; the glimpse I get of heavenly order in the simple complexity of computer technology; the flavor of bubbling, savory soup on the stove; the impossibility of a new leaf and a delicate blossom from that dry twig on my cherry tree and then that juicy red globe that not only causes anticipation but provides fuel for my body.

Like friends and lovers torn apart are my God and I. He finds little ways of making Himself known and real to me in beauty, friends, and everyday miracles. But I must remember to look for more than the surface beauty in them; *He* is in them. I must make the effort to be on the receiving end of this, His personal communication with me.

I shall refuse to depend only on the comfortable familiarity of clichés and pious phrases that we have invented and named "prayer" and that sometimes have a feeble relationship to real life. I shall also consciously find Him in the hundreds of little glimpses of Himself that He gives to me each day in raindrops, whiskers, rainbows, and mittens. And in joy I shall answer with thanks and obedience. I shall live in prayer. SUSAN SCOGGINS

NOVEMBER 15

STRANGERS

When he saw them, he hurried from the entrance of his tent to meet them and bowed low to the ground. . . . Let me get you something to eat, so you can be refreshed and then go on your way. Gen. 18:2-5, NIV.

I could see them from my kitchen window, and every bone in my conservative body shuddered. The orange hair, the myriad of tattoos showing beneath the strangest outfits I had ever seen. I just stood at the sink staring in disbelief as they strolled down our circular driveway right up to my front door. My not-as-conservative husband stood beside me staring.

The evening before, my stepson had called to say that he and a few of his friends were going to the hot springs about 30 minutes north of our house. Would it be all right if they stopped to see us? And so they had arrived.

As I stood staring at the strangers, the story of Abraham entertaining angels popped into my mind. Though I knew beyond the shadow of a doubt that these were not angels, I felt compelled to be hospitable. By the standards of these young college students I appeared wealthy; certainly I could afford the courtesy of providing them with a meal.

"Ask them to stay for breakfast," I urged my husband.

"What!" he replied in disbelief.

"I can't help realizing how much we have when I look at them. A good breakfast will save them money, and we have plenty of food," I replied.

Soon a mountain of pancakes, fruit salad, scrambled eggs, vegetarian breakfast sausage (all but one of the five were vegetarians), juice, and milk graced our table. They all bowed respectfully as our 3-year-old asked God to bless the food.

I admit I was surprised. The way they *looked* had deceived me. Each of them was respectful, polite, and thankful for the hospitality that was offered. They stayed through the morning, playing with our daughter, making conversation, and doing the dishes.

As they piled into the car to head for the hot springs, I realized that by serving these strangers I had received the biggest blessing of all! It did not matter whether they were angels or not—they were children of the King, and they deserved whatever I could do for them. I silently thanked my loving God for gently teaching me the value of giving even when I did not have to give. He had once again used circumstances to shape me and had given me a blessing in exchange.

"Do not forget to entertain strangers, for by so doing some people have entertained angels without knowing it" (Heb. 13:2, NIV).

CAREL SANDERS CLAY

NOVEMBER 16

THE BASIS OF FRIENDSHIP

I give you a new commandment, that you love one another. Just as I have loved you, you also should love one another. By this everyone will know that you are my disciples, if you have love one for another. John 13:34, 35, NRSV.

I like to think about the life of Ruth in the Bible. Ruth was a woman capable of rare friendships, and this gift changed Naomi's sourness into sweetness. Naomi was angry and bitter. After her long journey to Bethlehem, she said to old friends who met her there, "The Lord has made my life very bitter. I went away full, but the Lord has brought me back empty." One of Ruth's most outstanding characteristics was her abiding love that embraced the person you would least expect: her mother-in-law, Naomi.

One day while I was at a church conference I rushed out of the building with my young son. We had a plane to catch, and I did not want to miss it! Just then my little preschooler ran over to the beautifully manicured flowers near the building to chase a grasshopper. Hurriedly I began chasing my 3-year-old, while he was chasing his grasshopper!

After he successfully caught the green grasshopper, I said to him, "Please put it down. You will not be able to take it on the plane!"

"No, Mommy!" he replied. "I want to take it home and put it in my bug box!" (At home James-Pierre had a bug box with a frog in it.) "I want to put it in the bug box so the frog can have a friend!"

Friendships are important to 3-year-olds, and even more important to adults! But often as adults we become afraid, distrustful, hurt, unable to build meaningful friendships. We end up lonely. I recently heard that loneliness is the most serious problem facing our world today.

The powerful witness of Ruth's story is that the basis of her friendships was love. She was loved by all because she was so lovable. Love worked the miracle in Ruth's life. Love overcomes all.

The story of Ruth teaches us that attractive graciousness is worth cultivating, that strains and differences in relationships (marital, racial, parental) can be solved through a right relationship with Him who made of one blood all people. If we choose to develop unity and love in relationships, angels will cheer, just as the crowds cheered when Boaz married Ruth. As Boaz took his bride home, so God will take His bride, the church, home to live with Him forever!

The challenge to us, then, is: build, don't tear down; praise, don't criticize; include, don't exclude; create unity, not division; celebrate diversity! Build a solid unity of Christian women in which there is mutual love and devotion to God and to one another. Then we can say with Ruth, "Thy people shall be my people, and thy God my God" (Ruth 1:16).

RAMONA PEREZ-GREEK

November 17

Treasures of the Snow

Hast thou entered into the treasures of the snow? Job 38:22.

It is true that *treasures* in this verse might better be translated as "storehouses." And it is true that God meant for His string of questions in chapters 38-41 to broaden Job's perception of his Creator. But having grown up where winter equals snow, I can't help recalling real treasures of the snow I have experienced.

First of all, I anticipated its arrival. As a child, from the second the weather forecaster predicted even the possibility of a slight flurry, I would stand ready—snow gear stationed handily at the door, myself often at attention in front of a window to witness the first flakes. Only the approach of Christmas could rival my expectations concerning the advancing army of white-clad soldiers that would liberate me from the winter doldrums.

Then there were the treasured patterns of snow angels. My friends and I created these by lying on our backs in new-fallen snow, then swishing our arms and legs back and forth. We would then arise carefully to gaze upon impressions that looked like flying angels.

Third, there were the snowflakes themselves. The most treasured thing my third-grade teacher taught me was to wear dark-colored mittens when it snowed. Why? Because when the white snowflakes landed on your darkly mittened hands, you could see clearly the unique design of each individual flake.

And last, the very whiteness of the snow was itself a treasure. Glittering in the noon sun, cradling the long shadows of shivering trees, or glowing faintly pink against the gray horizon of winter twilight, the brush of snow could paint a landscape as breathtaking as any work of the great masters.

Now that I live where it doesn't snow a great deal, I must rely upon my memories of these snow treasures. Like the questions God asked Job, my reflections concerning these treasures often point me to the Creator. First of all, for every moment I recall anticipating snow, I wonder if I now spend an equal or greater amount of time longing for the Second Coming. Am I as prepared for that event as I was for a white countryside? How much do I desire that first glimpse of an advancing heavenly host coming to set me free from the doldrums of sin?

Then for every angel I remember swishing into the snow as a

child, I think of the thousand times ten thousand angels and thousands and thousands of angels who constantly travel between earth and heaven. Some of them have protected me from danger or evil. And one of them is even my very own. I believe this guardian has led me since birth, has observed my first steps, and, if I should die before Christ returns, will be the first to greet me at the resurrection. Together in heaven we will review the history of this being's intervention on my behalf, and my perplexities will vanish like snow in early-spring warmth.

Third, each individual snowflake I recall examining on my navy-blue mittens reminds me that God has created us all with a unique blend of talents and abilities. And just as each snowflake is needed to blanket the ground, so are we all needed to cover the earth with the good news of salvation.

And last, there is the snow's whiteness, defining the dull winter landscape with strokes of brilliance. Such alabaster memories remind me that "though your sins be as scarlet, they shall be as white as snow" (Isa. 1:18). And this is truly the greatest treasure of all—that the landscapes of our sinful lives could ever be as brilliant as a field of snow sparkling in the sun. LYNDELLE CHIOMENTI

NOVEMBER 18

LAST WORDS

Bless the Lord, O my soul: and all that is within me, bless his holy name. Ps. 103:1.

I am happy for my family
I am happy for my faith.
   But also I am happy because I am a woman.

Today I want to put my life at the foot of the cross.
Today I want to receive the transforming presence of Christ
   in my life.
Today I want to make a commitment to Jesus.
Today I want to consecrate myself to a life of action by the
   Holy Spirit.

This commitment and action means I want to be a ray of sunshine in my home, reflecting the light of Jesus to my beloved family. It means

I want to be the salt of the earth, carrying the taste, the delight of the transforming love of Christ to this drab, evil, and sinful world.

>   Today I want to be a blessing.
>   Today I want to waste myself in this ministry.
>   But I do not want to be alone.
>
>   Today I want you to be with me, my dear devotional companion.
>   Today I want you to be with me, my dear churdh friend.
>
>   Come, now, forward so that we can be together.
>   We want to consecrate ourselves to God, together.
>
>   Ask Him to be with us so that we can go forward together.
>   We can take up this commitment for effective action, together,
>   Our God, you, me. —MAILENE FERREIRA MOROZ

NOVEMBER 19

ABIGAIL AND HER LORD

She was a woman of good understanding, and of a beautiful countenance: but the man was churlish and evil in his doings. 1 Sam. 25:3.

Abigail's arranged marriage to Nabal must have been one filled with unhappiness and loneliness. Her story, recorded in 1 Samuel 25:3-42, teaches many lessons about unselfishness, courage, strength, humility, hope, faith, and how to love. As told in the biblical narrative, Abigail had the chance to escape her unhappy life, but instead she chose to save hundreds of lives, including that of her selfish husband. The day she met David on the trail she saved him from the guilt of having destroyed hundreds of innocent men, women, and children in response to her husband's evil actions.

In Abigail's speech to David, she reminded him of God's way of love, of peace instead of violence, of turning the other cheek when wronged, and how to forgive the person that hurt him. By choosing to follow those actions, David found peace of spirit and oneness with God instead of a tormented spirit.

As for Abigail, long before when she'd found herself in a difficult, unhappy marriage, she had two choices. She could let her arranged marriage with an evil man destroy her by becoming bitter and disillusioned, or she could draw nearer to the Lord and become the child of the King He wanted her to be. She chose to turn to the Lord. He strengthened her, sheltered her, and loved her with ceaseless love. God's love told her, in effect, "You can come to Me just as you are, and I will always be here for you. I'll never forsake you or leave you. Come to Me and let Me heal your broken spirit. Let Me love you, and with My love a great hope and joy that won't die will dwell in you."

The harder her life, the sweeter Abigail's disposition. It expressed the peace of righteousness and blessings only the Lord can give. She brought joy to the household servants, the neighbors, and everyone else who came in contact with her.

God can do this for you, too. God is telling you to come, to come home. "Let Me shelter you during your storms; let Me wipe away all tears. Let Me love you and strengthen you and fill your life with joy. I am the way, the truth, the life."

When you become disillusioned with your life, remember Abigail and ask God to fill your life with peace and joy.

KAREN ANN KNIGHT

NOVEMBER 20

MY NEIGHBOR

Listen! I am standing at the door, knocking; if you hear my voice and open the door, I will come in to you and eat with you, and you with me. Rev. 3:20, NRSV.

Now that I was a single parent, returning to college seemed a necessity to me. My young daughter was excited about getting to play with others at the campus nursery at the university. An eager 3-year-old, Jocelyn somehow seemed very mature for her age. After watching me spend endless nights of studying and endless days of lugging books around, we came to the week of finals.

Now it was time to explain to Jocelyn that I really needed her to help. I explained that I had to spend extra time with my books that week, but when it was over we would do something really special together. She agreed to help by asking Jesus to help her mommy in school, and by going to bed a little earlier.

Throughout the semester I had prayed and asked God for strength, wisdom in time management, help to be a Christian example and parent, and to help me recall what I had studied and learned.

Here it was, the last and most difficult final exam of the week. I said a quick prayer before I began. My heart raced and my hand felt uneasy as I began to answer the questions. As I finished, I thought, *The rest is up to You, Lord.* As the instructor graded my exam, I was hesitant yet anxious to find out my final grade. The floor dropped from under me as I saw B+ at the top of my exam. My instructor saw the look of relief on my face, for he knew I had struggled with the class all semester.

While driving home, I began to think of how wonderful my Lord and Saviour is. As we turned onto our street, I became overwhelmed with emotion and began to cry. Lifting my hand in praise, I said, "Thank You, Jesus." Jocelyn, too young to quite understand, responded, "Mommy, why are you waving?" I explained to her that I was thanking Jesus for helping me pass my classes. A wide-eyed, puzzled look came on her face as she asked, "Did we just pass Jesus' house? I didn't know He lived on our street."

As I smiled I thought, *Jesus wants to be in all the avenues of our lives.* He lives on your street, in your house, and in your heart. He wants to be your neighbor.

"Behold, I stand at the door and knock: if any man [or woman] hear my voice, and open the door, I will come in to him and will sup [or study] with him and he with me." DAVENA WELLINGTON

NOVEMBER 21

TENDER HEART—HELPING HANDS

Do good, . . . be rich in good works, ready to distribute, willing to communicate. 1 Tim. 6:18.

It was the smallest of the four young trees that I'd planted one spring day three years ago. It struggled to survive, so I spent more time on it than on the others. I watered and fertilized it faithfully, placed a protecting wire fence around it, and nurtured it carefully. When it finally began to show signs of growth that first year, I rejoiced.

Last year the little tree really grew rapidly and soon was taller than its companions. Stretching its leafy branches outward and upward in perfect symmetry, it was a pleasure to see.

This year it again spurted upward and outward in new growth, and I had to buy longer supporting stakes for its branches. It was giving a promise of a long, healthy lifetime of much-needed shade for our yard, which we looked forward to with delight. Even a neighbor friend looked at it also and remarked to me how nicely it was doing.

Then late one evening a sudden, severe thunderstorm visited our town. High winds, thunder and lightning, and small hail pelted our area for a long period of time. During the evening, television newscasts reported that a lot of damage had been done in our region, and I worried about what I would find in our yard in the morning.

As I looked out our kitchen window the next morning, I was dismayed. A large eight-foot top section of the cherished tree had been broken off and was lying on the ground beside it. I stood by the window and cried.

Upon examining the downed treetop, I found it had a hidden defect. It had grown so rapidly that it didn't have enough inner strength to withstand the 60-mph winds, and so had snapped off as it was bent low upon itself.

Now the tree is a shell of its former beauty, but the trunk and its branches seem to be doing well. I will continue to give it loving care; there are still signs of new growth, and for this I am thankful.

I am also thankful for the lesson that God is teaching me with this tree. I have always been willing and able to sorrow quickly over damage to a prized object, and then try to restore it to its original condition. But I wonder if I am as quick to show the same degree of sympathy and aid for people?

When a family member, friend, or neighbor's life is being damaged by circumstances, am I available for help? Can I be counted upon for spiritual and physical support in *all* types of situations? Do I offer assistance to those who sorrow and have shattered lives and need to recover to "normalcy" again? Do I see needs and show love?

O Lord, give me a tender heart and helping hands that You can use for others!

Rosemary Baker

November 22

Handling Anger

A fool gives full vent to [her] anger, but a wise [woman] keeps [herself] under control. Prov. 29:11, NIV.

Ruth Graham was once asked if she had ever thought of divorcing evangelist-husband Billy Graham. "Divorce? No!" she quipped. "Murder? Yes!"

How about you? Are you angry at someone or something? Before you answer, hear me out. If you say you are not angry and never have been, you are simply not being honest. Ruth Graham gets angry with Billy, admits it, and deals with it. This is healthy.

Anger is energy. When you become angry you can swear, spit, cry, throw things, slap someone, kick the dog, or seek any number of other inappropriate and unsuccessful methods of acting out your anger. But instead of turning your anger into an attack, turn the energy into something that will benefit you.

Find a safe, physical method that will allow you to vent your newly discovered energy to accomplish something positive. You can swim, jog, bicycle, do aerobics, mow the lawn, make or knead bread, pull up stubborn weeds, rake leaves, wash windows or woodwork, scrub floors, or any of a hundred other things that will relieve the physical stress of anger in minutes. You can write out your feelings and then tear up the paper, or simply take a walk.

On his fiftieth wedding anniversary an elderly man was asked the secret of his lengthy marriage. "We agreed early on," the old man drawled, "that if we disagreed, she'd tell me off and I'd take a walk. The secret of our marriage lies with the fact that I've largely led an outdoor life."

No one but you is responsible for your anger. The other person's behavior may have precipitated your feelings, but you are responsible for your response. Don't allow the other person to dictate how you respond. You are not at the mercy of anyone. You can and must accept ownership of and responsibility for all angry responses, regardless of what precipitated them.

Now you are prepared to share your anger in an acceptable manner. Avoid a you-message such as "You make me so angry when you . . ." Instead, state your anger in an I-message form: "I really get angry when you give the children permission to do something without checking with me first, because it undermines my authority."

When you learn how to reduce angry feelings, assume responsibility for your own anger, and share your anger in an acceptable manner, you regain the freedom to be in control of your life. And having dealt with the physical aspects of anger, you can now deal with the intellectual and analytical components of any anger-producing situation. Resolve today to turn any anger-producing events in the present or past over to our Saviour, who knows all, sees all, and is able to resolve all anger problems.   NANCY VAN PELT

NOVEMBER 23

UKULELE WITNESSING

But you shall receive power when the Holy Spirit has come upon you; and you shall be my witnesses in Jerusalem and in all Judea and Samaria and to the end of the earth. Acts 1:8, RSV.

God has had faithful witnesses to Him down through the ages. The lives and testimony of many are recorded in the Bible. God allowed Daniel and his friends to become slaves so they would have the privilege of interacting with the great men of Babylon. Through their witness, God's character was made known to that idolatrous nation. Tentmakers Priscilla and Aquila traveled with Paul, helping in the early establishment of the Christian church. When they witnessed to Apollos, who was an "eloquent" preacher, "mighty in the scriptures," he obtained a clearer understanding of the Scriptures and became one of the ablest advocates of the Christian faith.

Just prior to the time our eldest daughter, Patricia, was to be taken into surgery at Loma Linda University Hospital, a young nurse came into the room carrying a small ukulele. She came in rather timidly and, seeing several of us around Patricia's bed, turned around to walk out. "I'll come back later," she said quietly.

Sensing what she planned to do, my husband called her back and asked, "What were you going to do?"

"Well, I usually try to sing a little song of comfort and courage for the patients just before they have surgery," she told us.

We urged her to go ahead, and so, accompanying herself on that little ukulele, she beautifully sang the song "I've Found a Friend in Jesus." We'd felt great concern as Patricia faced surgery, for she had problems with her blood clotting properly. Tears came to our eyes as we listened to the words of that simple song sung in such a sweet, unpretentious manner. We deeply sensed the presence of the Holy Spirit, who gave us a feeling of assurance that all would be well.

Everywhere in the world people are longing for peace and happiness. How true are the words of the song "What the World Needs Is Jesus." Perhaps God is calling you to witness for Him right where you are. It may be to your neighbor, your own children, those across the sea, or those in your own church. Even a telephone call or writing a letter of encouragement to some lonely person is a beautiful way to witness for Jesus. Wherever it is, accept the challenge, through faith, with the full assurance of God's presence and help. MARIE SPANGLER

November 24

Praise, and Answers to Prayer

Pray without ceasing. 1 Thess. 5:17.

In an effort to become more caring and active on a personal level, those of us in my Bible class are given an opportunity to share what the Lord has done for us in the past week.

When this exercise first began, many people wanted to share what had happened to them as the result of prayer. But as the weeks passed, it seemed that the number of prayers decreased, until now only occasional answers are shared. I have thought about this and wondered why. I am absolutely certain that the God who did all those wonderful things for class members when the sharing started has neither stopped working in their lives nor gone on vacation, so there must be a different reason.

I have always had a secret fantasy, now not so secret, that someday I would present a "pearl of great price" to the Lord, just as a love offering. I would say something like "Thank You for loving me and putting up with my behavior, and for forgiving me, so here is a check for $1 million. Please use this in whatever way You see fit." Or maybe, "Lord, I know that I have been the kind of child that only a heavenly Father could love, and while I was tramping around the diamond mines in Africa I found this exceptionally large, perfect diamond. Here, it's Yours. I hope that You can use it."

But reality beckons, and my thoughts turn to the widow who gave her mites; Jesus commended her because she gave all that she had.

I think that we get into the same mode of thinking when talking about what God does in our lives. When we think of telling others about answered prayers, we reason that it must be some earth-shattering thing that the Lord has miraculously done. We forget that it is the "mites" that make up everyday living. In Philippians 4:6 Paul tells us to "be anxious for nothing, but in everything by prayer and supplication with thanksgiving let your requests be made known to God" (NASB).

One day I had to take my large, heavy typewriter in for some repairs. It is difficult to carry, so before I left home I talked to the Lord about the fact that I needed a parking place close to the store. The store is on the main street, and parking places are difficult to find.

Sure enough, when I came around the corner, there was a parking place waiting for me. I am sure that the Lord answered my prayer and saved that place for me. However, God's finding a parking place for me does not sound like a very dramatic testimony, and so it is easier not to share such a story. After all, our Lord is capable of doing great miracles, and parking places just don't qualify as major events. We hold back from sharing what is really going on in our lives in favor of waiting to tell about some big event that may be just around the corner.

If each of us were to tally up the "little" answered prayers we have each week, I'm sure that the length of the list would surprise us all. So try it. You'll like what you find. "Rejoice always; . . . in everything give thanks; for this is God's will for you in Christ Jesus" (1 Thess. 5:16-18, NASB).

SHEILA SANDERS

NOVEMBER 25

MAKE HIS PRAISE GLORIOUS

Sing forth the honour of his name: make his praise glorious. Ps. 66:2.

I will sing of thy power. Ps. 59:16.

God's blessings—I was struck one day by how much I take them for granted. I was in church, and as we stood to sing a familiar hymn, "All Hail the Power of Jesus' Name," I started singing the words with rote enthusiasm. As I glanced around the congregation my eye caught sight of movement. Near the front of the church a woman was lifting her hands, gracefully transcribing the words of the hymn into sign language in beautiful time with the music. She was hearing-impaired and mute.

As I watched this moving praise response, the tears in my throat forced my voice into silence. My voice means so much to me. I love to sing and to listen to music. I can't imagine being without the sense of hearing or the ability to express myself through song. Yet how many times do I remember to thank God for these blessings? Do I use my voice to sing forth the power of His name?

I have so much for which to praise God, yet I often neglect to do so. Singing is one way I can praise God, but I can sing forth the honor and power of His name in other ways as well:
- By sharing with others God's miraculous intervention in my life.

- By remembering the times God directly answers my prayers.
- By recognizing God's hand in my life.

Thank You, Lord, for this lovely woman who uses her talents to sing forth the honor and power of Your name. Thank You that she touched my life with her song of praise. Please bring me into a closer, more appreciative relationship with You and help me to make Your praise glorious.

JOYCE NEERGAARD

NOVEMBER 26

SAVING "JUNK"

And God will wipe away every tear from their eyes; there shall be no more death, nor sorrow, nor crying; and there shall be no more pain, for the former things have passed away. Rev. 21:4, NKJV.

My parents were savers. As an adult, when I'd go home to visit them I felt depressed by the accumulation and tried to get them to throw the "junk" out. They had decades of magazines and letters piled up in their house, and when they moved from place to place, the stacks went with them. Then in the early eighties Mom, blinded by cataracts and glaucoma, agreed to move from Wisconsin to Tennessee to be near her oldest daughter, Judy. In preparation for the move, my sister Beth and I went through her belongings. What a job!

Daddy had been laid to rest a few years prior to this, and we didn't feel comfortable having Mom living alone. She was fiercely independent, and the only condition under which she would make the move to the South would be if she could still live in a home of her own. We agreed to this, and thus Beth and I started the monumental task of sorting through her things. As we decided what to save and what to throw out, we filled garbage bag upon garbage bag. For once we were happy Mom couldn't see well and so didn't know what we were tossing out. But what a treasure our parents' "junk" was to the six of us children. Many of us were in the habit of writing weekly letters, and as we sorted, we made six piles of these treasures.

In my spare time, while getting some rest and relaxation in southern Texas, I put these old letters I had written in chronological order. As I read them, I kept a notebook by my side and recorded the events that were important to my husband, Dennis, and me and our four children. What a wealth of memories I found in those old letters. I have recorded this history in our computer and given a copy to each of our offspring, a very special reminiscence of their early years.

The letters refreshed my memory of things I'd thought I could never forget. I'd written my parents when our daughter Gwen, at ages 6 and 7, had recurring bouts with pneumonia. I couldn't keep the tears back as I remembered her in the hospital. The letters brought it all back.

Gwen had asked, "Do you think I'll die, Mommy? I don't want to die yet. I'm too young." As I embraced her weakened body, I assured her she wasn't going to die. Even 2-year-old Linden uttered a childlike prayer, "Help Gwennie get better." I'll never forget her worried little voice. What a treasure those letters are to me. They hold a wealth of information about our family.

Lord, thank You for Christian parents who saw the value in family letters and other things, and forgive me for my comments to them about "all this unnecessary junk."

Someday there will be no more death, neither sorrow nor crying. I'm looking forward to the time when I can personally express my appreciation to Mom and Daddy for the treasure they preserved for us in the form of junk.   MARGE LYBERG MCNEILUS

NOVEMBER 27

GIVING THANKS IN ALL THINGS

Rejoice in the Lord always. I will say it again: Rejoice! Phil. 4:4, NIV.

Have you ever been in prison? Imagine yourself locked into a small concrete cell with nothing but damp walls and a few rats. You decide to write a letter to your friends back at your home church. What would you say? Would you write of the joys of prison life? Or would your response be "Help—get me out of here, quick"?

Most of us haven't been physically incarcerated, but at times we all feel imprisoned by life's circumstances. Financial dilemmas, family problems, uncomfortable relationships at school or work, loneliness, or poor health can cause you to feel like a prisoner of life.

Is your consistent response to the less than ideal circumstances in your life joy? If you're human, probably not. Do you sometimes feel chained by unmanageable problems, frustrated because you're not in control as you'd like to be? Are mountainous difficulties blocking joyful sunshine from your life?

Paul found a way to live as a free man, even a joyful man, while physically imprisoned and in the worst of circumstances. In his letter to his friends at the church at Philippi, written while Paul was in prison in Rome, he outlines the formula he used to maintain a sense of joy while a prisoner of life (Phil. 4:4-7).

The apostle Paul's joy formula begins with a command: "Rejoice in the Lord always. I will say it again: Rejoice!" This might seem like an impossible command, but Paul goes on to explain how it can be done:

Relate to all people (even surly jailers) with a noncondemning gentleness. Paul says to do this because "the Lord is near" (verse 5, NIV), i.e., "Jesus is coming soon."

Don't worry, and last but not least, with confidence and thanksgiving, continually bring your cares before God.

Paul promises that if you will follow these steps, God's peace, transcending all your previous combined experiences of peace, will stand guard to protect you from all discouragement. This peace will so comfort and soothe you that you will continually find ample reason to rejoice!

As the year-end holidays usher in the year's grand finale, I encourage you to focus on the theme of joy in Philippians. Think "thankfulness" every day. Love gently and generously. Don't worry—that is so very important—but allow God's peace to surround, soothe, and support you. And finally, remember, no matter how difficult your circumstances, find some reason to rejoice. I'll say it again: Rejoice!

SALI JO HAND

NOVEMBER 28

DOVE'S WINGS, EAGLE'S WINGS, GOD'S WINGS

I said, "Oh, that I had the wings of a dove! I would fly away and be at rest—I would flee far away and stay in the desert." Ps. 55:6, 7, NIV.

King David wrote this section of the Psalms during a time of deep discouragement. He expressed the feeling common to all of us at certain times of life—the desire to get away. Like David, we may have feelings of sadness and fragility. We may need time for solitude, to rest our spirit, and even to escape reality.

Perhaps you may be feeling as David did, an intense need to escape to a faraway place. The fact is that life often wounds us, and we are left without motivation or enthusiasm. What can we do? Our womanly responsibilities—taking care of necessities—compel us to continue. But there is no joy in our work. Like David, we yearn to have the "wings of a dove" to "fly," to escape and remain in the desert.

The psalmist used as a symbol of his "escape" a dove, a bird that does not want to be left alone in the desert. Neither do we want to be isolated. We want only to rest, or have strength to continue, courage to live one more day.

Because God knows us so well—our emotions and needs—He made a unique promise. To encourage and strengthen He used a similar argument, that when we want to flee with "dove's wings" He will give us eagle's wings! "But those who hope in the Lord will renew their strength. They will soar on wings like eagles; they will run and not grow weary, they will walk and not be faint" (Isa. 40:31, NIV).

The Lord wants to give us wings like those of an eagle, the queen of birds. Not to escape from life—or to see it from the ground as we hop around looking for a crumb—but so that we can soar in a surprising flight to see life from above, with a panoramic view, as with the eyes of an eagle.

May we not become discouraged by a blundering day, or when annoyances remove the glow of life, or even when sorrows drain away our energy.

The one who waits on the Lord will have renewed strength.

However, if even with this promise you still feel incapable of believing that strength will be given to proceed, and you still want to "escape" and be alone, God offers you His own wings to sustain and comfort you. "He will cover you with his feathers, and under his wings you will find refuge" (Ps. 91:4, NIV).

God's love and care are infinite. Believe it!

As you contemplate heaven and you see a bird flying, with wings outstretched, soaring, remember that "as birds hovering overhead . . . so the Lord is hovering over you to shield you . . . He will protect you and save you, He will preserve you and will free you" (Isa. 31:5, paraphrased).

Courage, dear one! MARIA CRISTINE VICENTE

November 29

A New Song

Praise the Lord. Sing to the Lord a new song, his praise in the assembly of the saints. Ps. 149:1, NIV.

There it was again—that same old voice inside my head, singing that same old song. The tune first popped into my mind that morning while I emptied the dishwasher. As I lifted a glass from the rack, I discovered it had broken during the cleaning process. Disgusted, I tossed the goblet into the trash.

The shard from the glass had dropped to the bottom of the dishwasher, beneath the jet sprayer. Grumbling, I pulled the tray of clean, dry dishes from the machine and set them on the floor, then felt around in the cold, clammy residue of water still in the dishwasher.

"Stupid! How could you be so careless? This happens every time you forget to allow for one peg between each glass." My fingers brushed against the shard. It slipped away. "You know better! When will you learn? What a waste! Wait until Richard hears that you want to buy a new set of water glasses." I located the glass chip and held it up to be examined. "You think you have money to just throw around? I can't believe you could be so careless. At your age!"

And the song went on and on and on all morning while I vacuumed, dusted, fed the dog, and even wrote a chapter in my latest book. By midafternoon I'd exhausted the verses I'd learned from my mother and grandmother, and had composed a number of new ones of my own. My eloquence waxed great when Richard arrived home from work.

I met him at the door with the bad news, deprecating myself to the proper depths of my stupidity and slovenliness. "We'll have to buy some new goblets before next week. Remember, we invited the pastor and his wife for lunch. I am just so sorry that I was so . . ." The old familiar ditty started playing its worn-out tune once again. And the lyrics rolled from my tongue.

Richard frowned as he listened. Suddenly, without warning, he kissed me on the lips and said, "Shhh, I don't like it when you talk about my wife that way. You can talk to yourself about you all you want, but I won't let you talk that way about the woman I love."

Tears sprang into my eyes. Over the years he'd listened to my old song of failure and frustration, without complaint. Tenderly he took my hand in his. "You never criticize me that harshly when I make mistakes. You'd be the first to spring to my defense if anyone else did. And I love you too much to listen when you injure yourself."

He took me into his arms and held me until the old melody faded away. We didn't talk about the incident again. That night, as I read Jesus' warnings about injuring His little ones, I discovered a new depth of meaning to my Saviour's words. When I speak evil against any of His children, including myself, I injure Him. Emotionally abusing myself hurts Him just as much as if I were emotionally abusing my children. Overcome with emotion, I fell to my knees and asked forgiveness for the horrid way I treated myself, hence treated Him.

"Please, Lord, retrain my tongue. Erase that old dirge of death from my mind and give me a new song to sing; one that praises and glorifies You."

Sometimes, I confess, I forget and catch myself humming melodies of destruction instead of praise, but I'm learning. Through His Word and the power of the Holy Spirit, the new songs He's given me to sing are ever-present in my mind, just waiting to be sung.

KAY D. RIZZO

NOVEMBER 30

LOVE RETURNED

If anyone acknowledges that Jesus is the Son of God, God lives in [her] and [she] in God. And so we know and rely on the love God has for us. 1 John 4:15, 16, NIV.

It had been a day to remember. When less than 24 hours old, our newest grandson, Eric, had come home. For the first few hours we all took turns examining his tiny toes, button nose, and funny-looking tummy button. His 4-year-old brother, Ryan, and 2-year-old sister, Heather, were his most devoted fans.

Finally at bedtime my daughter offered her two older children a reward for getting ready for bed without delays. The reward—one last chance to hold their new brother! It was a prize they couldn't resist. Soon they both reappeared bathed and pajama-clad. With obvious delight they took turns cradling the newest member of the family.

When it was Ryan's turn, his mother suggested that because he was the "big brother" he could hold the baby on his shoulder—the way she liked to hold him. So with one hand supporting tiny Eric's head and the other around his waist, Ryan rocked the baby.

All of a sudden the baby began to awaken. Arching his neck and drawing up his tiny legs, he began to squirm in Ryan's arms. When Ryan felt his brother moving against his own small chest he called out excitedly, "Look, Mom, he's loving me back!"

Many times since, I've thought about this simple exchange between two brothers and Ryan's delight over Eric's unconscious movements—accepted as his own love returned. How wonderful to be "loved back" by a loved one or a friend. How we search for this response in even the simplest acts.

In a beautiful book entitled *The Desire of Ages* I found a moving description of how our Saviour longs to be "loved back."

"Our Redeemer thirsts for recognition. He hungers for the sympathy and love of those whom He has purchased with His own blood. He longs with inexpressible desire that they should come to Him and have life. As the mother watches for the smile of recognition from her little child, which tells of the dawning of intelligence, so does Christ watch for the expression of grateful love, which shows that spiritual life is begun in the soul" (p. 191).

What an incredible truth—the Saviour of the world longs for His children to "love Him back," in simple ways—every day.

Rose Otis

December 1

GLORIOUS MORNING

For the Lord Himself will descend from heaven with a shout, with the voice of an archangel, and with the trumpet of God. And the dead in Christ will rise first. Then we who are alive and remain shall be caught up together with them in the clouds to meet the Lord. . . . Therefore comfort one another with these words. 1 Thess. 4:16-18, NKJV.

The other day our family went to the funeral of a friend from our church who had died unexpectedly. We took our sons, ages 5 and 8, with us. While many times families might leave their children at home, we had no one with whom to leave them, and felt that allowing them to go see what happens at a funeral would help them to understand death more.

They had a lot of questions. Before we went, we talked about their questions, including how to behave at a funeral and what would happen there. We told them that the person who died did not know anything anymore, but that the family left behind would be very sad.

As we got ready to go, both boys ran to the edge of the woods near our home and came back to the car with fistfuls of tiger lilies. At the funeral home our friend's wife and daughter were greeting people as they entered (their faith and strength in the Lord is incredible). My sons ran up to these ladies and hugged them both, then gave them each a bunch of tiger lilies.

So often I am not sure what to do for or what to say to someone who is grieving. My sons knew. You show them that you love them and care for them. You do not have to say a word. Just trust the love in your heart.

After my husband and I hugged each woman, expressing our sadness and love, I took the boys to the casket. In their innocent curiosity they looked and looked. (How often I barely look and then move on.) Our younger son, Zachary, looked at me seriously and said, "Mama, he's just sleeping till God tells him it's morning."

To him it was so simple. One day God would call Mr. Richard and tell him it was morning, time to get up. And oh, what a morning that will be! The dead shall be awakened by the sound of the trumpet, and they shall open their eyes to see Jesus smiling at them, calling them to come home.

Loved ones reunited. Families parted by death, together again. Children returned to their mother's arms. Surprises, as those who died before find loved ones there who came to the Lord later. What a glorious morning!   TAMYRA HORST

DECEMBER 2

DO YOU APPRECIATE YOU?

As the Father has loved me, so I have loved you. Dwell in my love. John 15:9, NEB.

Excitement was in the air as my granddaughter and I made pizza for her birthday party. Eager little fingers patted the dough into the pan. "I appreciate your help, Elannah. Doing things with you is so much fun."

"And I appreciate you making a nice party for me, Grandma."

The golden head came up as she thoughtfully added, "Grandma, do you appreciate *you*?"

The profound question seemed to come from a higher source than 5-year-old lips. What could I say? I was sensitively aware of the preciousness of the little girl beside me, but not of my own value. "Well, I appreciate the person Jesus is making of me," I told her.

Traveling home after the party, I had time to reflect. I am quick to appreciate all of God's creation—the uniqueness of people and the beauties of nature—but so slow to recognize gratefully my own value. Self-criticism needs to be replaced by affirmations that celebrate my worth. Maybe I need to say "I love who you are, really love who you are" to myself, as well as to my grandchildren.

Can we be sensitively aware of our own preciousness? The Godhead that sits in heavenly places is. Jesus loves us as the Father loves Him (John 15:9), and God loves us as He loves Jesus (John 17:23). The One who knows the worst about us loves us most. How can we fathom the depth and richness of such mercy and love? We accept it by faith, and dwell joyfully as precious princesses—cherished daughters of the King.

LILA LANE GEORGE

DECEMBER 3

MY GYPSY AUNT

As it is, they desire a better country, that is, a heavenly one. Therefore God is not ashamed to be called their God, for he has prepared for them a city. Heb. 11:16, RSV.

I'm just a gypsy," my aunt Jimmie would say with a laugh. "I carry my home in a suitcase." And she did. Widowed, she spent her summers working in Michigan, living one summer with a son and his family, another with a good friend. Winters found her in Texas at yet another son's, or with one of her two sisters.

"I'm just a gypsy," she would laugh. "I carry my home in the trunk of my car."

Aunt Jimmie had a ready laugh and was always eager to see the happy side of life. Her life had not been easy. After being married to an abusive, alcoholic husband for 20 years, she gave up on the marriage to save her family. The next years were equally difficult, as she struggled to work, to rear two young boys, and to keep food on their table. Prayer and angels—the human kind—kept her going when things were at their worst.

Then she remarried. A young stepson was added to her family, and for a time her life stayed secure.

Then came the death of her husband, the loss of companionship and security. By then her sons were grown, scattered across the United States. She found herself in the sisterhood of widows. A cheerful gypsy. Never having a home of her own.

Diabetes had been a constant companion for many years. She measured her days in pills, then insulin injections. Dependence upon the doctors and their care never stopped.

After some years, the disease took its toll. Nerve damage and loss of eyesight. Infections that never quite cleared never went away. Then her lower leg was amputated. That helped her condition for a short while. But her eyesight was almost gone. With little sight and without feeling in her fingertips, she could no longer read nor play music or sermons on the cassette player that had brought her so much comfort.

During those last long days when she hardly knew who she was or where she lived, she talked to God. It was a lifelong habit, these conversations with God as with a much-loved friend. "I often wake up during the night and can't go back to sleep," she'd told me many years before. "I just use that time to talk to God. I'm so busy during the day. Working. The boys. But at nights, when it's quiet and I'm awake, it's just the Lord and I. Instead of struggling to go back to sleep, I just talk to God."

The end did not come easily. Pain-racked, restless, her mind grew fractured and foggy. And she knew it. That was the worst thing, trying to keep hold of reality as it slipped, like sand, through her fingertips.

The end came a short time later. Today she sleeps in Texas near her parents and a sister. And her hope, like that of mine or yours, could be summed up by the promise in 1 Thessalonians 4:16: "For the Lord himself will come down from heaven . . . with the trumpet of God, and the dead in Christ will rise first" (NIV).

PENNY ESTES WHEELER

DECEMBER 4

"I'M A LITTLE AFRAID, LORD"

He shall call upon Me, and I will answer him; I will be with him in trouble; I will deliver him and honor him. Ps. 91:15, NKJV.

The flight from the East to the West Coast had been crowded but uneventful. I'd looked forward to spending a couple hours with our children, enjoying their company, when they'd suggested they'd drive up to meet my plane. But good things always end.

"Here's the map we promised you and the routes written down for quick confirmation," my daughter-in-law said as she gave me the much-appreciated bundle. How blessed I felt not only for having two sons, but also for gaining a very special daughter.

"Mom, I hope you like traffic," my son teased lightly.

"I'll just go with the flow," I promised, appreciating his concern and yet feeling his support.

Now I had to get on with my journey. More family awaited my arrival. My eagerness to get to them dimmed slightly as I considered the next couple hours before we'd be together. Traffic. Miles and miles—lanes and lanes—of unfamiliar freeway. Even with the gift of three extra hours, darkness swiftly descended.

As the miles sped by, darkness settled and my apprehension grew. "You can do this. Relax," I chided myself. Yet much of the journey loomed before me.

"Please, Lord, give me peace," I prayed with eyes straight ahead and a strong grip on the wheel. "If You could just help me to find my way without making wrong turns or getting on any wrong freeways."

I longed for the comfort of music, but going from station to station was an effort in futility—until I prayed. Almost immediately the radio tuned perfectly to the strains of "God Will Take Care of You."

"Be not dismayed whate'er betide," the voice sang. "God will take care of you."

Stiff hands relaxed. A smile formed on my lips. God cared. He'd take care of me. My angel rode beside me. The miles melted away in the glow of promise. GINGER MOSTERT CHURCH

DECEMBER 5

SWEET INNOCENCE

Even a child is known by his doings. Prov. 20:11.

It was my birthday. The children in my third-grade class always brought treats to share on their birthdays, so I decided to do the same. Cupcakes would be good, but they could also be messy—the janitor frowned upon crumbs on the floor. "The kids smash 'em, and I have to scrub to get 'em up," he'd say. *Well, then,* I thought, *I'll take cookies.* So I did.

Blue-eyed and blond, 8-year-old Dennis lived up to his nickname—Dennis the Menace. I knew he was up to something when he grinned at me and held up one of the cookies I had distributed to the class. "Teacher," he grinned, "you make us tell, so you have to tell too. How old are you?"

"I'm 100 years old, Dennis," I lied. "One hundred years old today." I said it with a straight face, knowing I couldn't fool him for long. But he would get no grin from me!

He stared long and hard at me, looking at my face, my hair, then back at my face. As I stood there trying to keep from smiling, he walked around me, staring steadily at my every feature. It was such a temptation to laugh at him. I almost did, then resolved that I wouldn't. After what seemed like minutes, but couldn't have been, his eyes grew large as he looked into my face and exclaimed in all sincerity, "Really, Teacher? You don't look a day over 50."

Dennis had the last laugh after all. It was my thirtieth birthday! Though I eventually told him the truth, Dennis taught me a lesson I would not soon forget. "Lie not one to another" (Col. 3:9). Not even in jest should I have misled him. Nor would I do so again.

Patricia A. Habada

December 6

Ready for the Day

For in this hope we were saved. But hope that is seen is no hope at all. Who hopes for what he already has? But if we hope for what we do not have, we wait for it patiently. Rom. 8:24, 25, NIV.

The sun was coming up bright and beautiful. It made me feel good all over. I drove to my office, thinking about the many things I needed to do to get up-to-date with business demands.

As I walked through the door of the hospital my beeper signaled me to the emergency room. A gurney was being rolled in; on it was a human being covered in blood from head to toe. His arm lay separately on his chest. He was groaning and retching.

"This isn't what I had in mind for today," I said to myself as I flew into action: getting information, calling parents, helping whenever I could. Then it was time to go to the main door to open my arms to anxious parents and other family members.

It was such a gory, bloody mess that even the nurses had to take turns working with the patient. I spent the next hours going back and forth between the parents and their son's bedside, giving them information in a selective way to help them adjust to the shock.

I had no time to prepare for the moment. I had to trust former preparation and prayers to get me through this experience. God worked through me to give Todd and his family strength through the ordeal.

I made it through this tough time. And although he lost his arm and spent much time in the hospital, our young patient made it through also.

As we leave our bedrooms in the morning, we always hope that we will have a good day. A day that will bring satisfaction that we are productive people. We might even hope that the day will bring joy, peace of mind, and even happiness.

But we must prepare for this day by learning and applying health concepts, education, and experiential learning. We must allow the Spirit of God to infiltrate our lives. We will have often opened our hearts in prayer. We will have recognized God's Spirit making changes in our life.

Yes, with all the background preparation, we are ready for this day. It is the hope for a good day that inspires us to invest ourselves to the limit, to be the best person possible, and to follow our Lord's command.

There is another great day coming—when Jesus comes in all His glory to take His loved ones home. It is the hope that we will be among the saints that inspires us to patiently prepare, so that God can claim us as His own. MARY CASLER

DECEMBER 7

PINK PIGEONS AND PEOPLE FROM PONTYPRIDD

But now they desire a better country, that is, an heavenly. Heb. 11:16.

"Come and see the fantastic tropical gardens!" However, "fantastic" is not how I would have described them. OK, it was almost the end of the season, but I *do* think they could have kept things blooming until the season actually ran out! The seaside resort of St. Brelade looked lovely the day we saw it, though. A real taste of heaven there. But there are so many cars and other vehicles all over the island that you can't help wondering about the pollution you can't see.

My mom lives in a different time warp. I avoid all museums like the plague. Well, we had only six days, and Mom looks at every exhibit. But it would be lovely to look at things as long as you want to. That's one of the main things about heaven that attracts me. If I want to stare at a butterfly all day, I can do so.

We met some lovely people, too. There was the delightful couple from Pontypridd in Wales, who obviously thought the world of each other. We kept running into them all day. An idyllic couple, you'd think, but as we talked I discovered that the lady had been seriously ill and wasn't all that strong yet.

The carnation and butterfly farms were like a touch of heaven. The coastal scenery was breathtaking, and because of the ultra-clean waters, there was an abundance of sea life. I couldn't get Mom to go snorkeling, but I bet I'd have been able to if we really had been in heaven! But I don't see heaven as just a glorified holiday. Every aspect of our lives here is marred in some way. How wonderful when we will be able to go "into the city" and not see high-rise flats (four of them, even on Jersey), not breathe dangerous fumes (55,000 vehicles on an island with an area of 45 square miles). How great to be able to climb to the top of the highest hill and not be out of breath or in agony from painful knees.

And we won't have to go looking for places of worship. The glory of the Lord will be everywhere, and there will be nothing to spoil, ever again. And all the time of eternity to enjoy it.

I'm planning to be there. You're coming too, aren't you?

ANITA MARSHALL

DECEMBER 8

"CREAM OR LEMON IN YOUR NOSE?"

Help each other with your troubles. . . . Each person must be responsible for [herself]. Gal. 6:2-5, NEB.

When her daughters were very small girls, Mrs. Dwight Morrow gave a high tea at which one of the guests was to be the senior J. P. Morgan. The girls were to be brought in, introduced, and ushered out. Mrs. Morrow's greatest fear was the possibility that Anne, the more outspoken of the two, might comment audibly upon Mr. Morgan's celebrated and conspicuous nose. She therefore took pains beforehand to explain to Anne that personal observations were impolite and cautioned her especially against making any comment on Mr. Morgan's nose, no matter what she might think of it.

When the moment came and the children were brought in, Mrs. Morrow held her breath as she saw Anne's gaze fix upon the banker's most prominent facial feature and remain there. Nevertheless, the introduction was made without incident. The little girls curtsied politely and were sent on their way. With a sigh of relief, Mrs. Morrow turned back to her duties as host and inquired of her guest, "And now, Mr. Morgan, will you have cream or lemon in your nose?"

As a hospital pastoral caregiver, I sometimes become a burden bearer of others' hurts. I know that to stay emotionally healthy I need to consciously maintain a distinct identity that gives me boundaries to others' pain.

It seems to me, however, that a caregiver cannot be a caring person and not take on a portion of others' pain. Sometimes the pain will "get to me" as it touches some of my own painful history. Then I must find loving friends who will let me talk it out and process this pain.

As I open up and get my disappointments and fears out, they lose some of their power over me. Whatever our emotional turmoil, we cannot repress or mask it. In fact, the more we try to hide our "negative" thoughts, the more certain it is they will find a way out, as Mrs. Morrow found out.

It is much better to choose how, when, and to whom we want to talk about our emotionally charged issues.   SHARI CHAMBERLAIN

DECEMBER 9

BRIEFCASE ON ICE

God is faithful, and he will not let you be tested beyond your strength, but with the testing he will also provide the way out so that you may be able to endure it. 1 Cor. 10:13, NRSV.

I could see the light in my garage. Warmth and safety was within reach—but I just couldn't get to it! Not life-threatening, but just one of life's "little messes"—this one created by an unexpected late-night ice storm.

The freezing rain latched onto the road as if pulled into place by a giant magnet. I watched in horror as ice began to blanket my car. *Please, Lord, let me get home safely.* By the time I reached my street my heart was pounding—both from fear and excitement as I saw my house. *Whew! I barely made it. Thank You, Lord!*

Turning into my driveway, I pressed the garage door opener. To my surprise, my wheels started to spin. *Oh, no.* I tried again. *Whirrrrrr* was the only response. After allowing the car to roll back onto the street, I really gunned it and got halfway up the drive—only to slide back down.

After several more failed attempts, I decided to get out and let my husband deal with the car. But as soon as I stepped out, I knew I couldn't let go of the car or I'd find myself sprawled on the ice like a cartoon character. I was wearing sneakers, and sneakers and ice just don't mix!

I don't believe this. I can't get to the house! I could see the light in the garage. Safety was just a few yards away, but I couldn't get to it.

"Lord, help me?" I whispered.

Use your briefcase, the answer came, direct and clear. *My briefcase? How?* Then it came to me. I set the briefcase down on end right in front of me. Its rough texture held to the ice, and, holding on to it, I inched forward a few steps. I stabilized, set the briefcase down again, and inched forward. Finally I made it to the house. Upon seeing me, my dear husband gave me one of those "What happened to you?" looks.

"I've just spent 20 minutes at the base of the driveway trying to get into the house!"

Properly attired, we both went out to see what we could do about the car. Michael tried, with no success. Then he had an idea. He drove up on the grass until he reached the level part of the driveway, and then into the garage.

Often the Lord places solutions to life's little messes right before us. We just have to be willing to use what's available in a rather unusual way. A briefcase to shore up my steps? Driving on the grass? Certainly not my regular routine. But those were the "way of escape" for us that night.

Your solutions to life's little and big messes are probably right before you. Look around. Ask the Lord to open your eyes to them. Be willing to use the unusual. — Barbara Jackson-Hall

December 10

THE PALMS OF MY HANDS

Behold, I have graven thee upon the palms of my hands. Isa. 49:16.

I remember how as a little girl in school, whenever I secretly liked a special little boy, I would take a ballpoint pen and write his initials on my hand. It might be "N.C. + M.V." or something similar. It sort of gave me a feeling that that person was mine, even though he might not have even known I existed.

As might be expected of a young child, my affections changed periodically, as did the initials in my hands.

Do you know that Isaiah tells us that God has "engraved" us on the palms of His hands because He loves us so much and thinks we're very special? But we're not written there with washable ink—there today and gone tomorrow. Our names have been engraven on His hands with the spikes of Calvary, dipped in the blood of the Lamb. And unlike my childish fickleness, God's affection for us never changes. He is the same "yesterday, today, and forever." And His love for us will last forever. He pledges this to us: "Yea, I have loved thee with an everlasting love" (Jer. 31:3).

So when we're tempted to think that we're not worth much to anyone or that no one cares, let's remember to look at the palms of God's hands. Written there in divine love is "God + Nancy" and "God + _____ (supply your name)." And as we look, we can know that His jealous love is wrapped around us, for He says: "I have called thee by thy name; *thou art mine*" (Isa. 43:1).

NANCY CACHERO VASQUEZ

December 11

LESSONS FROM MY LAB

Go to the ant, O sluggard; consider her ways, and be wise. Prov. 6:6, RSV.

Some couples pray for children; we prayed for a dog. One month after getting married, my husband and I got a 90-pound black Labrador from the animal shelter.

Jake, as his previous owners had named him, was not our first choice, however. After being offered two other dogs and being turned down both times because of a mix-up in paperwork, or because someone else was ahead of us on their list, we felt that when Jake—a 10-month-old housebroken puppy—was offered to us, our prayers had been answered.

Mind you, Jake is not without fault. He sheds hair, attracts fleas, tramps mud through the house, and ruthlessly barks at old ladies walking down the street.

But in spite of his idiosyncrasies, Jake has been my teacher. Here's what I've learned:

Loyalty. This is something to be reserved for the one who provides for your needs. It grows by spending time with the Master.

Contentment. There's no need to run away if all your needs are met. Don't go out searching for tomorrow's needs if food is there today. Whoever provided it today will provide it tomorrow.

Friendliness. Any friend of the Master's is a friend of yours. And by sharing your bone with strangers, you can make them your friends.

Helpfulness. If someone needs help or is hurting, go and be with the person and quietly listen. Helpfulness sometimes consists of just sitting there and doing nothing.

Happiness. It isn't dependent upon circumstances. You can be happy in the middle of the night, first thing in the morning, or in the midst of a rainstorm.

Temperance. Care for your body. Don't eat more than is good for you. Eat the right things. Get plenty of rest. Exercise daily. Clean your body regularly. Lick your wounds, and forget them so they can heal.

Forgiveness. Be quick to forgive when someone forgets to feed you or accidentally steps on your tail.

Love. Sit at someone's feet to show that person your love. Dare to let the person pat your head, scratch your tummy, or rumple your coat. After all, any friends of the Master's are friends of yours, right? Wag your tail, rub up against them, and surround them with unconditional love.

Sometimes I wonder who's training whom.

When I look at Jake now, I see not only a special dog sent from heaven, but a teacher. And I pray that with God's grace I can exemplify the same happy Christianity that Jake has shown me.

JACKIE ORDELHEIDE SMITH

DECEMBER 12

FLYING LESSONS

But they that wait upon the Lord shall renew their strength; they shall mount up with wings as eagles; they shall run, and not be weary; and they shall walk, and not faint. Isa. 40:31.

Weekday mornings at our house are not full of philosophical musings. Routine is reduced to the essentials, and conversations are filled with such phrases as "Hurry, Jaime; find your shoes" and "Lauren, have you brushed?"

I sat on the edge of the big cast-iron bathtub in our mountain home, putting the finishing touches on a stubborn curl that wouldn't.

In the mirror I saw Jaime's reflection. Wistful blue eyes peeked out from below angel floss hair.

She was humming one of the songs again.

It was from the TV classic *Peter Pan*, the one with Mary Martin playing the leading role. The girls loved it. Especially Jaime. She seemed to have an affinity for Peter. She didn't know he was played by a woman. Or about the invisible wires. Peter was her friend.

Almost 3 years old, she would often break into a child's version of "I Won't Grow Up" or "Think Happy Thoughts."

When dressing, she would carefully lay out her sweatpants on the floor, plop down on top of them with baby legs outstretched, and declare to me that she had found her shadow!

Jaime stopped humming.

"Mommy." She turned her cherub face toward me expectantly.

"Yes, honey."

"Mommy, would you teach me how to fly?"

I chuckled and hugged her, enjoying the joke. But then I immediately realized that she wasn't joking. And she wanted an answer.

Of course, I was teaching my children how to fly—figuratively speaking. At least I thought so. Evan and I worked hard at helping our children to grow "roots" and "wings." You know, instilling and encouraging self-esteem, creativity, social skills, and moral and religious values. Mostly we tried to introduce these miraculous creations to their Creator and make Jesus real for them, too.

"Mommy." More insistently this time. "Will you teach me how to fly?"

She wasn't interested in figurative flying. She wanted to learn how to honest-to-goodness fly.

"Well, honey . . ." I hesitated. "Right now we have to use airplanes to fly. But someday, when Jesus comes on the big cloud to take us to heaven, we'll be able to fly."

I looked at Jaime. She didn't seem to be devastated by my inability to match aeronautics with Peter. She was thinking about Jesus coming on a big cloud.

"Mommy, will it be a *very strong* cloud?"

"Yes, sweetheart, a *very strong* cloud!"

I hugged her and thought of how heaven might be. In heaven, will flying be an immediately acquired skill? Or will we take lessons? Who will teach us? Our guardian angels?

Will we feel cool breezes as we travel through the air about Paradise? Or will we simply "think" ourselves to desired destinations?

I hugged Jaime again and determined that, by God's grace, I'd be there to see her first flight. SHEREE PARRIS NUDD

December 13

WOMEN OF WINTER

But Jesus said, "Someone touched me; I know that power has gone out from me." Luke 8:46, NIV.

I like Max Lucado. His book *God Came Near* is good stuff. Last Friday night a woman friend called from Idaho to share Lucado's three vignettes in "Women of Winter." (They are worth the price of the book.) My friend is the sort who calls for no particular reason except love. But God had His reasons.

The three women she read to me about were the widow of Nain, the woman at the well, and the woman with the 12-year hemorrhage. I'd never seen myself in quite their classes before. I've never lost a husband or a son. I'm still married to my first husband, and I go to the doctor once a year for a physical. But it is likely that I would have been slow to understand even if I had lived back then. Slow to feel my own deep need. Slow to recognize the real miracle.

As my friend read, I found myself lost in the imagery of the stories, merging into the scenes, becoming the woman upon whom the spotlight rested:

"I hurt a friend really badly this week trying to convey the strength of my feelings. For genuine warmth to be resurrected in our relationship, I'm afraid God Himself will have to say, 'Arise!'"

"I know what it feels like to be used. I also know how good it feels to be both fully known and fully loved. I came to bed late last night, exhausted but sleepless with responsibility. A streetlight illumined the face of my companion of nearly 28 years. Thank God there are men in my life who are trustworthy."

"I'm 48 years old. Old enough to know better. But the gospel keeps breaking over me in waves, each one playing itself out across my innermost being like none that has gone before. At last I think I am awakening to my need. I need the reassuring presence of a robe I can touch—again and again and again."

That's why I'm falling deeper and deeper in love with Jesus. A Jesus who stops, not because He wants to impress a large crowd, or even to raise up a young man with years of potential, but because He couldn't walk past a woman with red, puffy eyes. A Jesus who reads wrinkles and understands the pain of broken relationships from hard experience. A Jesus who holds the other end of my rope in His hand. A Jesus whose presence melts winter into spring. KAREN FLOWERS

DECEMBER 14

THE END OF MY ROPE

I will strengthen thee; yea, I will help thee; yea, I will uphold thee with the right hand of my righteousness. Isa. 41:10.

"O Lord, it's no use," I sobbed. "Why am I failing all the time? Why is the Christian life so hard? You know I've been trying my best to live up to what I know is right. And the harder I try, the worse I get. I'm so tired; I just can't keep on this way . . ."

With all the advantages of a devout, happy Christian home background and a Christian education, I knew there was something better than what I had experienced in Christian living. As a missionary and a minister's wife, I was awash in shame and consternation that all my efforts these many months to turn a humdrum spiritual experience into something really meaningful had come to nothing.

"Lord," I pleaded, "I don't know what's holding me back from the closeness with You that I'm longing for. If You'll just show me what it is, I'll be glad to give it up."

Immediately I sensed that I'd been holding Him off at arm's length from a hidden fear that if I surrendered everything, He'd fill my life with unpleasant things such as soliciting money and passing out tracts. I smile at that fear now, but at the time a serious struggle ensued—there was nothing I loathed as much as soliciting money. Finally admitting that such programs come infrequently, and trusting the Lord to strengthen and accompany me, I gave in.

Then it was explained to me that the experience I longed for is a covenant relationship. There are promises on both sides. God is my Father and promises to meet all my needs. I can choose to become His child. However—as is proper in parent-child relationships—the child obeys the father. I longed to hurry into His waiting arms and promise my willing obedience, but I'd lost faith in myself.

The evil one's caustic comments seemed all too true: "You promising to obey? Your promises are like 'ropes of sand' . . . your friends will think you've gone overboard . . . you'll always have to put duty first . . ." But there was another Voice persistently, patiently promising His presence and help.

When at long last I chose to trust my Father's love, I surrendered and promised my cooperation. I thanked Him for receiving me as His child, and climbed into bed. Peace that indeed passes understanding stole over me as text after text from the Bible filled my mind:

"Fear thou not; for I am with thee: be not dismayed; for I am thy God: I will strengthen thee; yea, I will help thee; yea, I will uphold thee with the right hand of my righteousness. . . . For I the Lord thy God will hold thy right hand, saying unto thee, Fear not; I will help thee" (Isa. 41:10-13). "Behold, I have graven thee upon the palms of my hands" (Isa. 49:16). "Fear not: for I have redeemed thee, I have called thee by thy name; thou art mine" (Isa. 43:1).

Norma Hilliard

December 15

"Be Strong and Take Heart"

Wait for the Lord; be strong and take heart and wait for the Lord. Ps. 27:14, NIV.

It was another night when sleep was somewhat restless. I was away from home to present a seminar for hurting women. The ministry dealt with a delicate and sensitive issue and could be emotionally draining. Yet I always looked forward to the weekends because of the spiritual focus and the peace we all experienced there.

As the need grew for more seminars, I felt pressured to expand

and commit to doing more: speaking, writing, training. Sometimes I felt overwhelmed.

Yet it seemed that God kept cutting our potential staff members. I woke up around 4:00 a.m. and couldn't go back to sleep. As I wrestled in my mind with God, I kept thinking that if God would just give us some answers and help, I could have peace of mind and get the needed rest to strengthen me for the next three days.

As I often do when I can't sleep, I took my Bible, opened it, and started reading. My eyes fell on these words: "Wait for the Lord: be strong and take heart." As my heart raced and I became wide awake, I realized that I had never read this verse in the New International Version before. It burned into my mind, as "Take Heart" was the name of my spiritual ministry.

What was God telling me or preparing me for? The next morning I again awoke at 4:00, this time with a severe case of intestinal virus. I had no control over my bodily functions and felt completely exhausted. How could I ever spend the next two days presenting a seminar?

When my copresenter came to my door early, I told her of my problem and that she would have to go on without me. She immediately rallied the troops, and suddenly I was the one being nurtured and prayed for.

I wanted God either to heal me so I could go on with the weekend or let me stay sick, rest, and let the staff go on without me. As often happens, in God's all-knowing ways He had His own agenda for us. By midmorning I felt strong enough to go on with the seminar. I was unable to eat any food for two days, and yet I experienced more strength and vitality and peace than I had ever experienced before. By the end of the weekend God had made clear to me the direction that He had for my ministry. I discovered He was already providing in ways that I hadn't even considered.

My own personal lesson learned is that God has not promised to take me out of every difficult circumstance, but He has promised to give me the strength to go through those difficult circumstances. He will give you the strength you need too. Oh, how I love Him!

JANIS VANCE

DECEMBER 16

YES, HE DOES CARE ABOUT LITTLE THINGS

Are not five sparrows sold for two farthings, and not one of them is forgotten before God? But even the very hairs of your head are all numbered. Fear not therefore: ye are of more value than many sparrows. Luke 12:6, 7.

"Where could that ticket possibly be?" I grilled myself. For more than two months now I had searched frantically for the return trip ticket for my niece Heather, who had been living with me and attending academy for the past year and a half. Her parents resided in California, and the ticket was for Heather's trip home for the Christmas holidays.

Every inch of the house had been scoured—upstairs, downstairs, every possible location. Even the not-so-possible areas had been examined thoroughly. But no ticket. What was I to do? It was now Thursday, the day before Heather's flight.

I'd been praying constantly during the past two months, asking that God, who knew exactly where that ticket was, would simply show it to me. For Him, that was an uncomplicated task. But was He still aware of my predicament? Did He realize that I had very little time left to search? Had He forgotten my desperate plea, or did He even care about little things? I knew I didn't have the money to replace the ticket, and I knew Heather's parents didn't have the money, so there was no alternative. I just had to find it!

That evening I planned to take up the search early, retracing my steps once again. But unexpected company arrived and visited until 9:00. The moment they left I started my search downstairs in the basement, looking into everything, even those places I knew were not places the ticket would be. As I proceeded to inspect every box and suitcase available, I continued to move through the house until at last I arrived at the final site—the third garage. Of course, the ticket wouldn't be there, but I had to make one last attempt.

I reached to pull the dirty light string, illuminating the area, and slowly gazed around the cluttered room, discouraged with my efforts. I made little move because I *knew* the ticket wasn't there. As I stretched once more toward the light string, conceding that there was nothing left to do but somehow come up with the money to purchase another ticket, I noticed a rather large suitcase.

Could it be? No, I'd looked in it on another occasion for something else, and I was certain I would have seen the ticket. But . . . I had this strong, overwhelming sense that perhaps one more quick glance wouldn't hurt. With misgivings, I opened the suitcase and discovered something else that had a connection to the time when Heather had arrived in August.

Maybe . . . just maybe . . . I reached down toward a blue envelope and anxiously scanned the contents. You can guess the rest of the story. I grabbed the ticket, pressed it to my chest, and verbally thanked God for leading me through all the clutter to show me that yes, He does care about little things!

There are many times when discouragement comes to all of us in our day-to-day efforts, but when we question if God really is concerned, let's remember that even the very hairs of our heads are numbered. Yes, our confidence is in Jesus! — KARON SCOTT

DECEMBER 17

GOD'S MEMORABILIA

How precious also are thy thoughts unto me, O God! how great is the sum of them!" Ps. 139:17.

Good morning, Father. Today I plan to decorate my Christmas tree. It isn't big or showy—just tall enough to hold some of the memorabilia I've saved all these years. Like that piece of ribbon from my wedding flowers; my little daughter's folded-up love note; a golden curl saved from my father's first haircut; a napkin ring made by my first-grade son; my husband's army insignia; and a few other things money could never buy.

And, heavenly Father, I like to imagine that You've collected memorabilia from Your children too over these past several millenniums. Forgive me, Lord, but would You place some of them on an evergreen this year? A very tall one, touching the ceiling of the celestial court? Oh, it would be a lovely sight, sparkling with 10,000 stars—left over after You made our universe.

And because You love us, Father, wouldn't those little treasures we've given You make Your tree look nice? Take the two little mites the poor widow gave You, and the ball of fleece Gideon presented. There's the axhead You caused to float on water for Your seminary students. It's a bit heavy, but You took care of that once before.

There's the tiny little needle Dorcas used—probably still attached to a garment she was making for needy people. And David's sling, with the pouch that held five stones. Four of them may still be inside.

I know You have room for the battered old rod Moses carried for 40 long years. Once he struck the rock with it against Your will, but You did forgive him. He tried so hard to be like You. Then there's the widow's cruse of oil You blessed when she drained it to prepare food for Elijah. And You kept right on feeding her!

You might want to add Joash's money box. And Father, here is an exquisitely carved alabaster box that still carries that heavenly fragrance! It was terribly expensive, but it was broken by Mary because she loved You so very much. Even though it's shattered, I know You won't reject it, for You didn't reject her. Then around that tree You could drape the red cord Rahab used to help two of Your Israelite children escape. All of these gifts are meager, Father, but they represent Your children. In Your hands they look exquisite!

Then, please, dear God, on the topmost branch, would You place Your star? You used it nearly 2,000 years ago to guide Wise Men to the manger. There, they found Your beautiful Gift wrapped in swaddling clothes and tied with Your own heartstrings. It cost You so very much.

And Father, because You've sacrificed it all for me, I give my heart to You with all my love. *It's the only gift You've ever asked for.* May Your Christmas be as joyful as You have made mine! Amen.

LORRAINE HUDGINS

DECEMBER 18

THE ONE WHO SERVES

You, my brothers, were called to be free. But do not use your freedom to indulge the sinful nature; rather, serve one another in love. Gal. 5:13, NIV.

Since my father was Jewish, as a child I often heard reference made to the traditional Jewish holidays. But it was not until I became an adult and had a child of my own that I became motivated to learn and understand the meaning of these celebrations.

Many people are familiar with the celebration of Hanukkah, which usually falls in December near the time when Christians are celebrating Christmas. The story of Hanukkah centers on the Jewish Temple. The king of Syria had taken the Jews captive, forbidden them to practice their religion, and defiled their temple. A brave band of farmers led by Judah Maccabee got fed up and decided to fight back.

Although they were up against the most sophisticated army of the time and were very ill equipped, the small band conquered the Syrian Army. The triumphant Maccabees led the Jews back to the Temple, only to find it defiled.

The sacred candelabra was unlit and there was only enough oil for one day, but they lit the lamp anyway. It continued to shine for eight days until more oil could be obtained.

Today Jewish people celebrate by lighting a candle on the menorah—a special candleholder that has room for eight candles—every day for eight days. The Hanukkah menorah is different from other menorahs in that there is a place for an extra candle. This candle is called the "shamesh," which means "the one who serves." It is used to light all the other candles on the menorah.

Many things could be compared to the shamesh. Certainly Christ has been the greatest server of all. "The Son of Man did not come to be served, but to serve, and to give his life as a ransom for many" (Matt. 20:28, NIV). Using Him as our example, we too must be "ones who serve."

A woman's role of giving service to our families, to the community, and in occupations of service has been devalued in our society. Oftentimes the way to "success" is by competing with men or acting like them. But women have been given certain natural abilities in regard to compassion, caring, and nurturing—all qualities that are service-related.

Let us not sell ourselves short and seek to be what we are not. Serving is a gift. Paul says that "we have different gifts, according to the grace given us. . . . If it is serving, let him serve" (Rom. 12:6, 7, NIV). Jesus served us with the greatest gift of all. Surely it is an honor to be able to serve Him by serving others.

CAREL SANDERS CLAY

DECEMBER 19

THE ANGEL OF THE LORD

The angel of the Lord encampeth round about them that fear him, and delivereth them. Ps. 34:7.

At Christmastime our family has a special ritual of going to San Francisco to see the sights in the big city. Many of the stores have animated characters parading across their windows. The beautifully decorated streets all lend their lights and color to a happy, festive mood.

It was the first day of Christmas vacation for our children, so with the help of our two younger sons we packed a lunch and loaded ourselves into the station wagon. We were eager to be on our way.

We first went to Rio Lindo Academy, where we picked up our other daughter. Just after we left the school it began to rain. Within minutes the rain turned into a downpour. But despite the bad weather, the four-lane, divided highway was filled with cars. Then just as we passed a car on the right, everything became quiet. We no longer heard the swish of the tires on the pavement, because we were hydroplaning on the inch of water that covered the road. As the car went into a spin, I sent up a silent prayer: *O Lord, please protect us and our car.*

The car spun across two lanes of southbound traffic, turning two and a half times and then coming to rest with the back end up against the bank on the right side of the freeway. We each had the feeling of angel wings wrapped around our car, protecting us. We never knew what happened to the car that was beside us when we began the spin. Perhaps it was the car we saw in the dividing strip of the highway, or maybe the car stopped in front of us.

A slightly bent tailpipe under the car was the only damage we could find. The pot of baked beans had traveled from the back corner of the wagon up to the back of the seat without spilling a bean. As we counted our blessings, our family was reminded of our heavenly Father's love in sending His angels to protect us. What a wonderful promise we have!

FREDI RAYLINE JONES

DECEMBER 20

HE HEARS US

Commit thy way unto the Lord; trust also in him; and he shall bring it to pass. Ps. 37:5.

One afternoon we crossed the border from Syria to Lebanon. We really didn't have a map that showed every road, but kept watching, and somehow it seemed we were going around a mountain. My husband finally said, "We'll just have to get on a road by the coast."

As we kept going, I hoped there wouldn't be any problem. Sometimes it took an hour to get permission to get into the country. We recalled the time we were going to a wedding in a village up on a hill. As we approached a turn, we were met by a group of people (mostly women) with stones in their hands, ready to stone us.

The afternoon wore on, and as I watched the sun getting lower and lower in the west I grew anxious about crossing the border. I began praying, "Lord, help us to get to the border before dark. May the guards not recognize us. Lord, please let us go through without any interrogation."

I kept praying as I watched the sun go down over the Mediterranean. I prayed until we arrived at the outpost and continued to pray as we gave the guard our Lebanese identity cards. He shouted, "Two Lebanese!" and we were in Lebanon. God answered my prayer in every detail.

Many times I have committed my plans to Him, trusting Him and praying that He would bring them to pass if it was His will. Then I bring out the special jewel of Psalm 37:5, "Commit thy way unto the Lord; trust also in him; and he shall bring it to pass," and renew my trust in Him. In a life of difficult pathways, I use that verse as a guide. May you enjoy it today.   MARGARET MONDICS GIBBS

DECEMBER 21

ANGELS IN AN ICE STORM

The angel of the Lord encampeth round about them that fear him, and delivereth them. Ps. 34:7.

In December of 1989 our son sent us airline tickets to come to Chicago to be with him for Christmas. At that time Mountain Home, Arkansas, had no regular passenger service, so we had to drive to Little Rock to catch our flight. Because this was a three-hour drive, we decided to go in the afternoon before our flight the next morning.

By the time we got to Interstate 40 a freezing rain had started. After driving slowly and carefully for several miles, we decided to pull off on the shoulder and wait for a salt or gravel truck, but no such truck came. As we sat there, several 18-wheelers pulled off on the shoulder ahead of and behind us. We kept on waiting, hoping and praying that the storm would let up. A truck driver behind us went up to talk to the driver of the truck just ahead of us. As he came back by us, I asked him if he thought we could make it. He said that if we could get across the highway to the left-hand lane and drive with two wheels in the grass, perhaps we could.

We managed that, but before long we came to a bridge, and had to move into the middle of the lane. We could see an exit ahead, but before we could reach it our car spun out of control. We came to a stop blocking the middle and right-hand lanes, and facing the oncoming traffic. The least movement of the car seemed to make our situation worse, so my husband flashed our lights to warn oncoming cars as they came over the hill.

We were helpless. Understandably, no drivers stopped to help. I prayed in agony for God to send us some help. Then we saw something that amazed us. A pickup truck came toward us, driving the wrong way on the left-hand lane.

The young driver came over to us and said, "My wife and I saw your car go into a spin, and we've come to help you."

Then the man's wife got out of the truck, and together they pushed our car, giving us enough traction and motion that my husband was able to get it moving. Carefully we drove to the exit ramp. We didn't see how they got back into traffic and we don't know if they were angels, but we do know that God sent them to help us. Prudent, unselfish persons don't drive the wrong way on an ice-covered freeway to help a stranded driver—but they did. We thanked God from the bottom of our hearts. And when we all get to heaven, we hope to thank personally whoever it was that helped us out of that terrifying experience. ELLEN SWAYZE-WARD

DECEMBER 22

HE MADE THE STARS, ALSO

Give thanks to the Lord, for he is good. . . . Give thanks to the Lord of lords, . . . who by understanding made the heavens . . . , the moon and stars to rule over the night, for his steadfast love endures forever. Ps. 136:1-9, NRSV.

Soft, pulsating, and almost tangible, the stars hung over us like ripe fruit—ready to fall into our outstretched hands if we could but reach a few feet higher. We sat outside a stone hut high in the Atlas

Mountains of Morocco. Not a light shone from the village below, and the clear night sky wrapped around us like a giant planetarium. Only the sharp-edged silhouettes of the mountain edges broke the illusion.

The day had been unforgettable, in more ways than one, for the four of us who were spending our Christmas holidays in Morocco. Early that morning we'd bundled mere essentials into two backpacks, stored the rest of our stuff at our hotel, and begun our trip from Marrakesh down on the plain to the mountain village of Imlil. The day was warm with an indigo blue sky. Two breathtaking car rides put us in the village just after noon. We were to stay at the home of our guide, who lived a short hike further up the mountain.

There was so much to catch our attention as we picked our way along the stone-strewn hillside path that I wasn't as careful as I should have been. One moment I was balancing on the edge of the stone walkway. The next I swung, quite literally, by the seat of my pants from a pointed rock in the wall from which I'd slipped.

Up at the hut Annette assessed the damage—a raw, red six-inch scrape down my right thigh. She cleaned it up the best she could, but the physical pain was nothing next to the fears created by my hypersensitive imagination—fears of parasites, or who knew what else, from the water used to clean the cuts. I'd heard too many stories of missionaries who'd returned home with hard-to-cure diseases from contaminated water. The fears followed me along the mountain trails, nibbled at my dinner, and parked themselves securely at my feet inside the hut.

Now it was night. The air was as sharp as the pain in my leg. Our warmth had set with the sun, but as if in compensation, out had come the stars—stars shining with a clear brilliance that we'd never seen before. We huddled on the balcony, wrapped in blankets against the night cold, to admire them. I found the Big Dipper and then the Little. Gavin pointed out the constellation of Orion to Lisa, and my eyes followed his finger and directions to the belt of three stars that swung at the waist.

Orion. Gradually my pain and the fear receded into the distance, replaced by the comfort that showered down on me from the light of the stars. Old and unchanging, they stood for beauty, power, and hope—and the God of all three. ROBYN WHEELER

December 23

The Dancing Rag Doll

And I heard the voice of the Lord saying, "Whom shall I send, and who will go for us?" Then I said, "Here am I! Send me." Isa. 6:8, RSV.

I remember the rag doll I got for Christmas when I was 10 years old. I'd gone to spend Christmas Eve at my grandfather's home across town with my 10-year-old cousin Sandra. We were both so excited that we giggled and talked late into the night before we finally fell asleep. We were awakened early by the sound of voices coming from the living room, and sleepily made our way to the Christmas tree.

Under the tree and all around it were beautifully wrapped boxes. Grandpa, playing the part of Santa Claus, called out our names and handed us our presents. Sandra and I had very large, identical boxes that we opened as fast as we could. Inside the identical boxes were identical four-foot-tall rag dolls. The dolls were wearing beautiful dresses, their hair was made from yarn, and their faces held sweet, hand-painted smiles. Their arms and legs were very long and slender, and had elastic bands on them. We put the bands over our feet and hands, and we danced, jumped, and ran with the dolls until our bodies were too tired to play anymore. It seemed to us that our dolls could and would do *anything* we wanted them to do. We were so delighted with them, and they remained our favorite toys for many months.

As I was reminiscing about the dancing rag dolls Sandra and I enjoyed so much, I thought about God and us. How pleased He is when we are willing to be connected to Him by the elastic of His love, and do the things that please Him. I can just imagine Him smiling contentedly and laughing with joy at our willingness to be His hands and feet and reach out to others here on earth. So many will spend Christmas alone and forgotten. Some are in nursing homes, some are street people, others are in orphanages and shelters. Some may even be in your own church. Ask God to help you find someone to reach out to this Christmas, and then listen for His voice. It's not too late to give Jesus a *real* birthday present!

Celia Cruz

DECEMBER 24

FROG SHOES

It is more blessed to give than to receive. Acts 20:35, NASB.

Christmas 1939 approached, but things were different this year. Dad's mouthwatering pastel-tinted divinity, chunky with walnuts, was absent from our log-house kitchen, and he was troubled and irritable. I watched my mother's discouragement, feeling deep sympathy for both of them as they struggled to make ends meet.

We older youngsters understood. (I'd turned 13 that year.) But the "little kids"—as we dubbed the four youngest—full of faith, looked forward to the great day. Excitement tickled their small middles with delightful anticipation. (I well remember the feeling!)

How I wanted to get them all gifts! Brows knit in deep concern, I sat idly contemplating my feet, determined my brain would spawn some feasible solution.

Suddenly I knew! Grabbing my loose-fitting moccasin-type shoe, I examined it critically. Its three parts—sole, vamp, and sides—didn't appear difficult to duplicate.

Meticulously I drew a pattern. Mom donated some old coats, from which I cut several layers of each piece, gathered and sewed, copying my moccasins. My big project, however, remained a secret, even to Mom.

The first pair of slippers fit me perfectly. I stitched another pair the same size. These would be for Morna and Una. Painstakingly seven more pairs of warm slippers materialized—very small ones for 4-year-old Leda, increasing in size for Vernon, Sharon, and Clement. I made Mom's quite large, and BIG ones for Daddy.

As an afterthought, a ninth pair for myself completed the stack. I reasoned that by giving a pair to myself, the donor's identity would be forever a mystery. Also, my parents might feel badly if everyone received slippers except me. Then, too, I felt a need to protect myself from the embarrassment of receiving no gift. (I needn't have worried. Ingeniously, Mom and Dad came up with several little gifts for each of us.)

Christmas morning Vernon awoke about 6:00 and tiptoed in to inspect the stockings, whose bulges secreted the long-awaited surprises. Previous solemn vows dictated that he must awaken all the others before peeking into his own.

As each found his/her gaily wrapped package (paper and ribbons salvaged from an earlier holiday), my happiness belied my innocence.

The slippers fit amazingly well, until it came to Mom's and Daddy's. My careful examination of various shoes, as I'd worked, had been dispensed with when I'd cut the larger patterns. In my mind Mom was BIG and Dad was BIGGER! And so were their slippers.

How we laughed when Mom tried hers on! When Daddy stuck his short, broad feet into those size 12s, four inches remained empty behind his heel!

Mom, tears in her eyes, hugged me and confided that seeing my enthusiasm had helped her have the courage to make the effort to have a happy holiday.

I felt their deep love for me, and mine for all of them, in spite of the comedy of Mom's and Dad's big "frog shoes."

My most memorable Christmas? The year I poured out my love for my family with an idea from an old moccasin.

Roberta Sharley

December 25

Looking for the Christmas Yet to Come!

If ye then, being evil, know how to give good gifts unto your children, how much more shall your Father which is in heaven give good things to them that ask him? Matt. 7:11.

A few years ago while my husband and I were attending a seminar held at Andrews University in Michigan, we took a few hours to retrace my "roots."

How exciting it was to once again visit the old farm where I grew up! There were so many memories and impressions from bygone but oh so happy days of long ago!

It was in this old farmhouse that my sister and I had experienced our first real Christmas with our new parents.

I was just 5 years old, and everything about Christmas seemed magical. My folks selected a beautiful floor-to-ceiling Christmas tree. Mother had gone all out buying strings of twinkling lights and yards of rope tinsel. She carefully selected boxes of beautiful hand-blown and decorated ornaments. A traditional angel and star crowned the topmost branch. I was sure I had never seen anything so beautiful.

The weeks before Christmas were especially busy with several trips to the big city as well as to our small town stores.

Packages filled the trunk and sometimes overflowed to the back seat of Mother's faithful old Buick. Once we arrived home and Mother carried the packages inside, a strange phenomenon occurred. The boxes and bags seemed to disappear—which only added to the excitement and anticipation of two little girls.

Finally, the night before Christmas arrived. It was a long time before our excitement succumbed to slumber—but not for many hours. Very early Christmas morning we awoke to mysterious sounds coming from the living room below us.

In a moment our little feet were on the floor, and we quickly made our way to the top of the stairs.

Our new parents were standing at the bottom of the stairs drinking in our look of surprise, joy, and wonderment. It was indeed a once-in-a-lifetime thrill for both little girls and Mother and Daddy.

I am told that as we made our way down the stairs, our eyes wide with wonder, we hesitated for a moment as we exclaimed, "Is this all for us? Is this all really ours?"

For you see, under the tree were gifts and toys that fulfilled every wish we could ever have had! Our parents had gone all out to give their newly adopted girls a truly unforgettable Christmas!

What did they get in return? They experienced the wonderful thrill of seeing their little girls receive the fruits of their loving efforts. They also saw the look of pure wonderment and excitement of little dreams come true. They were left with no doubts that their sacrifice of time, effort, and money had been worth it all.

One day our heavenly Father will also hear His adopted children exclaim, "Is this all for us? Is this all really ours?"

Hazel Marie Gordon

December 26

Angel Wings

For He shall give His angels charge over you, to keep you in all your ways. They shall bear you up in their hands, lest you dash your foot against a stone. Ps. 91:11, 12, NKJV.

Our 17-year-old son was in the driver's seat heading out of Spokane, Washington. We were on the last leg of our trip back from a Christmas spent in North Dakota where I grew up. Our 12-year-old daughter was sleeping in the back seat, while my husband and I occupied the front seat with our son.

It was dark as we drove down the icy mountain highway. Suddenly we hit a slick spot, and the car spun out of control. First to the left side toward a high bank of snow, then to the right, where a cliff faded into the darkness. We felt the car and ourselves hurtling swiftly over toward the abyss. Loose clothes in the car fell to the right, and our awakened daughter screamed in terror. I knew we were destined to roll into the blackness.

Bob struggled in vain for control when suddenly the car straightened up, climbed back onto the road, and went straight down the highway. Trembling, we stopped down the road and walked back to the edge of the bank. We found a 20-foot-wide wash, which our car had passed over. In those terror-filled moments, it had felt as if the car were digging in its front wheels like claws struggling for a hold.

We breathed a prayer of gratitude. We walked back to our car and saw a deep dent on the back right fender. There had been nothing on that side of the car to cause a dent as it sped across the wash. I believe an angel's hand made it as our car was pushed gently back onto the icy highway.

Faith Keeney

December 27

Power in a Small Package

Are not two sparrows sold for a penny? And not one of them will fall to the ground without your Father's will. But even the hairs of your head are all numbered. Matt. 10:29, 30, RSV.

Do you ever feel insignificant? Does it seem like you're a tiny molecule in this vast universe? Did you ever ask, "What difference do I make, anyway?"

If your answer to any of those questions is yes, then today's thought is for you. I heard a quotable quote recently that both made me laugh and gave me courage. Here it is:

"One excited flea can worry a whole dog."

Is there something in your neighborhood, your family, your work setting, that needs changing? Does your profession need some new paradigms? (That's a word we're going to hear more. It means a model or pattern, a way of looking at or doing things.) Do you have a vision for improving a procedure? an idea of how to enhance customer service? a way money can be saved? an idea for your church?

You are significant. You are of consequence. Your ideas matter. You have power to change those things that need to be changed. Think what one excited flea can do to a pet dog!

BEULAH FERN STEVENS

DECEMBER 28

ALWAYS POSITIVE

A word fitly spoken is like apples of gold in pictures of silver. Prov. 25:11.

She was not really our grandma. In fact, she was not a blood relative at all, but we adopted her and she became a very dearly loved member of our family.

"Grandma's" only and greatly beloved daughter and her family were missionaries who later settled in America. They unselfishly shared her with us, so that our own family was extended to include her grandchildren and later her great-grandchildren. Now that Grandma has gone, the family bond still remains strong between us.

Having two teenage boys in the home plus one of their friends who lived with us for a time could have posed problems, with a generation gap. But there was never a gap with Grandma—who was in her 90s! When the boys' clothes were a bit on the outrageous side she never criticized, but instead found something to admire—the color, the buttons, the shape—something. If there was just nothing in the clothing she could fix on, then she would find *something* positive to say—even if it was only "You have such a nice smile." The same was true of every aspect of their lives, from their music and their behavior to their girlfriends.

It was a marvelous gift and one that made my job as a mother so much easier. Instead of having to reconcile two generations with differing views, Grandma taught me always to look for the positive in every situation. Confrontation was avoided, and we were able to discuss issues and arrive at amicable solutions most of the time.

Grandma wasn't perfect. She could be manipulative as only older, wiser people can be, and sometimes I felt frustrated at the ways in which she got her own way. However, because she never said an unkind word and was always so gentle and loving, one could only be the same to her.

Consequently, when Grandma died we had no remorse, no thinking, *I wish I hadn't said that.* That was Grandma's gift to me and one for which I am very thankful.

I wish that I could say that I am like Grandma and always find something positive to say in every situation, but I'm not. Sometimes criticisms slip out, or I'm not as positive as I could be. But I am trying, by God's grace, to paint "apples of gold in pictures of silver" so that I can build people up, always, as she did.

Audrey Balderstone

December 29

Rainy Day Musings

The water I give will become a spring of water flowing inside.
John 4:14, EB.

Across the street from my home is a large city park. Mostly undeveloped, its only improvements are crudely graded dirt paths, a few foot bridges spanning small gullies, and several scattered picnic tables huddled for shade under the sparse oak trees. As this area of California is dry most of the year, I'm not attracted to the park because of its lush beauty, but because it provides me the space to exercise.

However, with the arrival of the winter rainy season, I am irresistibly drawn to the park to enjoy the transformation of the tired, dusty hills to new life and beauty. Shod in boots and armed with an umbrella, I'm equipped to watch God's "liquid renewal project" firsthand. The creek, its parched, stony bed so long silent, now raises a musical babble of praise, perfectly accompanying a chorus of very excited and vocal birds. Grass blades and tiny, vivid wildflowers emerge, awakened by incessant raindrops drumming on their earthen roof. Tiny rivulets join hands as they dance uninhibited down the hillside and across my path.

Even as nature rejoices in the freshness of a new beginning, the gentle reminder comes that I also may be washed, cleansed, renewed. No matter that sin, like layers of dust, has at times choked my joy in the Lord. No matter that life's periods of drought have caused my spiritual experience to become arid and brittle. For I know that as surely as the freshness of the Creator's rains is renewing the arid landscape, I too may be renewed. Beauty truly can come "out of the ashes" of my life. As my heart yields to the softening showers of the Holy Spirit, its parched, lifeless existence will be transformed into "a spring of water flowing inside."

> Flow through me.
> Show through me
> That when we give You all our pain,
> You will make us whole in Jesus' name.
> Give through me.
> Live through me.
> I want to be a channel of Your saving love.
> Flow through me.
> Flow through me.
>
> DEBBY GRAY WILMOT

DECEMBER 30

MY CROSS

If any want to become my followers, let them deny themselves and take up their cross and follow me. Matt. 16:24, NRSV.

My heart felt as if it had been kicked, trampled on, and left bruised and bleeding. I struggled to maintain an inner balance and forgiveness for those who had unknowingly hurt me and for the injustice I felt I had suffered. I prayed to be forgiven for those things I'd said and done.

I clutched at Bible verses, saying James 1:2, 3 over and over. "Count it all joy when ye fall into divers temptations; knowing this, that the trying of your faith worketh patience." I praised God and thanked Him that He considered me worthy to be tested. Anything I endure, I reminded myself, is nothing compared to what Christ endured for me.

Peace like a river began to wash over me, and words flooded to the surface. The tears stopped. I regained my composure and started to write.

My cross is not the pain I suffer from earthly ailments. It is not the up-and-down rough road of daily living. My cross is not poverty, lack of worldly possessions, the loss of a loved one, or the coldness of a friend.

My cross is Jesus' cross, to love as He loved. Jesus loved and forgave those who crucified Him. He gave His life to pay our sin debt so that all who believe in Him will live in this life and the next. His love knew no barriers of sex, race, creed, or color. He was spit upon, lashed, rebuked, ridiculed, called insane, foolish, and a liar.

Even His most trusted friends denied and deserted Him in His darkest hour, but He forgave them. His love was, and is, endless.

> This, then, is my cross, to love others as He loved.
> To take up my cross is to forgive as He forgave.
> To carry my cross is to walk the narrow way with Christ in my heart, oblivious to the taunts of others.
> My cross is to share His gospel with others by loving those around me in such a way that Christ shines through and God gets all the glory.
> My cross is light.
> Christ carries my burdens.
> My cross is not a hardship—it is joy, peace, and gladness.
> With Christ my cross becomes a song in my heart and sunshine in my soul.
> With Christ I know the power of sin is broken and I need not sin against God.
> With Christ I can glimpse the glory of things to come when Christ shall reign as King forever and ever. Praise the Lord! Hallelujah!   DORIS JENNER EVERETT

DECEMBER 31

PRIORITIES

If [our gift] is to encourage others, we should do so. Whoever shares with others should do it generously; whoever has authority should work hard; whoever shows kindness to others should do it cheerfully. Rom. 12:8, TEV.

Another year has evaporated like the morning fog, and I find myself wondering where it went. It will never be back in quite the same way again. Opportunities missed are often gone forever, and I find myself wondering how I personally could have contributed more.

Have I neglected to say something encouraging to someone who needed it? Have I been so involved meeting life's daily challenges that I neglected the Lord of the work? How about the note I should have sent but never got around to writing? What about the chances I missed to show my husband and children how special they are to me?

It all comes back to priorities. Every moment of our lives we need God close to continually remind us of what is really important. How weak we are; how often we forget how much we need His presence.

When we face serious problems in our lives, it makes us even more aware of how much we need Him and the encouragement of others. Life in this world is shallow and often painful, yet by the simple act of caring—a note, a word, a prayer—we can bring joy to others. I want to be an "encourager" in the remaining time God grants me. Won't you join me? — ELLEN BRESEE

Scripture Index

Genesis
1:1-3	Jan. 7
1:1-31	July 1
1:25	Mar. 26, June 27
9:13, 14	Apr. 28
18:2-5	Nov. 15

Exodus
25:31-33	Mar. 13

Numbers
32:23	Feb. 22

Deuteronomy
6:5	Oct. 28
32:11, 12	Nov. 2
32:35	Apr. 24

Judges
4:9	Sept. 21

Ruth
1:20	July 19

1 Samuel
3:7	Mar. 8, Mar. 14
3:10	May 6, July 27
16:7	Feb. 4
25:3	Nov. 19

1 Kings
18:21	May 25

2 Kings
20:5	Nov. 10

1 Chronicles
16:33	Mar. 6

Nehemiah
8:10	Mar. 10

Job
23:10	Jan. 6
38:22	Nov. 17

Psalms
1:3	Sept. 11
2:12	Sept. 20
4:1	Jan. 18
5:11	June 9
5:11, 12	Mar. 12
7:1	Sept. 20
16:11	Aug. 3
20:1	Apr. 22
23:1	Apr. 2
23:2, 3	Mar. 15
23:4	June 5, June 28, Aug. 26
27:1	Sept. 24
27:4	Jan. 19
27:11	Oct. 14
27:14	Oct. 6, Dec. 15
29:11	Jan. 25
31:3	Sept. 7
32:8	June 8
33:18	Oct. 5
34:7	Jan. 28, Mar. 1, Apr. 14, Dec. 19, Dec. 21
34:8	Mar. 28
34:17	Aug. 31
37:4	Jan. 8, Jan. 22
37:5	Dec. 20
37:23-25	Sept. 23
46:1	Jan. 23
46:10	May 17, Aug. 21
50:15	Apr. 21, Aug. 7
51:7	July 9
51:10	Jan. 4
55:6, 7	Nov. 28
59:16	Nov. 25
61:2	Jan. 16
61:2, 3	Sept. 28
62:5	Apr. 11
66:2	Nov. 25
73:25	Apr. 26
73:28	Mar. 27
89:47	May 9
91:1	Aug. 13
91:3, 4	June 13
91:9	Oct. 31
91:11	Jan. 5
91:11, 12	Dec. 26
91:15	Oct. 12, Dec. 4
92:4, 5	June 4
102:1, 2	Sept. 12
103:1	Nov. 18
103:2-4	Feb. 5
104:33	July 17
107:28-30	June 10
108:3, 4	Sept. 4
118:7	Mar. 30
118:23	Jan. 13
119:47	Oct. 7
119:105	Aug. 30, Oct. 20
120:1	Mar. 24
124:8	Feb. 13
126:3	Feb. 16
126:6	Apr. 29
127:3	Aug. 17
128:3-6	Aug. 17
136:1-9	Dec. 22
139:9, 10	Apr. 18
139:17	Dec. 17
139:23, 24	Aug. 23
147:16	Jan. 21

149:1	Nov. 29	40:1	Mar. 14	6:8-7:7	Mar. 20
149:1, 2	Aug. 11	40:11	June 15	6:12	July 2
		40:31	Dec. 12	6:19-21	May 29
PROVERBS		41:10	Feb. 10, Dec. 14	6:25	Jan. 17
3:5, 6	Oct. 18			6:28, 29	Apr. 6, Apr. 30
3:6	May 19	41:13	Mar. 16		
6:6	May 25, Dec. 11	42:6-16	Apr. 12	7:3	May 20
		43:2	Feb. 23, Aug. 28, Oct. 8	7:7	May 18
11:25	Jan. 31			7:9-11	Feb. 8
12:15	Jan. 12	43:10	July 20	7:11	Dec. 25
12:25	Aug. 18	49:16	Apr. 17, Dec. 10	8:1	Nov. 11
14:1	June 24			8:26, 27	Mar. 7
14:15	July 3	50:7	Mar. 5	10:29, 30	Dec. 27
16:9	Feb. 9	51:11	Oct. 21	10:29-31	July 13
16:31	May 5	52:7	Jan. 30	11:28	Apr. 4, July 4
17:17	Apr. 23	55:12	Sept. 17		
17:22	Aug. 16, Sept. 22	57:15	May 1	11:28-30	Mar. 11, July 5
		58:11	Apr. 27		
18:22	May 4	60:1	Apr. 5	13:15	Oct. 11
20:11	Dec. 5	61:10	Nov. 13	13:33	Feb. 2
20:12	Aug. 4	65:22, 23	Sept. 30	13:43	Oct. 15
22:6	July 8	65:24	Feb. 15, Mar. 23, May 31	13:45	Sept. 25
25:11	July 16, Dec. 28			13:52	May 14
				14:31, 32	Nov. 8
25:20	Oct. 29	**JEREMIAH**		16:24	Dec. 30
25:25	Mar. 25	1:4, 5	Oct. 16	18:2, 3	Jan. 3
29:11	Nov. 22	29:11	Jan. 16, Feb. 14, May 21, Nov. 12	18:14	Aug. 1
31:12	Aug. 22			21:15, 16	June 22
				22:9	Sept. 26
ECCLESIASTES		30:17	June 1	23:37	Sept. 27
2:24	June 16	31:3	July 11	25:21	June 23
3:11	Mar. 2, Oct. 2	**DANIEL**		25:37-40	Nov. 9
				25:40	Oct. 19
4:10	June 30	6:21, 22	Feb. 12	25:45	Sept. 18
				26:73	Apr. 15
SONG OF SOLOMON		**JOEL**		27:22	Apr. 16
2:11, 12	Mar. 21	2:28	Feb. 18	28:19, 20	Feb. 27, Sept. 29
ISAIAH		**AMOS**		28:20	Oct. 10
6:8	Dec. 23	2:9	July 30		
9:2, 3	May 7			**MARK**	
26:3	May 2, Oct. 17	**ZECHARIAH**		4:37, 38	Nov. 4
		8:13	Aug. 27	4:40	Jan. 20
30:21	Nov. 7	**MATTHEW**		5:29	Aug. 19
35:1, 2	June 3			5:34	Sept. 15
35:3, 4	Oct. 25	5:13	June 11	6:30, 31	July 6

6:31	Sept. 3	15:15	Sept. 19	6:2	Sept. 8
8:36	June 7	15:16	May 24	12:9	June 18,
8:36, 37	Apr. 10	16:21	July 23		June 25
10:14	Jan. 27,	16:24	Oct. 3		
	June 17	17:23	July 28		

Galatians

3:28	Oct. 24
4:22, 23	May 3
5:13	Dec. 18
6:2-5	Dec. 8

11:24	July 7, Aug. 8
14:8	May 30

Acts

1:8	Nov. 23
9:15	Sept. 14
9:40	Nov. 3
20:35	Dec. 24
27:44	Feb. 19

Luke

6:38	Jan. 9
8:46	Dec. 13
8:47	May 15
8:48	June 19
10:20	Jan. 24
10:40	Nov. 1
10:42	Oct. 26
11:1	Apr. 19
12:6, 7	Jan. 24, May 11, Dec. 16
12:22-24	Oct. 22
12:40	Feb. 17, Apr. 20
15:8, 9	Feb. 28
19:10	May 23

Ephesians

1:11	Jan. 15
2:10	May 10
3:17-19	May 16
4:29	Mar. 17

Romans

5:8	Apr. 25
8:24, 25	Dec. 6
8:28	Mar. 31, June 6, Aug. 10, Sept. 5
10:9	Mar. 4
12:2	July 26, Aug. 29
12:8	Dec. 31
12:10	Apr. 7
15:7	Mar. 9

Philippians

1:6	June 26
2:15, 16	June 20
4:4	Nov. 27
4:6, 7	Aug. 24
4:7	June 14
4:8	Aug. 6

Colossians

2:3	May 22
3:23, 24	Oct. 13

John

3:16	Apr. 13, July 12
4:14	Dec. 29
4:29	May 26
6:26	Mar. 3
6:35	Feb. 21
10:4	Nov. 5
10:10	Mar. 22
11:25	Jan. 29
11:33-35	May 13
12:24	Apr. 8
13:8	Feb. 3
13:14, 15	Sept. 2
13:34, 35	Nov. 16
14:1-3	Feb. 11, Apr. 3, Oct. 4
14:3	July 21
14:14	Sept. 22
15:9	Dec. 2

1 Corinthians

1:25	July 14
2:9	July 31
2:12	Aug. 12
3:18	Jan. 2
7:22	June 2
10:13	Mar. 18, Dec. 9
10:31	Sept. 6
12:4	Feb. 1
15:26	Aug. 2
16:13	June 12

1 Thessalonians

4:16-18	Dec. 1
5:17	Sept. 16, Nov. 14, Nov. 24
5:23, 24	July 22

1 Timothy

6:18	Nov. 21

2 Timothy

2:20	Sept. 13
4:18	Feb. 26

2 Corinthians

2:14	Nov. 6
3:3	Sept. 9
4:16	July 15
5:7	Feb. 7, July 10
5:17	Apr. 1

Hebrews

1:14	Jan. 11
2:6	Oct. 9
4:16	Feb. 25
11:8	Feb. 6

11:16	Dec. 3, Dec. 7	**2 Peter**		4:19	July 29
12:1	Oct. 27	3:3, 4	June 29	5:16	Oct. 1
13:5	Jan. 10, Oct. 30	3:13	Feb. 20	**Revelation**	
		3:18	Aug. 25	1:17, 18	Aug. 14
13:5, 6	Mar. 29			3:18	May 27
James		**1 John**		3:20	Nov. 20
1:22-25	July 18	3:1, 2	June 21	7:14	Apr. 9
4:6	July 24	3:18	Aug. 9	18:4	Aug. 15
4:17	Sept. 1	4:7	Sept. 10	21:4	Jan. 14, May 12, July 25, Oct. 23, Nov. 26
5:13-16	Feb. 24	4:7, 8	Aug. 20		
		4:11	Mar. 19		
1 Peter		4:15, 16	Nov. 30	21:4, 5	May 8
5:8	May 28	4:18	Aug. 5	22:5	Jan. 26